Making American Art

Making American Art presents a thematic, interdisciplinary examination of art in the United States from the seventeenth century to the present day.

The themes and issues explored in *Making American Art* pull together documentary material, artworks and contemporary theory to enliven what can often be a complex and geographically overwhelming history. The abiding and connective theme of the book is an extended and multidimensional examination of the perennial and vexing question: what is American about American art? In attempting an answer, the book draws upon topics that are not always present in conventional art-historical accounts – the education of the artist, the mechanisms for promoting and institutionalising artwork, the facilities for reproducing and disseminating American art, and the organisation of artistic activities. In considering the quest for an authentic expression of Americanism in the visual arts this book incorporates areas that normally fall outside the remit of high art, such as the conditions under which American art was produced.

Chapter topics include:

- Education and the American artist
- Art into reproduction
- Touring America
- The art of American landscape
- Accommodating American art
- Writing about American art.

Pam Meecham has worked as an art teacher in schools and universities since 1971. She currently teaches museum and gallery studies, is course leader for the MA Museums & Galleries in Education and has a number of doctoral students researching aspects of art education and museum studies at the Institute of Education, University of London.

Julie Sheldon is Reader in Art History at Liverpool John Moores University. She is the programme leader for BA History of Art and Museum Studies, a collaborative undergraduate course with Tate Liverpool. Previous publications with Pam Meecham include *Modern Art: A Critical Introduction* (2005).

Making American Art

Pam Meecham and Julie Sheldon

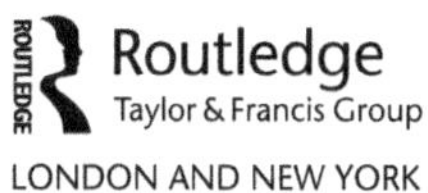

LONDON AND NEW YORK

First published 2009
by Routledge
2 Park Square, Milton Park, Abingdon, Oxon OX14 4RN

Simultaneously published in the USA and Canada
by Routledge

270 Madison Ave, New York, NY 10016

Routledge is an imprint of the Taylor & Francis Group, an informa business

Typeset in Sabon by Saxon Graphics Ltd, Derby

Printed and bound in Great Britain by TJ International Ltd, Padstow, Cornwall

British Library Cataloguing in Publication Data
A catalogue record for this book is available
from the British Library

Library of Congress Cataloging in Publication Data

Meecham, Pam.
Making American art / Pam Meecham and Julie Sheldon
p. cm.
Includes bibliographical references.
1. Art, American. I. Sheldon, Julie, 19630 II. Title.
N6505.M37 2009
809.73--dc22
2008019127

ISBN10: 0-415-42069-5 (hbk)
ISBN10: 0-415-42070-9 (pbk)

ISBN13: 978-0-415-42069-3 (hbk)
ISBN13: 978-0-415-42070-9 (pbk)

Contents

Plates

Plate section can be found between pages 118 and 119.

The following were reproduced with kind permission. While every effort has been made to trace copyright holders and obtain permission, this has not been possible in all cases. Any omissions brought to our attention will be remedied in future editions.

Acknowledgements

The authors would like to thank colleagues for their support. In particular Josephine Borradaile, Lynn Halliday, Kelvin Gwilliam and Peter Thomas. The authors have also profited from their conversations with Nick Addison, Lesley Burgess, John Reeve, Claire Robins and Elena Stylianou. We extend our personal thanks to Neil Hall and Colin Fallows.

Introduction

In 1943 Joseph Cornell collaged a set of images for the cover of *View*, one of the artist/writer led magazines that endorsed surrealism in the Americas.[1] Like other such publications, *View* was an artwork as much as an art magazine and exemplary of the commerce between writers and artist, a hallmark of European surrealism. Titled *Americana Fantastica*, (Plate 1) Cornell's cover shows, against a backdrop of the Niagara Falls, iconic American images: King Kong battling hostile airplanes at the top of the Empire State Building, Native Americans posed for portrait painting, early drawings of colonialists, cut-out photographs of trapeze artists and a vertiginously angled tightrope walker traversing the Falls (Parker Tyler 1943). The editorial by Robert Parker Tyler draws attention to the importance of the universalism of the fantastic (or marvellous) but also to the way that artworks, presented under the banner of *Americana Fantastica*, are made locally but are 'not so much indigenous to America as susceptible to it, just as oranges are not indigenous, but could grow here' (Parker Tyler 1943). The magazine, which stressed the term *fantastic* rather than the European-derived surrealism, together with its visual homage to the American landscape, architecture, athletic inhabitants and indigenous communities, can be read as an attempt to distance America from European surrealism: to create an independent American surrealism or *fantastica*.[2] While not the only visible register in the making of American art, the recurring aspirations to 'be different' and to be 'exceptional' from an Old World, make up much, although not all, of the history of American art presented in this book.

We are not Gombrichian enough to call this book the 'story' of American art but rather incline to a view. But even a view, like all histories, is contingent

1 Along with *View* (1940–47), *VVV* New York (1942–44) (representing victory over fascism, oppression and alienation), *Semina* Los Angeles and San Francisco (1955–64), and *Dyn* in Coyoacan, Mexico, 1942–44 disseminated surrealist art, literature and politics across the Americas.

2 See in particular Dickran Tashjian (1995) *A Boatload of Madmen: Surrealism and the American Avant-Garde 1920–1950.*

and partial, art histories no less than history proper. National visual histories, the case that occupies us here, can simply mirror the values of a nation, as Nancy Anderson suggests in relation to the western landscape, 'a natural resource, a raw material ... could be used to construct seductively beautiful works of art that reflected, in both direct and subtle ways, the material and spiritual needs of ... culture' (1998: 208). Art can be literal transcriptions of the material and physical culture that surrounds us. But artworks can also define: give representation to aspirations rather than trumpet achievements or celebrate physical geography. Moreover, visual arts can run counter to received or legitimate history, and in doing so act as gentle criticism that legitimates dominant liberal values. Perhaps less commonly art can also be deeply subversive and derail a nation's sense of itself. Visual art therefore contributes to the construction and re-construction of identities personal, regional and national. Camnitzer observed in 1996 that cultural diversity was an important part of the myth of American national unity:

> In its comparatively short life the USA has both adapted and developed a great variety of cultural paradigms and myths that give cohesion to a national identity. These constructs, by no means always a product of a conscious strategy, overshadow and help to reduce the diversities in population identity, a diversity that would normally tend to undermine a sense of unity. Some of the ideas are notorious and past their prime, like the 'America Dream' and the 'melting pot'.
>
> (Camnitzer 1996: 10)

Such clichés as the 'America Dream' and the 'melting pot' have however contributed to productive fictions and dissensions about what an American art and even artist might look like, and crucially what role both were to play in the aspirations of a 'new' nation.

It needs to be acknowledged that 'intangible culture' is also an important constituent of culture per se. We consider, albeit briefly, those that predate any geopolitical construction of America to look at artworks, including those of the Amerindian culture that appeared so often in surrealist magazines. This includes traditions by which history, myths, and personal stories are passed down by generations in visual, oral and performed forms. This book draws on often conflicting representations in imaginative ways, making connections between time and place, art practices and theoretical perspectives.

We are aware that in discussing American art we are considering the United States, but that America is more than a geographically defined space. The term America originally embraced the Americas in a more pan-American sense than is possible today. If, as in Jan Van der Straet's (Johannes Stradanus) *Arrival of Amerigo Vespucci in the New World*, we could conceptualise and visualise from a late sixteenth century imagination, it would confound most of our understanding of the distinct divisions between the countries that make up the Americas[3] and the terms used to distinguish their inhabitants. All the Americas in the Italian Vespucci's terms were simply the 'new world', with the point of discovery somewhere around present-day Venezuela and Brazil. The image appeared, reworked by Theodore Galle, Philippe Galle and Jan Collaert in *Nova Reperta*, in 1580, probably the product of an early publishing venture (Plate 2). It is from Amerigo Vespucci that the hemisphere's name is derived. Notwithstanding the image of cannibalism in the background, by the end of the sixteenth century the new world was already fabled: Eldorado, a land of milk and honey, arcadia, utopia and a new Eden. The wilderness was a wonder, rather than the later Puritan reconceptualisation of it as a place to both purge and be purged. But although seemingly unified by such a term, the 'new world' was always diverse and pluralistic and far more expansive than early cartographers and adventurers imagined. Moreover, art produced in Canada, Mexico, the West Indies and South American countries is also 'American', in a non-nationalistic sense. If we extend America to the imagination and the realm of fable as the surrealists did, or even through new technologies, geographic location is rendered obsolete.

It is necessary to remind ourselves that even in the nineteenth and twentieth century divisions between nations did not always result in writing and art divided along nationalistic lines. For instance, in writing of the mid-twentieth century, and the work of Joaquin Torres-Garcia (1874–1949), Cesar Paternosto refers to a time before 'the hardening of the arteries of art history', which had posited a more complex 1940s, replete with commonalities between north and south, which 'flies in the face of a bifurcation of 'American' (US) and 'Latin American Art'' (1998: 6).

However, we do not restrict our location to the fifty states and the work of expatriates but rather accept that much of the most exciting work produced in America is found in real or imagined borderlands, and produced by groups and individuals who fit uncomfortably within mainstream United States. There is no easily definable essential *Americanness,* but characteristics often used to define America in terms of its exceptionalism are shared by many. The sheer diversity of cultures along with the shifting and contingent rewriting of who and even what is American are issues to which we will return.

3 See in particular Felipe Fernadez-Armesto's (2003) *The Americas: The History of a Hemisphere*. He argues the case for understanding the Americas (North, South and Central) as a whole landmass with shared histories bound by migration, trade, politics, religion and culture.

America made and remade

This book is also about the relationship between practice and imagining, with a concentration on the visualisation of imagining. The imagining and practice of nations is the central theme of Benedict Anderson's *Imagined Communities* (1991), where he argues that nations are symbolically conceived and historically constructed. Moreover, the idea of nation, according to Anderson, coincided with the development of institutional practices and technologies. Although Anderson concentrates on the importance of new reproductive technologies, especially print, the visualisation of nationhood through original paintings is also important and central to much of this book. Accepting the imagined nation is not to write of a chimera. The nation, although constructed, is 'real', with a contemporary reality and changeable signifying practices. The active process of imagining the nation and at times alternatives to it has been a compelling feature of the making, display and writing about American art. The terms 'nation' and 'nature' are related at an etymological and semantic level, and are also discernible in nationalist ideology, most infamously in Third Reich primordial notions of 'blood and soil' (Blut and Boden in German). Indeed ideas about nature and the subsequent visualising of it through art are used in the formation and the subsequent shaping of a nation, and so the American landscape and attachment to or rejection of it is an important signifier in the transformation of European traditions into a specifically American experience. America like other nations is at once 'real' and constructed, and the local and international meanings attached to the narratives and dialogues that have been constructed historically make up the complexity of its visual culture. It is also worth remembering that it was not until the nineteenth century, with the 1803 Louisiana Purchase of French-speaking country, and the Treaty of Guadalupe of 1848, when large tracts of Mexican land were absorbed into the United States, that we see anything like the modern United States: making it a very young nation.

This book is a history written not from within but from without, with the caveat that few cultures have been immune to American influence. We hope to reveal something of the history of American art by looking at its reception beyond America. As well as looking in the borderlands and border cultures of America for art under-represented in consensus art history, we look at the reception of American art and culture in a range of other contexts, via dissemination through biennales, travelling shows, media and written text. America has travelled for centuries, both within and outside its borders, and we refer to some of the earliest encounters with what purported to be authentic, if unofficial, American culture: for example the Buffalo Bill Wild West and Congress of Rough Riders of the late nineteenth century that toured Europe. At his death in 1917, feted by popes, emperors, queens and presidents, it was estimated that Buffalo Bill (William Frederick Cody) was the most famous international celebrity of the age. Also revealing are the officially sanctioned showcases of international fairs and exhibitions, the staple of nation-state identities, where ideological battles can be fought through culture. Few international biennials in recent years have retained national pavilions: the Venice Biennale is a notable exception, and so the new internationalism is one site from which to view contemporary US art. In 2002 the curator Okwui Enwezor reconceptualised *Documenta*, the international quinquennial contemporary art show held in Kassel in Germany, by redrawing its geographical, social and artistic boundaries to stage an interdisciplinary show on what were termed 'platforms' across four continents. Moreover, the themes of the show marked a radical departure from established norms, and raised issues such as transnational justice, democracy and cultural translation: themes that emerge and re-emerge throughout the history of US art. The reception of American and most other art is currently mediated through new technologies. Wooden packing cases in transit have not been entirely replaced by digital technology, but electronic highways have altered the balance between unmatched cultures in terms of financial resources. The global dissemination of American culture via electronic media has been matched by the ability of 'peripheral' cultures to represent themselves with equal ease. An incomplete utopia, the much lauded democratising of culture through new technologies needs the caveat that there is still a digital divide.

All art histories are partial, exhibitions too are necessarily selective, but some question received wisdom and seek out alternative stories, creating new fictions, fables and orthodoxies. It is the intention of the two English authors of this volume to write an untidy history of American art: one appropriate for a period that lacks consensus and one that questions a contradictory and fractured heritage. We hope however that this history will illuminate a culture that has been envied and despised in about equal measure: one that has copied and innovated in much the same way. American culture has helped define those outside America, exposing commonalities and differences. A book on American art, written at a distance that attempts to represent the diversity of US culture, needs to acknowledge that local battles can take on particular significance when viewed from abroad. The tensions arising over the orthodox validation of differing forms of artistic expression can be received as more widespread that they actually were, but they can also be reinterpreted.

What is American about American art?

> One of the most American traits is our urge to define what is American.
>
> Lloyd Goodrich,[4] in Lipman (1963: 8)

When in 1958 Lloyd Goodrich, director of the Whitney Museum of American Art, posed the question 'What is American in American art'[5] in an essay for a book of the same name, his subheading 'Common denominators from the Pilgrims to Pollock' (Lipman 1963: 8) made his trajectory and ideological position clear. Goodrich offered a framework for charting American characteristics recognisable though subject matter, viewpoint, emotional and intellectual content, and through artistic concepts, style. Native subject matter could be found in the work of artists such as Copley, Mount, Homer and Eakins. For American emotional and intellectual content he referred to Albert Pinkham Ryder. For artistic concepts and a degree of naïveté he called upon folk art. Pitting contemporary art in the 1950s, against standardisation through film and television, he praised the wide range of artistic responses to the modern world as part of a national pluralism and diversity: the very lack of unity was, for him at least, evidence of a democratic society.

Barbara Novak, writing in the 1960s, was asking the same question, but in her preface to the first edition of *American Painting of the Nineteenth Century: Realism, Idealism, and the American Experience* she elaborates on it, to ask whether there can be 'a particular artistic identity that can be defined in terms of both American traditions and experience and of the Western world at large'. She determines that it is not *what* is American, but *how* it is, that is the important question to ask. Of course very little of any tradition is uniquely the preserve of one nation or group, and Novak maintains that 'What makes them indigenous is not their uniqueness to America but rather the *frequency or constancy of their occurrence within continuing American traditions to which they also contribute*' (Novak's italics) (1979: 7). Looking for the common denominators that consistently occur in American painting, Novak like Goodrich draws exclusively on an East coast trajectory (beginning with John Singleton Copley), defined and limited by European aesthetics: a history that is conditioned retrospectively by the inexorable move towards the New York School of the 1950s and beyond to the pop art of Rauschenberg, Oldenburg and the beginnings of conceptualism.

From a similar perspective in the 1940s, Jackson Pollock was also casting

4 Lloyd Goodrich was director of the Whitney Museum of American Art in New York in the 1950s and 1960s.

5 The question mark on the cover of *What is American in American Art* was supplied by Alexander Calder via a schematic humanised red, black and blue question mark.

doubt on what had seemed to be a defining feature of the homespun values of the 1930s, as Depression culture sought ways to celebrate seemingly indigenous values then under threat. Pollock stated:

> The idea of an isolated American painting, so popular in this country during the thirties, seems absurd to me, just as the idea of creating a purely American mathematics or physics seem absurd .... And in another sense, the problem doesn't exist at all; or if it did, would resolve itself: An American is an American and his painting would be qualified by that fact, whether he wills or not. But the basic problems of contemporary painting are independent of any one country.
>
> (Pollock 1944)

Mecklenberg has pointed to the 1930s as a decade when art was directly informed by American life:

> For over a century popular ideas about art had been shaped by the belief that art served as 'anthropological' evidence of a nation's philosophical and intellectual condition...As apparent from the immense popularity of John Dewey's writings and of Regionalist paintings during the thirties and of the relative public and political success... post-office murals, the idea that American art could accurately capture American values had reached new heights.
>
> (Austfield and Mecklenberg 1984: 41)

It was not uncommon to expect American painting of American subject matter to mirror the lives of the people and so in some way contribute to the nation's democratic idealism. In reality mirroring through authentic American subject matter was more of a hybrid and complex affair, as we can see from the American scene painter Stuart Davis's acceptance of 'influence' and Thomas Craven's rejection of it.

Davis replied in the negative to his own question 'Is there an American art?' Annoyed at a critic's undermining suggestion that 'he was a swell American painter (but in a French style)', Davis defended cultural borrowing in a period intent on an authentic expression of Americanness. He asked 'Has any American artist created a style which is unique in painting, completely divorced from European models?' He cited numerous examples of nineteenth-century American artists working successfully and originally within a tradition that derived from France (1941, in Chipp 1968: 523). He identified subjects that provided the 'originating impulse' in his own work:

> American wood and iron work of the past; Civil War and skyscraper architecture; the brilliant colors on gasoline stations, chain-store fronts, and taxi-cabs ... electric signs, the landscape and boats of Gloucester,

> Massachusetts; 5&10 cent store kitchen utensils ... Earl Hines' hot piano and Negro Jazz music in general, etc.

He continued:

> In one way or another, the quality of these things plays a role in determining the character of my painting; not in the sense of describing them in graphic images, but by pre-determining an analogous dynamics in design which becomes a new part of the American environment.
>
> (1943, in Chipp 1968: 524)

In the same period that Davis was working unashamedly on French-derived formal innovations applied to American subjects such as a packet of Lucky Strike cigarettes, critics such as Craven defined the American artist as one who had rejected all foreign (particularly French) influence. Writing of the 'abortions of surrealism – the culminating rot of European gadget makers [who] have found their proper level as eccentric window dressing for department stores', Craven valorised what he termed the 'thingminded' pragmatism of the American people, and lest he be thought overly nationalistic and close to fascism, he discarded 'the word nationalism' and supplied 'an unimpeachable substitute-localism' (Craven 1939: introduction). The language that Craven deployed is telling. Rejecting the conceits of the aesthete, his worker-artists were craftspeople, drafters technically competent at rendering the *anatomy* of the human figure and the *topography* of the landscape. Representing the American artist as more concerned with accurate and therefore 'realistic' representations, he pathologised his Americans as 'trial and error people', less interested in ideas and 'fatal dogma', who had rejected European precedents. For Craven, writing in defence of the Federal art projects of 1930s Depression America and Americanism in the arts, the American artist needed 'the vast panorama of American life, uncensored and unrestrained' produced in a definable American 'style' (1939: 3). 'Race nationality and art', an article written by Meyer Schapiro three years before Craven wrote his introduction to a collection of *American Prints* which included the work of regionalists such as Thomas Hart Benton and Grant Wood, made clear the dangers inherent in searching for essential racial characteristics in art, preferring cosmopolitanism.

Asked to write about the art of Mexican Americans, or Chicanos, in 1969, Jacinto Quirarte reasoned that he 'was not overly concerned with nationality and even less with ethnicity .... These matters were simply not important in the assessment of works of art' (1973: Preface). However, he came to the view that:

> While nationalism has been downplayed in matters of artistic production, it has nonetheless determined the way we perceive the art of the

> past and the present. Certain notions of art and architecture in the American Southwest have been ignored because they did not fit into our notion of what constitutes American and Mexican art.
>
> (Quirarte 1973: Preface)

Quirarte wrote his history of Mexican art as a riposte to received history rather than as an acknowledgement of the importance of distinctions and commonalities in terms of national identities. His stance stands in stark contrast to our understanding of art production in contemporary culture, where gender, sexuality and ethnic identities intersect. Ideas of nationhood are often subordinated to more local identities. Particularly, but not exclusively, in America, regional and ethnic loyalties have played a powerful role in the 'democratic experiment' that characterises the country and is another of this book's themes.

There is a further consideration when searching for anything that might be identifiably 'American'. Linda Nochlin, writing in 1994, made a strong case that both Mary Cassatt and Thomas Eakins had in their own very different ways transformed nineteenth-century American art from a 'provincial' undertaking to a 'world-class enterprise' (1994: 272). In doing so she remarked on the 'difficulty of making clear-cut stylistic distinctions in high art based on either national origin or gender' (Nochlin 1994: 255). She noted that reading art through gender had superseded what is American about American art, and yet was unwilling to forgo the:

> vexed issues of American-ness versus the cosmopolitanism represented by the French vanguard of the period or male versus female production ... [instead] exploring, in detail, the lives and works of these two artist-contemporaries, so alike in their ambitions and stature, so unlike in their choice of milieu and their pictorial language.
>
> (Nochlin 1994: 255)

Wanda M. Corn's *The Great American Thing* (1999), a phrase borrowed from Georgia O'Keeffe, also reflected on the question of 'What is American about American art?' Tracing the roots of American exceptionalism amid early modernists, Corn presented seven case studies to illustrate the variances and debates about what constituted national identity. Opting for a thematic rather than case-study driven model, we offer a range of interpretations from the earlier days of colonial rule to the present.

The extent to which any specifically national art can be called upon has never been simple. Essentialist notions of an American artist who expresses an American vision needs to be approached cautiously. Even the use of the less problematic term 'quintessential American' needs to be tempered. A country virtually defined by migrants since the colonial period to the present day is necessarily a pluralistic one. We should guard against the quintessential as some sort of essentialism. For instance Ben Shahn, often referred to as the quintessential American painter during the 1950s, was Russian-born, arriving in the United States in 1906 when he was eight. In 1968 he declared, 'I am the most American of all American painters ... maybe because I came to America and its culture and was sort of swallowing it by the cupful' (in an interview with Forrest Selvig).

Arriving via the Atlantic and Pacific ports from the late 1890s, large numbers of European and Asian immigrants contributed to the American avant-garde of the twentieth century. What émigrés brought with them in terms of experience and education varied: Dutch-born Willem de Kooning for instance did not arrive in the United States until he had completed his art education at 22. He often talked of the burden of Americanness in relation to his art making.

While American art is often presented as a dialogue between Europe and the United States, the influence of the East should not be underestimated, particularly in relation to avant-garde culture but also in relation to the enormous collections of Asian artefacts amassed by wealthy industrialists and museums in the nineteenth century. The influential art educator and artist Arthur Wesley Dow (1857–1922) encouraged in his students the appreciation of oriental art through Eastern artefacts to be found in collections at the Boston Museum of Fine Art. Educators such as Dow did not just appreciate the craft of Oriental cultures but drew on their methods of composition. In his teaching, he emphasised the importance of two-dimensional design, which he gained from studying Japanese culture in particular. Ultimately informing the aesthetics of the American Arts and Crafts movement, Dow's enthusiasm for Eastern aesthetics also informed the development of artists such as Georgia O'Keeffe and Max Weber. Closer to the modern period, Isamu Noguchi (1904–1988), born in the United States, was partially educated in Japan and deeply influenced by many aspects of its culture including Zen Buddhism. He travelled widely, was apprenticed to Brancusi in Paris, worked with ceramics master Uno Jinmatsu in Japan, and studied brush painting with Qi Baishi in China as well as visiting India. Seeing no distinction between fine and applied arts, Noguchi's fusion of East and West through sculpture, ballet set design, sculpture, gardens and the table lamp, contributed to a utopian vision of what art might be in a new world.

It is also noteworthy that a sense of *belonging* is not easily achieved in the modern world. Although he considered himself a global citizen, Noguchi was frank in his autobiography that unhappily he belonged everywhere and nowhere. The taxonomies of population movement – guest-worker, migrant, immigrant, émigré, emigrant, settler, refugee, expatriate, colonist – are often, in an American context, morally pitted against the seemingly authentic, rightful heirs, the indigenous, colonised, native, first peoples. Notwithstanding a brutal past, the toing and froing between cultures undermines any binaries of authenticity and displacement. Disabling liberal guilt and the stereotype of the native being closer to the earth, and therefore more 'real', have both played their part in the production of artworks and the writing that surrounds them.

Conversely, Louise Bourgeois, born in Paris in 1911 and coming to America after marriage to the art historian Robert Goldwater, is still after 60 years a 'foreigner', obsessively reworking in her often phallic-like sculptures themes that refer back to her French childhood and troubled relationship with her father.[6] Bourgeois's work retains many European theoretical influences.

In 2002 Erika Doss, writing in *Twentieth-Century American Art*, also returned to the old cliché, suggesting that what is American about American art is about trying to 'come to terms with American national identity' and 'what American is' (2002: 14) and cannot be answered by 'settling for misleading assumptions about national myths, or simplistic accounts of a modern-art canon'. She is also writing in a period when national, cultural and ethnic identity is a defining feature of the self rather than something to be laid to one side as redundant in the quest for universal significance. To ask now from a distance is also to look at the reception of such debates outside America. If for William Dunlap writing his first history of American art in 1834, the American artist was easily defined by place of birth, SAAM (the Smithsonian American Art Museum) has extended the eligibility to include artists working in America such as the English David Hockney and the Korean-born Nam June Paik.[7]

This history of American art does not start from the premise that America was an artistic backwater, only invigorated by European beaux-arts classicism in the nineteenth century or by the first Armory show in the twentieth century. The International Exhibition of Modern Art held at the 69th Regiment Armory on Lexington Avenue in New York in 1913 is often credited with bringing modernism to America, and in doing so sweeping aside a parochial, backwoods culture. Nor does this book subscribe to the view that American art 'came of age' after the Second World War, which was evident in the jubilant tone of Irving Sandler's 1970 *The Triumph of American Painting: A History of Abstract Expressionism.* Reading about American art, the phrase 'coming of age' is ubiquitous as competing claims are fought out in nationalistic and patriotic circles. For instance, on 31 October 1938 *Life* magazine ran the feature 'American art comes of age.' The article presented its case for a 'native school' from colonial to modern times through

6 See in particular Louise Bourgeois (1998) *The Destruction of the Father, The Reconstruction of the Father: Writings and Interviews, 1923–1997.*

7 Nam June Paik's 1995 *Electronic superhighway: continental US Alaska, Hawaii*, is a neon-lit map of the United States comprising over 650 working monitors and TV sets. It appears on the cover.

twenty-eight small black-and-white reproductions and eleven larger images printed in colour. The colour (and therefore more privileged) images included George Caleb Bingham's *Verdict of the people*, Thomas Eakins's *Max Schmitt in a single scull (the champion single sculls)* and Eastman Johnson's *Negro life at the south*. Illustrations of work by William Zorach, J. J. Audubon, Currier and Ives, Frederic Remington, Maxfield Parrish, Grant Wood, Trumbull and Winslow Homer augmented *Life*'s case for an indigenous history of American art.

In certain respects the European gallery goer would be untroubled by a visit to an American art museum displaying work from the history of American fine art. The sculpture would look reassuringly familiar, with the usual academic repertoire of mythological or historical subjects. The paintings would appear to cover the usual categories – genre, flower and still life, gesturing generals and figures from military history, children, landscapes and abstractions. But then, peering more closely, the works are punctured by decidedly un-European subject matter: slaves hoeing a field, a dying Indian, a mountain beyond the scale of anything in Europe, unfamiliar flora and fauna. Moreover there are subtle and sometimes startling formal differences, as European, Eastern and Caribbean cultures became 'susceptible' to America. So what we are extracting are commonalities and differences, but also art and cultural practices that stand on their own terms.

Culture in transition

There are inherent difficulties in writing about a culture in transition, particularly from an outsider perspective. Pico Iyer,[8] optimistically writing at the beginning of 2007, and commenting on recent shifts in international power, observes:

> the United States – though still the strongest power in the world – is by no means the largest or even the central one. One in every three people on our planet lives in China or India, and for those worthy souls the new century is a time of possibilities unimagined before.

He concludes that 'We live now in a global, not an American, century.'

This shift can be read out of a 2006 exhibition, *Uncertain States of American Art in the 3rd Millennium*, curated by Daniel Birnbaum, Gunnar B. Kvaran and Hans Ulrich Obrist, and held at the Serpentine Gallery in London. It presented an eclectic mix of works, from familiar pop to the endless referencing of appropriation art to the overtly socio-political, at the

8 In an article in the *Los Angeles Times* reprinted in the *Sydney Morning Herald*, 5 January 2007 (p9).

same time registering the interconnectedness of global cultures. The exhibition reminded the viewer that there was unease about the official political culture of the United States, and that artists were able to register their discontents under a banner of Mission Accomplished. The exhibition, on a two-year world tour ending in China in 2008, atypically showcased young American artists or at least artists working in America: a generation toying with their discontents within a media-saturated world. Notable for the use of new technologies, artists sampled, appropriated and collaborated. They also commented on contemporary America: the Argentinean US resident Mika Rottenberg's performance video *Dough* (2005) explored obese bodies through the metaphor of the bakery and dough production. Performing in a bakery in a studio, an obese woman kneads dough before its elongated mass joins the conveyer-belt below. Meanwhile Hong Kong-born Paul Chan's *1st light* (2005), a digitally animated film, like much in the exhibition in debt to surrealism, offers insights into a Christian fundamentalist's conceptualisation of heaven and hell, and the apocalyptic end of the world. Visualising the sifting of the virtuous from the damned on the day of judgement, an image designed on a computer and projected onto a floor shows bodies falling and consumer objects rising. It is an unsettling commentary on the doctrine of Christian Rapture combined with images of consumerism in an uncertain post-9/11 world. *Uncertain States of America*, the reader that accompanies the show, is at least in art history terms an indication of the distance travelled since Henry Luce's 1941 confident assertion that the twentieth century was the 'American century', the dynamo that drove the globe: 'the intellectual, scientific and artistic capital of the world' (Haskell 1999: 8).

We offer a history that we hope will take its place alongside others. Our intention is to present a view that relates present disquiet and reassessments of the past triumphs of America art to a more complex history than is normally the case. We look at art forms forced to fly under the radar of institutional art history as well as presenting, in critical terms artists, writers, curators and historians whose practices have contributed to the tributaries or deltas[9] that make up a less orthodox, heterogeneous history.

9 The analogy used in Robert Storr's lecture at the Royal Academy in 2006.

Chapter 1

Education and the American artist

In the nineteenth century respected American artists were often honoured with appellations that tied them firmly to the past and to Europe: Benjamin West was the 'American Raphael', Samuel Morse was the 'American Leonardo', Augustus Saint-Gaudens the 'American Michelangelo', Eastman Johnson the 'American Rembrandt', and both Washington Allston and William Page were granted the epithet of the 'American Titian'. In honouring its artists in terms of Old World standards the American art world may have revealed itself as a nation in thrall to its European past, but there is also an emergent confidence in the articulation of its native equivalence to European excellence. The period of the American Raphael, Leonardo, Michelangelo and Titian is not, as so often represented, just one of borrowing and imitation: it is also one of a growing faith in an indigenous national school of art.

The history of the organisations and institutions for teaching and promoting fine art in North America is long and geographically complicated, and largely absent from conventional histories of art. Art history regards the training of the artist as important, especially when one artist has been educated under the tutelage of another well-known artist (for example, Jackson Pollock studied under Thomas Hart Benton). However, the considerable training that most artists receive merits little separate attention. This is not to say that there is a dearth of literature on art education in America. On the contrary, there are rich sources of material in the periodical and book literature of the last hundred years, although it has yet to be integrated into accounts and analyses of American art history in the colonial, revolutionary and republican eras.

This chapter offers what at first might appear to be a familiar art history, which parallels the developments in European art history from the eighteenth century onward and charts the struggles for the admission of women to American academies, changing attitudes to the life model and the introduction of other formal teaching organisations to regulate art training. However, there are local and national circumstances that make the history of educating artists in the United States an unparalleled one. To this end we examine the efforts to promote and to standardise art instruction in the United States. The chapter also discusses the uneasy relationship of educational schemes in America with Old World teaching, and highlights the various attempts and initiatives to form a distinctively American, egalitarian and progressive school of art.

The self-taught artist

In presenting any discussion of American art education one needs to start with the caveat that art education existed in pre-Columbian America, and art education exists outside of formal establishments for art tuition, with a rich Native-American and Hispanic-American tradition.[1] It would be equally negligent to present a historical examination of art education for the American artist that overlooks the local arrangements for art education and the impact of amateur artists upon the narrative. Naïve animal painters, creators of military battle scenes and picturesque topographers of the Old West often have a history that is every bit as interesting as the types of institutional training of artists. And while it would be reductive to divide American artists into those who received formal art training and those who did not, it would be manipulative to say that it did not matter.

The educational coordinates that mapped an artist's practice are more often than not highly significant. In an environment where there were limited outlets for art training, education in fine art skills was a compromised *ad hoc* experience, arranged locally and in the spirit of fitness for purpose. The unrecorded and untrained artists active in the English American colonies of the seventeenth and eighteenth centuries normally came from the limner tradition. The term 'limner', coming from illuminator, described the anonymous activities of enamellers, coach and sign painters, and the artists whose portraits of wealthy plantation owners, merchants, industrialists and shipping line owners are not attributable to any one hand. For example, Edward Hicks began his career as a coach painter and sign painter; Matthew Pratt had been apprenticed at age 15 to his uncle, James Claypoole, who advertised as a 'Limner & Painter in general'; and the portraitist Thomas Badger (1792–1868) and landscape artist Alvan Fisher (1792–1863) were trained in the workshop of the decorative painter John Ritto Penniman (1782–1841). Art training for limners was conducted under the apprenticeship schemes of artisan workers. Apprentices learned their trade by assisting more experienced painters in the workshop, contributing to ornamental decorations on clock faces, militia standards and shop signs.

1 Peter Smith asks 'What was the art education of, for example, the peoples who created San Xavier del Bac? I cannot recall an answer to this question anywhere in the literature of American visual art education' (1996: 12).

Only a fraction of the artisan painters of the colonial and revolutionary periods crossed over into the realm of fine artists, but at least they had been trained in the skills of the painter. A number of American artists claimed no formal training whatsoever. Howard Finster, Grandma Moses, Bessie Harvey and Joseph Cornell, and the creators of tin whirligigs, wooden polychromed sculptures, and folk paintings in the Smithsonian American Art Museum are part of a rich tradition of outsider art in the United States. Deprived of the conventions of a formal art education, self-taught artists sometimes hit upon something novel, visionary and, if they become known at all, commercially valid. Jean-Michel Basquiat, Joseph Cornell and Grace Hartigan had little formal training in art; Andrew Wyeth was home schooled and largely self-taught; Ansel Adams was privately educated, Martin Wong self-taught. And some artists studied subjects other than fine arts: Vito Acconci studied creative writing at the University of Iowa; Robert Motherwell took a degree in philosophy from Stanford University before starting a PhD at Harvard, then studying under Meyer Schapiro at Columbia University; Frank Stella went to Princeton and majored in history.

Artists in early American art history could also be trained within a family unit. The profession of the artist in the United States was often connected to family. Gustavus Hesselius's son John Hesselius (1728–1778), also a successful portrait painter, was one of Charles Willson Peale's teachers. The Peales were the prime example of the artistic family; Charles Willson Peale's children included the painters Raphaelle, Rembrandt, Rubens, Titian and Angelica Kauffman Peale. John Rubens Smith was from a long line of English artists. Two of William Wetmore Story's sons were artists.[2]

For the amateur artist, it was possible to learn something about art through drawing manuals in the antebellum period. The proliferation of art instruction manuals in the nineteenth century has been characterized by Peter Marzio as an 'art crusade', and its chief crusaders – Rembrandt Peale, John Gadsby Chapman and John Rubens Smith – advocated not only that everyone was capable of drawing but also that the activity of drawing was a civilising one. Marzio has estimated that there were more than 145 drawing manuals published in the United States between 1820 and 1860 (1976). Rembrandt Peale in Philadelphia and William Bartholomew in Boston promoted a philosophy of art education which derived from two parent sources, Sir Joshua Reynolds' *Discourses on Art* and Johann Pestalozzi's *How Gertrude Teaches Her Children* of 1801. Pestalozzi taught drawing through the mastery of line and simple outlined forms, while Reynolds taught drawing by copying old masters in the tradition of the art academies. As Efland has phrased it:

2 Thomas Waldo Story (1855–1915) was a sculptor, and Julian Russell Story (1857–1919) a successful portrait painter.

> From the synthesis of these two traditions they had hoped to establish a new form of art education suitable for a democratic nation, one in which the ageless ideals of beauty perpetuated by the academy would be made available by means of a practical and efficient pedagogy.
>
> (Efland 1983: 155)

Most of the art instruction manuals advocated exercises in line drawing, a schoolroom exercise to train the hand and the eye in outline and tonal drawing. There was, as Glick has observed, less interest in colour, although the growing familiarity with Chevreul's colour theories gradually changed attitudes.[3] Colour exercises were difficult to achieve through books printed in black and white, and colour was also off the syllabus in the early stages of academic art training.

One of the first American art manuals was the *Juvenile Drawing Book* designed by John Rubens Smith (1775–1849), a painter and printmaker, and published in a three-volume set in 1822. Selling at $72, it was prohibitively expensive, but a cheaper alternative, *An Introduction to Linear Drawing* (1825) by William Bentley Fowle, became the first formal text book for teaching art in the US public school system.[4] Unlike Reynolds, Smith and Fowle were aiming their instruction at the school aged population. Fowle had introduced drawing in the public-school curriculum in Boston in 1821, and over the subsequent years art was gradually introduced in schools in the cities of the East. In the *Juvenile Drawing Book* Smith established that the purpose of his book was to contribute to the liberal education of the upper classes (assuming that the price of the book made him conscious of his limited readership), and he announced in his preface that:

> The book is predicated on the principle that drawing ought to form an integral part of liberal education .... It is not expected that everyone who learns to read will become a poet or writer ... anymore than by learning to draw they must become an artist.
>
> (Smith 1822: 147)

Smith followed with a series of books on perspective, colour and figure drawing which were more specific in their remit, but it is his idea about the contribution of drawing to a liberal education that it of interest. The authors of the drawing manuals shared, according to Marzio, a belief that the 'moral

3 Chevreul's complete text was not translated into English and published in America until 1857. Glick however has identified 'a summary of some of Chevreul's concepts' that was published in the American Repertory of Arts, Sciences, and Manufactures in January 1842 (Glick 1995: 102).

4 Fowle was not an artist and his book was really a translation of M. Louis Francoeur's original French text, supplemented with illustrations, exercises and instructions.

power of art came from a strengthening of mental and moral powers' (1976: 57) The writer and critic James Jackson Jarves considered that art education contributed to the individual's taste and virtue:

> Art education, rightly conducted, is not only a delight, but a source of virtue. Apart from the discernment of the false or superficial, or the appreciation of pure sentiment, the eye is exercised to detect error in design, or lack of harmony in color, and the mind notes whether it be of ignorance or wantonness. By such practice, a standard of correct taste in fundamental principles of the head and heart may be formed.
>
> (Jarves 1861: 11)

Mary Stankiewicz has described education in drawing as an accomplishment and a sign of cultivation. Borrowing the American philosopher George Santayana's derogatory phrase, the 'genteel tradition', Stankiewicz looks for its vestiges in 'common sense beliefs about the value of art education' that prevail today in notions of character building and citizenship (1999: 102). In antebellum America the wealthy may have been preordained to participate in the rituals of the 'genteel tradition', but through the educational initiatives of the second half of the nineteenth century, participation was extended.

European academies

The first professionally trained artists in America came from Europe and settled on the east coast. For example, one of the first noted portrait artists in America, the Swedish-born Gustavus Hesselius, settled in Philadelphia in 1712.[5] As colonial America began to produce native-born aspiring artists, a one-way transatlantic trade in art training commenced. Customarily the aspiring American artist in the late eighteenth and early nineteenth century went to Europe to train. Many from the colonial and post-colonial era went to England's Royal Academy of Arts, a relatively new establishment, founded in London in 1768. The curriculum at the Royal Academy relied on learning through a consistent and thorough imitation of the art of Greco-Roman culture and Renaissance Italy. Having spent a period of time studying copies of the great artworks of the past, students at the Academy were encouraged to travel to Italy to see the originals. Its first president, Sir Joshua Reynolds, explained the role of the past as a source of inspiration and improvement: 'It is vain for painters or poets to endeavour to invent without materials on which the mind may work, and from which invention must originate.

5 Hesselius's painting of the *Last Supper* (1721–2) for the St Barnabas Church in Prince Georges County, Maryland is normally cited as the first public art commission in the United States.

Nothing can come of nothing' (Discourse VI, 210f.). The Royal Academy had a monopoly on professional art practice, and it provided the reassurance to young American artists that success here would certainly mean success in America. During the colonial and early republic periods of American history, artists such as John Singleton Copley and Benjamin West (1738–1820) settled in England and both were highly successful painters there. West was particularly amenable to young American artists, and those that trained in his studio included Matthew Pratt, Charles Willson Peale, Gilbert Stuart, John Trumbull, Ralph Earl, Washington Allston, Thomas Sully and Samuel F. B. Morse.

Matthew Pratt's painting *American school* of 1765 is a conversation piece depicting a group of young American artists in West's London studio. West was a Pennsylvania-born artist who became a charter member of the Royal Academy when it was founded, and its president in 1792 and in 1807. All of the young men depicted in *American school* would have been British subjects, and they were among three generations of Americans sent to study under West. The image of the American artist projected at this point is rooted in the professional aspirations of artist-citizen. West, like his contemporary Copley and Trumbull, was self-taught and rose from humble origins to become the 'American Raphael'. But it would be wrong to give an impression here that *American school* shows American painters as part of an artistic enclave in London, and merely an ancillary part of art education in England.

John Vanderlyn (1775–1852) has the distinction of being the first American painter to study in Paris, the first American to exhibit at a French salon, and the first to win a medal at a salon. Vanderlyn was primarily a portrait painter but he also painted history and landscape subjects. As was mentioned earlier, despite being born to a wealthy family and being classically educated, Vanderlyn was apprenticed to a coach painter and print dealer, Thomas Barrow, in New York. During his apprenticeship he took classes at the Columbian Academy (see below), where he met and entered the studio of the American portraitist Gilbert Stuart (1755–1828) in 1794. Vanderlyn's patron, the US Senator Aaron Burr, advised him to study in Paris, and unusually for the period, he went there rather than to London.[6] He studied at the Académie de Peinture at the École des Beaux-Arts, where he followed a prescribed programme of study that included life drawing, drawing from casts of Antique and Renaissance sculpture, and copying old master paintings.[7] The École des Beaux-Arts was a state-supported organi-

6 Burr was a Democratic-Republican, who regarded revolutionary France as a more appropriate place for artists to learn how to develop a suitably national art for the new American republic than England.

7 Albert Boime discusses the teaching curriculum in the academies in *The Academy and French Painting in the Nineteenth Century* (1971).

zation that was free to both Frenchmen and foreign artists, although it did not admit women.

The case of John Vanderlyn also demonstrates how the first professional artists in America were charged with numerous tasks, in addition to rounding off their education. When Vanderlyn returned to Paris in 1803 he was funded by Edward Livingston, president of the newly formed New York Academy of Fine Arts, with the arrangement that he should obtain copies of Old Master paintings and casts of Antique sculpture in Paris, Florence and Rome for the Academy's collection. This also shows that artists did not sever links with Europe once they had completed their formal education. On the contrary, and even once there were home-grown organisations for teaching art in public schools and academies, artists maintained strong links with Europe. It is worth noting that numerous American modern artists continued to go to Europe. Thomas Hart Benton, Philip Evergood, Thomas Anshutz, Childe Hassam, Charles Demuth, Arthur Wesley Dow and Robert Rauschenberg all studied at the Académie Julian.

Academies in Germany became popular with American art students in the mid nineteenth century. Düsseldorf Academy attracted Americans such as George Caleb Bingham, William Morris Hunt, Worthington Whittredge, Richard Caton Woodville, William Stanley Haseltine, Enoch Perry and Eastman Johnson, as well as German-Americans such as Emanuel Leutze and Albert Bierstadt. The Düsseldorf School was noted for its stringent programme of 'indefatigable and minute study of Form'. William Morris Hunt remarked on his experience of Düsseldorf that the academy's philosophy was 'that the education of art genius, of a mechanic, and of a student of science were one and the same thing – a grinding, methodical process for the accumulation of a required skill' (Hoopes and Kalnein 1972: 24). The emphasis on meticulous attention to detail and a high degree of finish was influential on the Hudson River school of painters. Towards the end of the nineteenth century the Düsseldorf School was superseded by the Munich School. Unlike the precision drawing of the Düsseldorf School, Munich permitted a greater freedom of brushwork. American students in Munich included David Neal, Toby Edward Rosenthal, Walter Shirlaw, Frank Duveneck and William Merrit Chase. A number of Munich-trained artists became teachers at the Art Students League of New York. In contrast to the influence of the Düsseldorf school over the Hudson River painters, the Munich influence tended to assert itself in more modest American landscape art.

The Pennsylvania Academy

In the 1790s Philadelphia was the seat of the federal government, which accounts in part for its propensity to found cultural and scientific societies and institutions. The Pennsylvania Academy, founded in 1805 by Charles

Willson Peale and William Rush, was established to collect, exhibit and teach fine art in America. Although it was one of the first academies of art in America, it had been preceded by a number of projects. An early plan to educate potential American artists was devised in Boston in 1729, when Dean George Berkeley arrived in the United States with plans to establish a missionary college in Bermuda.[8] John Smibert was to be its first professor of painting and architecture.[9] Although the proposed college never materialised, Smibert settled in Boston and had a more indirect impact on art education: he was the first professional portrait painter to live there.[10] He supplemented his income by running an art shop from his home, selling artists' materials and engravings of Italian art. To return to Joshua Reynolds's observation that 'nothing can come of nothing', Smibert's shop provided something for artists to imitate in Boston.

Another Scottish artist, Archibald Robertson (1765–1835), was invited to teach drawing in New York City in 1791. With his brother Alexander, also an artist, he set up one of the first art schools in the United States, the Columbian Academy of Painting. During the thirty years of its operation the school taught artists such as Francis Alexander and John Vanderlyn. Robertson was also an active participant in the scheme to establish the American Academy of Fine Arts. Charles Willson Peale had also been involved in an earlier scheme to form an academy: he established the Columbianum, or the American Academy of Painting, Sculpture, Architecture, and Engraving in 1795. In 1805 Peale and his son Rembrandt were part of a committee that founded the Pennsylvania Academy of the Fine Arts. Robert R. Livingston (the minister to France in 1801) developed the plans for an art academy in New York. The plans included the importing of plaster casts of Ancient sculpture to New York as instructional aids for art students (Dunlap 1918: 104–5). The New York Academy of the Fine Arts was opened in 1803 and shortly afterwards became known as the American Academy of the Fine Arts. The Academy acquired full-size casts, including the *Laocoon*, *Castor and Pollux* and *Hermaphrodite*. Since drawing from the nude model was basically outlawed in American art academies until the last quarter of the nineteenth century these casts caused problems during the short period in which they were open to public display.

In 1804 a congressman from Philadelphia, Joseph Hopkinson, saw the cast collection at the American Academy and was inspired to help establish the Pennsylvania Academy of the Fine Arts (Dunlap 1918: 106). The

8 Berkeley had outlined his plans in 'A proposal for the better supplying of churches in our foreign plantations and converting the savage Americans to Christianity by a college to be erected in the Summer Islands, otherwise called the Isles of Bermuda' (1724).

9 Smibert commemorated the venture with a group portrait, *The Bermuda group* (1728, Yale University Art Gallery).

10 See Foote 1935: 14 for exceptions to the statement.

Pennsylvania Academy was the first purpose-built art school to also be an art museum in the United States (Searing 1982: 22). The remit of the Pennsylvania Academy was comprehensive, and linked the functions of collecting art to the training of artists, and the processes of exhibiting art to the profession of the artist. Like the European models on which it is based, there was an assumption that artists should learn by contact with historic works of art, and preferably that those examples should be experienced in the original.

Peale was among the first to recognise that the training of future American artists was a cultural imperative, having unsuccessfully made several attempts between 1791 and 1795 to establish art schools in Philadelphia (Dunlap 1918: 104–5). He had studied fine art with Benjamin West at the Royal Academy in London and was fully familiar with the pedagogic tools of a classical education – the use of plaster casts, and copying from European Old Master paintings. However, the only cast that Peale could obtain in Philadelphia was a cast of the *Medici Venus*, belonging to an expatriate English painter Robert Edge Pine. One of the stated purposes of the Pennsylvania Academy was to introduce Philadelphians to 'correct and elegant copies from works of the first masters of sculpture and painting'. With a budget of $1,000 the board of directors acquired plaster casts of Ancient statues from the Louvre. In 1807 the Academy's first exhibition presented full-size casts including the *Apollo Belvedere*, the *Laocoon* group, the *Medici Venus*, the Borghese *Gladiator* and a *Crouching Venus*, and busts of numerous historical figures in its rotunda.

The intrinsic usefulness of plaster casts and anatomical observation to training artists was unquestioned, but there was some nervousness about the place of the life model in academies and art schools. A successful artist such as the sculptor Hiram Powers resided principally in Florence where it was socially acceptable to employ models. However, matters were different in the United States, where the anxieties attending the establishment of life drawing at newly opening academies demonstrated a New World unease with the Old World's changing customs. The chances of securing a life model were slender in America, since there were no professionals. In the event Peale, 'finding nobody who would exhibit his person for hire to the students, whipped off his frills and ruffles and bared his own handsome torso for the class' (quoted in Sellin 1975).

James K. McNutt (1990) has detailed the history of the use of plaster casts as an educational tool in colonial American history. However, and as McNutt has amply demonstrated, there were social mores that rendered the display of the nude figure (which was, with a very few exceptions, the subject of the plaster casts) highly problematic in early nineteenth-century America. Pine's cast of the Medici *Venus* was, the librarian at the Academy later remembered, 'kept shut up in a case, and only shown to persons who particularly wished to see it; as the manners of our country, at that time, would not tolerate a public exhibition of such a figure' (McNutt 1990: 161). A tortuous etiquette was established whereby the drawing of casts of sculptures of nude figures could be used as part of the training of artists; opportunities to view the nude outside the formal class were limited and access by women was policed by academy officials. Peale was to acquire further deposits of casts for his collection,[11] but delicacy dictated that men and women should be segregated in order to view them. A similar arrangement at the New York Academy of the Fine Arts also stipulated for ladies' days, when the genitals of statues of the male figure were covered by plaster fig leaves.

So casts were then a staple in American academies. As late at the 1860s, art students were relying on them for their drawings of the human figure. Some enterprising students at the Pennsylvania Academy of the Fine Arts formed their own life classes, paying their models by subscription (as they did in the independent ateliers in France). But this was an exception to the rule. When an art school opened in San Francisco in 1871 it was given a collection of casts of sculptures from the Louvre and the Parthenon frieze by the French government in recognition of the $289,000 that San Franciscans had raised for the relief of the French during the Franco-Prussian War of 1871. The Chicago Academy of Fine Arts was founded in 1879.[12] The new Academy imitated established European models and, unsurprisingly, acquired an impressive collection of plaster casts.

The National Academy of Design, in New York City, now called the National Academy, is an association of artists, plus a museum and a school of fine arts. It was founded by members of the American Academy, Samuel F. B. Morse, Asher B. Durand and Thomas Cole, to 'promote the fine arts in America through instruction and exhibition'. Colonel John Trumbull, the Academy's director since 1817, regarded the education of students as a secondary concern of an art academy, although students of art were permitted to draw from the Academy's collection of antique casts (Thayer 1976: 38). Students began their studies by drawing from engravings. Once they had gained proficiency here, they progressed to drawing from the casts, then to drawing from live models and from nature. At many art schools, and in imitation of the beaux-arts tradition, there were regular competitions scheduled for the award of gold and silver medals.[13] Morse had studied at the

11 Joseph Allen Smith presented his collection of casts of Antique sculpture to the city of Philadelphia in 1804. Since there was no suitable space for the collection, Peale exhibited the casts in his natural history museum until a permanent building could be constructed (Sellars 1947 (vol 2): 242–3).

12 In 1882 it partnered with the Chicago Museum to become the Art Institute of Chicago. The School of the Art Institute of Chicago trained or contributed to the art education of Joan Mitchell, Elizabeth Murray, Georgia O'Keeffe, Claes Oldenburg, Mark Tobey, Richard Estes, Robert Indiana and Jeff Koons.

13 Lois Fink and Joshua C. Taylor, in *Academy: The Academic Tradition in American Art* (1975), discuss the curriculum at the National Academy of Design.

Royal Academy in London and transported many of its organisational principles including 'professors' in art, science and anatomy.

The National Academy of Design was patterned along the same pedagogic lines as European academies, and the first lecturer to be appointed there was Dr Frederick Gore King as professor of anatomy. Donald Thayer has thoroughly discussed the place of anatomical instruction within the curriculum at the National Academy, and shows that his time was so filled that a second professor of anatomy, Dr John Davidson Godman (1794–1830), was invited to alternate with King as a lecturer. Godman was married to Rembrandt Peale's younger daughter, Angelica (1800–1858), and presumably familiar with the workings of the artist's studio. Thayer is unable to establish either way whether Godman performed dissections for the students of the National Academy, 'But it is a reasonable conjecture that his duties toward that group were a carry-over from those to his medical students' (Thayer 1976). What Godman seems to have been most interested in, and taught to his students, was muscular action, and in his first lecture at the National Academy in 1827 he discussed the effect of muscular energy on the external surface of the body.

There is an illuminating, if inconclusive, story to be told about the attitudes of Americans to statues of the nude or partially clothed figure in the early to mid nineteenth century. In *Prudery and Passion*, Milton Rugoff writes, 'It is difficult to overstate the extent and intensity of prudery in America in 1840' (1971: 46). But we wonder just how consistent and insistent prudery was in America. Vanderlyn's best known painting, *Ariadne asleep on the island of Naxos*, was exhibited in 1816 at his first American exhibition in New York. Although the exhibition included several history paintings and portraits of Monroe and President Madison, as well as copies of Old Master paintings, the travelling show was noticed mainly for the display of the nude. Customary separate viewings were arranged for men and women. Whether these observances were rooted in native prudery or strict religious codes, the unflappable English writer Frances Trollope could not fathom the fuss when she visited the room marked 'Antique Statue Gallery' at the Pennsylvania Academy of the Fine Arts during 'Ladies Only Hour':

> I never felt my delicacy shocked at the Louvre, but I was strangely tempted to resent as an affront the hint I received, that I might steal a glance at what was deemed indecent. Perhaps the arrangements for the exhibition of this room, the feelings which have led to them, and the result they have produced, furnish as good a specimen of the kind of delicacy on which the Americans pride themselves, and of the peculiarities arising from it, as can be found.
>
> (Trollope 1839)

As we shall see in Chapter 3, Hiram Powers's *Greek slave*, the first life-sized nude to be toured in the United States between 1847 and 1848, excited cautious approbation. So it is not possible to say with absolute conviction that Americans were horrified or impressed by the nude, or that there were locations where the nude was tolerated and areas of the country where it was not. The supposed prudery of the Americans insinuated by Frances Trollope was probably no more universal than anywhere else.

However, there are stories to be pulled from the narrative of American art history that undermine the conclusions offered thus far. And there are nuances and special mitigating circumstances in each extracted story. For example, the forced resignation of Thomas Eakins (1844–1916) from teaching at the Pennsylvania Academy of the Fine Arts by the Board of Trustees in 1886 is such a case.[14] When Eakins became an assistant professor of painting and anatomy for the Academy in 1876, he set up a class in which students of both sexes could draw from a nude model, if not at the same time. Speculation has persisted that it was Eakins's prurience that led to the trustees' intervention. Stories abound that he used male and female life models together, or that he encouraged his students to pose naked, or that he revealed the genitals of a male model to a group of female students (Doyle 1999). There is even a photograph of Eakins undressed and carrying (presumably) a female life model in his arms. Elizabeth Johns (1983) has reassessed the reasons for his resignation, concluding that it was his advocacy of a 'pure art education' that was the cause of his troubles with the trustees. Johns argues that it was Eakins's stringently fine art outlook that led to charges of narrowness in the curriculum. At a time when progressive art education was looking to holistic schemes (see Sartain below), the view could be taken that Eakins's teaching of fine art was narrow and was neglecting a large constituency of the Academy. The Trustees saw that not only fine art students enrolled at the Academy – there were lithographers, graphic artists and photographers.[15] For their industrial art and applied art training Eakins argued students should look outside the Academy; he was only teaching the classical study of art based on the study of the nude through life drawing and supplemented by lectures on anatomy, given by the surgeon Dr William Keen. Although attendance at dissections was optional, it appears that most of the students, including the women, attended them.

Educating the sculptor

Although pedagogic models for training painters might still be based on European teaching, it was becoming increasingly possible for American painters to be educated to a standard that guaranteed professional acceptance

14 Eakins was an assistant teacher between 1876 to 1879, a professor of drawing and painting from 1879 to 1882, and director of the schools from 1882 to 1886.

15 Johns also cites Eakins's hands-off approach to tuition.

in America. However, in the training of American sculptors the connections with Europe were slower to break. There was still an expectation that sculptors should not only study in Europe but often practise in Europe. Saint-Gaudens and Lorado Taft studied at the École des Beaux-Arts in Paris, Moses Ezekiel went to the Royal Academy in Berlin. Many sculptors supplemented their training or settled in Europe, Hiram Powers and Horatio Greenough both lived for periods in Florence, and Thomas Crawford, Harriet Hosmer and William Wetmore Story lived in Rome. Edmonia Lewis, although trained at Oberlin College in Ohio, mainly worked in Rome.

Not all American sculptors were integrated into the prevailing style of European beaux-arts classicism. Clark Mills and Erastus Dow Palmer had no formal training; and Thomas Ball learned his art after being apprenticed to a wood carver. John Rogers followed the custom and went to Paris and Rome in 1858 for his training, but was utterly dispirited by the prevailing neoclassical style and by its lack of interest in incident and narrative (Wallace 1972: 60). Henry Kirke Brown was also an advocate of an American national school of sculpture, which could be better expressed through a naturalism of style and subject matter rather than the artificial poise of neoclassicism.

Lorado Taft (1860–1936) received his Master's degree in the United States before going to study at the École des Beaux-Arts in Paris from 1880 to 1883. On his return he taught at the Art Institute of Chicago, before teaching art and the history of art at the University of Chicago. In 1903 Taft published the first survey of *The History of American Sculpture*, in which he identified the Civil War as a turning point for American sculpture:

> Aroused from their dreams by the drama in which they lived, our sculptors felt emotions that they had not known before, and a few of them ventured to seek expression for these feelings in their art. Timidly but hopefully American sculpture began to grow contemporaneous in spirit; the 'actual' crept at last upon the stage, while classic themes gradually receded into pale obscurity.
>
> (Taft 1924: 131)

Taft remarked upon the number of sculptors who chose not to go to Europe to train.

Art leagues, clubs and artists' colonies

The convivial and social image of the artist is often at odds with the image of the artist as a lone outsider. Notwithstanding the pervasiveness of the solitary artist within art-historical narratives, there are many instances of artists thriving in the company of like-minded individuals. The studios of contemporary artists Jeff Koons and Julian Schnabel are busy spaces populated by a team of assistants. Andy Warhol's Factory was not just a mischievous anti-art term – it described a production line of assistants. Similarly artists often group themselves according to interests. There are numerous organisations in the United States devoted to genres, materials or artistic concerns. Most are incorporated as non-profit, tax-exempt organisations seeking to promote their particular art form.[16] At their best clubs and societies share and disseminate ideas. For example, Chiura Obata (1885–1975) co-founded the East West Art Society in 1921, ostensibly to facilitate cross-cultural exchanges of ideas about art. Obata was to become professor of art, with a short break necessitated by the US internment of Japanese citizens during the war, throughout the 1930s and 1940s at the University of California at Berkeley. His presence as both an art educator and a practising artist led to a discernible influence of Japanese art techniques and styles on the California watercolour school.

Art leagues have been an important way of organising and promoting activities in the visual arts in America. Virtually every town and city has an art league which provides classes, organises exhibitions and nurtures the arts. The Art Students League of New York was established in 1875 after the National Academy of Design closed its art school. William Merrit Chase, who had studied at the Royal Academy in Munich, became a teacher there in 1878. The League had been formed to compensate for the shortcomings of the National Academy of Design, principally that it could neither accommodate nor show the work of as many artists as wished to be there. Like the Academy, the League was a membership organisation, but unlike the Academy members did not have to be elected. For the sum of $5 per month artists could attend classes each day. Chase was considered to be bold and progressive in both his art practice and his teaching. His years in Munich had given him a painterly approach to painting at odds with the academic style. There was a difference between Munich and Paris-trained artists, but the League appeared to accommodate both styles of painting.

Art colonies had emerged throughout the United States at the end of the nineteenth century, especially in the Midwest and along the East Coast, and by the start of the twentieth century they were appearing in New Mexico. Artists' colonies offered two incentives for artists – a retreat from the urban areas that they normally resided in and the company of other creative, if not always like-minded, people. The Taos Society of Artists, for example, put Taos, New Mexico, on the art world's map. California's Monterey Peninsula

16 The American Society of Marine Artists, founded in 1978, promotes and encourages cooperation among marine artists, historians and enthusiasts. The American Society of Aviation Artists, founded in 1986, does the same for artists creating works that are unique to aviation and aerospace. Another, the American Society of Botanical Artists, Inc. (ASBA) dating from 1995, does promotes botanical art, and yet another, founded in 1999, the Society of American Mosaic Artists (SAMA), promotes mosaic art.

was home to several art colonies in the towns of Monterey, Pacific Grove and Carmel, and between 1890 and 1920 artists and writers settled in a coastal section of Greenwich, Connecticut, founding the Cos Cob Art Colony.

The drawing act

The nineteenth-century designation of a discipline called 'fine art' was problematic, and in some respects it still is. The term 'fine art' is the English language equivalent of what the French term *beaux-arts*, the Italians *belle arti* and the Germans *die schönen Künste*. The word 'fine' or 'beautiful' in its continental equivalents is not so much a sign of the value of a painting or sculpture, but more a reference to the purity of the discipline. Fine art is art produced primarily to fulfil aesthetic rather than utilitarian ends. Fine art refers to a limited number of art forms, and it has connotations of exclusivity and appears to be unrelated to industrial skills. Consequently there was a separation of fine arts from applied arts education, although as we shall see there was considerable crossover, with artists such as Ed Ruscha, Andy Warhol and Ben Shahn having trained in commercial art. Fine arts were taught in academies and applied arts in trade schools, common schools and schools of design.

The 1870 Massachusetts Drawing Act provided for mandatory free drawing classes for women, men and children in all communities with populations over 10,000.[17] As a direct result, twenty-three cities provided drawing classes for their communities. The Massachusetts Drawing Act also made it mandatory for state schools to incorporate art as one of the required subjects of the curriculum. The appointment of Walter Smith as director of art education for the state of Massachusetts, to in effect oversee the implementation of the Act, heralded the start of what became known as industrial drawing. Smith's interpretation of the Act advocated industrial drawing, predicated on a notion of drawing for a purpose, which in turn was rooted in art practice aligned to trade and industry.

All industrialists needed skilled drafters somewhere in their company. Since no institution for training them existed in America, Smith helped to form the Massachusetts Normal Art School in 1873.[18] Smith had trained at South Kensington in London under Henry Cole,[19] and his system of drawing imported British pedagogical ideas, but it would be misleading to say that it

17 Paul E. Bolin (1995) has shown that proposed amendments to the Act would have reduced this figure to 5,000.

18 Now called the Massachusetts College of Art.

19 The National Art Training School at South Kensington in London was established for the purpose of training art teachers, but also to train students in drawing, applied design and modelling to meet the requirements of trade and manufacturing.

was only English teaching systems that had an impact on American art instruction. For example, Horace Mann's publication of Peter Schmid's system of drawing instruction in 1844 was indicative of the impact of German pedagogical drawing systems on America. Arthur Efland and Peter Smith have acknowledged the influence of Henry Cole's views on drawing in the American system of art education, through Walter Smith. Art education was not an imaginative, personal or self-expressive activity, it was a way of teaching observational skills based on empirical and vocational terms. Its intention was to enhance the drawer's skills in accuracy of imitation, improved hand/eye coordination and following instructions with precision. Like the methods originally developed by the European design schools, industrial drawing began with the school pupils copying simple geometric shapes and then progressing to more complex designs.

In linking art education to a perceived need for industrial training, American educationalists knew of precedents and parallels in Europe. But we would argue that there is something distinctive about the attitude of Americans to their emerging industrial economy. Many Europeans were ambivalent about the industrial revolution, and we suppose rank and file Americans may have been too. But the difference is that Americans appreciated and anticipated the growing importance of industry to their country's economy and to its cultural life. Teaching art that had no overt fine art pretensions and did not attempt to give students aesthetic insights characterised a system of art instruction that emphasised the instrumental attributes of drawing – manual dexterity, delineation, recollection and measurement. Smith's influential reference work, *Art Education, Scholastic and Industrial* (1872), sequenced exercises for teachers and children which began with freehand drawing and moved to memory exercises, and geometric and perspective drawing. Learning by rote, through copying and repetition, Smith's method was part of broader efforts to standardise art instruction in the normal schools, technical schools and teacher training schools.

Dual-scheme fine art (picture making) and applied art (geometrical drawing) education developed different curricula, which according to Efland 'began to replicate certain aspects of the social class structure. High academic art was for the art student with upper-class aspirations while geometric drawing was for the working class' (1983: 156). This would reveal itself in the orientation of drawing in private and public schools: the aesthetic and liberal culture presented to upper-class Americans in collegiate and museum art education contrasted with the functional drawing taught to students from less fortunate economic groups. This separation between fine and applied art, with all its implied class bias, sits oddly however with the subsequent dismissal of Walter Smith from his post in Boston. Peter Smith summarises the various explanations for Smith's dismissal (1996: 29–31), and we would not wish to choose between them. Suffice it to say that Walter Smith's classical content appeared to be at odds with the desire for a democratic American culture, and that Smith's rarefied instruction in beauty was at odds with a useful industrial art training. Peter Smith has shown that Walter Smith's emphasis on teaching mimetic skills to potential industrial designers was already outmoded (1996: 38).

Pestalozzian drawing methods were popularised in North America through early nineteenth-century art instruction manuals.[20] However, the industrial drawing method advocated by Walter Smith dominated drawing instruction in the late nineteenth century. Louis Prang recognised the potential for art education material, opening the Prang Educational Company in 1878 with branches in New York City, Philadelphia, San Francisco, London, Berlin and Melbourne. Characteristically the drawing manuals of the nineteenth century detailed rigid exercises in line and perspective, although these later yielded to less prescriptive methods that encouraged spontaneity and self-expression. Louis Prang published Walter Smith's *American Text-books of Art Education*, which largely maintained Smith's industrial system of drawing, but later revisions to the Prang series in 1904 began to introduce some Froebelian exercises such as paper folding and weaving, and to suggest subjects for children to draw and paint.[21] 'This edition eliminated the lessons in drawing straight lines or geometric blocks; now children were asked to paint such natural forms as grasses, trees, and flowers without outlines, and were encouraged to explore mixing colors' (Tarr 1989: 119).

Prang's support for art education was not solely predicated on a desire for commercial gain. In fact he protested vociferously that his contribution to art education was done out of the goodness of his heart and at a financial loss to his business (Prang, 1882, quoted in Stankiewicz 1999). In an indirect sense there was no great loss to his business since its success was dependent upon skilled labour. In a roundabout way it could be seen that Prang's elementary course instilled the requisite drawing skills in the future labour market. The Prang Educational Company, as distinct from the lithographic company discussed in Chapter 2, developed the material published in its manuals from a largely female body of experienced art teachers. The best known was Mary Dana Hicks (1836–1927), who became Prang's wife. Mary Dana Hicks had been a drawing teacher in the Syracuse public schools, and had also established a teachers' training course in drawing. The

20 Pestalozzian ideas continued to exert their influences through Froebelian pedagogy. For example Prang's *The Use of Models: A Teacher's Assistant in the Use of the Prang Models for Form Study and Drawing in Primary Schools* (1887) was essentially Froebelian (Wygant 1983).

21 Pestalozzi's follower, the German pedagogue Friedrich Froebel, best known as the originator of the 'kindergarten system', expounded the theory children's understanding of the conceptual could be enhanced by drawing or by manipulating tangible objects (such as shaped wooden bricks and balls).

Syracuse schools had adopted the Walter Smith system of drawing, and Hicks was employed by Prang to revise Smith's drawing series.

Arthur Wesley Dow's art manual *Composition: A Series of Exercises in Art Structure for the Use of Students and Teachers*, first published in 1899, became the standard text for the study of art and design in the first half of the twentieth century. Dow was an influential teacher at his own Ipswich Summer School of Art, and also taught at various institutions including the Pratt Institute, the Columbia University Teachers College and the Art Students League. Programmes such as those at Pratt Institute and Columbia University emphasised practical skills in design and the decorative arts, and Dow's tuition was highly informed by the Arts and Crafts movement, which sought to blend an eye for beauty with a regard for utility. Nowhere perhaps is this more apparent than in his book *Theory and Practice of Teaching Art* (2nd edn 1912), aimed at art educators. Dow's separation of art appreciation and art practice stressed that the real aim of art education was aesthetic refinement rather than the development of artistic skills.

Women and art education

Remarking on the nineteenth-century art world, Laura Prieto observed that 'Women might draw or paint or sculpt, but they could not be Artists' (2001: 3). Coupling Prieto's distinction between women who drew or painted and 'Artists' with the wide-ranging activities of nineteenth-century women throws into sharp relief the inadequacies and inconsistencies of western art education.

One compelling statistic is that a majority of students in American art schools in the late nineteenth and early twentieth century were female. For example, the majority of students in the first year of admission to the first art school in the west, the San Francisco Art Association's California School of Design, were women (Wilson 1982: 47). But what special provisions were made for women artists in the United States, and how do they compare with European models? In the main, women artists in Europe fared no better than American women artists. For example, the École des Beaux-Arts did not admit women. Trainee female artists in Paris studied at private ateliers run by French academic masters, such as Julian's, Colarossi or Carolus-Duran, or Krug's. Women artists often paid a premium: the monthly charge for male students at Julian's was 50 francs per day, while women paid twice that sum. (Wein 1981: 42).

As we have seen, art leagues have been an important way of representing special interest groups. These non-profit organisations were not the special province of women but were often associated with specialised groups and shared local interests. After the short-lived experiment at the Pennsylvania Academy of the Fine Arts, the Art Students League of New York was the first school in America to permit women to take life classes, albeit separately from male students in the first years of the policy. The League also stipulated in its constitution that half its board should be made up of women. The Plastic Club in Philadelphia was formed in 1897 as a women's group (membership was extended to men in 1991) which hosted exhibitions and lectures. These local efforts at marshalling artistic activity are only part of the story. There were also national attempts to foster and promote common interests. For example the National Association of Women Painters and Sculptors (NAWPS), founded in 1889, not only promoted their interests through an annual exhibition in New York, it also sent travelling exhibitions around the country.

Mary Dana Hicks was elected first president of the Syracuse Social Art Club in 1875. Its forty members collected reproductions of works of art, visited art galleries and organised exhibitions. Blair calls Hicks and other women organisers 'torchbearers', asserting that 'women ... used the arts, no less than they used political skills to effect their vision for social change in America' (1994: 11). Blair argues that women may at first have organised themselves into social clubs for the purpose of self-development, but they came to see participation as a means for improvement of society in general and their communities in particular.

Vassar College, opened in 1865, was the first to offer a full liberal arts curriculum to women (although other colleges had admitted women before 1865). The college building, designed by James Renwick, had its own gallery, and from the outset it may be seen that studio practice and exhibition were twins of education. Under the tutelage of Henry Van Ingen, Vassar became the first college to offer courses in art history. It was also at Vassar that the first MA in fine arts in the United States was awarded (Askew, in Smyth and Lukehart 1993: 60).

William Morris Hunt returned to America in 1855 after a prolonged period in Europe, studying in Rome, Düsseldorf and Paris. He had worked alongside two famous European artists, Thomas Couture and Jean-François Millet,[22] and he had some success at the Paris salon. As he was a successful and accomplished painter, his reputation in America, in first Vermont and then Rhode Island, attracted young artists. When Hunt settled in Boston, he occupied a large studio where the walls were covered not only with his own paintings but with the work of Millet and other French artists. His studio became an unofficial art centre, and he was a generous teacher. He taught large numbers of female students in Boston after 1868. Boston still had no academy of its own. Women could attend the Boston School of Design, but as the term 'design' indicates, that school was geared towards preparing students for employment as designers in manufacturing industries (Hoppin 1981).

22 Hunt was an enthusiastic advocate of Millet's art and purchased a number of his paintings.

The first coeducational degree-granting college of fine arts in the United States was at Syracuse University.[23] This was the second US college, after Yale, to grant degrees in fine arts. The College of Fine Arts was inaugurated in 1873, and run by Dean George Fisk Comfort. Comfort's provision for female students has been described 'virtually as a women's finishing school' (Stankiewicz 1982: 48). Comfort was professor of esthetics and modern languages, and Stankiewicz has argued that he allied a collegiate education in aesthetics with a moral belief in the role that women were best suited to play in society. That is, cultural refinement was the core business of a fine arts college.

Emily Sartain (1841–1927) was among the first group of student artists who were permitted to draw from the male nude at the Pennsylvania Academy of the Fine Arts in 1868–9 (Peet 1990). Sartain set out for Europe with Mary Cassatt to further her studies. Cassatt had finished at the Pennsylvania Academy in 1866, before the Ladies' Life Class was formed. With Eakins's encouragement Sartain applied for the post of principal of the Philadelphia School of Design for Women (now Moore College of Art) in 1886.[24] Her plans for updating the curriculum were implemented by new appointments, of Alice Barber Stephens (1858–1932), Lucy D. Holme, Samuel A. Murray (1870–1941) and Thomas Anshutz (1851–1912) – all former pupils of Eakins.[25] Her distinctive contribution to art pedagogy at Philadelphia was that when two new areas of teacher training and fine arts were added to the programmes, Sartain stipulated that fine art, training teachers and industrial or commercial art students participate in the same progressive curriculum.

Philadelphia's School of Design offered industrial arts training aimed at widening career opportunities for women who had already received some education. The emphasis on vocational art training for women was a response to a wider social need to make women employable and escape the poverty trap in which even socially higher-class unmarried women might find themselves. The vocational training was to help respectable women escape from the poorly paid professions of needlework and school teaching. Many cities (Philadelphia had followed Boston) had incorporated 'industrial drawing' into the common school curriculum by the end of the nineteenth century.

23 The first coeducational institution of higher education in the United States was established in 1787 at Franklin College in Lancaster, Pennsylvania. The longest continuously coeducational school is Oberlin College in Oberlin, Ohio, which has been running since 1833, and awarded the first degrees in the United states to women in 1841 and the first degree to an African-American woman in 1862. The coterminous establishment of women's colleges included the Seven Sisters – Vassar, Radcliffe, Wellesley, Smith, Mount Holyoke, Bryn Mawr and Barnard colleges.

24 Emily's niece, Harriet Sartain, took over as dean in the 1920s.

25 She appointed Robert Henri (1865–1929) in 1892, the same year that Henri and other painters exhibited their controversial impressionistic paintings.

Black Mountain College

Black Mountain College, an independent coeducational college, was founded in 1933 in a small town in North Carolina. Combining the values of a solid liberal education with training in the creative arts, Black Mountain was passionately committed to the principles of interdisciplinary practice and formal experimentation. What was most remarkable about Black Mountain in the 1930s was its integration of creative and performing arts. Perhaps wrongly, it has come to be thought of as an art school, but its director John Andrew Rice strenuously resisted that narrow view.

The place of John Dewey (1859–1952) on the college's advisory board is indicative of, rather than conclusive proof for, the positioning of the fine arts within a general curriculum of creative and performing arts. Dewey's theories of progressive education had garnered support in the previous decades, so much so that the Progressive Education Association was established in 1919, in part to promote his and other progressive ideas. Under the aegis of the Association, art education in schools shifted from the nineteenth-century emphasis on picture study, correct drawing and hand-eye coordination to exercises for unlocking children's creative capacities. The student-centred, holistic and experiential curriculum advocated by Dewey and adopted by John Andrew Rice in founding Black Mountain College is best illustrated in the interdisciplinary and experimental nature of education there.

The College's commitment to interdisciplinary practice is evident from the accounts of teaching and projects that have survived. One of the best remembered now is John Cage's staging of the first multimedia happening at Black Mountain in 1952.[26] Cage had joined the faculty in 1948, and in 1952 devised his *Untitled event*, also known as *Theatre piece no. 1* or the *Black Mountain piece*. Conceived, planned and executed between lunch and evening, *Theatre piece no. 1* was a busy and unrehearsed platform for simultaneous performance. Cage read to the audience while perched on a ladder at the side of the room, as Merce Cunningham danced in the centre and David Tudor played the piano and radio. The room was adorned with Robert Rauschenberg's white paintings, and Nick Cernovich's movies were projected onto a side wall and the performers. The only predetermined part of the happening was the performers' agreement about the duration of their contribution as it was improvised to the audience.

Much has been written about the presence of Josef and Anni Albers[27] at Black Mountain College, and certainly Josef Albers is the pivotal presence

26 'Happenings' were live events that sought to bring audience and performers together in unusual venues. See Allan Kaprow, *Assemblage, Environments and Happenings* (1966).

27 There were few women teachers at Black Mountain, although there were many female students. Mary Gregory (b. 1914) did however take over the running of the woodworking shop when a number of male members of the faculty enlisted in the Second World War.

in the history of the college. It was not just that the Alberses transported Bauhaus ideas of education and art foundation training from Europe to America, but also that they resettled the Bauhaus belief that education must be gained outside the classroom, and that it might also be experienced through the ethos of communal living. Calling it an 'education in a democracy', Black Mountain promoted the idea of democracy not only through its independence and self-governance, but also through its approach to teaching the creative arts. To illustrate the application of its pedagogic principles, subject areas such as drama, music and the fine arts were regarded as an integral part of student activity and experience. Outside the subject-specific domain, staff and students participated jointly in extracurricular schemes such as running the college farm, serving meals and maintenance of the building on campus. To facilitate this wider engagement with the college community, no classes were held in the afternoon and many ran in the evenings. However, it was perhaps at its summer schools that the most significant teaching took place. The renowned summer institutes attracted some of the best-known artists of the period onto its teaching faculty – including Walter Gropius, Jacob Lawrence, Willem de Kooning, Robert Motherwell, John Cage, Buckminster Fuller, Merce Cunningham, Charles Olson, Robert Creeley, Robert Rauschenberg and Franz Kline.

Josef and Anni Albers were two of a number of artists to flee Nazi Germany after the closing of the Bauhaus and to be appointed to teaching positions in America. For example, Walter Gropius was appointed to Harvard and László Moholy-Nagy and Gyorgy Kepes to the New Bauhaus in Chicago. The New Bauhaus, founded in 1937, continued the work started at Weimar and Dessau by former Bauhaus masters. Moholy-Nagy was its founding director and encouraged the same level of experimentation with materials among students at the New Bauhaus as he had at Dessau.

In the mid-twentieth century the provisions for art education were reviewed in response to changing national and global contexts. In the immediate aftermath of the Second World War large numbers of soldiers returning home to the United States were lured into art schools and universities by the GI Bill (the Servicemen's Readjustment Act) of 1944. Artists who benefited from the scheme included Leo Krikorian, Robert Rauschenberg, Kenneth Noland and Ed Rossbach, and many, including Jules Olitski, Ellsworth Kelly and Sam Francis, used the funds available to go to Paris during the late 1940s and early 1950s.

The review considered the needs and special interests of various groups that had not been accommodated within existing educational schemes. For example, the congressionally chartered Institute of American Indian Arts (IAIA) was established in 1962, in Santa Fe, New Mexico. Although the idea of a separate education for Native Americans that focused on native arts and crafts was a laudable one, the scheme has been perceived to have been subsumed within overarching modernist art practices. Joy Gritton has investigated the early years of the IAIA, and exposed a disparity between the curriculum it advocated and the practice it engendered. Although the school advocated a cultural pluralism, its adoption of modernist individualism impinged upon Native tribalism, and modernist art practices and aesthetics came to dominate the activities of students. As Gritton puts it:

> Students were asked to be at once the 'Primitive' and the 'Primitivist' in a Western discourse wherein form took precedence over meaning, product over process, and 'universal' aesthetic (and market) value replaced cultural context. Within such a framework the recognition of the equality of divergent aesthetic systems, values, and beliefs was precluded.
>
> (Gritton 1992: 35)

College art and the MFA

> A College education for an artist is absolutely necessary to learn that it isn't absolutely necessary.
>
> (Reinhardt 1953: 249)

Diego Rivera began studying at the Academy of San Carlos Mexico City in 1898, when he was 12 years of age. As Jean Charlot has observed, he was as much interested in 'What went on back of the school building' (Charlot 1950: 10). Rivera's apparent lack of interest in the Academy predates Ad Reinhart's (1913–1967) mischievous assertion above, that colleges teach artists that a college education is unnecessary. Indeed Rivera is presumed to have left the Academy of San Carlos at the age of 16, objecting to the emphasis of the curriculum.

This idea of the artist at odds with his or her educational provider is not a modernist phenomenon per se. It is perhaps indicative of the fact that modern artists had choices – choices of where to study, choices of how to study, stylistic choices of operation and choices of patron. But more tellingly, the troubled relation between artists and the education system is indicative of a view that art education did not meet the needs of modern artists. After all, Paul Cézanne and Vincent van Gogh received very little art education, and their example lent credence to the view that artists were born rather than taught. Moreover, the kind of education modernists appeared to require was one directed more toward developing perception, awareness, self-expression and individual creativity rather than honing mimetic skills. This opened up the activities of the teacher of art in the twentieth century, and permitted wildly different educational approaches to emerge, represented at one end by those who expounded formal exercises in art, and at the other by those who upheld the view that art was 'unteachable'.

When the College Art Association (CAA) was founded in 1911, there was some debate about the relationship between art history and practical art training, which Howard Singerman has characterised as a split between practitioners and teachers within the ranks of the CAA.[28] But this discrepancy between art history and art practice is only one aspect of the changing provisions for art education in the twentieth century. Arguably more insistent was the seeming irrelevance of established patterns of art education within the modern art period. In 1946 the CAA sponsored a committee report, 'The practice of art in liberal education', recommending a new kind of educator, the 'artist-teacher', who would unite the liberal arts education and studio training in working with art students.

A number of twentieth-century modern artists worked as teachers. The immigrant artist-teacher Hans Hofmann (1880–1966) opened his first school in Greenwich Village, New York in 1933, later called the Hans Hofmann School of Fine Arts, and in 1935 he established a summer school in Provincetown, Massachusetts. Hofmann's students included Lee Krasner, Helen Frankenthaler, Larry Rivers, Allan Kaprow and Marisol Escobar. Hofmann's teaching, often referred to as a 'push and pull' technique, combined principles of cubism and German expressionism, and influenced the first generation of abstract expressionists. The influence of his teaching (and teaching by surrealist émigrés) upon a generation of New York painters is often minimised in histories of the mid twentieth-century art that emphasise American lineal descent. And there was a buoyant history of American artists as teachers. The various community centres established by The Works Progress Administration Federal Art Project (WPA/FAP) during the depression provided work for artist-teachers. One example the Harlem Community Arts Centre provided art classes for its local Community of African Americans as well as a much needed venue to showcase artists like Jacob Lawrence. In addition to artists paid as teachers under the Federal Art Project William Zorach and Thomas Hart Benton taught at the Art Students League of New York. Clyfford Still, Ad Reinhardt and Mark Rothko taught at the San Francisco Art Institute. Ad Reinhardt also taught at Brooklyn College. Robert Motherwell, Mark Rothko and William Baziotes founded a short-lived art school in 1948 called 'The Subjects of the Artist', which contributed to the development of abstraction in American painting.

In 1973 Harold Rosenberg, the critic who championed action painting in the 1950s, discerned an appreciable shift in art practice among students educated in university art departments as opposed to those trained in art schools. Remarking in particular on how the short-hand teaching of modernist abstract painting had contributed to 'the cool, impersonal wave' of

28 Citing a 1927 survey by the Association of American Colleges, Singerman points out that schools in the South and West were more practically oriented, while the older liberal arts colleges of the Northeast gave priority to art history.

1960s art, Rosenberg observed that 'Josef Albers' impacted color squares have become the basis of impacted-color rectangles, chevrons, circles, stripes – works bred out of works, often without the intervention of a new vision' (1973: 92–3). He was critical of the emphasis upon training artists in the methods of other artists, notably Albers, and expressed concern that the systematic observance of grids and circles would herald a generation of problem solvers rather than artists. In the specific case of art students taught by Albers, Rosenberg's fears seem to have been without foundation. Robert Rauschenberg, Cy Twombly, Nancy Graves, Richard Serra and Eva Hesse (all taught by Albers either at Black Mountain or at Yale University) worked in a variety of styles and media, and none appears to have been in thrall to Albers's own art practice. However, Rosenberg was promoting the unfettered and imaginative art of abstract expressionism, and his hostility to pop art or to hard-edged minimalism is grounded.

The great majority of contemporary American artists are now educated in the colleges and universities of North America. The Bachelor of Fine Arts (BFA) for students of the visual or performing arts usually consists of two-thirds study in the arts, with one-third in more general or liberal arts studies, taken over four years. The Master of Fine Arts (MFA) is an additional two or three-year graduate programme in visual, applied or performing arts. Singerman has found it impossible to conclude exactly what skills are gained by graduate art students in the college arts departments. He refers to the ideas of Pierre Bourdieu and Thierry de Duve, who have both argued that contemporary art practice is driven by critical engagement and a high degree of self-motivation, so that the commitment to art practice is of itself a sign of its intellectual gravity. The advent of more conceptual and discursive art practice leads Singerman to conclude that 'the failure of the M.F.A. lies ... in the lives of individual students who are neither disciplined nor skilled' (1999: 211). So, we suppose, we have come on a circular and circuitous route by which art changes drastically (in terms of style, medium, concept and so on) but the exhortations to artists learning how to be artists remain fundamentally the same – discipline, skill and commitment.

After attending Hartford Art School in Boston, Mark Dion moved to New York and, in his own words:

> Attending the School of Visual Arts and then the Whitney Independent Study Program .... I met extremely generous teachers like Tom Lawson, Craig Owens, Martha Rosler, Joseph Kosuth, Barbara Kruger and Benjamin Buchloh ... the third stage took the form of my travels in the forests of Central America that led to my renewed interest in the biological science which I studied at home and at the City College of New York.
>
> (quoted in Corrin, Kwon and Bryson 1997: 8)

Dion's summary of his education suggests that he has negotiated a medley of schemes, programmes and self-tuition. Hal Foster has written about 'The artist as ethnographer' (1995), but Dion's art practice requires the skills of the anthropologist, ethnographer, archaeologist, natural scientist and team-worker as well as a thorough grounding in theory. The contemporary artist may still only gain an entrée into the art world through a formal educational training, such as the BFA and MFA; however, current art practice often requires additional skills that are beyond the remit of either qualification. The early nineteenth-century aspiration to a distinctively American art education in the academies and art colleges has been realised in a significant measure. But art practice and the range of media employed are so varied that perhaps no one institution or organisation can ever prepare contemporary American art for the scale and range of operations of an artist such as Mark Dion.

Chapter 2

Art into reproduction

When Thomas Jefferson was planning his classically inspired home on his Virginia plantation at Monticello, the designs proposed a gallery for the display of plaster casts after antique sculptures and copies of paintings by European Old Masters. Around 1771 Jefferson compiled a wish list in his building notebook for 'Statues, Paintings &c.' (Howard 1977: 583). Since he was not to make his long-desired Grand Tour to Europe until 1784, Jefferson's list consisted entirely of items he had not seen in their original incarnations. So where did his knowledge of antique statues and Old Master paintings come from? How did he prioritise items on his list? And what status did reproductions of works of art have in colonial and republican America?

The relationship between Americans and the Old Masters was often forged through intermediaries. Jefferson's knowledge of works of art came either from a trade in prints and reproductions or from the collections of his friends and acquaintances on the East Coast, in Williamsburg, Annapolis, Philadelphia and New York. Since the North American continent was such a vast landmass, from whose eastern seaboard Europe could only be reached after a sea journey of some months, the connection to cultural beacons of European art was secured through casts, copies and prints. This chapter considers the place of surrogates and simulations of the actual artworks – prints, copies of Old Master paintings, engravings after paintings and sculptures, lantern slides, plaster casts of original sculpture, and photographs – in the history of American art, and the status of the reproductions as they increasingly came to deputise for the originals.

Copies of Old Masters

For a wealthy collector such as Jefferson, at the high end of the market in reproductions, there was a growing trade in plaster casts after well-known statues and watercolour or oil painted copies of Old Masters. To facilitate the latter there were numerous professional copyists in Europe who could be commissioned by American collectors, and at the start of the nineteenth century there were a growing number of American copyists sent to Europe for the express purpose of copying Old Masters. Amateur copyists were a common sight in European galleries – copying from the Old Masters was, after all, part of an artist's formal training. The profession of the copyist, however, was not an entirely desirable one. On the one hand they were highly trained, technically accomplished artists who could make their living by copying the work of others. On the other hand, the professional copyist was not always an entirely reputable figure since their skill could also prepare them for a career as a forger. However, there was a genuine demand for 'legitimate' copies in the United States, and many American artists supplemented their income by legally copying European paintings when abroad.

Generally speaking, American art patrons had conservative but discerning tastes in paintings. They knew the canon of art and they knew which artists were most highly regarded, both aesthetically and fiscally. The copies most demanded by collectors were of well-known pictures, particularly by Italian Renaissance and Baroque painters. Jefferson's Monticello gallery list stipulated, among a number of items, a *Holy Family* after Raphael, a *Descent from the Cross* copied from Rubens and a copy of Ribera's *Penitent Magdalen* (Howard 1977: 598–600). Jefferson's tastes were not exclusively biblical, and his collection included many mythological subjects and engraved pictures after classical sculpture, including a considerable number of nudes. As was evident in Chapter 1, there was some ambivalence in the United States about exhibitions of nudes, but they were clearly popular with private collectors. For example, John Vanderlyn made a copy of two Correggio paintings, *Antiope* and *Leda and the swan*, for undisclosed patrons.[1] Vanderlyn himself painted copies after Raphael and Rubens for American patrons when he travelled to Rome, perhaps as part of a committed effort to study the Old Masters, or perhaps in response to a private commission.

Copies of Old Master paintings were one-offs, and copying was a time-consuming process for the artist. A painting that illustrates both of these points is Samuel Morse's *Gallery of the Louvre*. This large painting (over 6 x 9 feet) depicts the Salon Carré, one of the grandest rooms in the Louvre, hung floor to ceiling with Old Master paintings from the fifteenth to the eighteenth century. Three walls of the gallery are visible, and toward the back of the scene is a view through to the Grand Salon. The Louvre was frequently populated by copyists, both trainee artists and professionals. When the Louvre was first created, its collection was reserved in the main for the purpose of permitting artists to copy and study Old Masters, only later

1 The original *Antiope* was painted in 1524–5 and is now in the Louvre, and Correggio's *Leda* was painted in the 1530s and is now in the Gemäldegalerie, Berlin.

being opened to the public. The sheer volume of artists arriving at the Louvre to execute copies became so large that the gallery instituted a rule that no more than three copyists could work on the same painting at the same time.

Morse was in Paris between 1831 and 1833 to fulfil a list of commissions for copies of paintings which he hoped would finance his trip to Europe, including one of Rembrandt's *The angel leaving Tobias* for his friend the American novelist James Fennimore Cooper (Tatham 1981: 40). He copied several of the paintings located throughout the museum and brought them together in his original painting, this imaginary museum. Each of the thirty-eight miniature copies of the original paintings was worked over the spring and summer of 1832 from a series of scaled-down studies. Morse wrote a guide identifying the paintings, but he failed to provide a key to the figures in the foreground of the painting. It is generally, although not unanimously, thought that they include James Fennimore Cooper with his wife, and their daughter Susan Cooper seated at the easel. The other unspecified figures include a teacher (perhaps Morse himself) advising his pupil and a seated, turbaned artist sitting in front of an easel before a landscape (Tatham 1981: 44).

An engraving by Winslow Homer shows *Art-students and copyists in the Louvre Gallery, Paris*. The engraving, which appeared in *Harper's Magazine* in 1868, depicts several copyists, including in the foreground women artists, who have set up easels and platforms to permit the close copying of the work from the salon. The image is revealing in two respects. Like Morse's rendition of the Salon Carré some thirty-five years earlier, Homer's Louvre explicitly connects women's creativity with the twin skills of diligence and mimesis. In the latter half of the nineteenth century there was an increasing number of educational facilities founded for the purpose of teaching art. The dispatch of copyists to Europe therefore fulfilled a dual brief – to copy as part of their own education and to copy Old Masters in response to a growing need for copies of paintings in educational establishments in America. Throughout the nineteenth century many art academies, art colleges and museums formed their own, sometimes extensive, collections of copies and casts. Vassar College was among the first of the US colleges to be founded with a programme of study in art and art history. It was also one of the first to have a permanent art collection which included both copies and casts from European sculptures and copies of Old Master paintings (Plate 3). The hiring of female copyists in Europe was entirely within the norms of the time. Many women were making a living from copying artworks. For example, the American painter Emma C. Church was commissioned to make copies of Italian Renaissance and Baroque paintings to be part of Vassar College's collection. In Rome she copied Guercino's *Unbelief of Saint Thomas*, Carlo Dolci's *Madonna and child* and Raphael's *Madonna of Foligno*.

Plaster cast collections

The first examples of European sculpture to reach the United States arrived with a Scottish portrait painter, John Smibert (1688–1751), in 1728. As we have seen Smibert's plan had been to use his collection (which comprised copies of Old Master paintings and engravings as well as casts) as teaching aids in Dean George Berkeley's unrealised college for instructing the Indians of Bermuda (Foote 1935: 17). In 1730 he opened an engraving studio and artists' supply store in Boston. In the room above the store he displayed his copy collection together with his own portraits, establishing what might technically qualify as America's first art gallery (Hagen 1940: 45). His collection was by no means comprehensive but he did have a cast after the *Medici Venus* and his casts were consulted by artists. It is known that on occasion, his casts were copied by John Singleton Copley, Charles Willson Peale and John Trumbull (Flexner 1947: 130). Recalling that Smibert's collection had originally been transported with the express purpose of educating native American Indians in the beauties of the classical tradition (Foote 1935) the casts served as surrogates for colonial artists who were not imbued directly with the Western classical tradition but would be receptive to its representatives in Boston.

As we saw in Chapter 1, nineteenth-century collections of plaster casts after key European sculptures formed important pedagogical tools in the beaux-arts educational model. At the core of fine art training was the educational given that students of architecture and fine art were to be inspired by their commerce with European classicism. Since there were limited opportunities to do this directly, students were exposed to collections of plaster casts and engravings to augment their knowledge of the classical. Plaster casts are facsimiles of sculptures, either actual size or in reduction, made from plaster of paris cast into clay moulds. Moulds were often reused, and permitted plaster workshops to manufacture limited editions of plaster casts. There were several established European manufacturers in Italy, France, Germany and Britain, including Antonio Vanni of Frankfurt and the Domenico Brucciani firm of London. Typically these firms provided the goods for an increasingly vibrant America market in the mid-nineteenth century. American museums and art colleges could consult an illustrated catalogue of casts and order copies as required. However, towards the end of the century the firm of P.P. Caproni & Brother in Boston became the most widely used manufacturer of plaster reproductions of classical and contemporary statues in the United States. Caproni was the chief supplier to American University collections and installed the cast galleries at Harvard University, Yale University, Princeton University and Cornell University. Caproni's distinctive brass hallmarks bearing the tag 'PP CAPRONI & BROTHER PLASTIC ARTS, BOSTON, MA.' were a familiar feature in the turn of the century art classroom. The firm attracted for a time well-known sculptors who worked with the Caproni brothers, such as Daniel Chester French, Lorado Taft and Leonard Craske.

Visual copies created expressly for the purpose of pedagogic transmission are discussed in the context of art education in Chapter 1. What is interesting here is the way in which many museums treated their cast collections like original works of art. For instance at the Corcoran Gallery of Art, casts were displayed alongside original sculptures as an enhancement to its collection. Similarly the Boston Athenaeum, founded in 1807, included plaster casts alongside its collection of original statuary. When some of its collection was transferred to the Boston Museum of Fine Arts (BMFA), founded in 1870 and opened in 1876, the combination gave the new museum the third largest collection of plaster casts in the world. It was not until more works became available from private European collections (and finds from successful archaeological digs) that original pieces began to displace the plaster casts, removing them from display. By 1927 all the casts had been deaccessioned: that is, formally disposed of or given away to art schools.

In 1867 Vassar's first professor of art, Henry Van Ingen, recommended to the college that Vassar adopt a policy of systematically purchasing casts after Greco-Roman sculpture, and the collection grew to over 200 examples, including copies of the *Venus de Milo*, the *Apollo Belvedere* and the *Nike* of Samothrace, but also of less well-represented Renaissance works including Lorenzo Ghiberti's *Gates of Paradise*, and architectural details from classical and gothic European buildings. Vassar was the first of the colleges founded in America to have its own gallery and a permanent art collection.

There are also instances of plaster casts deputising for original artworks in the collections of wealthy Americans. For example George Washington, like Jefferson, owned casts.[2] Jefferson's plans for a gallery at Monticello contained plaster cast copies of some of the most esteemed examples from the classical canon, including the Farnese *Hercules*, the *Apollo Belvedere* and *Medici Venus*. As we have seen there was however a social problem with the exhibition of the nude in America. A strong puritanical streak in middle-class, provincial America meant that many Americans were unused to displays of nudity and uncomfortable with statues of naked bodies.

In much the same way that some aficionados would react badly to the perceived ersatz culture of chromolithographs, some critics reacted to the treatment of plaster casts as though they were works of art in their own right. Those who had visited Europe and had seen the original beacons of Western civilization in the British Museum, the Louvre and the Uffizi were dismayed by the plaster copies in New York, Pennsylvannia and Boston. In July 1831 the *New England Magazine* contrasted the cast with the original

2 In 1759 George Washington ordered busts of military leaders such as Caesar and Alexander the Great from London.

as like 'an idea of a living flower by a dried specimen in an herbarium, or of a handsome man by his shadow on the wall' (Tyro 1831: 21). The writer was concerned that the undiscerning American might 'look with equal emotions of pleasure, on the Laocoon or the Belvedere Apollo, and a barber's block, or the painted head of a China mandarin, wonder what earthly good can arise from an Academy of arts, or how the world is to be improved by a mutilated Torso' (ibid: 537). But as with chromos, the quality was variable and there were both cheap and expensive copies. The quality of casts was aligned to the techniques of reproduction in cast workshops, and a trade in reproductions of reproductions removed casts further from the original. The increasing mechanisation of copying, through pointing machines and factory conditions in the workshops, caused some cheap copies which offended James Fennimore Cooper when he saw 'attenuated Nymphs and Venuses, clumsy Herculeses, hobbledehoy Apollos and grinning Fauns' in premises in Livorno (Haskell and Penny 1981: 123).

Various reasons are given in the literature for the decline in the fortunes of the plaster cast collection in the last years of the nineteenth century. Some see that plaster casts lost their centrality to art education as the importance of classicism ebbed in the advent of modernism. Others regard the growing acceptability of the life model as an instructional instrument as a factor in its demise. And some suggest that the greater contact with Europe in the years leading up to the First World War reduced the need for copies. The early twentieth century was also a time when there was an upsurge of acquisitions of original artworks. For example, between the 1920s and the 1940s Vassar's plaster cast copies went first into storage, and later most of the casts were dispersed or destroyed.

The decline of the plaster casts in public museums was a little slower. The improving zeal of civic-minded individuals endowing museums in East Coast cities was anchored to the hope that plaster casts of Western sculpture would elevate public taste. For example, the Carnegie Institute in Pittsburgh enthusiastically collected plaster casts of sculpture and architectural sections of Gothic and Romanesque buildings. However, the de-accessioning of plaster cast collections has been linked to the shift in museum policy away from education and towards art collecting. Alan Wallach, in an essay on 'The American cast museum: an episode in the history of the institutional definition of art' (1998b), discusses how American art museums have pensioned off their collections of reproductions in order to house original works of art. The influx of artworks donated by 'Gilded Age robber-barons', he argues, has marked a 'crucial shift' in the status of exhibits underwritten by the hand of the artist. Thus he argues that 'cast culture', where the exhibit has an indirect connection to the artist, was valued less than the 'cult of the original', which is grounded in the celebration of the artist as genius.

Parian miniatures

As we shall see in Chapter 3, Hiram Powers's publicly acclaimed sculpture *Greek slave* was not only reproduced in several identical versions by the artist to allow its simultaneous exhibition, it was also reproduced in scaled-down versions made from Parian porcelain or marble, bronze and plaster. Parian marble, originally called statuary porcelain, had been invented in England in the 1840s and was widely used in the Staffordshire pottery industry.[3] It was relatively affordable and a popular medium for figurines and busts which adorned middle-class homes. A number of British potteries made small-scale Parian copies of the *Greek slave*, including Minton, but the archetypal copy by Copeland appeared in 1852. The thousands of reproductions of the *Greek slave* in American homes caused Henry James to wonder about the presence of 'the Greek Slave, so undressed, yet so refined, even so pensive, in sugar-white alabaster, exposed under little domed glass covers' in respectable American homes. A number of scholars have speculated on the cultural and moral acceptance of the *Greek slave*'s nudity in America, when otherwise the Americans were widely regarded to be men and women of stern propriety. Most writers conclude that the moral of the *Greek slave*'s story (that of Christian inner strength through captivity) redeemed the work and certainly sanctified the reproductions of a chained female nude.[4]

Parian was to statuary what print was to painting: that is to say, its invention led to the commodification of the reproduction. The invention (in 1836) and patenting (in 1844) of Benjamin Cheverton's reducing machine, which scaled reproductions of larger statues, greatly assisted the Parian replica industry. Parian was less expensive than bronze, and Americans returning from tours in Europe frequently brought home Parian statues after Antique sculptures. As with other reproductive technologies, American manufacturers soon replicated the processes at home. One of the primary manufacturers of Parian ware in America was Christopher Webber Fenton with his brother-in-law Julius Norton. Their pottery was in Bennington, Vermont. Fenton and Norton began manufacturing Parian figures in 1846, and issued portrait busts, ornamental statuary and scaled-down copies of artworks. Parian ware was generally bought from china and glass dealers in America's larger cities, and promoted through exhibits at the many regional, national and international fairs that proliferated in the mid-nineteenth century.

One of the artists to systematically reproduce his own sculpture in America

3 Several potteries developed imitation marble but it was Minton that gave Parian ware its name.

4 Vivien Green, 'Hiram Powers's "Greek slave:" emblem of freedom (1982). See also Carl Bode, *The Anatomy of American Popular Culture, 1840–1861* (1959), and two works by William H. Gerdts, 'Marble and nudity' (1971) and *The Great American Nude* (1974).

was John Rogers (1829–1904). Rogers came to public attention and acclaim for two pieces – *Checker players* and *The slave auction* – exhibited in Chicago in 1859. Fittingly in the context of the present discussion, the composition and idea for *Checker players* was also a form of reproduction, since it was taken from an engraving that Rogers had seen after a painting by the British genre painter, Sir David Wilkie. In exhibiting and disseminating the piece Rogers established a twofold reputation, first for his detailed and naturalistic depiction of American genre subjects, and second for his accessible and affordable reproductions of clay groups. In 1860 Rogers moved to New York and began reproducing his sculptures in plaster and selling them for around $14 to $20.[5] Some 80 different so-called 'Rogers groups' were patented after 1860, and thousands of plaster statuary groups issued from his New York factory. His heyday was during and after the Civil War, in response to which he designed and reproduced plaster groups of *The picket guard, One more shot* and *How the fort was taken*, copies of which were displayed on General Custer's desk in his study.

Aside from the prolific output of plaster copies from Rogers's factory, which made him one of the best-known artists of his day, he merits attention for his contribution to a distinctively American type of sculpture. David Wallace's appraisal of Rogers's work reminds us 'that John Rogers came on the scene at a time when American sculpture was noticeably out of step with the other arts [painting and literature], still looking to Europe and the classical past for its standards and its inspirations' (1972: 62). Citing the observations of the anti-slavery journalist James Redpath in 1870 that 'Fine art has long lagged behind literature in America in becoming distinctively American, but sculpture has been pre-eminently non-American' (ibid.: 65), Wallace claims that Rogers was making distinctively American statuary. In the second half of the nineteenth century, as the plaster and Parian porcelain industry grew exponentially, the subject matter frequently drew on American life and history. Aside from popular historical figures such as George Washington and Ulysses Grant, sculptors such as Daniel Chester French (1850–1931) often modelled sentimental genre subjects and animal groups for replication in Parian porcelain. Isaac Broome's (1835–1922) celebrated *Baseball vase*, made for the firm of Ott and Brewer in 1875, enjoyed the distinction of being the first American ceramic work to be 'officially' classified as a work of art when it was exhibited in the Art Building of the Centennial International Exhibition in Philadelphia in 1876. The leap in status of the *Baseball vase* from Parian ware to work of art signals that art's long association with expensive materials had been undermined; however, the special status of the vase was preserved since there were only a small number created.

5 Rogers only occasionally issued works in Parian porcelain.

Engravings

Artists often tried to trade in engravings based on their art, and the reasons for their frequent entrepreneurial failures provide an object lesson in the tensions between art and its commercial reproduction. John Vanderlyn was the instigator of multiple enterprises that were commercial failures.[6] An early enterprise was to sell engraved views of Niagara Falls. Although other artists had painted and drawn the falls, Vanderlyn was the first professionally trained American artist to paint at Niagara, in 1801, completing two large canvases in 1803. He hoped that making aquatints after his paintings would bring him fortune. After all few Americans had even been to Niagara, images of the falls were scarce, and even scarcer were images signed by a distinguished artist. His aquatints, issued in both coloured and uncoloured versions, were made in Europe rather than America. The circuitous route that Vanderlyn had to take in order to print his views of Niagara, coupled with a series of misfortunes that dogged the enterprise, demonstrate the problems of reproducing works of art in America. First the artist tried unsuccessfully to locate an engraver in France, then he travelled to London in order to have the plates prepared by two different engravers, before returning them to France for printing. However, the plates never made it back to France, and only a limited number of prints were struck in London before being sent to New York in 1805. Vanderlyn spent 12 years trying to recover the missing plates.

It is difficult to apportion the blame for Vanderlyn's commercial failure to a specific error of judgement – the subject matter, the medium or plain bad luck. Engravings of famous paintings were rarely the bread and butter of a professional engraver, and much of the lucrative engraving trade was for business cards, lottery tickets and banknotes. The painter Asher B. Durand began his career as an engraver of printed matter such as banknotes. In 1820 Trumbull commissioned him to engrave his painting of the *Declaration of Independence* in the Rotunda of the Capitol.[7] Initially Trumbull had considered the London engraver James Heath, but the asking price of $6,000 was considered prohibitive, so he engaged Durand at half the cost (Dunlap 1918, I: 382). The engraving was a critical success and in 1823 the *New York Evening Post* anticipated 'a great desire in every American to ornament his parlour with so beautiful a representation, and thus furnish a topic of

6 When Vanderlyn's rival John Trumbull was commissioned to paint four history paintings to decorate the Rotunda of the United States Capitol, Vanderlyn pointedly made his own rotunda – ostensibly the first purpose-built space for exhibiting art in New York – to show his panorama of Versailles. The venture was not the success he had hoped for, and he took the painting on a tour that included Philadelphia, Montreal, Washington and Boston in order to recoup his investment.

7 Trumbull painted three *Declarations*: the first for the National Capitol, and two others which are at the Wadsworth Atheneum at Hartford and the Art Gallery of Yale University.

never ceasing interest to his family, or his guests' (quoted in Hendricks 1971: 71). However, as Gordon Hendricks has pointed out, despite the relative affordability of an image that was seminal to American history, it did not sell as well as expected and few engravings have survived (1971: 71).

One of the most successful venues of circulating prints after works of art was the American Art Union. The Art Union began life in 1839 as the Apollo Association for the Promotion of the Fine Arts in the United States, an organisation headed by James Herring, director of the Apollo Gallery in New York City. The following year Herring changed the rather august name to the Art Union, a venue and an opportunity for New Yorkers to appreciate the American school of artists. During its years of operation, the Art Union purchased around 2,500 works from the artists, exhibiting them at its Broadway gallery before distributing them to subscribers by means of an annual lottery.[8] The venture was highly successful and in 1849 there were 18,960 subscribers, 460 works purchased and distributed by lottery, and $100,000 taken in receipts (Troyen 1991: 26).

The American Art Union was conscious that traditionally the ownership of art was predicated on wealth, and that in order to give as wide an audience as possible the opportunity not just to experience its free exhibitions but also to collect images, it would have to disseminate reproductions of artworks.[9] The Art Union used the revenue it generated to purchase paintings from American artists. For a yearly fee of $5 subscribers received engravings after its purchases, including works by Thomas Cole, George Caleb Bingham, John Vanderlyn, Asher B. Durand and William Ranney. Members also received an admission ticket to a biannual art distribution and a copy of its *Bulletin*. About 3 million people visited the Art Union's gallery during its thirteen-year history, and the constituency of its visitors was regarded, by its Bulletin, to be very democratic, ranging from 'the retired merchant from Fifth Avenue, the scholar from the University, the poor workman, the newsboy, the beau and the belle, the clerk with his bundle – all frequent the Art-Union' (cited in Troyen 1991: 26). As Carol Troyen remarks, its democratising mission was also deeply patriotic, and bound up with a long-term aim to create a National School of Art. Indeed, enthusiasm for reproductions extended to wood engravings and photography, which Charles Eliot Norton felt could elevate popular taste to unprecedented heights (Vanderbilt 1959: 145).

The dissemination of reproductions of works of art through the American Art Union certainly broadened public knowledge about American art, and viewed collectively, the paintings it bought had wide appeal. One of the

8 The seeds of its demise lay in its success. In 1852 the Art Union was declared to be illegal in New York State because it was operating a lottery.

9 There were art unions across the United States, including Chicago, Philadelphia, Boston, New Orleans and the Western Art Union.

best-known engravings it produced, of which it sold around 14,000 copies, was after Richard Caton Woodville's painting *War News from Mexico*, first exhibited in 1848 and issued as an engraving in 1851 (Plate 4). It is perhaps not without coincidence that such a popular image should be a scene that represented the American struggle for independence in Texas from Mexico. Art Union paintings were often aligned to the organisation's views on advancing American ideals and traditions. The United States had annexed Texas in 1845, inciting war with Mexico and generating the hostility of many in the North.[10] The outcome for the victorious US side in the Mexican War was that the nation gained new territory including California and the American Southwest. Woodville's painting shows the various reactions of a group gathered in the doorway of a frontier town hotel as a well-dressed man reads out the latest news of the war.

Engravings and printed depictions of historically significant events were produced in great numbers for dissemination to all classes of Americans. Emanuel Leutze's enduring image of *Washington crossing the Delaware* has been so widely reproduced that the American audience is very familiar with its composition, and artists from Norman Rockwell to Larry Rivers have borrowed from it (Plate 5). The engraving of Leutze's painting by Paul Girardet was published in 1853, although the publishers, the Parisian firm of Goupil, Vibert & Co., were advertising it in 1851. The print was available in different impressions and on various grades of paper, at prices from $15–40. This enabled different socio-economic groups to purchase it, and other cheaper impressions that followed in subsequent years ensured that all but a few homes were adorned by it. The quality of the reproduction was linked to the price, and the ownership of consumer goods such as these reproductions, bought either in a moment of unprovoked patriotism or in imitation of perceived upper-class lifestyles, was allied to a perception of upward mobility or enlightened superiority. As we shall see, the commodification of art through reproductions of *Washington crossing the Delaware* may have made shrewd business sense but purchasers were not correspondingly cynical at the point of purchase. They often had very genuine patriotic or self-improving motives.

The chromolithograph

The firm of L. Prang & Co., founded by Louis Prang (1824–1909) in 1860 in Boston, was one of the most prolific and influential of all publishers of chromolithographs in America. It dominated an increasingly buoyant trade in colour reproductions in America. Chromolithography used the same

10 The best known protester was Henry David Thoreau, who went to jail in Massachusetts for refusing to pay the taxes that supported the war.

reproductive processes as lithography but could achieve a far greater range of colours. In the early days of chromolithography it was the custom for American publishers to outsource the task to European, and particularly to London-based, printers. For example Charles Risdon Day's chromo after Frederic Edwin Church's highly regarded painting of the *Great Fall, Niagara* was actually published in London by the firm of Day & Son in 1857.

Although initially specialising in small prints, of a size suitable for albums, Prang expanded his business and became the main publisher of colour-printed copies of famous paintings. His first successes were prints of maps of Civil War battle sites and portraits of military figures. Prang had a nose for popular tastes, and after a series of Cuban scenes proved a flop, he made his first commercially successful chromo, a reproduction of Arthur Fitzwilliam Tait's *Group of chickens* issued in 1866, which ran to almost 30,000 copies. Similarly, when it came to selecting designs for Prang's famous Christmas cards, Louis appointed a jury and conducted a poll to decide which to print. Prang issued around 800 art prints, showcased in his own magazine, *Prang's Chromo: A Journal of Popular Art*, where he advertised them on the basis of their authenticity to the original and their democratic potential. He also ran newspaper advertisements for his fine art prints:

> PRANG'S AMERICAN CHROMOS. 'THE DEMOCRACY OF ART' ... Our Chromo Prints are absolute FACSIMILES of the originals, in color, drawing, and spirit, and their price is so low that every home may enjoy the luxury of possessing a copy of works of art, which hitherto adorned only the parlors of the rich.
>
> (Clapper 2002: 20)

The operative word 'democracy' is intriguing here. Although chromos were by no means the cheapest reproductions, they were within the economic reach of middle-class Americans. The great benefit of chromolithography over other forms of printing in the mid-nineteenth century was that it could be used for large-scale folio images. Once framed, these larger images could be hung in the parlours of the not so rich. The chromo then is not only deputising for the original, it is claiming a status as art in its own right.

But Prang's advert is eager to do more than simply democratise the fine art object. It also guarantees the faithfulness of the reproduction by inserting the word 'facsimile' in upper case. A further property of chromolithography was that it was possible to obtain a wider range of tonal effects than with other forms of colour printing. Chromos were made in a process very similar to black-and-white lithography, with the printed image laid out on stone. However, chromolithography was built up from a series of layers of transparent ink until a full range of colour was achieved and using sometimes dozens of separate stones. Achieving the correct colour separations was a specialist job since it was done by eye and without any hand colouring. For pictorially complex images as many as twenty or more workings might be needed, but although this was a laborious process, the upside of these efforts was that the process yielded thousands of prints without image degradation (unlike copper plate engravings, which lost resolution after thirty to fifty pressings).[11] In post-bellum America the chromo was cheaper to mass produce (although high-quality chromos continued to be manufactured at a higher cost since they were made on expensive equipment and cost months of work for the manufacturer). Even cheap chromos required a heavy initial investment; since it took up to three months to draw the colours onto the stones and it could take up to a further five months to print a thousand copies. Eventually their success led to their routine appearance in advertisements and greetings cards. But chromo's first incarnations, as reproductions of paintings, were a clever print contrivance. The aim of Prang and other chromolithographers was to make the print look as close to painting as possible, so the chromo was frequently coated with an oily varnish and then embossed with a canvas-like pattern, to emulate the texture of an oil painting.

The reassurance of the closeness of images to the original, guaranteed by Prang in his advertising copy, is also worth noting. After all, why should a printer make claims about the adherence of the copy to the original when it was highly unlikely that most purchasers of the chromolithograph would ever be able to make any direct comparison? Before Walter Benjamin's articulation of auratic encounters with original and one-off artworks, and before the mass mobilisation of the middle classes into Europe, why would anyone care about the proximity to the original?

As we have seen with the trade in engravings, there was a correlation between quality and price. The advertising claims of publishers provided reassurances of likeness, but there was an implicit claim that greater veracity could be purchased at a higher price. Prang's particular area of expertise was in attaining a high level of technical refinement in his imitation of an oil painting. 'Prang's American Chromos' were guaranteed by a trademark and became the national leader, and his prints after popular contemporary paintings were remarkably successful (Clapper 2002). As Clapper has showed, these efforts were not universally well received (2002: 20–6). Charges of deception and commercialisation recurred in the hostile press, where writers generally expressed the fear that homes were being invaded by poor substitutes for the original. Chromos had their critics in the United States, just as they did in Europe. The weekly journal *The Nation* referred to 'the sensation of sham, of a swindle which disappoints even while it deceives'. The journal was particularly offended by Prang's copy of what

11 The firm of Storch and Kramer in Berlin were able to make 5,000 copies at a time.

was at that time thought to be a work by Correggio, chiding the printer for its audacity in trying to mechanically replicate the hand of the master.

Peter Marzio's study of the chromolithograph in antebellum and post-bellum America, *The Democratic Art* (1979), sees the chromo as a correlative to democracy, and particularly to the democratic belief that mass commerce with the fine arts could be a device for improving mass culture. What the constant appeals to democracy highlight, however, is a divide in post-bellum America between popular and elite tastes. Marzio concludes, 'In introducing paintings to the masses [the chromo] forced Americans to grapple with the concept of a culture for all, or art in a democracy' (1979: 211). It is debatable whether Americans were ever forced to grapple with the concept of a culture for all, but Marzio is persuasive in his claim that 'At the peak of America's Victorian age, the mass-produced color lithograph waved unchallenged as the flag of popular culture .... Chromolithography was a technical accomplishment with a vibrant social presence' (1979: xi).

The 'vibrant social presence' of the chromo made the reproductive technology highly visible. Many of the chromos were purchased for homes in urban America. If a household had a parlour, then more likely than not it had a chromolithograph on its walls. Not for the first time in this chapter we encounter a reaction to the mass production of what had once been high culture. In the case of chromos, the critics of the prints typically thought that they were garish or that they diluted, and therefore weakened, the culture they sought so faithfully to represent through mechanical reproduction. At the root of these criticisms lie two fundamental, and recurring, assumptions. The first was that so-called 'chromocivilisation' was grounded in the inferior taste of mass culture, and the second that the multiplication of the original work of art through mechanical reproduction degraded art. Louis Prang, so often on the defensive in his promotional literature, insisted that 'the business of this age is to make the products of civilization cheap ... what the people want and admire are not the dry bones or the syntax of art, but life pictures, full of the bloom and brilliancy of nature, to brighten their homes and make their own existence more pleasant' (Marzio 1979: 1–2).

Most of the severe criticisms of chromolithography were articulated in an elitist journal, *The Nation*. This was an opinion-forming American weekly journal, and the leading liberal magazine of its kind. It was founded in 1865 by Edwin L. Godkin. Godkin supported liberal and progressive causes, and *The Nation* was an advocate of women's suffrage, equal rights for African-Americans and public education. However, on this issue of cheap reproductive technologies Godkin was intolerant, seeing chromos as representatives of 'the confusion of ideas which assumes that "what the people want and admire" is the same thing as "what the people need and ought to admire" [which] is strange to see' (quoted in Marzio 1979: 5). Chromolithography for Godkin represented the conflict of interests between indulging and improving the nation. The distinction between 'want' and 'need' is telling in this respect. For Godkin, cheap reproductions were pandering to the half-formed tastes a market of people who are ill equipped to judge art, let alone to choose artworks, but at the same time who are buoyed up with an 'unprecedented self-confidence in dealing with all the problems of life, and raise them in their own minds to a plane on which they see nothing higher, greater or better than themselves'. The perceived diminution of art and the lack of authenticity of the copies rendered them merely 'merchandise'.

Godkin was not the only critic to cross swords with Prang in the periodical press. Clarence Cook, critic for the *New York Daily Tribune*, objected to chromos in 1866, suggesting that they were only fit for children, or the immigrant and lower classes who would be attracted by their bright colours (Stankiewicz 1999: 108). Prang's response was to point out that chromos were the same as issuing copies of great literary works for the libraries of hundreds of homes. The most vocal of the chromo apologists was the American novelist Harriet Beecher Stowe. In the domestic manual she co-wrote in 1869 with her sister Catharine, *The American Woman's Home*, she advised readers to adorn their homes with chromos, suggesting that a quarter of their decorating budget be laid aside for pictures that represented the nation's best artists.[12] James Parton, in the *Atlantic Monthly* (1869), also argued in opposition to Cook and Godkin, with the optimistic observation that the mass market for chromos would conversely grant a great distinction to original works of art.

As we shall see in Chapter 4, between 1873 and 1875 Moran accompanied the Hayden Expedition to Yellowstone. Moran's commission was to paint a portfolio of watercolours for chromolithographic reproduction by Prang, with Hayden providing the supporting text. *The Yellowstone National Park, and the Mountain Regions of Portions of Idaho, Nevada, Colorado and Utah* (1876) consisted of fifteen brightly coloured images of the American West. These portfolios were not cheap, retailing at $60 each, but a thousand copies were produced. There had been black and white engravings of Yellowstone but colour, as well as Moran's artistry, was a unique selling point. As Hayden put it in his preface:

> All representations of landscape scenery must necessarily lose the greater part of their charm when deprived of color; but of any representation in black and white of the scenery of the Yellowstone it may truly be said that it is like Hamlet with the part of Hamlet omitted, for the wealth of color in which nature has clothed the mountains and the springs of that region constitute one of the most wonderful elements of their beauty.

12 The Stowe sisters' support brought Harriet to the attention of L. Prang & Company. His own short-lived quarterly *Prang's Chromo: A Journal of Popular Art* (five issues were published from January 1868 to April 1869) printed a letter from Stowe thanking Louis Prang for giving her complimentary chromolithographs.

Prang was not the only firm to profit from art images of the West: the catalogue of Currier & Ives prints also testified to the popularity of the subject. The printers Nathaniel Currier and James Ives published around 7,000 hand-coloured lithographs and prints,[13] many depicting America from 1840 onwards. Like Prang's claims to democratising the image, the firm of Currier & Ives styled itself 'Printmakers to the People', and created lithographed prints to be sold for framing and display in the homes of the American public. Taken in its entirety the stock issued by Currier & Ives forms a pictorial history of the United States, charting landmark events in its history. The firm produced popular scenes of frontier life, or vessels hunting whales at sea, or as in 1876, historical prints that celebrated the American Centennial. Currier & Ives generally commissioned illustrations from a stable of artists associated with the firm – Frances Flora Palmer, who was responsible for the majority of landscape views, John Cameron, Louis Maurer, Thomas Worth, Charles Parsons, Napoleon Sarony, Otto Knirsch and occasionally Arthur Tait. Currier & Ives prints were not just reproductions of well-known paintings; they were created especially for the firm. Its most prolific artist, Frances Flora Palmer, made around 200 illustrations for Currier & Ives. Despite travelling no farther west than New Jersey, Palmer sourced scenes from books, daguerreotypes and photographs to create views of Yosemite, the Catskills and the Rocky Mountains, and to recreate views of Civil War battles entirely from written descriptions of events.

Currier & Ives prints were sold either directly from the firm's shop in New York or through printsellers across the United States, as well as overseas. Another retail outlet was itinerant street sellers equipped with pushcarts loaded with prints. The retail price of a Currier & Ives print ranged from 20 cents for a small print coloured by a team (these usually consisted of women who swiftly applied washes of colour) to the more expensive prints retailed for as much as $5 and were normally be coloured by an individual skilled colourist. In addition to the colourists employed by Currier & Ives the firm had hundreds of employees at the point of production and sale.

When the firm finally closed in 1907, after more than a decade of dwindling returns, it was partly because photographic reproduction had subsumed the functions of its commercial wing and partly because its collectors had formed different habits and had different expectations of quality.

Photographs of works of art

Within a few years of Louis Daguerre's invention of the daguerreotype in 1839, daguerreotype studios were established in US cities. By the 1850s

13 Although the majority of Currier & Ives prints were hand-coloured lithographs, the firm also issued limited numbers of monoprints and chromos.

there were in excess of 100 daguerreotype shops in Manhattan and Brooklyn. Mathew Brady (1822–1896) had been working as a jewel-case manufacturer when he somewhat opportunistically established himself as a portrait photographer with his own Daguerrean [sic] Gallery in New York City in 1844, later establishing other galleries in Boston and Washington, DC. Brady created a competitive edge by concentrating on improving the quality of his images and searching out a more elite customer. Although now better known as a photographer who documented the Civil War, Brady was also a portrait designer whose sitters included presidents, senators and celebrities. (He was not the camera operator; instead he designed the portrait, posing the subjects and rehearsing their expressions.) The main room of his Daguerrean Gallery, recorded in a woodcut of the early 1850s, shows a fashionable and respectable clientele assembled before his work. His visitors could view the 'Gallery of Illustrious Americans', a portrait gallery created in the context of, and contributing to, a craze for *cartes-de-visite*, small copies of portraits for pasting into albums. Brady was aesthetically if not commercially suspicious of these cheap *cartes-de-visite*, preferring the Imperial portraits he himself circulated once paper photographic prints replaced daguerreotypes. In 1856 he commenced 'photography on canvas', so-called 'Brady Imperials', which were large photographic portraits printed on canvas and coloured with oil paint, aimed at a higher-class market.

In photographic hierarchies the daguerreotype was at the high art end of the scale. It was produced without a negative and therefore each daguerreotype was unique, its status underscored by its presentation in a velvet-lined case. It is unsurprising that the 'poet of democracy', Walt Whitman (Plate 8), who frequented New York's daguerreotype galleries, should see the potential of photography to achieve an equivalence to his own poetic egalitarianism. The main photographic rival, the tintype, was made from a negative which yielded multiple copies, and was also much cheaper.[14] Tintypes, supported on an iron plate, were much more durable and resilient than daguerreotypes. Quick to make, inexpensive to produce, their affordability extended to all classes, and having a tintype taken was a particularly popular pastime at seaside resorts and county fairs. Tintypes were regarded as at the low end of photographic practice and lacking in any pretensions to art. Itinerant photographers extended the tintype business at fairs and carnivals across America and boardwalks on its coastal resorts. Sitters could pose against painted backdrops of Niagara Falls, or with an assortment of props.[15]

As we have said, the anxieties attending a printed reproduction's veracity to its original seem largely inappropriate given that most people would

14 Tintypes were called talbotypes or calotypes in Europe.

15 In 1863, tiny portraits (about the size of a small postage stamp) were popularised under the trade name Gem Galleries. The Gem was the most frequently produced form of photography in the 1860s, its images not only displayed in albums but also cut to fit jewellery.

never be able to make a direct comparison between a chromolithograph and an oil painting in a European museum – or for that matter between a privately owned American painting and the print after it. However, the advent of photography, a medium whose results could only be achieved in front of the original, did contribute to a sense that the copy of a work of art was 'authentic' or bore a close resemblance to its source. However there is less evidence that the photograph after the work of art was treated as a surrogate for the artwork; that is, that it was framed or displayed as a substitute. In fact the photograph was more likely to be used as a record or consulted for the purposes of verification. When André Malraux noted in the 1950s that 'For the last hundred years ... art history has been the history of that which can be photographed' (1974: 30), he was reflecting on the supremacy of photographs of artworks in the classroom. For example, when Lewis E. Pilcher succeeded Van Ingen as head of the Department of Art at Vassar in 1898, he initiated a policy of creating a photograph library. The photograph of a work of art, though not treasured as a surrogate in the same way that a chromo might be, has come to have a special place in the teaching of art and art history in the schools and colleges of America.

Several commercial photographers specialised in the photographic reproduction of paintings, sculptures and architecture; Fratelli Alinari in Italy, Goupil & Cie and Adolphe Braun in France are among the best known. The trade in photographs of works of art became increasingly an important part to the teaching of art history in American colleges and universities. For example courses in art history began at Harvard in 1874,[16] and at Mount Holyoke in 1878. The American art historian and connoisseur Bernard Berenson (1865–1959) routinely used photography as a tool of attribution.[17] His collection, begun in 1895, consisted of more than 300,000 photographs, mainly of works of the Italian Renaissance.[18] The photograph, increasingly supplemented by the lantern slide and later by 35mm slide, came to dominate university education, and in schools it remained the principal mechanism for transmitting knowledge about works of art, as well as enhancing visual literacy, as part of an educational scheme known as 'Picture Study'.

National support for mandatory art instruction grew out of a growing consensus by leading educators and social reformers of the nineteenth century that art had a place in the public schools because it was educationally valuable and socially worthwhile. The enhancement of children's cognitive

16 Berenson's tutor Charles Eliot Norton (1827–1908), the first chair in the history of art at Harvard, acquired a large collection of illustrative materials for the Fogg Museum, including photographs, although he was not fond of using them in his classes.

17 Berenson wrote an article for *The Nation* in 1893, 'Isochromatic photography and Venetian pictures' (reprinted in Roberts 1997).

18 The collection is housed at the villa he left to Harvard University, I Tatti in Florence.

learning through observation and visual reasoning is an allied outcome of art instruction. Aesthetic enrichment is not absent from educational discourses, however, and the phenomenon of picture study is a case in point. Advocates of Picture Study believed that school children could develop their personal and moral virtues through a systematic and sustained exposure to works of fine art. As Mary Stankiewicz has observed:

> Most of the leading advocates of picture study and schoolroom decoration were not male intellectuals but women. Told by Ruskin and other Victorian writers that they had a duty to refine the lives of those around them, women took an active role in organizing school art societies to promote the distribution and study of pictures. The growing feminization of teaching, coupled with women's role as guardians of culture, contributed to the development of the conservative museum of virtue.
>
> (Stankiewicz 1984: 61)

The Picture Study movement had its heyday between the last decade of the nineteenth century and the start of the 1920s. Improvements in the technologies of reproduction permitted widespread picture study, and one company, the Perry Pictures Company, located in a suburb of Boston Massachusetts (founded in 1897), became a national provider of material to aid picture study. Perry Pictures produced good-quality black and white or sepia pictures for school teachers to use in classes. Typically teachers introduced the painting reproduced for the classroom (often included as part of the Perry Pictures Series material) and the students would respond to set questions and exercises. Typically teachers selected reproductions of Old Master and nineteenth century paintings, with a moral message. This was, of course, also a period in which increasing immigration to the United States was adding to the school population. Picture Study was a means of educating prospective immigrant children, unable to speak English and unfamiliar with American ideas of citizenship and morality.

As early as 1937 Walter Benjamin in his seminal essay 'The work of art in the age of mechanical reproduction' distinguished between the quality of our experience of original artworks and their reproductions. 'Aura' was the term he used to describe the uniqueness of the single art object, occasioned by its lack of reproducibility. Mechanical reproduction potentially undermined the 'unique existence' of the art object – and the reproduced work of art loses its 'aura' and therefore its authenticity (Benjamin 1999). Benjamin's essay is not so very far off the thinking that informed Godkin and Cook in their estimation of the copy as a reminder of an original artwork but in no way a spur to aesthetic admiration in its own right. However, Benjamin's distinction between our experience of an original and a copy does not always hold up to scrutiny. For example, his discussion of the impact of mechanical reproduction on art does not mention photography of artworks or photomechanical reproductions of art in the nineteenth century. Benjamin's notion that copies and reproductions destroy the aura of the original has been questioned, and some writers think that quite the opposite is the case, and that copies contribute to the value of the original (Hughes and Ranfft 1997).

Outside of the art history lecture, photographs of works of art were keenly collected by tourists. In Europe photographing works of art had followed quickly on the heels of the various patented processes that mark the invention of photography. For example, daguerreotypes were used in the 1840s to record works in private collections. Photography was also a means of selling souvenirs to visitors to Europe, and middle-class tourists frequently collected *cartes-de-visite* of artworks, sold in sets and mounted for albums.[19] The stereoscopic view was the standard for reproducing images of sculpture and architectural views. Stereoscopic views were made using a special camera with two horizontal lenses set apart, and recording the image as seen by each eye. The resulting prints yielded twin images pasted on a piece of cardboard that, when viewed through the stereoscope, combined in the eyes to create a single three-dimensional image. The stereoscope had greater impact on American culture than in Europe. Oliver Wendell Holmes created a smaller and cheaper viewer that made the equipment accessible to middle-class homes, even leading to claims that every parlour in American had a stereoscope. The stereoscope itself also became more affordable. One of the main stereoscopic companies, Underwood & Underwood, sold them at the price of six for a dollar in the 1880s. Stereoscopes were sold in drugstores, and through mail-order catalogues. There were even canvassers who toured the country, selling images door to door.

The Index of American Design

The Index of American Design (1935–43), a pictorial archive constituting some 18,000 watercolour images representing traditional American arts and crafts, was devised and conducted under the auspices of the Federal Art Project (FAP) of the Works Progress Administration (WPA). The Federal Art Project operated from 1935 to 1942 to find employment for artists during the Depression. Its nationalistic agenda was thoroughly suited to the Index, which was part of a larger campaign to define national culture through the identification and promotion of what was called a 'usable past'. The images created for the Index of American Design, now in the National Gallery of Art, Washington, were ostensibly a pictorial survey of the history

19 The *carte-de-visite* was a popular and affordable format for circulating images of works of art. Hamber has shown how it was used by politician M. Witt in Columbus Ohio to circulate images of W. H. Powell's painting of the Battle of Lake Erie to raise money to assist soldiers wounded in the Civil War (1996: 138).

of American design. In the words of its website, 'The Index is one of the most significant and enduring products of a search for national cultural identity that was conducted in this country during the 1920s and 1930s.'

Presented in official WPA and FAP literature as a retrieval of crafts, processes and identities in danger of being lost, individual items of folk art and crafts were recorded with exacting realism. The Index, under the direction of Holger Cahill, employed between 400 and 500 'less able artists', people according to Jonathan Harris 'not considered accomplished enough for the easel or mural programs' (Harris 1995: 85) but fitted to fulfil the documentary brief of the Index. The artists employed on the Index were obliged to work to a prescribed format, not depicting backgrounds and only shading within the object rendered, suppressing their own visual proclivities. Despite these prohibitions, many individual hands are recognisable in the drawings to the knowledgeable eye (Plate 6).

The underlying idea of tapping a historical 'usable past' that could separate America from its cultural and artistic ties to Europe is one we have encountered before. Rather than trying to create a culture anew, Americans were looking for evidence that the separation had taken place long before. The term 'usable past' was coined by critic Van Wyck Brooks (1886–1963) in an article 'On creating a usable past', in 1918. A 'usable past' was a plea for a collective recognition that there was indeed a tradition of art and culture in America that went beyond mere derivation.[20] In terms of the Index the proposition that everyday life had yielded a 'usable past' through its vernacular culture in a way that high art had not, was not simply a piece of post-hoc reasoning. The patriotically inspired record of native folk and decorative arts lent credence to the idea that America had its own aesthetic traditions, and more importantly, that the new modern movement would be enhanced by the association. As Harris puts it, 'Not simply an illustrated chronology of American objects, the Index of American Design was expected to reveal the direction, purpose and destiny of the nation, which was assumed to possess an irreversible evolutionary trajectory' (1995: 86). On the surface of things, there might appear to be little common design ground between a hand-crafted wooden toy and an industrially produced kettle, but modernists shared their sense of aesthetic economy, immediacy of expression and utility of form.

> The Index helped to form collective assumptions of what 'American' means in the arts, and to construct a framework within which to gauge the American character of everything from abstract expressionism and pop art to home furnishings. Although its impact on American culture

20 See Wanda M. Corn (1999) *The Great American Thing: Modem Art and National Identity 1915–1935*, pp 12–14, 317–19.

> has been more indirect than its creators had imagined, the Index of American Design has nevertheless left us an important and enduring legacy: a truly usable past.
>
> (Clayton 2002)

The systematic documenting of folk art, also a passion with John Cotton Dana (see p 147ff) a generation earlier, served the purpose of creating an authentic regional distinctiveness that could be annexed to the needs of a nation state searching for unity and cohesiveness. Insisting on only indexing 'art which we could call our own without reservation', Gordon M. Smith settled on Shaker products as exemplars, representing values associated with 'Americanism – simplicity, economy, reliability, durability, solid good sense, and, finally, complete freedom from frills' (quoted in O'Connor 1973: 173). Regional and ethnic diversity were celebrated through a recovery of folk craft items and the processes by which they were made. Costumes typical of ante-bellum New Orleans, Swedish immigrant designs from Minnesota, saddle trappings, storefront figures including the ubiquitous cigar-store Indians, ships' figureheads, 'santos' from the old Spanish Southwest and the painted ornamentation discovered under old missions' whitewashed walls were all faithfully recorded, processes documented and attributions sought. The Index was displayed in departments stores such as R.H. Macy of New York and Bullocks of Los Angeles as well as museums, federal art centres, and universities from San Diego to Dallas, to Pittsburgh and Milwaukee.

Printmaking

Perhaps unsurprisingly the role of reproduction in the graphic arts was also annexed to democratic values. Described as 'multiple originals' by Rockwell Kent, prints were recalibrated during the WPA as popular and accessible. Putting a print-based artwork in every home was not attendant upon the validation of the art market or the sanctioning of taste by American museums. Developing new markets in the sale of prints was crucial in keeping the wolf from the door of unemployed graphic artists. The New York graphic division of the FAP was instrumental through its workshops of revitalising printmaking in America, according to Hyman Warsager (1973), with new innovations taking place in colour woodcuts, lithography and silk screen printing, the latter creatively using the medium in colour. In California there were technical innovations in lithography, contributing to the mass production of prints. 'Lithography in this country had no connection with fine art and meant only one thing, the flashy poster or the "chromo" reproduction of tenth-rate paintings' (Russell T. Limbach in O'Connor 1973: 145–7). Limbach along with others attempted to intervene in the dominant perception of reproductions as inferior, and restate them as worthy artworks against the snobbery of the art market and speculative stockmarket-minded dealers and collectors who lionised the unique status of the one-off original work of art.

Elizabeth Olds (1896–1991) worked as a printmaker for the New York WPA/FAP Graphic Arts Division between 1935 and 1940, a facility that was one of the best-equipped graphic art workshops in America. She also worked consistently as an advocate for cultural democracy, and as a member of several artists' organisations, including the Artists Union and the American Artists' Congress. Printmaking was a way of practising her egalitarian ideas for the democratisation of art, especially through the creation and dissemination of inexpensive colour prints of popular subjects. She identified that 'These average citizens are an audience for the artist new to our time. New methods of reaching them have to be devised [so that] art will at last flourish on a democratic scale' (Olds 1973: 142). In 'Prints for mass production', an essay written in 1936, Olds suggested that the wide circulation of prints produced in large editions would educate a culturally and visually impoverished population. Much of her own work was disseminated through screen printing – a relatively simple, inexpensive process that allowed for large runs of prints.

Olds's imagery frequently drew from everyday life and scenes involving ordinary men and women. For example, she made prints for a series that depicted the slaughter of stockyard animals. Like the writers Steinbeck and Caldwell, artists responded to the themes of the Depression. Another artist in the scheme, Hyman Warsager (1909–1974), made colour prints of workers *Gathering logs*, Rockwell Kent asked *And now where*, and Margaret Lowengrund worked on scenes such as *Breadline*.

The creation and dissemination of colour prints was a significant achievement for the Print Division. Hitherto, the processes of colour lithography or colour woodblock had been prohibitively costly. In the first half of the nineteenth century metal engraving was the predominant method of making fine art prints in the United States.[21] Lithography only achieved its artistic distinction in the 1920s and 1930s, when its nineteenth-century connotations of commercial reproduction ebbed and the lithographer could be valued as a creative artist, especially gifted by the process that allows the image to be drawn directly on the smoothed stone. Warsager in his 1936 essay 'Graphic techniques in progress' reported on the experimentation that underscored the work of the Print Division: 'In lithography, Project artists did not confine their efforts to crayon work on stone. They struck out boldly with washes of tusche or opaque tusche[22] and scraped with razor blades, sandpaper, or carborundum. Project artists took to this medium with rare enthusiasm.'

21 In the 1870s and 1880s there was a market acceptance that prints might be traded as original works of art, and etching, with its possibility for greater tonal variations, assumed a significance as the favoured medium for landscape artists.

22 Tusche is a greasy liquid used to produce dense black areas in the lithograph.

But it was colour silk screen printing that Warsager acknowledged as 'the most startling contribution to color prints'.

Helen Langa observes that the distribution system of fine art prints was not always equal to the egalitarian aims of the WAP/FAP. They may not have found their way into homes but they 'did reach a range of middle- and working-class individuals because they were routinely displayed in government offices, libraries and hospitals and were shown in WPAFAP exhibitions' (2004: 48):

> Printmaking was seen as both an elite and egalitarian form of art production, because fine art prints retained the aura of the artist's original touch and signature even while being produced in multiples and sold for less that unique original works. Originality was inextricably associated with value; Associated American Artists[23] often stressed the word 'original' in its advertising copy and explicitly urged prospective buyers to view prints as valuable original images.
>
> (Langa 2004: 48)

However, Langa also raises the issue of 'taste' for prints, especially modernist prints, noting that, 'In general, neither liberals nor radicals thought highly of the aesthetic judgment of most Americans' (2004: 51). The underestimation of the tastes of the American public perhaps summed up in Olds's pithy formulation: 'With freedom to choose his subjects [the artist] did not need to restrict himself to gamboling kittens and succulent nymphs beside a lake (sure-fire sales)' (quoted in O'Connor 1973). Olds's *Picasso Study Club* humorously illustrates the difficulties that museum-going public had with modernism. However, a number of key modernist painters were active printmakers: etching was practised by Edward Hopper, John Sloan and Reginald Marsh; drypoint and monoprint by Milton Avery; colour lithography by Stuart Davis; and practically every print medium by Ben Shahn.

Shahn designed posters for the Office of War Information (OWI) during the Second World War, although only two were ever published. In 1945, he became director of the Graphic Arts Section of the Congress of Industrial Organisation-Political Action Committee (CIO-PAC). During his career Shahn created numerous posters that had a sufficiently high status to be exhibited at MoMA. MoMA did not unanimously endorse his graphic work, and as James Thrall Soby's[24] unedited autobiography (nd) suggests, the reception of his CIO-PAC posters there was mixed. Prescott, writing in

23 Private presses such as the Associated American Artists (AAA) published etchings and lithographs for $5 each.

24 Soby, made assistant director of MoMA in 1943, and Director of the Department of Painting and Sculpture until 1945, was an advisor to the Committee on the Museum Collections from 1940–67. He supported Shahn and wrote widely on his work.

1973, considered Soby had defended Shahn's posters 'as the finest and most compelling posters yet seen in our period and country' (1973: xix). His work with the OWI and CIO-PAC, labour movements and political campaigns was mordantly anti-fascist and advocated social change through political action. For example, Shahn's eight CIO-PAC and OWI posters, most notably *We demand the National Textile Act* (1935) and *Warning! Inflation means depression: register/vote* (1946) were stirring invocations to the viewer, at odds with MoMA's conservative board of trustees.

New technologies of reproduction

The World Wide Web went live in 1995, and artists immediately began customising it as a venue or an exhibition space in its own right. Art museums, when budgets permit, have gradually come to see the internet as a place for the display of images of works of art. The website of the Metropolitan Museum of Art, for example, provides access to visual information about its large collection through an index. The internet has been viewed by museum educators as a place to provide public access to American art collections through searchable databases, and open up collections when the physical space of a museum prohibits ever showing more than a fraction of the collection at a time.

André Malraux's concept of 'the museum without walls'[25] is the proposition of a notional museum, one that is neither described by any physical space nor confined to a limited audience. As far as Malraux could envisage in the 1950s, any work of art that can be photographed can take its place in the museum without walls, and the lavishly illustrated art book was his model of the *musée imaginaire*. Malraux's coordinates for the 'museum without walls' are arguably close to those of artworks in cyberspace: that is, they offer the possibility to 'virtually' experience artworks, without ever setting foot inside the museum space. Many museums do not at present, however, have extensive websites that detail their collections or offer high-resolution images of works of art. Creating, designing and maintaining such a resource is expensive. Moreover, the suggestion that a two-dimensional interface would compensate for the museum environment is undermined by the continuing phenomenon of replicas after works of art. Today there are a number of firms specialising in copies of paintings. Paintings will be copied to order, scaled down if necessary, and shipped to anywhere in the world. Giclee printing, prints from a digital source using ink-jet technology, can be done on canvas or hand-painted oils on canvas. And digital reproduction can even simulate the craquelure finish: that is, it can deliberately imitate the hairline cracks that form on the surface of an old oil painting.

25 An English (mis)translation of his *musée imaginaire*.

In Las Vegas it is possible to experience three-dimensional equivalents to the art museum or the cultural site. The Las Vegas Strip is a succession of simulacra – outrageous and knowing copies of famous statues or buildings, purposely *not* real. The egregious and inauthentic representations of works in Las Vegas is unsettling at both the point of design and staging. They may resemble their original but equally they are wide of the mark on some essential – be it scale, colouring or situation. Arthur Danto has noted that 'Las Vegas employs as many sculptors as papal Rome' (1999). Daniel Boorstin's 1961 book *The Image: A Guide to Pseudo-Events in America* proposed that America was in an 'age of contrivance'. While he was ostensibly discussing pseudo-events in society, he noted that the tourist industry provided 'artificial products', safe versions of the experiences they imagined.

The sculptors in Las Vegas work in fibreglass and Styrofoam to make statues and architectural detailing for hotels. A scaled-down version of the Statue of Liberty in coated Styrofoam, a Sphinx, a half-scale simulacrum of the Eiffel Tower are not surrogates for the originals in New York, Luxor or Paris, they are fakes and appreciated as such. The phoney versions of Old World cultural beacons in Las Vegas have been treated with suspicion by commentators. Umberto Eco's identification of the 'blurring of the boundaries' between the original and its reproduction is presented as a negative state of affairs, a 'contamination' of the original (1995). But as Eco and Jean Baudrillard (1993) agree, the simulation eventually replaces the original, particularly in America where, according to them, Americans come to prefer the simulation or even, they suggest, fail to grasp the distinction between the real and the fake. However, Eco and Baudrillard have missed the humour and missed the point. As this chapter has shown, American culture has a long and distinctive regard for art in reproduction. To be sure, some individuals may have their boundaries blurred. But on the whole visitors relish the bizarre juxtapositions of icons on the Las Vegas Strip *en masse*, not as individual substitutes for the original.

Chapter 3

Touring America

From the first years of its discovery, new World culture, tangible and intangible, was toured in Europe to rapturous, curious, sceptical and sometimes hostile audiences. By the nineteenth century American artists, gifted with the promotional flair of showmen, also toured their art internationally. The pay-as-you-enter roadshow exhibitions, introduced in America after the 1776 Revolution, were vital to artists' livelihood in a culture lacking the relatively secure structure of European patronage. These entrepreneurial ventures were spectacles that patriotically combined scale of presentation with national pride. Promoting technical and artistic expertise, the touring shows also exported American values and ideology to the rest of the globe.

Among the first examples of American art to be toured nationally and internationally were large-format, spectacular paintings and panoramas. These crowd-pullers were precursors to the silent movies, since they often had piano accompaniment. For example, the sequential narrative of Thomas Cole's *The voyage of life* was a work that required the viewer to experience its unfolding moral message over time. Cole's ventures were highly lucrative, and *The course of empire*, another episodic series from 1836, earned around $1,000 for each show. In the nineteenth century, then, as paintings became a popular diversion nationally, the crossover between popular and high culture was evident.

Art in American nineteenth-century life was neither restricted to a small portion of the population nor entirely a story in which a degenerate second-rate art is peddled to the lower classes in lieu of high art. Lawrence Levine's *Highbrow/Lowbrow* (1988) has demonstrated how certain events could be both culturally significant and hugely popular in the nineteenth century and, for example, that museums could display paintings and sculptures alongside mastodon bones without leaving themselves open to charges of populism. John Banvard (1815–1891), who had begun his career as a frontier sign painter, produced what was hyperbolically known as a *Three mile painting* (see also page 103), and toured America and Europe, drawing large crowds to metropolitan and provincial theatres. The painting was installed in his own museum on Broadway in New York, which exhibited his collection of Egyptian artefacts and his so-called 'Cardiff giant'. This mixture of what might now be designated highbrow Egyptian art, medium-brow *Three mile painting* and lowbrow carnivalesque hoax clearly caused no anxieties to Banvard or the museum-going public. Indeed his ventures made Banvard, in monetary terms, the most successful artist of his day, with a million-dollar fortune at the height of his success. But Levine also shows that clearer distinctions came to be drawn between culture and popular entertainment towards the end of the century, and correspondingly culture became either highbrow or lowbrow.

In Europe the American expatriate John Singleton Copley speculated on topical subjects such as *The death of the Earl of Chatham* (1778–81), which he displayed in what was disparagingly called 'a raree show'. Sensational subjects such as *Watson and the shark* (originally *The youth rescued from a shark*) were not only profitably displayed, they were later lucratively engraved. Copley's sensational *Siege of Gibralter* [sic] (1791), a huge work at 18 by 23 feet, was displayed in an oriental tent in Green Park, London. The display of the painting, visible in an engraving by Francesco Bartlozzi (1791), shows the work framed as theatre, fitted behind a proscenium arch flanked by ionic columns and swagged by fringed curtains. Harold E. Dickson (1973) names John Trumbull, unsurprisingly an eyewitness to Copley's touring paintings, as the first (in 1789) to emulate the commercial exhibition in America, with another painting of Gibraltar: *The sortie made by the garrison of Gibraltar, the night of 26/27 November, 1781*, which was followed by paintings of American independence. The price of admission (25 cents) guaranteed something large, such as Edward Savage's life-size patriotic conversation piece *The Washington family* (1796).

Itinerant shows were common, with artists such as Rembrandt Peale and John Vanderlyn touring the country, seeking dwindling portrait commissions, and exhibiting picture shows as an alternative source of income. According to Dickson, the heyday of the *spectacular* painting came after the war of 1812, and reached its peak around 1820. Most popular with the public were moral allegories and biblical stories; episodes of patriotic derring-do were a less dependable draw. William Dunlap produced several touring canvases of religious subjects of immense scale: *Calvary* (1825–8) filled 250 feet of canvas and despite its bulk was ferried huge distances, travelling as far as Detroit. Benjamin West's *Christ healing the sick* was also shown to great acclaim in Philadelphia, as was his *Christ healing in the temple*, which garnered $4,000 in its first exhibition year. Claimed as the world's largest painting, the Atlanta Cyclorama was a cylindrical panoramic painting of the defence of Atlanta by confederate soldiers during the Civil War: the *Battle of Atlanta* (1887) measures 42 feet high by 358 feet long. Painted by a team of artists led by Germans F. W. Heine and August Lohr, the Cyclorama was based on eyewitness accounts including that of Civil

War artist Theodore Davis. Being cylindrical it rotates, enabling the seated viewer to see the whole painting. Originally toured with a circus that fell on hard times, the painting was bought and housed in Atlanta. A diorama, narration and a musical score were added in the twentieth century.

These were speculative works, and by no means without risk. For instance, Samuel F. B. Morse's ambitiously large painting of a *Gallery of the Louvre* (1832, 76 ft x 106.5 ft; see also page 42) was not entirely successful despite promising subject matter. Although ostensibly a travel-free way of seeing European art, looking at artists painting paintings evidently did not appeal, and the tour ended in the sale of the picture for an unremarkable sum. Death was popular, though, and Rembrandt Peale's *The court of death* (1820),[1] a classical allegorical work, broke all records, being seen by 32,000 people in a little over a year and accruing $8,886 (Dickson 1973: 11).

What is important here is that the travelling shows of the first half of the nineteenth century were a form of popular entertainment that combined the highbrow and lowbrow, helping to create a public for sculptures and pictures, and importantly (as we saw in Chapter 2) their subsequent realisation as reproductions. The touring works also acted as nascent tourist guides, sometimes depicting apparently untouched, virgin landscapes. Such works also contributed to a burgeoning sense of American manifest destiny and exceptionalism, as the landscapes depicted rivalled any European counterpart in scale and drama, becoming 'an effective substitute for a missing national tradition' (Novak 2007: 18).

Works travelled with explanations, inducting audiences in how to read them: a particular necessity in a country still accustomed to prurience when faced with the country's first full-scale female nude statue. Hiram Powers's neoclassical marble sculpture, *Greek slave*, toured the country in 1847–8 and was seen by over 100,000 people. As we have seen, Powers made six copies of the statue, and a widely produced miniature proved very popular. Lest the statue of a chained, naked women be misread as pornography, the artist's text and that written by the tour promoter, Miner Kellogg, emphasised the unfortunate woman's forbearance and Christian virtue as she awaited sale by the infidel. The *Greek slave* was also the centrepiece of the American section of the Great Exhibition of 1851 in London. It was displayed under a canopy complete with red plush swags, to huge acclaim. However *Punch*, the satirical magazine, was quick to point out the contradictions of so popular a work emanating from a slave-owning culture, a difficulty that was ameliorated somewhat in the 1860s when *Greek slave* was conscripted into the anti-slavery debate in America itself.[2]

1 The painting was based on a poem 'Death' by Beilby Porteus, Bishop of London.

2 Abolition was achieved with the Thirteenth Amendment to the Constitution freeing slaves in December 1865.

There were also artists who toured their work outside the mainstream for a range of reasons. As we will see, the distinct divisions between exhibition spaces for popular and fine art were not secure. For instance, the sculptor Edmonia Lewis (1845–1911) left New York to tour her work in Western fairs.[3] Marble sculptures such as *Old Indian arrowmaker and his daughter* (1872) were displayed on stands inside a form of wigwam, enabling Lewis to accentuate the relationship between the West and her Native American heritage. Originally named 'Wildfire', Lewis had a Chippewa Indian mother and African-American father, and although later an expatriate working in Rome, with another female American sculptor Harriet Hosmer (1830–1908), she represented her ethnicity in a period that excelled in caricature representations of both the minority groups she was descended from.[4] From a contemporary perspective it is possible to read some of Lewis's work, such as *Forever free* (1867), as classically derived and Europeanised representations of African-American people. Moreover in the representation of the newly freed women kneeling beside her man there could be read a continuation of subservience and ongoing gender oppression. However, in the years after the Civil War, African-Americans had few artistic progenitors to inform their images of emancipated slaves.[5] Atypically, Lewis was a financially successful woman working in marble,[6] in an art world hostile to female professionalism.

Other African-American women also toured works at fairs and venues that otherwise perpetuated stereotypes, particularly through the display of native huts and representations of so-called primitive peoples. Meta Vaux Warrick (Fuller) (1877–1968), born into a privileged black family in Philadelphia, was the first African-American to receive a Federal Commission to make an artwork (see Brundage 2003). Her task was to create a series of tableaux in the form of dioramas that illustrated 'in a true and artistic manner ... model groups ... to show by tableaux the progress of the Negro in America from the landing at Jamestown to the present time'. The narrative tableau was presented in the Negro section at the Jamestown Fair for

3 See in particular Albert Boime's *The Art of Exclusion: Representing Blacks in the Nineteenth Century* (1990).

4 See in particular Frances K. Pohl, 'Black and white in America' (1994).

5 The complexity of the debate around the representation of African-Americans in monumental sculpture during the nineteenth century can be drawn from the contemporary and continuing reception of Augustus Saint-Gaudens's *Memorial to Robert Gould Shaw* (1897). Son of an abolitionist family, Shaw was the Bostonian white colonel of an otherwise all-black regiment, who died and was buried with many of his men following a Civil War battle in 1863. Gaudens's black footsoldiers are individualized without recourse to racial stereotype, while Shaw is depicted on horseback in classic equestrian mode.

6 Much has been made of Lewis's depiction of black people realised in white marble, seemingly implicated in some sort of conspiracy against the black body. However there are historic precedents for the representation of figures in non-natural colours.

the Tercentennial celebrations of the first English settlement. The fourteen dioramas contained two-foot-high painted plaster figures set into modelled landscapes with painted backgrounds. Warrick initially trained at the experimental Industrial Art School, which combined traditional academic art with manual training, and was also educated at Pennsylvania Museum School of Industrial Art in 1896, eventually studying sculpture in Paris.[7]

Like many of her generation, Warrick excelled in allegory and mythical subjects: the dioramas therefore marked a departure for her in their representation of African-American people. W. Fitzhugh Brundage (2003) maintains that in avoiding caricature and exoticism, representing rather than displaying African-Americans, her work ran counter to the usual fairground representations informed by white supremacy. Although Warrick's dioramas won gold prize in the Fine Arts category at the Jamestown Fair, her dioramas were not without critics. In the final section of the series *Improved home life*, for instance, she presents the culmination of self-improvement for the prosperous black nuclear family: a middle-class setting with a woman doing needlework and a man reading. This comfortable, white vision of civilisation, it can be argued, did not take into account pluralistic notions of difference. The visitor shown in the tableau is however a black dissident poet, and the room's artworks have also been read as a challenge to the view that culture and African-Americans could be a seditionary combination. Brundage argues that the dioramas challenged what was termed the visual structures of white supremacy:

> by simultaneously adopting and subverting conventional turn-of-the-century images. Dismantling the stereotyped and caricatured images of African Americans reproduced in American popular culture, the dioramas recalled the long history of blacks in North America, resisted claims of racial purity by acknowledging the historical reality of interracial reproduction, and offered a teleological narrative culminating in black civilization, not in retrogression or criminality .... Her tableaux provided a vivid forum in which to challenge exhibitions of black subjectivity with unmistakable representations of black agency.
>
> (Brundage 2003)

The ephemeral dioramas were dismantled after the exposition, so today they are evidenced only by contemporary accounts and indistinct photographs.

7 Warrick was influenced by Augustus Saint-Gaudens, the African-American Henry O. Tanner and Rodin.

Touring America abroad

The first displays of indigenous American art and peoples date from the first encounters between Europeans and the New World. The travels of Martin Frobisher in what became Virginia brought 'curiosities' to Europe in the form of people, chattels and customs. As early as the 1590s there was an enthusiasm for wearing hair fashioned after the asymmetrical Powhatan male cut (shaved on one side and long on the other). As fashionable aristocrats had their portraits painted with their hair in lovelocks imitated from America, William Prynne blustered about the degenerate effects of the blurring of boundaries between genders, the modish haircut: condemned as 'Effeminate, Proud, Lascivious, Exorbitant, and Fantastique' (Kupperman 2000: 74). Karen Ordahl Kupperman has noted the positive exchanges between Europeans and Native Americans in the period. Europeans admired Indians for maintaining clear social distinctions of gender and class, which were apparent in their clothes, customs and behaviour. Their tangible culture was collectable: a deerskin decorated with shells referred to as Powhatan's (Pocahontas) mantle was part of the earliest public collection, Tradescant's Ark, and it appeared in the catalogue to the collection as the 'King of Virginia's habit all embroidered with shells, or Roanoke'.[8]

Arguably the most influential advocate of American popular culture in Europe in the nineteenth century was *Buffalo Bill's Wild West and Congress of Rough Riders of the World*. This extravagantly produced touring show introduced Europe to mythologies of the embattled west through sensational battles and Native American Indians. Buffalo Bill (real name William Frederick Cody) (1846–1917) was an international celebrity, painted on horseback in 1889 by the most famous animal painter of her day, Rosa Bonheur. By the time of his death the former bison hunter and soldier (during the Civil War), turned tireless promoter of the vanishing West, was the most famous American in the world. A poster for the Congress, 'Art perpetuating fame', records Bonheur posed at her easel flanked by two famous men, Napoleon and Buffalo Bill. She focuses on Buffalo Bill, captioned 'The Man on Horse of 1900 from the Yellow Stone to the Danube, From Vesuvius to Ben Nevis', as he faces forward into the future; while Napoleon, captioned 'The Man on Horse of 1796, From the Seine to the Neva. From the Pyramids to Waterloo', faces the past. In the background of the poster are two camps, one army, one Native American. Family groups of Native Americans travelled with the congress, and contemporary photographs show Buffalo Bill and numerous Native Americans in full tribal dress, on gondolas in Venice, or riding through New Street in Birmingham,

8 The John Tradescants Younger and Elder, gardeners and explorers, showed their collections of rarities in London during the seventeenth century. The cloak (with much of Tradescant's collection) eventually formed the basis of the Ashmolean Museum collection in Oxford.

England. There was a separation between the public and private presentation of Indians travelling with the Congress of Rough Riders. In the re-enactment of Custer's Last Stand, Buffalo Bill scripted his Rough Riders into stereotypical Indian roles. However, the Native Americans and women comprising his entourage led independent and culturally appropriate lives beyond the show. Entertainments of this scale were heavily dependent on advertising, and generated merchandise such as posters and comics portraying Buffalo Bill's exploits. Images of the West were also found in the 'blood and thunder' dime novels of the 1870s (Sides 2007: 306) (Plate 7).

As we have seen, the distinction between high and low art was not fixed until the early twentieth century. A further example of the compression of art into popular entertainment was the menagerie circus, which was often also an art show, with dioramas and waxworks. The modern circus that showcased skills (as opposed to the spectacles of the ancient world) had its origins in Philip Astley's (1742–1814) English equestrian display. Borrowing from Elizabethan theatre, equestrian performance circuses like Astley's were soon travelling across Europe. Perhaps unsurprisingly trick riding was also the highlight of the American circus, but it was its ability to travel light that was its real innovation. Not for the first or last time, innovation and pragmatism were the hallmarks of American adaptations of European ideas. The movement westward and the need to find new audiences required the circus to be mobile, and the canvas tent or the big top was in common usage by the 1830s.[9] By the end of the Civil War the familiar circus parade through the town to tout for custom had arrived. With its transnational appeal through mime, juggling, music and acrobatic skill, the circus was successful in communicating to large immigrant populations both at home and overseas.

The touring shows made a considerable impact in Europe, and contributed to Europeans' sense of the Americans, in particular through Phineas Taylor Barnum's (1810–1891) *Greatest Show on Earth: P.T. Barnum's Museum, Menagerie and Circus.* The range of Barnum's attractions of the early 1870s, when the museum was prominent in the form of a sideshow, included 'twenty vans of waxworks, dioramas, mechanical figures' (Bogdan 1988: 41). As we shall see in Chapter 5 when we return to Barnum, the museum, sideshow and circus travelled in tandem as education and entertainment.

The cold war and the atomic age: global pilgrims

While the interested reader might be convinced that during the 1950s and 1960s abstract expressionism swept all before it, since so much has been

9 In 1825 Joshuah Purdy Brown become the first circus showman to use the canvas tent.

written on the promotion of abstract expressionism as a signifier of American freedom and therefore its use as a diplomatic tool in the cold war, in fact there is another (if perhaps less compelling)[10] history: the promotion of diversity as a signifier of American values. Diversity can been seen as similar to assimilation: a sense that we are all alike if we use the same set of humanist values as a prism for viewing, standing in stark contrast to the differences that separate cultures and histories.

The extent of tolerance to dissent and the presentation of a mythical diversity through America art can be demonstrated by the history of *Advancing American Art*, an exhibition rarely referred to in revisionist histories.[11] Initiated and funded by the US State Department in 1946 for $49,000, and touring between 1946 and 1948, *Advancing American Art* comprised 117 paintings curated as a travelling show. There were two versions of the show, both with similar selections of artworks: one travelled to Europe, including the then Czechoslovakia, and the other to Latin America. Seventy-nine paintings from the show were exhibited at the Metropolitan Museum in New York (from 4 October 1946). *Advancing American Art* was a diplomatic disaster, and it was recalled after a hostile Hearst newspaper campaign.

The conceptual framework for the exhibition was determined by J. LeRoy Davidson, an art specialist from the State Department, to represent the 'newest developments in American art' (Littleton and Sykes 1989: 68). Although by 1946 there had been considerable growth in abstract expressionism it was not represented in the exhibition. Work by William Baziotes (1912–1963) and Adolf Gottlieb (1903–1974) was included, but it did not include the work of any of the abstract expressionists who were then in their 30s, such as Pollock, Motherwell and de Kooning. Virginia Mecklenberg has argued that Davidson deliberately forswore an allegiance to non-objective art in favour of an art that appeared 'socially engaged', even if figuration was absent and this orientation was only evident in the work's title (Austfield and Mecklenberg 1984: 35–64). The selection hinged on the presentation of American individualism and freedom through dissent, which was at odds with the exhibition's hostile domestic reception. The exhibition rejected local

10 Cultural pluralism (a Whitmanesque unity in diversity) offered a more complex history than that presented by Serge Guilbaut in *The New Adventures of the Avant-Garde in America* (1980) and its successor, *How New York Stole the Idea of Modern Art: Abstract Expressionism, Freedom, and the Cold War* (1983). Guilbaut's view is countered by Michael Kimmelman in 'Revisiting the revisionists: the modern, its critics, and the cold war' (1994).

11 Guilbaut curtly dismissed *Advancing American Art*, merely referencing it as evidence of interest in art by the State Department. He maintained that the process of dazzling the free world 'got under way in 1946 when the *Advancing American Art* exhibition was sent abroad. There were disappointments connected with this show, whose preparations were halted in midcourse for domestic political reasons' (1983: 118).

regionalism and concentrated on variations of a European-inspired expressionism and abstraction, usually wedded to social and political commentary. *Advancing American Art* included a high number of older American moderns: John Marin, Georgia O'Keeffe, Marsden Hartley and Arthur Dove.

An anti-fascist mandate is evident in Davidson's selections, which featured several artists best known for their politically oriented work, including Jack Levine and Ben Shahn, two 'artists of particular originality who reacted with power and maturity to the violence of Fascism and World War II' (Mendelowitz 1960: 417). Philip Evergood and William Gropper, artists often connected with the 1930s and a politically left past, although they had careers in the 1950s and 1960s, also found a place. Many works selected contained overtly anti-fascist texts, symbolism and imagery, as was seen in Mitchell Siporin's *Neapolitan nights* (1946) and Evergood's *Fascist leader* (1946). There were other anti-war works without overt reference to fascism, in particular Paul Burlin's *News from home* (1944) and Julio de Diego's *Under stiff rearguard action* (1942). Gropper's *Prey*, borrowed from Goya's *Third of May 1808*, and *The sleep of pure reason produces monsters* were often appropriated as anti-fascist imagery, and his *They fought to the last man* also registered despair at war and humanity in chaos. His 1945 work *Home* depicted a huddled, anonymous figure searching the rubble of a building in an unspecific landscape. Gropper, Evergood, Davis and Shahn had all had been members of the American Artists Congress, and apart from Davis all produced works that satirised big business. Their inclusion is significant because their political, anti-capitalist past made them vulnerable to censure by the late 1940s. However, as Mecklenberg has noted, Davidson selected 'paintings by these militants that reflected universal concerns about humanity rather than doctrinaire political views' (Austfield and Mecklenberg 1984: 42).

The domestic hostility to *Advancing American Art* resulted in calls to send portraits of George Washington and Abraham Lincoln as correctives to the perceived anti-democratic content of the exhibition. From the 1930s onward similar unifying symbols had been pressed into the service of democracy as a bulwark against fascism. Cécile Whiting (1989) remarks on how national icons such as American presidents, the Declaration of Independence and the Constitution were enlisted during periods of national unease. According to her, 'by the late thirties a Washington revival was in full swing' (Whiting 1989: 109). Perhaps the most salient feature of the Washington revival was his versatility. He was used by the Popular Front, for instance in Gropper's cartoon *The Delaware for them – The Atlantic for us*, published in *The New Masses* (no 44, July 1942), and in John Corbin's *Two frontiers of freedom* (1940), as a hero of democracy who saved America from fascism in 1783 and also 'rescued eighteenth century America from nascent communism' (Whiting 1989: 109).

Ben Shahn was an advocate of the dissenting tradition, as is evident in his statements like 'Our idea is Democracy ... but if we, by official acts of suppression, play the hypocrite toward our own beliefs, strangle our own liberties, then we can hardly hope to win the world's unqualified confidence' (1953). His work presented in *Advancing American Art* did not deal specifically with anti-fascism, although much of his work in this period did, and he was well represented in other touring shows, at the Venice Biennale (1954) and the Moscow Show (1959). The reason for his inclusion seems to have been his critique of social welfare, found in *Hunger* (n.d.) and *The clinic* (1944–5), which were both singled out for particular censure, although for quite different reasons. An article in the popular magazine *Look* (18 February 1947) censured *The clinic* because it was a reminder of the welfare state and social issues (a haunting reference to the Depression era), and *Hunger* because post-purchase Shahn allowed the CIO-PAC to use it with their text as the basis for a poster, *We want peace* (1946).

According to Mecklenberg, Shahn's *Hunger* and Kuniyoshi's *Circus girl resting* were two of the most widely reproduced images from the exhibition. The latter appeared in *Time, Newsweek*, the *Washington Post* and the *Republican News*, and both were reproduced in *Look* (Austfield and Mecklenberg 1984: 30). The inclusion of *Hunger* is indicative of the direct use of Shahn's work as a politically coercive tool in the face of a hostile government and press. It was not perceived as addressing a domestic issue, but as a reflection of a defeated Europe, one of several such images sent abroad. However, as hunger was a major issue in a post-war torn Europe, US food exports were identified as a more pragmatic response than culture. Parallels were drawn in the press and by Congress with Marie Antoinette's exhortation to 'let them eat cake'.

The un-American constitution of the artists was also cause for recourse by the popular press and Senate to myths of Mayflower origins and xenophobia: 'The names of artists – Shahn, Zerbe, Prestopino, Kuniyoshi, Guglielmi do not seem to have the flavor of an American background but bring visions of a transplanted European hodgepodge at its worst' (Henry Collidge Learned, in a letter to Representative George Bates, 10 February 1947, quoted in Austfield and Mecklenberg 1984: 20). The works in *Advancing American Art* were also publicly ridiculed by Presidential Truman, who famously said of Kuniyoshi's *Circus girl resting*, 'If that's art, then I'm a Hottentot' ('The Washington merry-go-round', *Washington Post*, 18 February 1947).

After the exhibition's recall William Benton, head of the State Department, told General George C. Marshall (then Secretary of State) that he would 'declare that art collection surplus property and throw it on the market' (Littleton and Sykes 1989: 152).[12] Fred Othman denounced the subsequent

12 The show was largely sold to Auburn University, Alabama, for extraordinarily low prices: Dove's work was priced at $30, O'Keeffe's at $50, Marin's at $100, with a loss to the government of over $50,000.

hasty sale, which inevitably held the exhibition up to further public scrutiny, as a 'Scrambled egg art sale' in the *Washington News* (14 May 1947). The national press had a field day. The *American Weekly* ran the headline 'Advancing American Art Dean Cornwall – a distinguished American artist tells why the State Department has decided to junk its $49,000 collection of weird masterpieces' (17 September 1949). The article condemned the State Department for its sponsorship of the exhibition, holding up as notorious examples Shahn's *Hunger*, Louis Guglielmi's *Tenements,* and *Mother and child* by Nahum Tschacbosov, maintaining that 'despite their appearance, they were done by adults who had been hailed as leaders of modern art' (Littleton and Sykes 1989: 22). The article points to the acquisition of Raphael's *Alba Madonna* by the Soviet government for $1,166,400, as a salutary example of prudent expenditure.

The exhibition predated the Marshall Plan by several months although it was implicated in the controversy surrounding it, and used in Senate debates as an example of fiscal imprudence when faced with the massive funding required by the Marshall Plan. As Secretary of State, it was Marshall who ordered the works to be held in Prague and Port-au-Prince, and returned to the United States. His battle cry of 'no more taxpayers' money for modern art' was a common cause for consternation amongst the liberal elite of art institutions as late as 1948 (Littleton and Sykes 1989: 58), a view borne out by correspondence between the Federation of Arts and museums.

Benton accounted for the recall of the works quite specifically, tying it to the communist past of the artists involved, even though this had been well documented before the work had been dispatched. He claimed that after his discovery that many of the painters in the exhibition were, justly or unjustly, on the attorney general's list of communists, allowing the exhibit to continue under State Department sponsorship would have allowed the Russians to exploit the matter, a move which in turn would have severely affected congressional attitudes (Littleton and Sykes 1989: 39). The State Department was charged with misappropriation of funds as a result of involvement in art exhibitions that year. There were a series of hearings before the subcommittee of the House Committee on Appropriations, which looked into the Department's budget proposals for 1948 (Littleton and Sykes 1989: 31). The projected figure for a cultural budget to send an alternative US image abroad was 'thirty-one-million dollars' (Littleton and Sykes 1989: 32). Accounts of the proceedings suggest many Republicans thought touring art was a poor weapon with which to halt the spread of communism in Europe.

The hearings indicated that the intention was to use art as a tool of diplomacy and propaganda. Benton specifically defended the selection of works at the hearings as more representative of 'the current artistic interests of this country than the more orthodox or traditional forms of art. Here you have the first reason underlying the theory behind this program' (Littleton and

Sykes 1989: 32). This is an important point. The selected works registered as modern art, at least to the organisers. This assertion flies in the face of the hostility that *Advancing American Art*, and a decade later the art exhibition at the Moscow Show, met not just in the popular press but even in the more liberal *New York Times*. *Look* for instance ran the headline 'Your money bought these pictures' (Littleton and Sykes 1989:30).

The pictures widely ridiculed were the modern 'distortions' that were still being singled out in the Moscow show a decade later. Four were social realist, two paintings were of circus subjects and one of a mother and child. They were the works of Kuniyoshi, Zerbe, Shahn, Tschacbasov, Guglielmi and Prestopino. The usual suspects, Shahn, Kuniyoshi, Stuart Davis, Gropper, Walt Kuhn, Jack Levine, Evergood and Anton Refregier, were causing havoc for two distinct, but subsequently conflated, reasons: first, the un-American nature of modern art, and second, their communist past during the New Deal.

To draw a correlation between communism and a New Deal past was a well-rehearsed activity at this time. The Congressional Record for 13 May 1947 contained this comment from the senator for Illinois, Mr Busbey:

> Mr Chairman, the so-called art exhibit that was sent abroad by the State Department is a disgrace to the U.S. ... [containing] communists and their New Deal travelers. I asked the House Committee on un-American Activities to give me a report on the artists. The records of more than 20 of the 45 artists are definitely connected with revolutionary organizations.
>
> (Barr Papers, no. 3)

The House Committee on Un-American Activities (HUAC) documents dated 22 March 1947 audit the political affiliations of the artists and their works. Paradoxically Shahn was also promoted as emblematic of American freedom at the same time as being censored by press and government:

> Shahn, one of the central figures in the [*Advancing American Art*] disaster, whose work only a few months earlier had been derided in the press and by Congress as alien to the American image, would complete in his stark expressionist style the striking cover illustration for a major summer issue of *Fortune* magazine devoted to this very subject of the struggle in Cold War Italy between capitalism and communism.
>
> (Littleton and Sykes 1989: 64–5)

The exhibition did receive the endorsement of the influential art critic Clement Greenberg, who was eager to show the world the advances in US art (and Greenberg was particularly concerned about the censure of Latin America). He commented on the:

> daring and plastic originality [rather] than ... the American 'scene' or our home-grown surrealism; [declaring that] 'it was up to the State Department to show people that ... we too kept keep abreast of advances in art'. Greenberg was at pains to praise Leroy Davidson as 'a good half of his show goes determinedly in the direction of the abstract'.
>
> (O'Brian 1986: vol. 2, 114)

The *Family of Man*

The American exhibition probably seen by more people globally than any other was *Family of Man*, a photographic show originally curated for MoMA in 1955 by Edward Steichen, director of photography at MoMA from 1947, with text provided by Carl Sandberg.[13] *Family of Man* contained just over 500 photographs by 273 photographers drawn from an international field: five copies of the exhibition travelled until 1965 under the auspices of the US Information Agency (USIA), which calculated that it was seen 'at eighty-eight venues in thirty-seven countries ... by seven and a half million people' (Szarkowski 1994: 13). In the introduction to the book accompanying it, which ran to over thirty printings and more than 3 million copies, Steichen's universalising and pedagogic agenda is clear:

> the art of photography is a dynamic process of giving form to ideas and explaining man to man. It was conceived as a mirror of the universal elements and emotions in the everydayness of life-as a mirror of the essential oneness of mankind throughout the world.
>
> (Steichen and Sandberg 1955: 3)

The biblical opening is: 'And God said, let there be light' Genesis 1:3'. The possibility of capturing the essential oneness of mankind appealed to MoMA's International Council:

> four near replicas of Family of Man, an exhibition ... on the theme of the universal oneness of mankind, were produced for the Agency and have been widely circulated throughout the world and the original version was also acquired by USIA for foreign circulation.
>
> (International Council MoMA press release 1958:3)
> (Source Tate London Archive)

Collated during the cold war, the exhibition presented a vision of unity,

13 Steichen and Sandberg had collaborated on an earlier 1942 MoMA wartime exhibition, *Road to Victory*.

with human beings bound by their essential humanity and intrinsic 'goodness' through the nuclear family and the 'American way of life', and its resolutely heterosexual normativity. Images of voting at the ballot box also abounded, and the whole was sanctioned by the image of a session at the United Nations, with a quote from the Charter about reaffirming 'faith in fundamental human rights, in the dignity and worth of the human person, in the equal rights of men and women and the nations large and small' (Steichen and Sandberg 1955: 184). Susan Sontag, writing in 1977, saw the *Family of Man* as a continuation of Whitman's 'program of populist transcendence, of the democratic transvaluation of beauty and ugliness, importance and triviality' (1977: 27). The images were of:

> Ordinary, unknown people, engaged in unexceptional activities. The photographs were arranged to suggest that all people's goals and problems were fundamentally similar, and to recapitulate in broad strokes the life cycle of the species, beginning with love and proceeding through marriage, childbirth, family life, play, work, aspiration and religious feeling, and death, followed by a brief survey of the bad news – hunger, barbarity, and war – and then a final reprise to the magic of childhood.
>
> (Szarkowski 1994: 13)

The ideological basis of the exhibition was cogently exposed by Roland Barthes in 'The great family of man', published in 1957 and using the reworked title the French gave the show when it moved to Paris (Barthes 1957:100–2). Barthes noted the exclusions operating to represent the world as a united brotherhood. Central to the original exhibition in 1955 was an image of a mushroom cloud, which was omitted from subsequent tours. The US hydrogen bomb tests in the South Pacific during the mid-1950s were a major source of international friction. The image of the hydrogen bomb was virtually the only image of modern technology in the entire photographic exhibition: it was accompanied by a statement from the US Atomic Energy Commission, '[n]uclear weapons and atomic power are symbolic of the atomic age: On one side, frustration and world destruction: on the other, creativity and a common ground for peace and cooperation' (Steichen and Sandberg 1955: 82).

Notwithstanding the absence of visible technology in the photographic exhibition, the first exhibition programme was also a denial of the power relations that existed between nations in that period. It was this aspect that Roland Barthes and latterly Allan Sekula have commented on (Sekula 1984). Barthes's 1950s criticism resurfaced, at a safe historical distance, in a MoMA article by Szarkowski in 1994. He revisited Barthes's observation on the exhibition's habitation of the 'realm of gnomic truths, the meeting of all the ages of humanity at the most neutral point of their nature, the point where the obviousness of the truism has no longer any value except in the realm of a purely poetic language' (Elderfield 1994: 33). The critical perspective is a familiar one coming from Barthes, who levied the charge of 'ahistoric' against the curators, for investing in the myth of the human condition and for placing 'Nature at the bottom of History' (Barthes 1957: 101). For Barthes, classic humanism produces a flawed 'solid rock of a universal human nature', instead of what he defines as, 'progressive humanism', which 'must always remember to reverse the terms of this very old imposture, constantly to scour nature, its "laws" and its "limits" in order to discover History there, and at last to establish Nature itself as historical' (1957: 101). Barthes's cautionary tale has resonances in the construction of the natural landscape and the changing of nationalism into the nation-state, themes we return to at intervals in this book. The exhibition, even now when viewed through historic installation shots and the concentrated, reduced format of the book, presents a constructed homogeneity, denying difference in favour of what Barthes terms 'Adamism', resulting in a sentimentalism that masked the ideological selections at play. Its very disguised neutrality made it the ideal vehicle to go travelling to Sokolniki Park, Moscow in 1959.

The *Family of Man* exhibition was not without its contemporary American critics. Hilton Kramer, writing in 1955, picked up the Whitmanesque elements in the show just as Sontag did later, describing it as the climax of Steichen's long career and consistent with his other work in that 'Steichen defines the exhibition as a mirror of the universal elements and emotions in the everydayness of life as a mirror of the essential oneness of mankind through out the world' (1955: 366). Kramer continued:

> his method of depicting this 'essential oneness' is to place in juxtaposition photographs from all parts of the world, playing up every superficial resemblance in custom, posture, and attitude, until he has whipped up a pictorial rhetoric very like Sandberg's [the prose that accompanied the exhibition] terrible parody of Whitmanesque sentiment .... He thus succeeds in making abstract an art which relies, above all, on the particular for its integrity.
>
> (Kramer 1955: 366)

Kramer's focus is specific: the apolitical pretence is most apparent in the images presented of European Jews. Kramer points to the paucity of 'political images', particularly those depicting violence. He argues that when such imagery does occurs, as in the case of a photo that showed Jews being marched through the streets of Warsaw, it brings the 'vacancy of thought which characterizes this notion of "relatedness" into sharper focus' (Kramer 1955: 366). The lesson of relatedness in the show he termed 'facile' when faced with the reality that:

> the most profound link between peoples today is their political link; that if races are 'as relatives' in any sense, they are political relatives. And in the presence of that fact, all pieties about the universal elements ... in the everydayness of life ... are revealed for what they are: a self-congratulatory means of obscuring the urgency of real problems under a blanket of ideology which takes for granted the essential goodness, innocence and moral superiority of the international 'little man', 'the man in the street', the abstract, disembodied hero of a world-view which regard's itself as superior to mere politics.
>
> (Kramer 1955: 367)

Although Kramer's political perspective is contrary to that of many other critics of the exhibition, his reading of the exhibition is an appeal to an 'illusionary image of the world' taking 'refuge in a supra-political realism'. He argues that instead the exhibition should engage in a 'real' world. His atypical perspective on the exhibitions circulating in the 1950s and 1960s is an important counterpoint to that being promoted by MoMA (Kramer 1955: 366–7).

There is an alternative view posited by John Roberts. Although he acknowledges both Barthes and Sekula's condemnations of *Family of Man*, which he describes as 'the now established radical positions', he suggests that they:

> fail to take account of the political contradictions out of which the exhibition was organised. The *Family of Man* may have celebrated the nuclear family and the American Way of Life but this does not mean that these ideologies were coherent or stable .... The affirmative humanism of the show, in fact, can be read non-positivistically as an attack on American Cold War policy.
>
> (Roberts 1998: 5)

Louis Kaplan has also argued that particular viewing audiences contested the notion of a unified global community, even though the images presented seem to have been mobilised to that end (2005).

American National Exhibition in Moscow 1959

> too many kitchens and not enough machinery
>
> Nikita Khrushchev, *New York Times*, 4 September 1959

In the year following the Geneva Summit Conference of 1955, the International Cultural Exchange and Fair Trade and Participation Act ratified the first exchange to take place in post-war Europe between the United States and the Soviet Union. Aborted in 1958, by 1959 the documentation had materialised into a cultural exchange: a US fair in Moscow with a corresponding Soviet exhibition in New York. The fair in Moscow was held at Sokolniki Park, famously referred to as 'the kitchen conference': the result of a well-publicised frank exchange of views between US Vice-President Nixon and Soviet President Nikita Khrushchev on the relative merits of their differing ideological positions, which took place in the display kitchen. The exhibits included American architecture, fashion, technology and culture, washed down with free Pepsi-Cola. An exhibition of contemporary American art was included as part of the officially designated American National Exhibition in Moscow. The art show was one element in a cultural package that included a Walt Disney Circorama, seven cinema screens, a colour television studio, the photographic exhibition *Family of Man*, outlined above, a book exhibit, a fashion show and twenty-two 1959 American automobiles. Newly developed Polaroid cameras and an American house separated into two parts to make it a 'walk through' were also conspicuous, widely advertised elements of the show.

The art exhibition was arranged by Edith Halpert of the Downtown Gallery, and Richard B. K. McLanathan. Lloyd Goodrich, Franklin C. Watkins, Theodore Roszak and Professor Henry Radford Hope completed the selection panel approved by President Eisenhower. The selection of fifty paintings and thirty sculptures from a thirty-year period (1928–58) avoided an over-emphasis on vanguard work. There was a conscious decision to select works so that early New York realists, American Scene painters, and American pioneers of modernist art and abstract expressionism could be represented. Goodrich declared that 'the committee feels justified in saying that it is the broadest, most balanced representation of recent American painting and sculpture so far shown abroad by our government' (1959: 3), opting for a broad survey, one work by many artists approach.

The significance of the exhibition can be gauged by attendance figures, although this should be mediated by knowledge of the Russian enthusiasm for exhibitions and fairs in this period. Figures for the overall exhibition were estimated at 2,700,000: the corresponding Soviet fair shown at the New York Coliseum over a 42-day period, closing on 10 August, drew less than half that, at only 1,100,000 visitors. The figures for the art exhibit were also high. Goodrich cited visitor figures of between 10,000 and 20,000 a day (1959: 5–6). The unexpected, overwhelming numbers required a shift system to be put into operation. Press and official opinions on the success of the art section of the show were deeply divided, and like the earlier exhibitions *Advancing American Art* and *Sport in Art* in 1952, the selections were subject to questions in the House, and requests for recall and removal of some works before and during the show.

The exhibition was due to open in Moscow on 25 July. As the artworks were being catalogued and shipped, some artists involved were subpoenaed to appear before HUAC. A newspaper photograph of Ben Shahn, under the caption 'Ben Shahn subpoenaed by House Committee', drew public attention to the selection issues. The article quoted the chairman of HUAC, Congressman Francis E. Walter, whose accusation was that more than half of the sixty-seven paintings and sculptures to be exhibited had been done by artists with records of 'affiliation with Communist fronts and causes' (*New York Times*, 27 June 1959).

Ironically, given the rhetoric of tolerance and diversity that issued from press releases, the reception of the modern works in Moscow, while mixed and at times hostile or derisory, was less uniform in condemnation than the comments in the United States. Many Russians displayed a depth of knowledge of American art and modernism that had bypassed the US Congress. McLanathan, reflecting on his own perception of the success of the *American Art Show in Moscow*, remarked:

> Among these young scientist intellectuals, Western artists in all fields are as well known as the great Russian writers and composers, and Americans such as Hemingway, Faulkner, O'Neill, Gershwin, Shahn, Pollock, and Stuart Davis are considered by them to be among the world's great and have won respect for the country that produced them.
>
> (McLanathan 1960: 77)

Young Russians were familiar with 'the Eight', the Ashcan school and many other American artists. One review ends with the comment, 'you in America have inherited the leadership, and you represent freedom and the future'. It was also a lament for the early Russian modernists and a Russian art that had become 'expatriate' (McLanathan 1960: 78). According to the article, those Russians 'open to new ideas' were very impressed with American abstract art. As his was the official voice of the exhibition, McLanathan's selection of quotes is perhaps unsurprising.

McLanathan's reliability is subject to further doubt since the general impression gleaned from a broader range of reviews gives other perspectives. It is also difficult to measure his qualitative moral high ground in naming those who were 'open to new ideas' as those who were 'receptive' (McLanathan 1960: 78). The official line however, as 'repeated in the press' and 'heard daily dozens of times, as well as written in the comment book' was that 'Such [abstract] pictures cannot please the Soviet people' (McLanathan 1960: 73). Nikita Khrushchev, who visited the exhibition, is reported to have observed that 'People who paint like that are crazy, but people who call it art are crazier still' (McLanathan 1960: 73). The polarisation along official party lines is hardly surprising; what remains a problem is the collapsing of terms, and treating modern art and modernism as synonymous with the 'all-over' abstractions. An unnamed and undated newspaper cutting with the headline 'Soviet expert hits abstract art at U.S. exhibit' quotes Dr

Keminov, director of the Pushkin Museum, complaining that the show 'includes too few works by realistic Leftist American painters'.[14]

What is clear, however, is that the critical attention heaped on abstract expressionism was out of all proportion to the number of entirely abstract works shown. Of the recent works shown at the exhibition, McLanathan observed that:

> less than a third can be considered ... abstract or non-objective. When older paintings are included [he was referring to the belated addition of eighteenth and nineteenth-century paintings], the fraction diminishes to nearly one eighth. Yet there was very little mention of anything but the modern or abstract or surrealist – all three adjectives being applied without discrimination as equally disparaging.
>
> (McLanathan 1960: 74)

Reviewers used 'abstraction' to refer to both social realist work such as Shahn's, and Pollock's work: both unsurprisingly failing to meet the expectations of exactitude and class politics expected of socialist realism. The heading 'Soviet culture's U.S. contemporary art on exhibition in Sokolniki Park' (11 August 1959) reveals an ideological fissure: the sub-headline read 'Realist trend suppressed and weakened'. The show also drew comments from Russian critics that the works sent were not of a high quality or even really representative of the artists' best work. In some cases, these critics and museum curators demonstrated a well-informed understanding of artists rarely discussed outside the United States (Kemenov 1959, McLanathan 1960: 77).

The publicity literature surrounding the exhibit as a whole, and the art exhibition in particular, was seen by the exhibition's organisers as crucial to the dissemination of US art. There were two catalogues to the exhibition, a small leaflet and a larger comprehensive catalogue. There was also a brief account of the art exhibit in the general guide to the whole exhibition given to every visitor. The brief reference to the art show in the introductory guide had a photograph of Watkins, standing in front of William Glackens's *Soda fountain*. The smaller of the two art catalogues began with a map showing the distribution of art museums across America, perhaps to counter the charge of East Coast hegemony. The eight black and white images showed only two 'abstract' works, a sculpture and a painting by Morris Graves, *Flight of plover*. McLanathan also used the Graves work as the frontispiece of *American Art in Moscow* (1960), together with Peter Blume's *Eternal City* on the front page. *Flight of plover* was also used on other publicity material. The choice of images in the small catalogue mostly belonged to a

14 Source: Public Information Scrapbook, MoMA Archives.

figurative realist tradition related to the 1930s: works by Hyman Bloom, Glackens, Walt Kuhn, Eugene Speicher, Seymore Lipton, and Jo Davidson's bust of Albert Einstein. There was a total absence of any 'American type painting' or New York School images. In fact, Eugene Speicher's *Red Moore, blacksmith* (1935) would not have looked out of place in an exhibition of Soviet socialist realism.

The presence of Graves's work is significant as he is another of the exclusions that buttress canonical modernism. Graves, a West Coast painter, is sometimes seen as representing a new American regionalism associated with a mystical 'natural' world influenced by Zen Buddhism. His works have been equated with a religious spirit that draws on Chinese and Korean painting. The emphasis on the mystical and the spiritual were not compatible with later Greenbergian formalism, and artists such as Richard Pousette-Dart found themselves outsiders even within the small coterie of abstract expressionists. According to Sam Hunter, Graves represented a 'distinct American artistic tradition, recalling the confined but powerful sensibility of Ryder[15] and the poetess Emily Dickinson' (1959: 147). Pollock and Rothko were represented at Moscow, Pollock by *Cathedral* (1947) and Rothko by *Old gold over white* (1956).

The exhibition also had a larger, much sought-after Russian-language catalogue which quickly became a black-market item. The English language translation started with Goodrich's essay 'American art today', in which he differentiated between the 'purism' of geometric abstraction and the 'free form', more 'expressive' agenda that he saw as more consistent with American values. Goodrich was at pains to point out that American art institutions accommodated more than abstraction. He maintained that 'In spite of the current predominance of abstraction an interesting feature of American art today is the number and strength of representational artists.' What he stressed in his essay was the tolerance awarded in the United States to artistic creation and opinion, which was condemned as a sham in Soviet circles in Moscow.

Goodrich quoted the fierce opposition to the show in the popular press but attributed the lack of government censorship to the immediacy of the Pasternak case.[16] The Moscow show went ahead, but not without revisions. At President Eisenhower's request, eighteenth and nineteenth century examples of American art and democratic virtues were reinstated, with Gilbert Stuart's *George Washington* and George Healy's *Lincoln*, along with works

15 Albert Pinkham Ryder (1847–1917) was an early American painter with Romantic predilections, who arguably anticipated abstract expressionism through his emotional exploration rather than representational exactitude in painting.

16 The United States had publicly denounced Russia for its suppression and censoring of the work of the novelist and poet Boris Pasternak a few months before the Moscow show opened: the event was still in the public eye at the time of the exhibition.

by Copley and Ryder. Also called upon were Remington's reassuring images of cowboys, Indians and settlers enduring 'the hardships of frontier life' (Goodrich 1959:4). Goodrich saw the lack of censorship as 'a great and encouraging difference from similar past incidence' (1959: 5). Like many other liberal gallery directors in this period, he wrote of the fear of ridicule from abroad because of the government's lack of clarity. President Eisenhower's condemnation of Jack Levine's *Welcome home*, which he dismissed as 'more like a lampoon than art' (Goodrich 1959: 4) found its way into the international press, where it was used as an example of government interference in art shows. Goodrich however held up the presence of Levine's satirical work as a telling demonstration of US freedom.

In a postscript to the Moscow show, MoMA's director, Alfred H Barr Jr., went to lecture on American art in Russia at the invitation of the Soviet Society for Cultural Exchange. His lectures emphasised 'abstractionist, expressionist and experimental techniques' (*New York Times* 11 June 1959). Barr gave slide lectures and showed film footage of Alexander Calder's *Circus*, or *Ballet Mechanique* and Hans Namuth's film from 1956 of Jackson Pollock demonstrating his drip painting. The newspaper report detailed the reactions of A. Zamoshkin, director of the Pushkin Art Gallery, who challenged the validity of the American abstractions, saying, 'we are glad to see the variety of American art, although not all of it is art with which we agree'. He remarked on the full-circle nature of the exhibition, maintaining, 'More than thirty years ago the Russian artist Malevich painted a famous black square. Now abstractionists, after two generations, have not advanced beyond that point.' Barr replied that 'each generation must have its own black square'. The gulf of incomprehension between the two nations during the cold war was exacerbated rather than tempered by the cultural exchanges.

The Venice Biennale

The Venice Biennale too was a venue for cultural sabre-rattling in the twentieth century. Frances Pohl's 'An American in Venice: Ben Shahn and United States foreign policy' (1980) and *Ben Shahn: New Deal Artist in a Cold War Climate 1947–1954* (1989) document how Shahn's work and writing were used as tools of cultural diplomacy. The American pavilion at Venice recalls Jefferson's Monticello: neoclassical symmetry with a central rotunda, rather than opting for the jewel in America's cultural crown, contemporary architecture.

At the 52nd Venice Biennale in 2007 a series of twelve huge billboards on sites across the city announced the posthumous American representative to the show, Felix Gonzalez-Torres (1957–1996). The image of a featureless grey sky punctuated by an indistinct bird in flight was replicated inside the US pavilion, where it was illuminated by Gonzalez-Torres's trademark string of light bulbs called *Untitled (leaves of grass)* from 1993. Taken together, the reference to Walt Whitman (Plate 8) and the solitary, soaring bird can be read as a paean to democracy and the individualism that underpins it. But there is also an ambiguity about Gonzalez-Torres's work which evades any easy reading of his ghostly attendance. The choice of artist to officially represent the United States has a long history of political interference, and also a sense of presenting to the outside world that which is liberal and most cherished and diverse. Gonzalez-Torres, a founder member of the activist collective Group Material,[17] started in 1979, died from complications caused by AIDS in 1996. The group's work includes *AIDS timeline* (1989–91), a piece critical of those in the Supreme Court of Justice who upheld the anti-sodomy laws in 1986. Moreover the group are committed to social justice and control over their own art work rather than being in thrall to the art market. The exhibition, 'Felix Gonzalez-Torres: America' was organized by the Solomon R. Guggenheim Museum, chosen by a jury of museum curators and directors, and overseen by the Federal Advisory Committee on International Exhibitions (FACIE) and the US State Department's Bureau of Educational and Cultural Affairs (ECA).

Gonzalez-Torres's work, offering take-away sweets and paper stacks, is a commentary on American consumerism and a form of participatory art. In other works such as *Untitled (monument),* ambiguously with and without interpretation Gonzalez-Torres's captions gracefully lead the witness. Inscriptions such as 'Memorial Day Weekend' and 'Veterans Day Sale' remind the viewer both of the organising principle of American holidays, related to acts of patriotism and nation building, and of the commercialism that pervades every act.

Importantly, although a US citizen, Gonzalez-Torres was Cuban-born, and his sexuality and untimely death were enough to cause a stir among those wishing to select works politically rather than through artistic criteria. The selection of the African-American Fred Wilson in 2003, with *Speak of me as I am*, was also a significant reconceptualisation of not just who could represent America but what kind of work was a suitable emissary. Far from the controversy that stalked the exhibitions above, for official artists such as Gonzalez-Torres and Wilson the issues to which they give visual representation were entirely the point. The official leaflet suggested that Wilson's installation was timely given:

> the increasing ethnic diversity in the West, growing xenophobia, and stricter immigration policies in both the United States and Europe. Making the case that Western culture is the result of historical multicul-

17 Group Material's founder members were Doug Ashford, Julie Ault, Tim Rollins, Felix Gonzales-Torres and Karen Ramspacher.

> turalism, Wilson believes that Venice, as a vital trading city like New York City today, was a place where people of various races and religions put aside their differences for the economic benefit of all.
>
> (*Speak of me as I am* (2003), US pavilion, 50th Venice Biennale)

'The first glimpse of the Promised Land of American art': modernism and Australia[18]

> Any study of the period should ... examine the process of consolidation of this [regional tradition] whose ideological character can be located in both its continuity and its specific historical changes. This consideration would effectively counter the notion of the 'arrival' or 'landing' of modernism as some monolithic force which was greeted by a reception party and proceeded effortlessly to sweep the country.
>
> (Burn *et al.* 1988: 44)

Nancy Jachec, writing on abstract expressionism and cold war politics, identifies problems with the orthodox view of the reception of new US art travelling abroad in the post-war period, which tended towards 'the bald conquest of Western Culture by American culture' (2003: 533). She questions the 'assumption that Europeans were passive in the face of American cultural expansion' and suggests that 'the blanket explanation of cultural imperialism has more or less overlooked the specific policy objectives that have been pursued by the United States government through its support for Abstract Expressionism' (Jachec 2003: 533). At the same time the 1950s were presented as an era when abstract expressionism was devoid of political relevance, and socially or politically relevant art was presented as devoid of aesthetic qualities. While this binary supports the first of Jachec's assertions about resistance rather than passivity to US cultural expansion, it contradicts the view that abstract expressionism was devoid of political radicalism, which is particularly represented by Elwyn Lynn in an article, 'Puritans in affluent America' (1967), who wrote 'true frontiersmen they [abstract expressionists] act as though art was part of Trotsky's permanent revolution; something of the apocalyptic attitude of the old left lurks in them'.

In Australia, which was both geographically and politically situated close to the war in Vietnam (1965–1973), abstract expressionism was considered at least by the left-wing press, to be implicated all too closely in politics. Noel Counihan, writing in *Tribune*, Sydney on 5 July 1967, decried the landmark show *Two Decades of American Painting* as representative of the values of Washington, the State Department and art dealers. We take issue

18 The heading quotes from Elwyn Lynn (1964).

with the assumption that the underlying problem is 'the specific policy objectives that have been pursued by the United States government through its support for Abstract Expressionism' by looking at the diversity of artworks that travelled the globe as cultural ambassadors. The time-lag (what was termed the tyranny of distance) in the critical reception of US art means that rather than a concentration on the immediate post-war period, the Australian context demands a broader time-frame and includes commentary from the 1960s as well as the 1940s and 1950s. The case of Jackson Pollock's *Blue poles* shows how, whilst not alone in this respect,[19] cultured Australians were critical but curious about American painting.

From early December 2003 to late February 2004 the National Gallery of Victoria in Melbourne exhibited Jackson Pollock's *Blue poles: number 11* (1952) as part of an exhibition to mark the thirtieth anniversary of the National Gallery of Australia (NGA) (Plate 17). *Blue poles* was allocated its own room, education programme and merchandising. The late Pollock painting[20] was purchased for US$1 million, with the intention of forming the cornerstone of the embryonic national collection. The painting was the most expensive international art purchase in Australia, sanctioned by Gough Whitlam's administration (1972–5), Australia's first Labour government. The acquisition stands as a marker for the government's progressive internationalist aspirations, where modernism was seen as a form of cultural advancement. In the publicity devised to accompany the 2004 exhibition, the NGA defended its purchase of the controversial work as 'a symbolic event in the movement towards cultural independence for Australia' (Public Programmes leaflet, National Gallery of Victoria 2003: 4). Moreover, in the introduction to the collection of the NGA the author recalls that the acquisition of *Blue poles* announced 'to the world a serious ambition to form a significant international collection' (Kennedy 1998: 41).

Although established, looking at and evaluating Australian art in terms of its dependency upon European English or American work had been challenged. The perception of the purchase as internationally significant is echoed by evidence from the period. As debate swirled around the status of *Blue poles*, Bryan Robertson, author of *Jackson Pollock* (1960), wrote:

> The presence of *Blue Poles* in Australia will inevitably change the course of Australian history, because it will effect the developing imagination

19 See in particular Jachec (2003: 546) on the hostile response of Jean Cassou (then director of the Musée de l'art moderne, Paris) to both *New American Painting* and *Jackson Pollock 1912–1956*.

20 It is worth noting that as the painting contains implied depth it was considered a failed painting by advocates of the earlier 'all-over' painting of the late 1940s. It was also subject of controversy, as being the possible progeny of a late-night drunken collaboration between Pollock and the sculptor Tony Smith.

> and awareness of successive generations of Australians, at the most profound level, it will become a talisman of a great nation.
>
> (Lloyd and Desmond 1992: 9)

The following year the NGA purchased another modernist work: Willem de Kooning's *Woman V* (1952–3). According to Lloyd and Desmond there were other American paintings on the museum wish-list including Helen Frankenthaler's *Other generations* (1957), 'which the artist was reluctant to relinquish because she felt that selling it to Australia was tantamount to consigning it to oblivion' (1992: 8). What is significant is the perception, supported by such luminaries as Robert Hughes, that purchasing US art would help end the deference to British art, and ameliorate what was termed the provincialism of Australian art in preference for the supposed internationalism of US high modernist art. Even during the 1950s and 1960s, Australia was open to America, losing patience with England's 'mandarin manners' and feeling affinity with America's egalitarianism (Horne 1967: 104). Attacks on the conservatism and aesthetic pitfalls of national schools of art within modernist theory are legion: in Australia the 'gum-tree' painters of the Australian bush, 'kitchen-sink paintings' in Britain and in the United States the 1930s Regionalists have all run the gauntlet of charges of mediocrity and failed ambition because of their attachment to location. What is significant here is the way an art that was affectionately referred to as 'Manhattan regionalism', the New York School, can register as international. That is to ask how one particular work rather than another can transcend its origins. The debate raises the stakes on what kind of art can be developed at a parochial or regional level that does not face the charge of being derivative and dependent on a dominate form developed at a centre at some distance.

There were voices raised against a purchasing policy that lauded the internationalism of US modernism and neglected the national, local and regional, although the arguments vary in complexity and political hue, from those tainted by chauvinism, philistinism and anti-American sentiment to concerns about cultural imperialism. Ian Burn's 'Buying cultural dependency: a note on the crazed thinking behind several Australian collections' (1975b) was not the only head above the parapet that questioned the shift of artistic dependency from Britain to the United States. See Bernard Smith's writing, and also Terry Smith's 'The provincialism problem', which appeared in *Artforum* in 1974. By the late 1980s 'The necessity of Australian art: an essay about interpretation' by Ian Burn, Nigel Lendon, Charles Merewether and Ann Stephen was arguing that in 'Australia emerging modernist attitudes were defined both in terms of and against the dominant regional consciousness'(1988: 41). The authors also disputed orthodox views and questioned the dependent and therefore derivative model of art (and art history), arguing against the idea that there was an uncritical acceptance of the 1960s form of American cultural imperialism. The article was hostile to the notion that Australian art should be dependent on any dominant international model, and defended what had largely been written out of Australian art history: attachment to place, and specifically regional landscape art.

Earlier in 1962 the Australian art historian Bernard Smith had debated the terms in which the reception of *Recent Australian Painting* shown at the Whitechapel Gallery, London had been written. In *Australian Paintings Today* he remarks on the different artistic outputs and artistic experience of two 'new' worlds, America and Australia, citing the legendary New York Armory Show of 1913, which took modernism to the United States, and the influence of Paris-based expatriates Gertrude Stein and her brother Leo on a generation of young Americans, at their fabled Saturday night soirees which celebrated French modernism. Smith argued that Australia had to wait until Sir Keith Murdoch's exhibition of 1939. He also problematised myths of national culture, and was critical of notions that Australian isolationism from international centres such as Paris, New York and London were a weakness. He commented that 'the Sydney band-waggon of abstract expressionism … had begun a kind of Juggernaut intent upon destroying every other kind of art in its path' (Smith 1962). Writing in defence of the Melbourne-based figurative work, Smith railed:

> if figurative painting was going to survive in this country as a creative activity some sort of vigorous counter-attack was necessary, otherwise the individuality that had developed in Australian painting during the preceding twenty years would be swamped by a provincial form of American abstract expressionism with a good public relations machine behind it. Sydney was already.
>
> (Smith (1962) in Stephen *et al.* 2007: 719)

It is not just the undue influence of particular styles of painting emanating from Paris, London and New York that caused concern: it was the financial apparatus that sustained and defined art which was called into question. Ian Burn noted that after the optimism (and art purchasing power) of the 1960s, art's commodification started at a work's inception, not merely at the point of sale, and that this precipitated a crisis by limiting the form and radicalism that art could take. While not laying the blame for the commodification of art entirely at the door of US capitalism, Burn observed that the power of market values distorted other values, arguing that:

> what is and is not acceptable as 'work' is defined *first and fundamentally* [Burn's italics] by the market and only secondly by 'creative urges'. This has been the price of internalizing [through the endless innovation and elitism of avant-garde growth] an intensely capitalistic mode of production.

(Burn 1975a: 34–7)

Burn saw the growth of market values as a fundamental and insurmountable problem, pitting elite art's valorising of individualism and a 'neutered formalism' at the expense of content erroneously against the idea of sociality and a social art practice (in Stephen *et al.* 2007: 936).

Identifying with nineteenth century alienation, Burn observes that the phenomenon is replicated with 'thousands upon thousands of artists in all corners of the modern art empire tackling American formalism in the belief that it is the one 'true art' – that's when it is possible to see how preposterous and finally downright degrading it has become!' (in Stephen *et al.* 2007: 936). The art market in Burn's terms was also implicated in the pathology of the artist, who under high capitalism was cast in the role of politically impotent, and through critics and historians as often merely a defender of the status quo.

As revisions to histories are rewritten in newer editions, the claims of pervious ages are often modified: earlier histories erased or made to seem less significant than formerly. During the 1970s and 1980s as US modernism gained in international focus, earlier histories were recalibrated with changed priorities. Burn and his colleagues claimed that one of the casualties of the rewriting of the interwar period by Bernard Smith was the shift away from discussion of 'contemporary realism' which had tended to be figurative to an almost exclusive focus on modernists (1988: 65). Taking as an example the work of the interdisciplinary group Angry Penguins, they maintained that these Australian artists, rather than being in thrall to modernism as it was constructed in the US version:

> forged a new relationship with modernism which allowed for a radical reworking of the Australian landscape and cultural traditions, reconstructing priorities around specific subject matter and a populist access to content. Thus the modernist source was utilised not as an end in itself but more as a resource in 'reinventing' or 'transforming tradition.'
>
> (Burn *et al.* 1988: 72)

Sydney Nolan's reworking of the mythic life of bushranger Ned Kelly in a series of quasi-modernist/ figurative paintings is paradigmatic. Nonetheless, during the 1960s and 1970s there was a widespread acceptance of the idea that innovation in contemporary Australian art was directly linked to the development of abstract art overseas.

Provincialism or a claim to an international stage was closely related to another question in the 1950s: what form could an international art take? *Blue poles*' arrival in Australia then needs to be contexualised against a dispute that had run for decades but gained more coherence in the 1950s, about what constituted valid art forms. One of the most tangible, if contentious, outcomes of the 1950s debate in Australia was the publication of *The Antipodean Manifesto*, written by seven artists and the art historian Bernard Smith in 1959 (Blackman *et al.* 1959) to accompany *Antipodeans*, an exhibition of the Victorian Artists' Society in Melbourne.[21] It was to be a clarion call: a critique of European modernism. It was also an impassioned response to what was perceived as a crisis in representation, and the hope of international recognition for Antipodean art: the term itself was to connote internationalism rather than the nationalistic-sounding Australian.

The heated debate that followed the exhibition and the manifesto now 'sounds strident and hysterical' (McDonald 1999: 4), and seem arcane in our postmodern writing of more inclusive histories, but a recovery of the argument does focus attention on what was at stake in 1959, when an overly polarised debate pitted Tachism or abstraction against, broadly speaking, figuration or image. This debate turned on a defence of humanist values depicted by a socially relevant figurative art, against the perceived social barrenness of an individualistic indulgent, profligate abstraction. *The Antipodean Manifesto* was defending the image against two perceived threats: non-figurative art in the West and socialist realism in the East. Caricaturing abstraction or Tachisme as being an emperor with neither body nor clothes but rather a 'a most colourful, elegant and shapely blot' (Blackman *et al.* 1959), the group did not wish to see a return to forms of naturalism. They were however, concerned that rather than an invention of a new language, what they were witnessing in the growth of abstractions was 'another attempt by puritan and iconoclast to reduce the living speech of art to the silence of decoration'[22] (Blackman *et al.* 1959). Although chary of creating a national style, they wanted work to 'draw upon our experience both of society and nature in Australia for the materials of our art' (Blackman *et al.* 1959).

Two Decades of American Painting

The influence of American art was part of an older debate which by 1967 had gained a sense of overpowering physicality with the arrival of a travelling show *Two Decades of American Painting*: literally the biggest exhibition ever to reach the 'remote' shores of Australia. In the year of the war film *The Dirty Dozen*, with its celebration of American individualism, machismo and anti-establishment alienation, this show of almost 100 paintings curated

21 *Antipodeans* ran from 4–15 August 1959. The artists and historian behind the manifesto were Charles Blackman, Arthur Boyd, David Boyd, John Brack, Robert Dickerson, John Perceval, Clifton Pugh and Bernard Smith.

22 This is not the first time abstraction has faced the charge of being decoration; Harold Rosenberg had famously described action paintings he found inauthentic as 'apocalyptic wallpaper' (1990: 76).

by MoMA's Waldo Rasmussen travelled to New Delhi, Kyoto and Tokyo. Word of the proposed tour reached Hal Missingham, the director of the Art Gallery of New South Wales, who had been trying to secure an exhibition of US art for six years. *The Australian* (22 July 1967) quoted Missingham on the protracted negotiations which went back to 1959. Missingham travelled to New York and unsuccessfully appealed to US ambassadors, politicians and officials. He was quoted as saying, 'we weren't able to get to first base. The Americans were using their exhibitions for propaganda then, and since we were on side, we didn't matter too much. We all got pretty cranky and then gave up.' News of the exhibition's itinerary, however, started a flurry of cables and a rescheduling to include sixty-two days in Australia, to be split between Melbourne and Missingham's gallery.

The exhibition cost $6 million and had an estimated 16,000 visitors before the official opening in August. The *Sydney Herald* reported, 'The young strolled by, impressed, rather inarticulate. The show, they said, was overwhelming, exhilarating. They had seen the paintings reproduced in books, but reproductions could never show the true colours, the technique. Every art student in Sydney seemed to be there' (19 July 1967). Viewing the real thing cannot be underestimated, and for many *Two Decades of American Art* was a revelation:

> A characteristic of western abstract painting from the 1950s onwards has been its comparative unreproducibility. Reproduction nullifies the physical presence of the work of art and so makes the conditions of viewing meaningless. For abstract art the unreproducible qualities of facture, scale, and visual distance were crucial. Knowledge about post-war abstraction necessarily had to be gained through actual sighting, rumour or report, or through painters following a set of instructions to produce their own models.
>
> (Eagle and Jones 1994: 271–2)

It was the sheer scale of the works that captured the press's imagination, which was unsurprising as they caused problems with shipping, transport and storage, and in Sydney resulted in an unscheduled route through the botanical gardens. The *Sydney Sunday Telegraph* under the headline 'American giants' noted that 'at the entrance [to AGNSW] an arrangement of huge blue crates are stacked like pop sculptures' (23 July 1967). A fine day was hoped for by gallery officials at the end of the show, according to the *Sun-Herald*, as the paintings had to be re-crated by the side of the road. The crates were too large to get through the not inconsiderable front door of the gallery (23 July 1967). It is noteworthy that a significant number of newspapers did not regard *Two Decades of American Painting* as being what the label implied. Some critics, for example, argued that it contained no West Coast painters.

A giant catalogue

As with the Moscow show, the proselytising catalogue for *Two Decades of American Painting* was also far greater in size and value than anything previously published. For instance earlier US exhibitions shown in Australia, such as *Abstract Watercolours by 14 Americans*, had only black and white thumbnail images barely 2 x 3 inches in size, with brief biographical details and a cursory introduction. In stark contrast *Two Decades of American Painting* had 10 full-page colour reproductions, three essays and de Kooning's *Woman VI* (1953) in colour on the cover. The essays were Irving Sandler's 'The will to renewal', Lucy Lippard's 'American painting 1946–1966: cult of the direct and the difficult' and G. R. Swenson's 'A view of an exhibition'. They were an important source of information and benchmarking. Lippard's scholarly essay emphasised the earlier generation of abstract expressionists and the colour field painters at the expense of any real discussion of the newer generation's work. She did however draw clear distinctions between the older generation and the younger artists while exploring several approaches to current avant-garde art: in the 'most currently viable, possibility renounces the dichotomies of action–reaction, form–content, conceptual–intuitive, objective–subjective in favour of an art of inaction, one that "simply exists between mind and matter, detached from both, representing neither"'. She was quoting Robert Smithson (1966) and referring largely to the work of Stella and Reinhardt.

Irving Sandler's contribution was symptomatic of the difficulties facing those who would question the orthodoxy of abstract expressionism. The language of heroism was tempered however by the necessity of accommodating younger artists who rejected the romanticism of abstract expressionism in favour of 'cool'. Cool and diversity were the principal themes attributed to the younger artists, standing in marked contrast to the hagiography deployed to explain the first generation of abstract expressionists. The cool detachment, standing in marked contrast to 'the anxious objects'[23] of the older artists, according to Sandler enabled artists such as Andy Warhol and Roy Lichtenstein 'for the first time in the history of art, to produce an utterly impassive figurative style'.

By 1967 the influence of the first generation of abstract expressionism had waned in the United States and Europe. Lippard wrote of the 'Oedipal ritual of action and reaction inherited from art history' and of the 'disaffection with "easy art" that had witnessed a reaction around 1960 by many young artists to the work of Abstract Expressionism' (1966: 5). Riddled with the language of self-denial, distrust and Puritanism, and the struggle against the orthodox, Lippard's essay toys with existentialist philosophy and notions of

23 The phrase is Harold Rosenberg's.

alienation. It might be relevant to question all the above concepts when transposed to 'the Lucky country'.

The most contentious painter in the exhibition, if the newspaper cuttings and cartoons were the only monitor of impact, was Ad Reinhardt. Lippard stressed Reinhardt's oriental scholarship and contribution to theory. She particularly emphasised how oriental art was assimilated by different painters in the United States, Mark Tobey being a notable example. She warmed to this theme of the orientalising of Western culture, and in particular the new painting and sculpture, from Warhol to André via Judd, Morris and LeWitt through the cool of the inscrutable (acknowledging the Western cliché), which, she concluded, 'suggests a dimension of difficulty hitherto inaccessible to American art' (1966: 6). The orientalising of western culture is an inversion of the usual understanding of the relationship between East and West.

In his review of the exhibition, 'Where the action is?' Lansell was not alone in picking up on the oriental qualities of Albers, Gottlieb, Reinhardt and Tobey. The oriental influence seems to have been significant enough for Lansell to question why Lippard's emphasis had not gained more widespread credence. He suggests:

> Clement Greenberg, the American art critic who is fortunately more revered than read, rubbishes this notion of an oriental slant to American painting. Its 'sources lie entirely in the West' he says, which is nonsense .... The other argument that 'there is nothing more to these paintings than formal values' rather misses the point. Many of these painters are also extremely barbed social commentators.
>
> (Lansell 1967)

What is important here is the extent to which writers on *Two Decades* felt that abstract expressionism and other forms of American modernism were assimilating Eastern belief and formal values.

Art and the Vietnam War

In the eyes of radicals and nationalists in Australia, American economic imperialists had become the most powerful opinion-formers in the country. American pop culture, with its money values, its emphasis on sex, and its presentation of material well-being and creature comforts as the greatest good in human life, were corrupting Australians, calling them to worship false idols (Clark 1986: 235–6).

Although *Two Decades* was held during the Vietnam War (in which Australians were conscripted), there were few direct references to the war during the show. John Henshaw, in a piece entitled 'A second look at the art of the new world', almost as a footnote observed, 'As a cultural pushover this show might in true Dada fashion be dropped on North Vietnam and the bombs sent on a gallery tour' (*The Australian* 29 July 1967). More urgently, the left-wing social realist artist and critic Noel Counihan argued that the New York bias in the show was a display of 'dehumanised values', maintaining that 'One can see the connection between the de-humanised values of this art and the prosecution of the war in Vietnam and the spilling of blood in the Middle-East' (*Sydney Tribune* 5 July 1967). By the early 1970s there were 'misgivings' from radicals and conservatives in Australia about the moral influence of what was referred to as 'American cultural imperialism' (Clark 1986: 235).

Clement Greenberg on tour

As a busy international advocate for abstract expressionism, Clement Greenberg, the influential American art critic most prominent from the 1930s to 1970s, visited Japan, Israel, South Africa and Canada. The Canadian artist Wilf Perreault observed:

> One can almost chart Greenberg's lecture engagements by the Post-Painterly residue. Canada itself had become lopsided because of the weight of bad abstractions inspired by Greenberg's repeated studio visits.
>
> (www.artsjournal.cam.artopia, 5 May 2006; quoted in Walker 2007)

Greenberg was in Australia for two months the year following *Two Decades of American Painting*. In the Australian context, Eagle and Jones (1994) claim that Greenberg was recognised:

> as the critic most responsible for promoting hard/edge/colour-field painting at home in the United States. Australians expected to hear a strong defence of the style. Instead, during the tour, Greenberg expressed his opinion that avant-garde styles (by their nature) had a limited life span. The remarks seemed significant coming from the senior advocate of the avant-garde style then being promoted with vigour in Australia. Because the hard-edge style was adopted rather late – it had begun in America in the fifties but was not practiced here in volume until the mid-sixties – the Australian movement had an artificial aspect, an adoption rather than a birth. Hard edge had legitimacy as an American movement. By the same token its fate was external to the Australian expression of hard edge. Just as no one cared to look back to a tradition of Australian abstraction, neither did it seem relevant to look forward to hard edge's local evolution into another style.
>
> (Eagle and Jones 1994: 268)

In 1950 the Australian Bernard Smith visited the 25th Venice Biennale. Although writing in retrospect, Smith maintained that of the artists representing the United States (John Marin, Hyman Bloom, Lee Gatch, Rico Lebrun, Arshile Gorky, Jackson Pollock and Willem de Kooning), he 'responded warmly to the work of Bloom and Lebrun but not the three paintings of Pollock' (2002: 443). He had felt even then that the dribbling technique was a cul-de-sac. But perhaps more importantly, Smith felt that for Pollock to 'ensure his position he ... needed an impeccable linage', which was to be found the catalogue essay by Alfred H. Barr Jr. Unconvinced by the linage set out by Barr, Smith also observed that:

> Barr and Clement Greenberg played-down the overwhelming importance of the surrealist contribution to Abstract Expressionism; it would not have helped their advocacy of contemporary American painting during the early postwar years. However, it is in the automatist aspect of their work that a better claim to innovation may be developed. They are better understood as oppositional to the Formalesque[24] rather than latter-day champions of it.
>
> (Smith 2002: 445)

It is clear that Australian critics and historians were unconvinced by several aspects of high modernism: there was no single response and the picture was more subtle and nuanced than that suggested by the 'swept all before it' hagiographies written in the 1980s.

Australian artist Albert Tucker, who lived overseas between 1947 and 1960, echoed some of the local as national debate, translated to an international stage, stating that:

> International style is an example of the old con game. Actually it is one of the most concentrated forms of regional art. Manhattan regionalism comes from a small island off the American coast .... I like Manhattan regionalism. But the things that are valid in Manhattan have no necessary validity here. [The United States] succeeds in culturally colonising those who submit to being colonised.
>
> (quoted in Thomas 1976: 296–7)

Cultures removed from the centre have rarely capitulated fully to another culture,[25] but take and rework within their own communities of practice. *The Field* (October-November 1968) was the first temporary exhibition

24 Formalesque is the term coined by Smith instead of formalism.

25 See in particular Gordon Bennett's reworking of Pollock's Blue Poles in *Myth of the Western Man (White Man's Burden)* 1992 in Meecham and Sheldon, 2005: 14–15.

held at the National Gallery of Victoria's new building, a year after Two Decades of American Painting and is an important barometer of the reaction amongst the younger generation of artists and those who were committed to contemporary art and an international art scene. Elwyn Lynn's essay in the catalogue acknowledges the changes then taking place in Australian art:

> There is a shift in sensibility; there is a change of creative focus; the sources of inspiration have sprung up in unlikely places, but the old wells have not dried up. We should, as Clement Greenberg urged in his final talk in Australia, enjoy our diversity.
>
> (Finemore 1968: 85)

Tony McGillick's 1968 *Arbitrator*, shown in *The Field*, was emblematic of the cultural borrowing and assimilation that took place in this period. The hard-edged abstract painting could be read as a schematic rendering of the map of Australia coloured in the burnt browns that are often used to represent the continent.

Chapter 4

The art of American landscape

John Gast's painting *American progress* of 1872 is an uncomplicated parable of manifest destiny (Plate 16). In this small painting (measuring just over 12 x 16 inches) hunters, prospectors and farmers are depicted amid stage-coaches, iconic covered wagons[1] and railroad stock, all moving westward, from right to left of the outer edges of the picture frame. To the far left of the picture frame Native Americans are being evicted from the scene. Floating above all this activity is an ethereal figure, the personification of America, stringing telegraph wire across the plains of the United States. The personified America holds in one hand a schoolbook and in the other a telegraph wire. Literally, Gast's vision is one of telegraph wires connecting the country, relaying transcontinental messages. Figuratively, the painting conveys the message that national enlightenment is transforming the land through the twin civilizing processes of education and technology. *American progress* is not one of the finest renditions of landscape, but it does unequivocally illustrate the way that the West (that is, the land west of the Mississippi) was treated simultaneously as a physical and a psychic space.

American progress was in fact the product of two minds. Gast's allegorical rendering of the push westwards was commissioned by George Andrews Crofutt (1827–1907), a publisher of magazines and travel guides to the West. Crofutt held fast to America's manifest destiny in the West, being both ideologically and economically implicated in Western settlement. He had been present at the Golden Spike ceremony on 10 May 1869, when the oriental and occidental halves of the Pacific Railroad were joined at Promontory, Utah. Within seconds of the spike being driven home, the news was relayed across the continent by the telegraph. Crofutt seized the moment and headed off to Chicago to found his own publishing company, and issue the first in a series of 'transcontinental' guidebooks to the – now relatively

1 The conestoga covered wagon became synonymous with western expansion. A staple prop of paintings, photographs and films of the west, the conestoga wagon was probably a Mennonite invention, first constructed about 1725 in Pennsylvania. Capable of moving nine tons, conestoga wagons were originally pulled by four to eight mules or oxen.

accessible – West. Between 1869 and 1893 he sold over a million copies of his handsomely illustrated and affordable guides, disseminating engraved images of yucca trees in the Mojave desert, huge cacti in the Arizona desert, geysers at Yosemite and unusual rock formations such as San Pedro's Wife to the American people.[2]

Crofutt's ekphrasis[3] for Gast's *American progress* simultaneously acted as advertising copy:

> This picture was the design of the author of the TOURIST – is National, and illustrates, in the most artistic manner, all those gigantic results of American brains and hands, which have caused the mighty wilderness to blossom like the rose.
>
> (Crofutt 1883: 243)

The agency of 'those gigantic results of American brains' in the West is a vexed issue. On what authority did westward expansions proceed, and to what extend was the uncultivated landscape in effect a *tabula rasa*, a clean slate waiting to be inscribed?

In several key respects, these were not questions that troubled the 'American brains' of nineteenth-century landscape painters. What is evident in both Gast's and Crofutt's transaction with the American West is that the visual experiences they represented are unprecedented and unparalleled in European art. And this distinction is at the crux of many artists' dealings with the West. Traversing the Mississippi to paint landscapes, American artists not only authenticated their own art practice on the basis of individual experience, they contributed to an emergent sense of national identity and belonging among the wider American public. In this chapter we examine the West as a stimulus for ideas about destiny and identity in America. American artists created an indigenous and often epic experience of the magnificent (and largely unrecorded) scenery of the West. In the rhetoric of American landscape painting, it was the very lack of historical associations with the falls, mountains and canyons of America that made the American West a source of national pride and identity.

2 Crofutt's guide described 'over one thousand three hundred cities, towns, villages, stations, government fort and camps, mountains, lakes, rivers, sulphur, soda and hot springs, scenery, watering places and summer resorts; where to look for and hunt the buffalo, antelope, deer and other game; trout fishing, etc., etc. In fact to tell you what is worth seeing – where to see it – where to go – and whom to stop with while passing over the Union, Kansas, Central and Southern Pacific Railroads, their branches and connections, by rail, water and stage. From sunrise to sunset, and part the way back; through Nebraska, Wyoming, Utah, Montana, Idaho, Nevada, California, Arizona and New Mexico' (Crofutt 1883, frontispiece).

3 Ekphrasis is a graphic description of a painting. Crofutt, drawing attention to his own skill in the design of the painting, is reminiscent of the literary advisers of European classical painting.

Sublime and supplemented sight

Gast's rendition of *American progress* lacks the credentials to be truly epic – and not simply because it is a very small painting. The work is also fundamentally illustrative and its narrative unsubtle. Yet *American progress* does conjugate the elements of the epic in America's sense of the West, and the figures are subordinate to the overwhelming rendition of space. However, many other responses to the landscape of the west in the nineteenth century either acknowledged or sought to approximate the epic: that is, having the quality of surpassing the usual or the ordinary, particularly by means of scale.

The epic is in the first instance associated with scale – either scale of representation or the scale of what is represented. Much of what is considered in this chapter is a discussion of the large scale represented on the smaller scale of a two-dimensional canvas. But the competitively proportioned images of landscape in the late eighteenth and early nineteenth centuries, it may be recalled, when linked to modes of visual entertainment, are quite remarkable. Eighteenth-century Europe had a predilection for panoramas, and wide-screen renditions of famous battles, views or expeditions attracted large crowds in urban centres. The panorama first came to America in 1795, when a copy of Barker's London panorama was exhibited in New York City. The first panorama by an American artist represented Europe also – John Vanderlyn's *Panoramic view of the Palace and Gardens of Versailles* (c. 1819, Metropolitan Museum of Art, New York), a work that now has the distinction of being the second-oldest surviving panorama. Vanderlyn's gigantic painting is 165 feet in length and was installed in a purpose-built domed rotunda on the northeast corner of City Hall Park.[4]

One of the visitors to Vanderlyn's panorama was a young scene-painter, John Banvard, visiting from what was then the frontier town of Louisville, Kentucky. The experience inspired, or contributed to his plans for, an ambitious scheme of his own – to make the largest panorama. Banvard's panorama was painted as a series of thirty eight scenes. When first exhibited in 1846 it depicted the eastern bank of the Mississippi from the mouth of the Ohio River to New Orleans, although it later also depicted the western bank of the river. Painted on a twelve foot high (3.6 metres) bolt of cloth, and around 1,300 feet (369 metres) in length, the panorama was later expanded to about half a mile.[5] The claim that it was a 'three mile picture' was an exaggeration, and part of the shameless hyperbole that American showmen excelled in. The moving panorama was the backdrop to a performance by Banvard. The cloth on which the view of the Mississippi was painted was

4 Later, other panoramas from London were exhibited in the rotunda. It was demolished in 1870.

5 The panorama was eventually cut up in to hundreds of pieces, none of which has survived.

rolled up, and rolled by on stage behind Banvard as his accompanying narration explained the locations depicted, adding anecdotes and local colour as he toured his monumental painting in Boston, New York, Paris, London and the British provinces. In London *The Times* remarked that 'life indeed was short but ... American art was very long'.[6]

Godfrey N. Frankenstein's 'moving panorama' of Niagara Falls opened to the New York public in 1853. Unlike the linear design of Banvard's panorama, where scenes along the Mississippi were arranged in topographical sequence, Frankenstein's panorama illustrated the most picturesque views of the falls in differing seasons and times of day.

Elizabeth Kessler (in her contribution to DeVorkin and Smith 2004) compared pictures of Eagle Nebula taken by the Hubble telescope with Thomas Moran's *Cliffs of the Upper Colorado River, Wyoming Territory* (1882). This may seem an artificial and contrived comparison until we consider that the Hubble images had been artistically rendered. What is transmitted back to earth in the form of raw data is a set of visually limited black and white electronic pictures lacking definition or detail. In order to make them visually palatable for magazine or television coverage, visualisation experts combine the information collected from three different Hubble filters, apply colour to each, remove imperfections and crop to a standard four-sided image. The resulting picture is not a visual fact but an artistic interpretation of gas clouds and stellar matter. Kessler concludes, 'The aesthetic choices made result in a sense of majesty and wonder about nature and how spectacular it can be, just as the paintings of the American West did.' Her suggestion that many of the results resemble paintings of the West by Albert Bierstadt or Thomas Moran makes us wonder how much the visualisation experts are consciously or subconsciously influenced by their knowledge of landscape art. 'Just like Bierstadt's or Moran's paintings, the hope here is that the final image will capture the feeling of awe and majesty and wonder about nature,' Kessler says.

Such an extreme example of supplemented sight, enhanced by the scientists on the Hubble team, is in some respects a tradition that traces its lineage back to the image makers of nineteenth-century landscape scenes. Supplemented sight – that is, sight enhanced by mechanical means – had been one way of approximating the sublime. Frankenstein and Banvard had tried to introduce the element of movement to their views of Niagara and the Mississippi, but the landscape of the West is largely incomprehensible to unassisted sight. For example, the vastness of the Great Plains is best appreciable viewed from an airplane, as one expanse after another of brown and green rectangles, neatly arranged and delineated. Robert Smithson's epic earthwork, *Spiral jetty* (1970) is only comprehended as a design if viewed

6 14 November 1849, p. 4, col. C.

from a helicopter or light aircraft. However, the unassisted gaze of artists who predated automobiles, airplanes and space travel was not without imaginative enhancements. Albert Boime's book *The Magisterial Gaze: Manifest Destiny and American Landscape Painting, c. 1830–1865* considers 'the magisterial gaze', as a conquering 'male earthmover substituting for God' (1991: 92). Boime demonstrates that the assumption of a raised viewpoint on the part of American landscape painters was a central feature of the art of the period from 1835 to the Civil War. In creating a high sightline the American artist communicated a mastery of all that the eye could see, consistent with the tenets of manifest destiny. The panoramic viewpoint, Boime argues, renders the land as simultaneously scenic and possessed by the viewer.

The explorer and painter George Catlin (1796–1872) began his travels west just as Congress had passed the Indian Removal Act, in 1830. During his travels Catlin drew and painted the native tribes of the Great Plains and tribes resettled by the terms of the Act. Before the invention of Uncle Sam as the personification of America in 1812, America was often symbolically represented by a Native American.[7] The native's body could signify on several levels including that of the noble savage in need of Christian interception. Many early paintings of the West include Native Americans fading into the distance with their backs to the future, as indistinct or shadowy groups, or as Rousseau's noble savage or Chateaubriand's natural man, distinct from European civilisation and cultivation. For instance in Albert Bierstadt's *Crossing the plains* (1867),[8] the settlers, covered wagons, sheep and cattle are depicted moving purposefully through the plains occupying the foreground and middleground, while a Native American is barely visible in the background. However there is also a tradition of powerful Native American portraits, represented by John Westley Jarvis's *Black Hawk and his son, Whirling Thunder* (1833) and Catlin's portraits, which counteract Bierstadt's conventional imaging. Even so the portraits of nineteenth-century Native Americans, for example those painted when Native American delegations came to visit Washington, frequently presented their subjects as figures of pathos. Catlin's portraits were conceived in such a spirit, and as historical records of a vanishing people. Catlin's Indian Gallery, which toured America between 1837 and 1840 (and London and Paris in the 1840s) was an exhibition that was tinged with nostalgia. It was believed that the ineluctable force of 'civilisation' would either wipe out the Native American or lead to assimilation. Either way a way of life was going forever. Catlin's presentation typifies a type of representation of the Native American

7 Other early emblems also included the rattlesnake, eagle, turkey and bucking horse.
8 Now housed in National Cowboy and Western Heritage Museum, Oklahoma City, OK.

that signifies victimhood or elegiac loss, and which would continue as a prevailing mode of representation until the late twentieth century.

Catlin also painted landscapes of the western territories, describing his particular 'magisterial gaze': 'I was lifted up upon an imaginary pair of wings, which ... held me floating in the open air, from whence I could behold beneath me the Pacific and the Atlantic Oceans – the great cities of the East, and the mighty rivers' (Dippie *et al.* 2002: 153). However, the possession of land, either figuratively or financially, is a fiction. The jury is still out on whether Catlin's motives for recording a perceived dying way of life among Native Americans were anthropological benevolence or merely mercenary chutzpah. Thomas R. Hietala regards Catlin as essentially ambivalent; on the one hand enthralled by what he called a 'splendid juggernaut', but rueful that 'one nation's glorious destiny necessitated other peoples' decline and demise' (1997: 49). Catlin's ideological complicity was part of his faith in a 'divine plan': he could 'rescue' the vestigial image of the Native American and preserve the record in his Indian Gallery, but he surrendered entirely to God's will for the American Republic.

'Part or particle of God'

> Standing on the bare ground, – my head bathed by the blithe air, and uplifted into infinite space, – all mean egotism vanishes. I become a transparent eye-ball. I am nothing. I see all. The currents of the Universal Being circulate through me; I am part or particle of God.
>
> Ralph Waldo Emerson (1971: 1, 10)

To return momentarily to Gast's visualisation of Crofutt's *American progress*, we have seen how the image illustrated the tenets of manifest destiny, advancing the rights of the American people over the land, indigenous people and animals of the continent. It is not possible to say with certainty whether Crofutt's advocacy of the westward thrust of progress was motored by his entrepreneurial or his ideological ambitions, but his presence in the West does encapsulate the alliance of these twin antecedents of American exceptionalism. Crofutt's instructions to Gast detailing the content of *American progress* give colour and dimension to one particular allegorisation of manifest destiny. 'Manifest destiny' was a proposition rather than a policy, predicated upon the presumption that white Americans were divinely sanctioned to settle in as much of the New World as they cared to.[9] However, both Crofutt's schema and Gast's painting are best viewed in the context of a rash of paintings making the same points about manifest destiny. Gast employs a similar visual scheme to Frances ('Fanny')

9 The term was coined by the journalist John L. O'Sullivan (1845).

Palmer's very popular lithograph for Currier & Ives, *Across the continent – 'westward the course of empire takes its way'* (1868), Andrew Melrose's *Westward the star of empire takes its way – near Council Bluffs, Iowa* (1867) and Emanuel Leutze's *Westward the course of empire.*

These paintings, each imagining the processes of empire building, take their cue from Thomas Cole's epic series of canvases collectively entitled *The course of empire.* Cole (1801–1848), one of the artists of the Hudson River school, was influenced by the panoramas that toured America.[10] *The course of empire* (now in the New York Historical Society) consists of five paintings of five imaginary landscapes, made from 1833 to 1836. The canvases read, in order, as an evolution of a classical empire, beginning with 'The savage state', proceeding to 'The arcadian or pastoral state' and the 'The consummation of empire', which is followed by 'Destruction' and finally 'Desolation'. The conceit of the series lies in the compression of aeons into five canvases, but individually each painting owes much to the etiquette of European landscape art. In Europe the representation of landscape was often subordinate to a literary or biblical idea – a *Flight into Egypt* or *Nymphs chased by satyrs.* Even when figures are rendered small in the composition, as they often are in the landscapes of Claude Lorrain, the story that they represent still dominates the presentation of the painting, and gives the work its title. Cole's *Course of empire* series belongs in many respects to the tradition of its European predecessors. However, Cole represented an attitude to landscape that valued nature as a powerful carrier of meanings and instrumental to his overall iconography. In Cole's painting it is nature that was the 'visible hand of God', rather than the characters inhabiting it.

Cole's epic cycle of rise and fall had, he believed, attained 'the sublimest of the sublime' (Sanford 1957: 445). The philosophical coordinates of the sublime were not stable in the early nineteenth century, and although the idea was an imported one, it evolved and produced sub-categories as it was debated and discussed among American intellectuals. Cole compared the challenges of the nineteenth century artist: 'The world requires much of us that was not demanded of the artist of antiquity .... He probably speculated little ... on the sublime and beautiful. His faith was fixed' (Sanford 1957: 439). The creation of an American sublime, anchored in European thinking but evolved specifically to assert American independence from European culture, is indicative of the transatlantic relations between Old and New Worlds. On both sides of the Atlantic the sublime was a facility for intensifying the emotional capacity of landscape art, but in America it assumed additional powers – the power to represent personal freedom and a statement of faith in God's special covenant with the Americans.

10 For a fuller account of the influence of panoramas and dioramas on Cole, see Ellwood C. Parry III, *The Art of Thomas Cole* (1988), 174–6.

The sublime – terror experienced from a place of safety – has an added dimension in the American experience. In the American West, the possibilities for terror were exponentially increased: many travellers west froze to death in an ice storm, or died of thirst in a desert. Therefore the capacity to represent the intensification of feeling in view of raging rivers, roaring waterfalls and precipitous cliffs or mountains is invested in the artist – someone who is temperamentally predisposed to the sublime, or who has a vocabulary equivalent or approximate to it. The sublime is ineffable; for example, Thoreau's description of his ascent and descent of Mount Katahdin in *The Maine Woods* (1864) dwells on the 'Matter, vast, terrific' of the barren summit (Thoreau 1864: 2). But painters had to find a visual vocabulary equal to it. Frederic Church (1826–1900) painted a wide-angled view of Niagara Falls in 1857. Unlike Hicks's or Alvan Fisher's views of the cataracts (see below), Church's view begins and ends with the cascading water, with the dark electrified sky underwriting the mood of the scene. According to McKinsey, *Niagara falls* fuses the 'meaning to be found in the sublime experience of American nature with the artistic rendering of the experience itself, presenting both to its viewers so that we too undergo the process of recovery of the sublime at Niagara' (1985: 247). In talking of 'recovery' McKinsey is arguing that something had been lost by the time Church painted the falls, that tourism and commercialisation had deprived the site of some of its sublime power. Church's uncompromising depiction of the massive sweep of the falls across eight feet of canvas reconnects the viewer to the sublime since there are no troubling distractions from the phenomenon of falling water.

The Hudson Valley had been represented in artworks before the so-called Hudson River school painted it.[11] But it was Thomas Cole, along with his pupil Asher B. Durand, who created its particularity. Durand's large painting *Kindred spirits,* now hanging in New York City's Public Library, is emblematic of the Hudson River school. The painting shows Thomas Cole and either Durand himself or the poet William Cullen Bryant on the edge of a rocky promontory looking over a gorge in the Catskills, snaked through by a running stream. Superficially the painting owes much to European classicism, and it shares the compositional arrangement of numerous Claudian landscapes, for example the foliage-framed arrangement of the composition, and the rendering of foreground, middleground and distance in the misty arrangements of a subdued palette of golds, browns and greens. But there are un-European features of the painting too. Whereas a Claudian landscape may feature biblical or mythological figures discreetly enacting a narrative, Durand's painting is contemporary and lacks an obvious narrative. Although it is not implausible that Cole and Bryant at some point in time stood upon that rocky ledge together, the scene is purely whimsical,

11 For example, by Thomas Doughty, Thomas Chambers and Jasper Francis Cropsey.

since the topography of Kaaterskill Falls and the Kaaterskill Clove is such that they can not be seen together from the point of view of the painting. Myers and Buff have alerted us to the fact that *Kindred spirits* is a caprice, an imagined scene that combines different actual sites in a topographical impossibility (Myers 1988: 70; Buff 1987: 108–10). In the painting Durand allegorises landscape – the river of life, and the shattered tree representing death (Cole's, who had died the previous year: his departed spirit indicated by the bird flying away). Cole's staff pointing to an eagle could be read as the impulse to a national art movement.

The role of science and geology and the preoccupation with 'creation' in American landscape art have been noted by Barbara Novak. Novak suggests that science was important to landscape painters as it confirmed the superiority of America in terms of primordial timespan over the younger Europe, and so came to stand for national superiority over the culture of Europe. With a little effort of metaphorical imagination it was possible to see geological rock formations as evidence of God's support for his chosen people. There were plenty of opportunities for landscape painters, preoccupied with finding God through science in the landscape, to read about geology or to attend scientific meetings. For example Cole, Durand, Church and Moran, were keen readers of scientific texts, and collected fossils and mineral specimens. Rebecca Bedell has examined the relationship between art, science and religion in a study of the Hudson River school (2002), demonstrating how many American artists Christianized science and approached geology as a means to understanding God.

The American luminist painters also looked to nature for a sign of deity. Luminism developed as an offshoot of the Hudson River school, and like its predecessor, became emblematic of the status of landscape as a carrier of American national identity. Luminism is John I. H. Baur's twentieth-century label for a style of painting in American landscape art of the 1850s to 1870s. As with other post hoc definitions, the artists included in this category did not articulate or espouse any common artistic goal. The movement is now noted principally for the recording of the effects of light on the landscape, but also for the use of aerial perspective. If any generalising claims can be made for luminist painters then it is that they tended to create serene and calm views of nature, the effect enhanced by their attention to detail and efforts to disguise brushstrokes, in contrast to European impressionism where hurried brushstrokes were a marker of modernism. In the radiant, light-saturated pictures of the American luminists the light effectively deputised for God.

Novak identified a shift from eighteenth-century European attitudes to nature as a 'reflex of Romantic thought' towards a Christianised and highly moralising view among nineteenth-century Americans. Landscape art was 'absorbed into a religious, moral and frequently nationalistic concept of nature, contributing to the rhetorical screen under which the aggressive conquest of the country could be accomplished' (Novak 2007: 33).

A landmark touring exhibition in 1980 entitled *American Light* demonstrated luminism's importance, especially between 1860 and 1875, although it only showcased painters resident on the East Coast. Luminism – in the sense of light-saturated sensibilities that readily lend themselves to metaphorical readings – was evident in early landscape painting in California, among painters such as Raymond Dabb Yelland, Norton Bush and Charles Donnon Robinson. A visitor to California, John Ross Key, in 1869 painted the *Santa Clara valley*, published as a large chromolithograph in 1873 by L. Prang and Company. The valley is depicted at the onset of evening, and Key's subtle handling of light tinting the distant hillsides and the distant fog brings the divine design of nature to a religious mind. The East Coast luminists are better represented in the literature, and Barbara Novak has found compelling parallels between transcendentalism and luminism. Other writers have also connected luminist painting perhaps unsurprisingly to Ralph Waldo Emerson. In Novak's discussion of luminists' handling of space, she remarks, 'There is little flow or sweep, but rather a containment of each part within its own spatial unit that arrests the moment in Emerson's "concentrated eternity"', and she also uses Emerson's phrase 'the transparent eyeball' as a benchmark for luminism (Novak 1969: 105).

Gayle Smith takes art historians and critics to task for isolating the 'transparent eyeball' idea and using it out of context, arguing that Emerson's rapturous oneness with nature was not the instantaneous transportation that art historians imagine:

> When Emerson celebrated the ecstatic oneness of seer and seen, artist and nature, he always depicted the singular process he went through to experience that merging. We do not get the finished, 'transparent' canvas of the luminist painter, but a text that traces the movements of his own mind as it interacted with reality.
>
> (Smith 1985: 195)

Smith does itemise what she regards as more compelling parallels between Emerson and the luminists, for example comparing the smooth handling of paint apparent on the surface of luminist painting to the careful rhetoric of Emerson's prose style, and the horizontality of luminist painting which seems to engulf the viewer to Emerson's interest in the experience of nature.

'All nature here is new to art'

> The painter of American scenery has, indeed, privileges superior to any other. All nature here is new to art. No Tivolis, Ternis, Mont Blancs,

> Plinlimmons, hackneyed and worn by the daily pencils of hundreds; but primeval forests, virgin lakes, and waterfalls . . . hallowed to his soul by their freshness from the creation.
>
> (Cole 1836: 2)

Cole did not always play his 'superior privileges' to advantage, and was criticised for not painting indigenous scenery. For instance, Charles Lanman's review of *The course of empire* for the journal *Democratic Review* of 1843 found Cole's debt to European art regrettable:

> He [Cole] has but set a noble example, which ought to be extensively followed. Mind, we do not mean by this that his subjects ought to be imitated. Far from it, because they are not stamped with a national character, as the production of all painters should be. Excepting his actual views of American scenery, the paintings of Cole might have been produced had he never set foot upon our soil.
>
> (quoted in Sanford 1957: 445)

In his 'Essay on American scenery' of 1836, Cole discussed the 'want of associations' in American landscape as no deterrent to the painter of the sublime. Arguing that American scenery has as great a potential for the artist to experience the sublime as sacred European sites, Cole promotes the belief that the experience of 'The hidden glory veiled from vulgar eyes' (Cole 1836: 12) is in the gift of the artist. Despite his apparent gift for discerning 'hidden glories', his landscapes are frequently imaginary views. This is in spite of his habit of sketching in the Catskills, White Mountains, Adirondacks and the coast of Maine before returning to his studio to work up the sketches into larger compositions. The proposition that an artist should venture outside to record his or her first-hand observations of nature is often represented in the history of art as a risible one until the nineteenth century. Therefore art history makes a great deal about the painters of the Barbizon school and the French impressionists, who were supposedly the first to contravene academic advice and paint *en plein air*. In fact, there is plenty of evidence to support the view that artists were painting *en plein air* long before the French avant-garde gave their permission.[12] The implicit suggestion of the artist's presence at the sight of the subject is important, and become more so in underwriting the credentials of the landscape painter.

12 For example, Joseph Vernet tied himself to the mast of a ship in a storm so that he could observe its effects first-hand; J.M.W. Turner also lashed himself to the mast of a ship, and as a railway passenger in 1844, held his head out of the window of a fast-moving train in a storm so that he could observe the effects of speed. John Constable meticulously researched his landscapes outdoors in drawings and oil sketches across hundreds of sketchbooks, faithfully noting down the dates and times of day for each.

However, popular images of the West were not always underwritten by the presence of the artist at the scene. Fanny Palmer (1812-1876) never travelled west but her lithographs included *Rocky mountains, emigrants crossing the plains* (1866) and *Across the continent, 'westward the course of empire takes its way'* (1868). Edward Hicks (1780–1849) visited Niagara Falls in 1819 and made a painting of the scene six years later in 1825. Although he had stood in front of the falls he had not, as far as we know, recorded the experience in a *plein air* sketch, and the composition of his painting appears to have been based on a well-known engraving of the falls that had appeared as a vignette on a map of North America published by Henry S. Tanner in 1822. The view is accompanied on all four sides by a textual frame:

> Above, below, where'er the astonished age
> Turns to behold, now opening wonders lie
> This great o'er whelming work of awful Time
> In all its dread magnificence sublime.

This combination of image and text is not entirely unusual, and the text compensates for Hicks's naïve (in the sense that the work is provincial imitation, and like most of his works, based on prints and copies of better-known paintings) rendition of the sublime. Hicks took the text from a poem – an excerpt from Alexander Wilson's 'The foresters' (1818).[13] Wilson's poem and Hicks's painting were but two of a spate of literary and visual responses to Niagara Falls. As McKinsey notes, the earliest artists and writers to treat the falls grappled with the literary models and visual modes of representation that had come from Europe, which seemed to be unequal to the 'powerful emotions' they felt in view of the falls (1985: 39).

In Alvan Fisher's pendant views of Niagara Falls of 1820, tourists are clearly visible in the foreground of the painting and their responses to the great cataract are discernible in their bodily gestures. The two paintings, *A general view of the falls of Niagara* and *The Great Horseshoe Fall,* may be generally said to fall best under the category of the picturesque. The facility for appreciating the picturesque and the sublime was imported from Britain. Virtually every nineteenth-century traveller would have been prepared for their experience of sublime and picturesque landscape by the Reverend William Gilpin's tourbooks (1782–1809), illustrated with aquatint engravings that demonstrated that paintings were greatly improved by picturesque detail. Craggy mountains were favoured over ordered classical compositions, feathery trees with knarled and knotted barks, zigzagging roads and

13 Hicks returned to the subject again in 1835, in a painting now in the Abby Aldrich Rockefeller Folk Art Center of Colonial Williamsburg, Virginia.

countryside littered with cottages, barns and wandering tribes of gypsies. The picturesque is therefore different from the sublime in that it represents nature as pleasingly irregular but never awesome. *The Great Horseshoe Fall* is therefore a picturesque rendition of a sublime landscape. It shows tourists variously gesturing, pointing and edging close to the chasm, some young men lying on their stomachs to peer over the sides of the horseshoe. These small figures may very well be experiencing the sublime as they peer into the misty chasm; but the viewer of the painting is experiencing a picturesque landscape.

Into the wild

Travel (with a few exceptions, notably Fanny Palmer) was a condition of American landscape painting. Steamboats and railroads first opened up the continent in the 1830s and 1840s, and the simultaneous development of fast and affordable steam transportation on land and water mobilised an increasingly large middle-class population with a discretionary income. But even before steam transportation, tourists were venturing into the American hinterland. Fisher's view of Niagara shows only a select party of visitors to the falls, but the introduction of a railroad line to Niagara increased visitors and heralded the start of mass tourism. The role of the artist, now that Americans could see sights for themselves, was perhaps to embellish the view. The year that the railroad to Niagara opened was the same year that Frankenstein exhibited his moving panorama of the falls.

The French visitor to the United States Alexis de Tocqueville (1805–1859), author of *Democracy in America*, was a minor aristocrat working for the French government ostensibly to research the American penitentiary system. The farthest west Tocqueville reached was Green Bay on Lake Michigan, although to get there the guides led his party through the wilderness. They also went north to Quebec and south to New Orleans, travelling during one of the worst winters. In Detroit Tocqueville encountered a grand excursion steamboat, the *Superior*, midway through a pleasure cruise for ladies and gentlemen from the East who wished to see the hinterland of the western lakes. Tocqueville joined the tour and made his way, finally, to Green Bay. On board he wrote an essay entitled 'A fortnight in the wilderness'. He was surprised that even though he had covered vast distances, the wilderness eluded him:

> Of all the countries of the world America is the least fitted to furnish the spectacle I came there to seek. In America, even more than in Europe, there is only one society .... The plane of a uniform civilization has passed over it. The man you left in New York you find again in almost impenetrable solitudes: same clothes, same attitude, same language, same habits, same pleasures. Nothing rustic, nothing naive, nothing

> which smells of the wilderness .... Those who inhabit these isolated places have arrived there since yesterday; they have come with the customs, the ideas, the needs of civilization.
>
> (Tocqueville 1959: 151)

John F. Sears's work on American tourist attractions of the nineteenth century, *Sacred Places* (1989), discusses the role that tourism played in forming, or contributing to formations of, a distinctive national culture between 1820 and 1880. In the absence of the historical remnants that the Old World used to support identity, Americans found a surrogate in landscape. The role of artists and writers in creatively transforming landscape into something more palatable to Americans in general is important, but so is the connection to the divine that underscores the commerce of the artist with nature. Sears calls tourist attractions 'sacred places' because they marked areas or sights where Americans might travel to find evidence of their God. He acknowledges that the imperatives of tourism and the desire to commune with the divine are not always compatible, and he discusses the unresolved tension between the impulse to develop and that to preserve.[14]

Even in the twentieth century, after the frontier was officially closed, the West continued to play an important role in the American painter's spiritual imagination. For some it was a place of spiritual redemption. Arthur Wesley Dow (1857–1922) worked on a series of seventeen painted views of the Grand Canyon between 1911 and 1913. The titles he gives each painting, *Bright Angel Canyon*, *Cosmic cities* and *The glory of Shiva*, are an indication of his conceptualisation of the landscape as a carrier for a cosmic spirituality beyond conventional Western religious experience. Visualising the geological formations of the Grand Canyon in works such as *Unpeopled cities*, it has been argued that Dow envisioned a 'new and pure social order' that imbued the landscape with an Eastern spirituality (Hough and Zakian 1992: 16).

Before mass tourism permitted curious visitors to experience the continent, there were professional travellers opening up the West through scientific and mercenary expeditions. The period of mass tourism was heralded by steam transportation in the 1850s. The exploratory impulses of the men and women crossing the American continent in the nineteenth century sprang from several different sources. Following the Lewis and Clark expedition, the next wave of trailblazers were fur trappers sent out to source and supply wealthy entrepreneurs. Then a period of military expeditions mapped more of the West. In the history of westward exploration and expansion there are several key expeditions. The Lewis and Clark expeditions of the

14 Sears's book is not just about natural 'sacred' sights. He examines prisons, asylums and cemeteries, and itineraries that were popular among visitors to urban areas.

Jeffersonian era were partially undertaken to take an inventory of the continent and its flora and fauna; assessing the viability of converting wilderness to a rural agrarian economy. There were four Fremont expeditions in the 1840s, led by John Charles Fremont and spanning the Rocky Mountains to California. The five Lander expeditions between 1853 to 1860 saw Frederick West Lander leading parties to the West Coast to find routes for wagon trains and railroads. Following the Civil War, there were four Great Surveys, led by Ferdinand Hayden, Clarence King, John Wesley Powell and George Wheeler, and in general terms identifiable with explorations in Yellowstone Canyon, the Sierra Nevada Mountains, the Colorado River, the Grand Canyon respectively.[15]

It is difficult now to reconstitute the scale of the operations that these expeditions faced. The West was of unknown proportions, uncertainty about its dimensions being best exemplified by the widely held belief in the years before the first expeditions westwards that California might be an island. The hazards implicit in the journeys west became embedded within mythologies of frontier. Artists were a presence in many of the early expeditions, either as official members of the party or as self-invited guests. While art and social history have tended to record the drama of western expansion through epic landscapes and settler conflicts with Native Americans, as we have seen, much of the recording of the West took place before settlement. Artists frequently travelled with explorer ships as illustrators, surveyors and mapmakers. The first illustrator to comprehensively record the American West was John Webber (1752–1793), who travelled with Captain Cook to Nootka Sound on the west coast of Vancouver Island, where he drew natives of the Nootka tribe. Samuel Seymour (c. 1796–1823) went on several exhibitions including the famous Long expedition of 1819–1820 (led by Major Stephen H. Long, on which the mastodon was found as we shall see in Chapter 5), where he made the first visual record of the Rocky Mountains. Titian Ramsey Peale was also on the Long expedition. Albert Bierstadt (1830–1902) and Thomas Moran (1837–1926) are now the best remembered of the artist-explorers. In the first instance, their presence was justified by the need to record in visual form the discoveries of each journey. Bierstadt's first expedition west was to the Wind River Mountains in 1859, as part of Lander's fifth outing. He not only made sketches, he also took stereoscopic photographs to record the landscape. But for both Moran and Bierstadt their on-site, *plein air* sketches were principally the starting points for compositions for wood engravings, etchings, chromolithographs and paintings, worked up into panoramic Western landscapes once they had returned to their studios.

15 Yosemite, conspicuously absent from the itineraries of the Great Surveys, is discussed below.

As we have seen, John Charles Fremont's first expedition (with Kit Carson) in 1842 was partly in order to produce a guidebook for settler's travelling the first part of the Oregon Trail. The resulting publication, *A Report on an Exploration of the Country Lying between the Missouri River and the Rocky Mountains on the Line of Kansas and Great Platte Rivers*, captured the public imagination and was reprinted in newspapers. Artists such as Church, who later became synonymous with the epic landscapes of the Rockies, often owned copies of reports of explorations and surveys carried out by railroad companies. Such reports included information on animals and botany as well as meteorological and geological data. Most of the early images of the West therefore were not those stock pictures of Western expansion we have already encountered, but more likely to come from railway surveys such as the Pacific railway and Mexican Boundary surveys, or connected to mining enterprises. Christian Nahl (1818–1878), for instance, recorded a mining prospect on the Yuba River set up in 1849, by the Rough and Ready Mining Company and named after the town of the same name in Nevada, California.

In a mutually dependent way, tourism promoted the settlement of the American West that followed on the heels of the survey parties. In the nineteenth century, newspapers, guidebooks, and popular magazines sold the attractions of Western territories to Americans in the East.[16] According to Fifer, Crofutt's *Great Trans-Continental Railroad Guide* of 1869:

> fairly crackled with exhortations to go, to experience the sense of space, the vistas, the wonders but also the realities of the West at first hand. The Guide, like the railroad, had cut a huge slice out of the centre of Western America for all to see.
>
> (Fifer 1988: 171)

Later the familiar apparatus of tourism – Thomas Cook's tours of the western territories and Baedeker's first American guidebook – facilitated mass tourism, just as the railroads were facilitating mass settlement. The connections between tourism and the pictorialisation of the West were exemplified by one railroad company, the Atchinson, Topeka and Santa Fe Railway (offering the only direct route to the Grand Canyon) in its purchase of Moran's painting of the Grand Canyon to use as an image in its marketing campaigns.[17]

16 Beyond the Eastern seaboard of America, images that illustrated technical and scientific explorations or imaginative reconstructions were also disseminated to the *Illustrated London News* by the 1870s, establishing images of the West and its frontier more widely.

17 Thomas Moran, 'Grand Canyon of Arizona from Hermit Rim Road', Chicago: Atchison Topeka & Santa Fe Railway System, 1913. Chromolithograph by American Lithographic Co.

In *Traveling South: Travel Narratives and the Construction of American Identity* (2005), John Cox argues that travel 'remained a central paradigm for imagining the freedoms granted to citizens of the new nation' (2005: 3). The emancipatory potential of travel for Americans is unlike that imagined by Europeans. In literature and art Europeans often 'go away to find themselves', but Americans appear to have travelled as an exercise of their freedoms. The designation of wilderness as a place of imagined freedom is deeply rooted.

Wilderness

> A wilderness in contrast with those areas where man and his works dominate the landscape, is hereby recognized as an area where the earth and its community of life are untrammeled by man, where man himself is a visitor who does not remain.
>
> Wilderness Act, 1964

The sense that amongst the European explorers into the heart of North and South America that the sparsely inhabited landscapes they encountered were indeed wilderness was an Old World conceit, a belief grounded in the assumption that indigenous peoples had not previously inhabited or altered the environment. William M. Denevan (1992) argues to the contrary that American landscapes had been subject to extensive deforestation and agricultural burning before the first settlers arrived. Denevan thus refutes the long-held notion of the 'noble savage' whose occupancy of the land was a symbiotic process of oneness with nature which did not impact upon the landscape. But looking at attitudes to wilderness historically, it is possible to trace the polarised view that Denevan resists, in which the untamed territories are either the site of savagery and temptation which threaten the authority of settlers, or a potential Garden of Eden if properly cultivated by European settlers.

The geography and ecology of the American continent have long been preoccupations among Americans, and wilderness one of its most cherished ideals. The American Wilderness Coalition was established in January 2001 to support and coordinate wilderness advocates and organisations nationwide. In an effort to protect America's remaining wild places, the American Wilderness Coalition lobbies Congress to grant the status of 'wilderness' as one that permanently protects these special areas of public land. There are currently 643 protected wilderness areas covering over 105 million acres of public land across the United States. Together, these wilderness areas make up the National Wilderness Preservation System. In his influential essay, 'The trouble with wilderness,' William Cronon questions the tendency to idealise the wilderness as:

> the false hope of an escape from responsibility, the illusion that we can somehow wipe clean the slate of our past and return to the tabula rasa that supposedly existed before we began to leave our marks on the world. The dream of an unworked natural landscape is very much the fantasy of people who have never themselves had to work the land to make a living.
>
> (Cronon 1995: 80)

The trouble with wilderness then is that it is dependent upon a notion of nature's otherness.

Freeman Tilden (1883–1980) was the one of the most important advocates for the modern national park. With books such as *The National Parks: What They Mean to You and Me* (1965), and his seminal *Interpreting Our Heritage* (1954), he contributed to America's understanding of its own relationship to the natural, and historical interpretation of the national parks. Current advocates of a rethinking of our relationship to wilderness, including Roderick Nash, optimistically look to an eco-centric future where human needs are subordinate to the needs of nature, ideas that challenge the Jeffersonian pastoral ideal which has lingered in the American imagination for three centuries (Nash 2001: 384).

In his definitive history, *Wilderness and the American Mind* (1967/2001), Nash compares wilderness to themes from the Bible, the 'antipode' to paradise, or the Garden of Eden. According to Nash, the first Puritan settlers of New England, brought with them their biblical views of the wilderness as 'cursed' land, or more extremely a 'kind of hell' on earth, and sought to transform it into an earthly paradise. He cites evidence from several seventeenth-century books and tracts to support this, such as Cotton Mather's *Decennium Luctuosum: An History of Remarkable Occurrences in the Long War Which New-England Hath Had with the Indian Salvages* (1699). Nash makes an important distinction between the romantic and the American wilderness in his book. The wilderness offered Americans their distinctiveness, since it was unparalleled in scale and diversity by anything from the Old World. New World wilderness offered the very real possibility of a basis for emerging nationalism.

The 1870 Washburn Expedition included Charles Moore and Henry Trumbull. While they were on the expedition they made pencil sketches of the sights they encountered, recording broad topographical facts. Neither was an accomplished artist, and when another member of the party, Nathaniel P. Langford, wrote 'The wonders of Yellowstone' for *Scribner's Monthly* of 1871, one of Scribner's staff artists, Thomas Moran, was employed to rework the Moore and Trumbull sketches into an image more suitable for the highly regarded and notably illustrated periodical.[18] Moran

18 The extant Moore and Trumbull sketches are in the Yellowstone National Park archives.

The following were reproduced with kind permission. While every effort has been made to trace copyright holders and obtain permission, this has not been possible in all cases. Any omissions brought to our attention will be remedied in future editions.

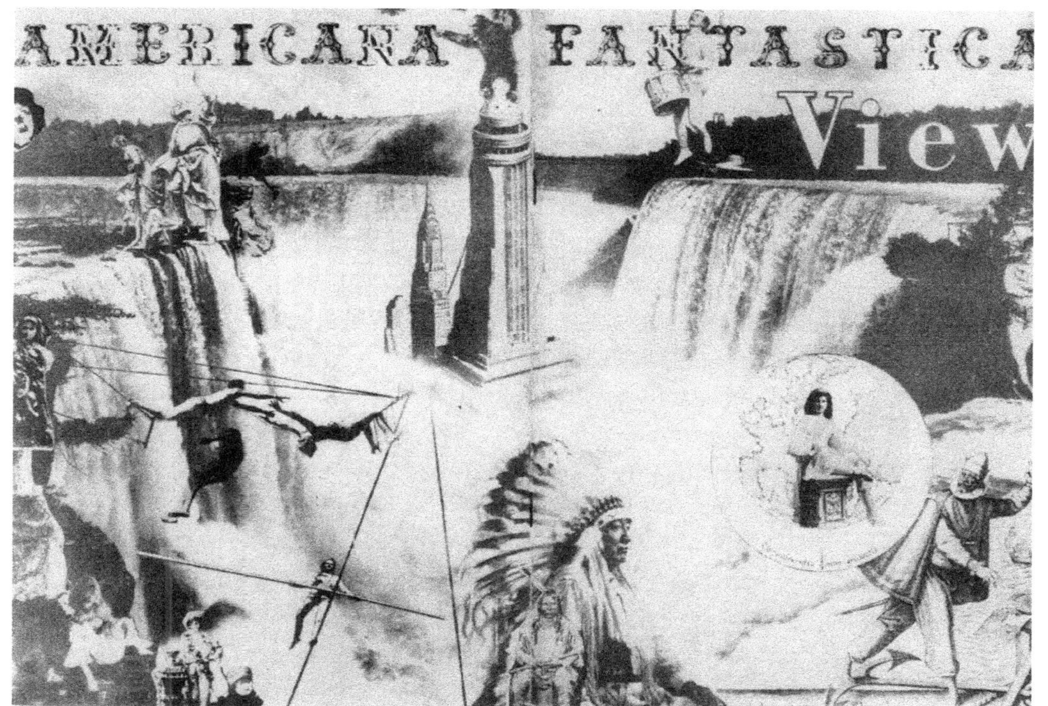

Plate 1 Joseph Cornell, 'Americana fantastica', *View* magazine, 1943.

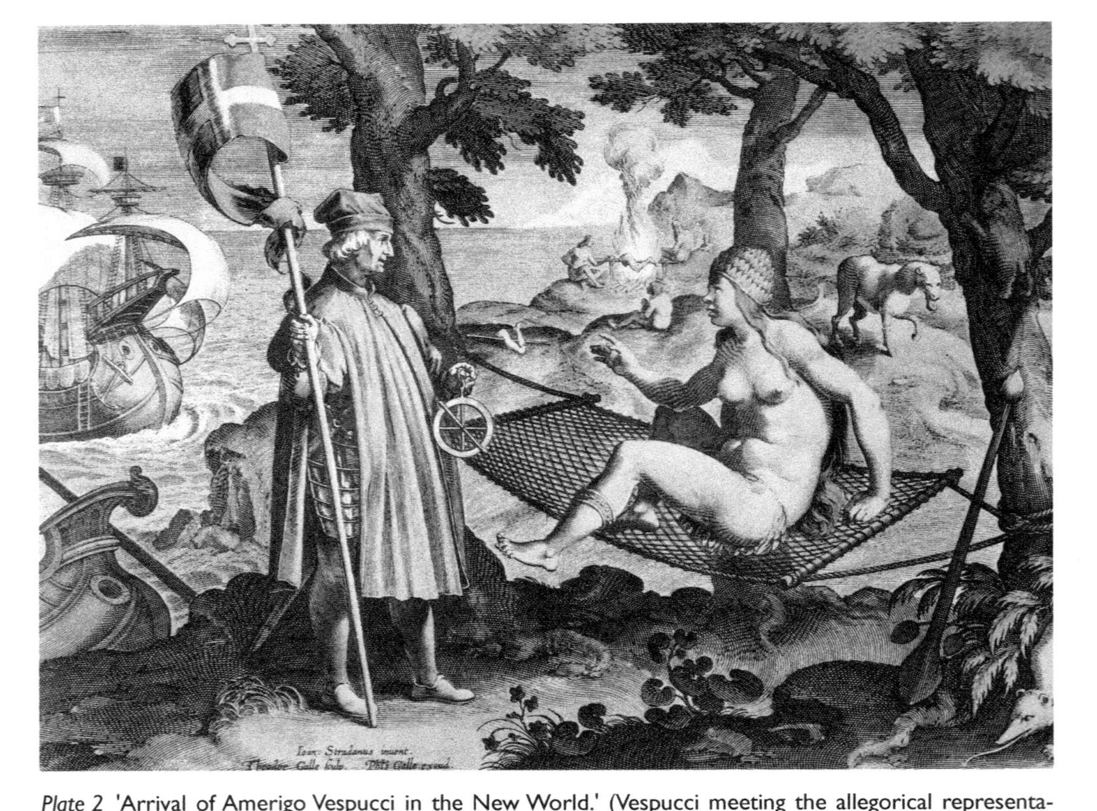

Plate 2 'Arrival of Amerigo Vespucci in the New World.' (Vespucci meeting the allegorical representation of America). Engraving by Theodor Galle after the drawing, c.1580, by Johannes Stradanus. Courtesy of the Granger Collection, New York.

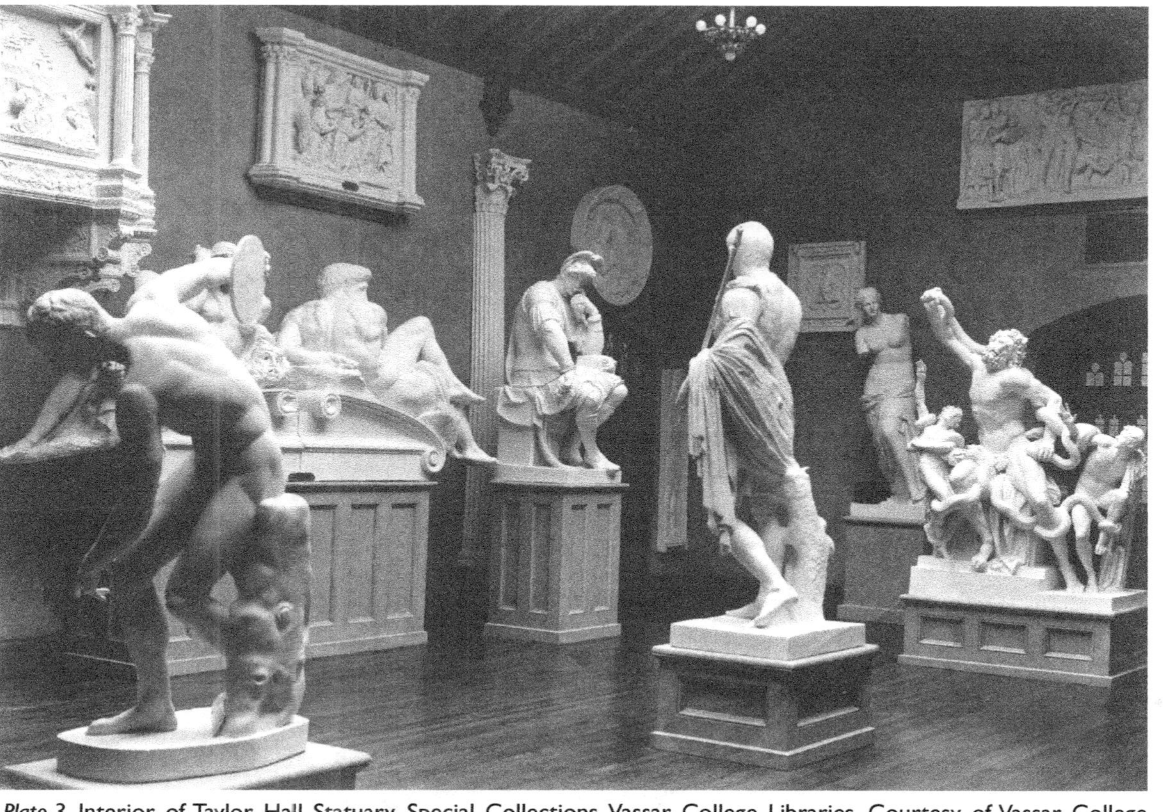

Plate 3 Interior of Taylor Hall Statuary, Special Collections, Vassar College Libraries. Courtesy of Vassar College Libraries.

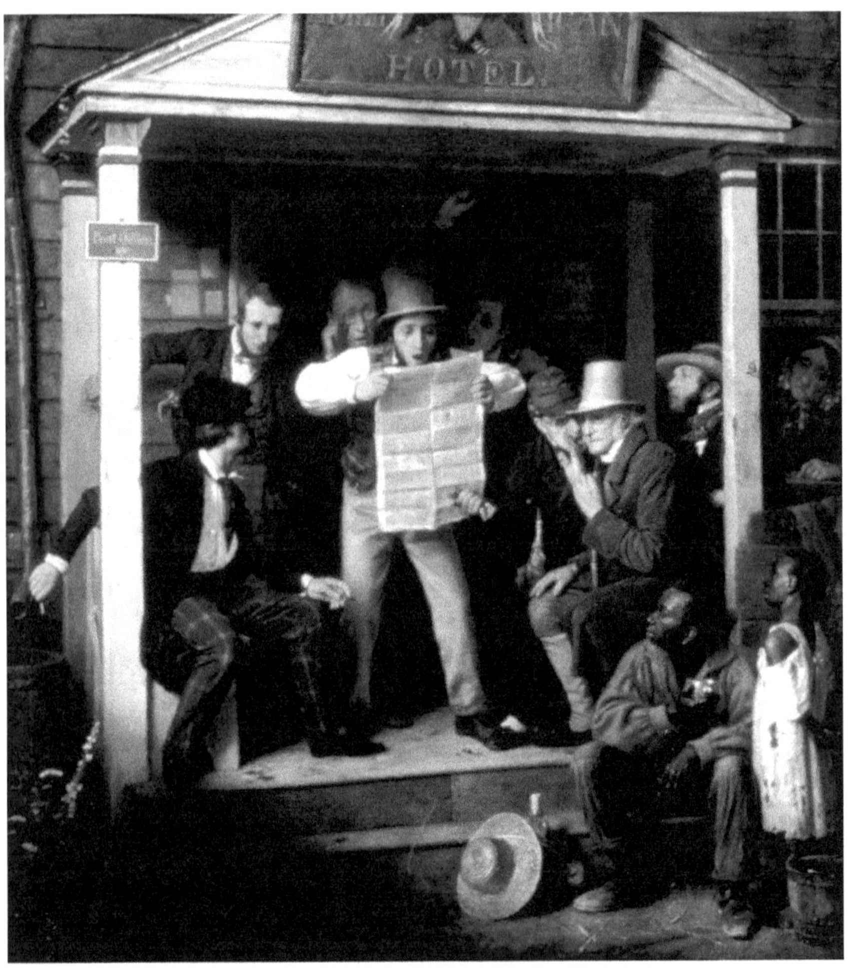

Plate 4 Richard Caton Woodville, 'War news from Mexico'. Oil on canvas, 1848. Courtesy of the Granger Collection, New York.

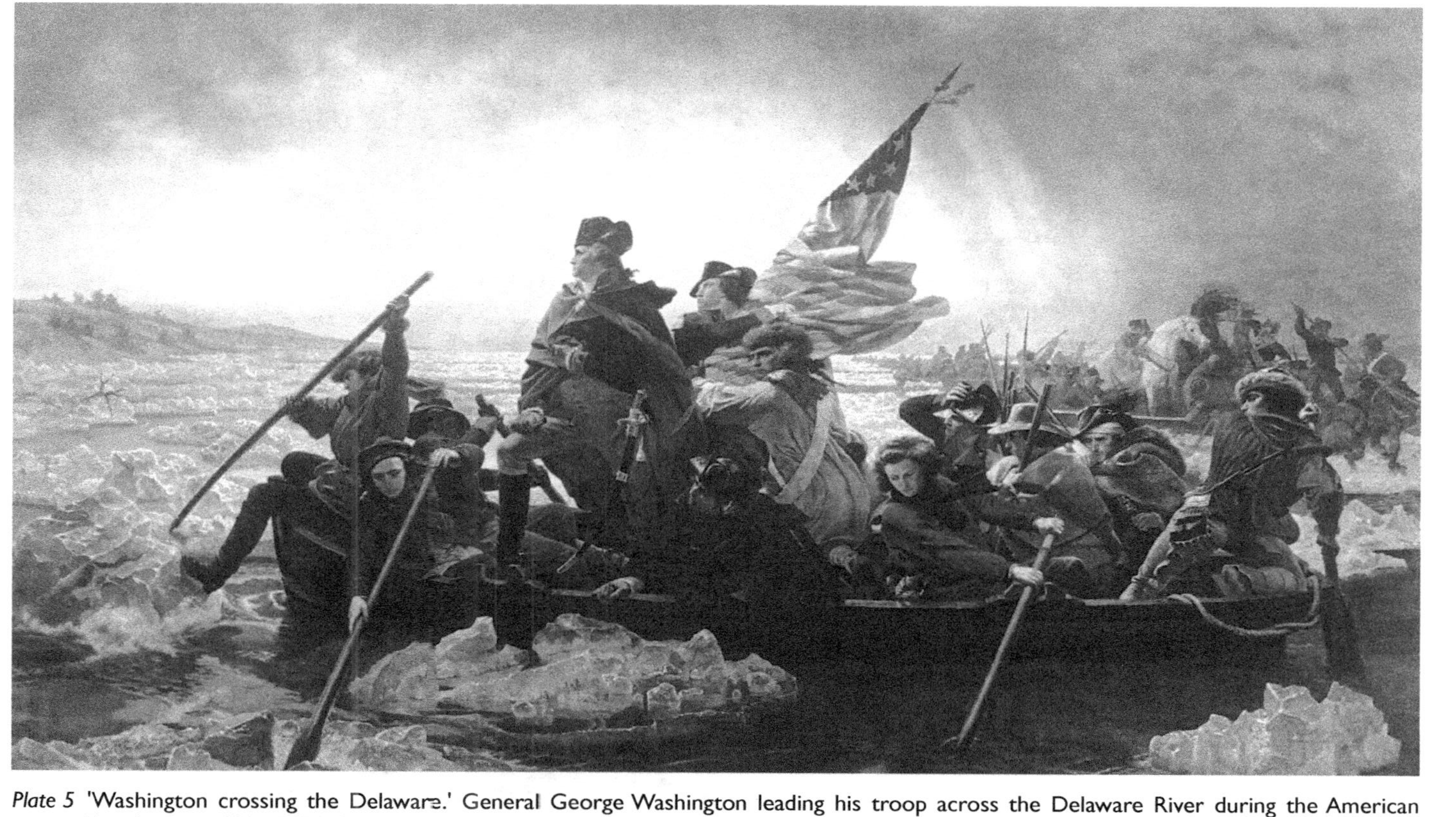

Plate 5 'Washington crossing the Delaware.' General George Washington leading his troop across the Delaware River during the American Revolutionary War, 1776. Oil on canvas by Emanuel Leutze, 1851. Courtesy of the Granger Collection, New York.

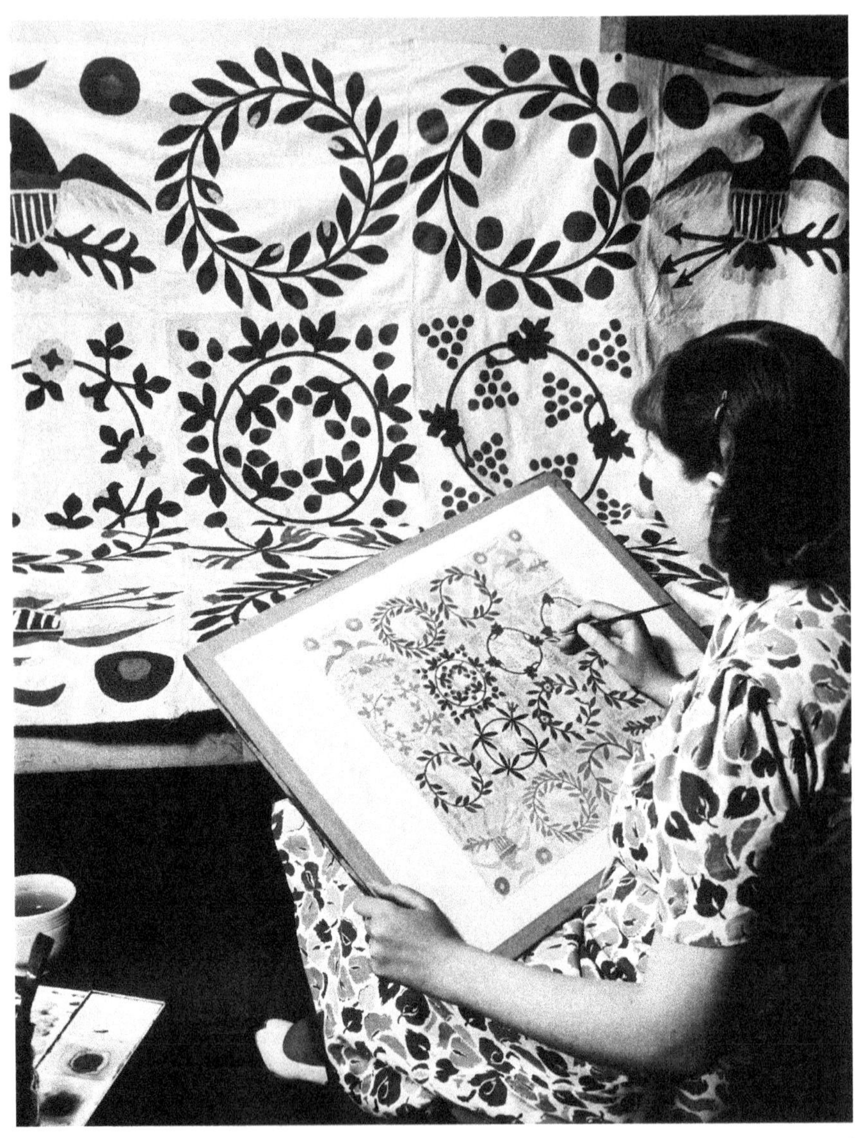

Plate 6 Index of American design artist Charlotte Angus at work on a rendering of 'Appliqué sampler quilt top,' 1940. Courtesy of National Gallery of Art, Washington D.C., Gallery Archives.

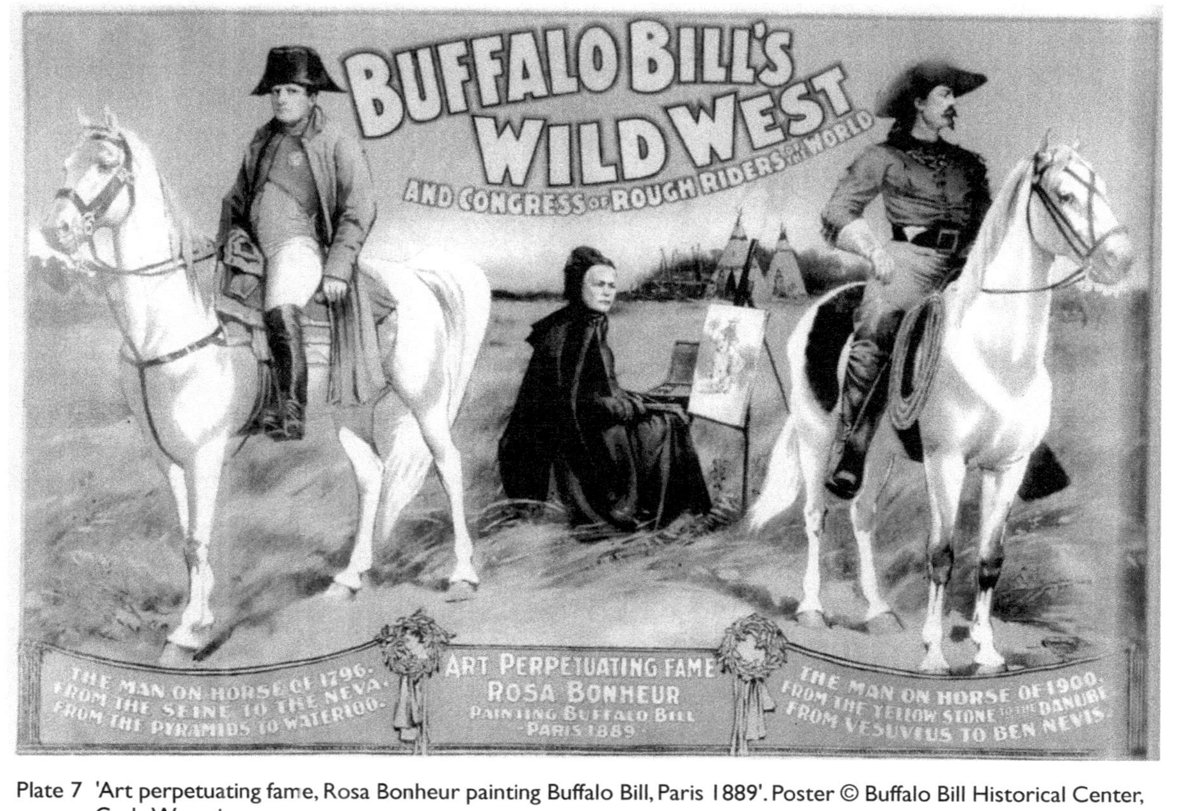

Plate 7 'Art perpetuating fame, Rosa Bonheur painting Buffalo Bill, Paris 1889'. Poster © Buffalo Bill Historical Center, Cody, Wyoming.

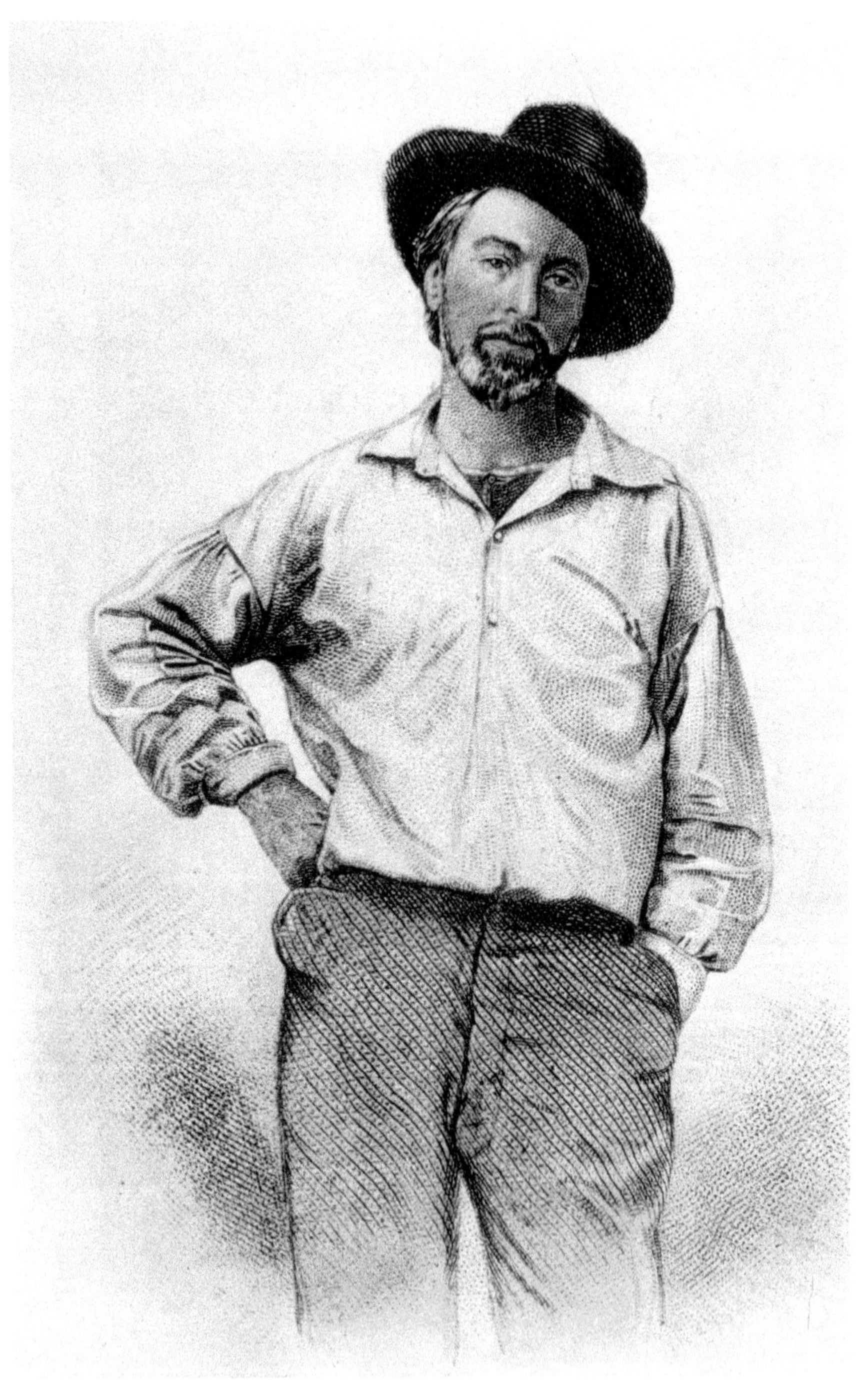

Plate 8 Walt Whitman (1819–1892). Engraved frontispiece, by Samuel Hollyer, to Whitman's first edition of Whitman's *Leaves of Grass*, 1855. Courtesy of the Granger Collection, New York.

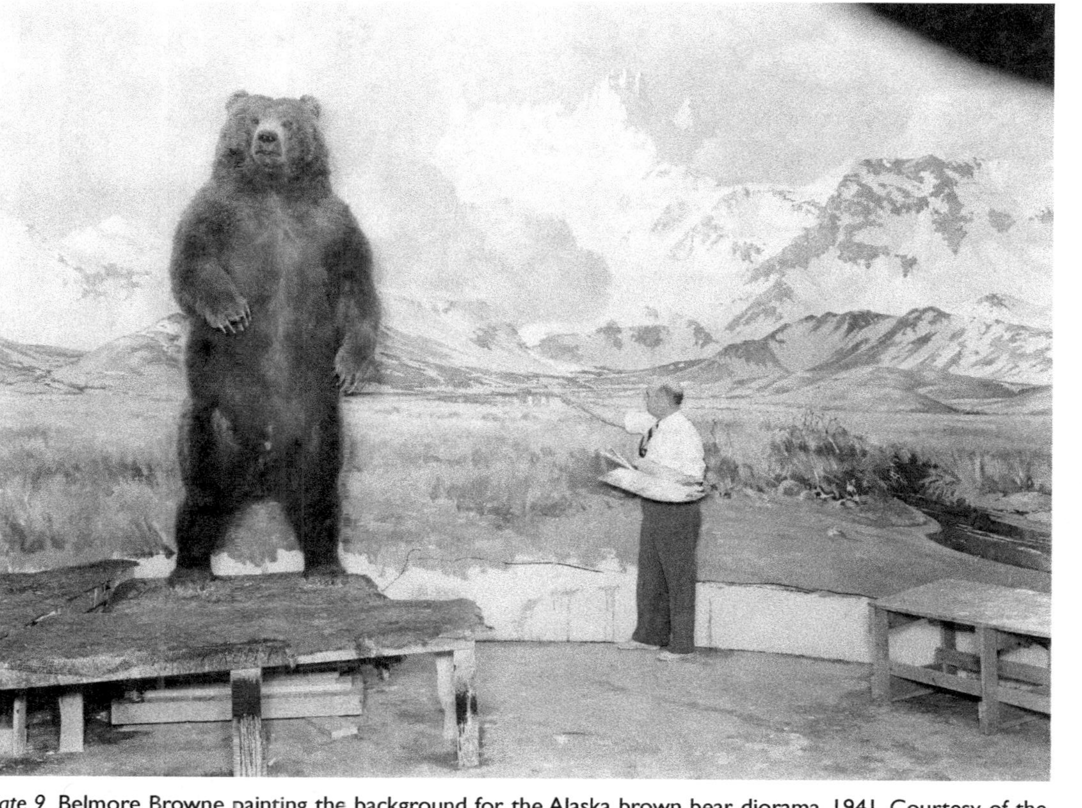

Plate 9 Belmore Browne painting the background for the Alaska brown bear diorama, 1941. Courtesy of the American Museum of Natural History.

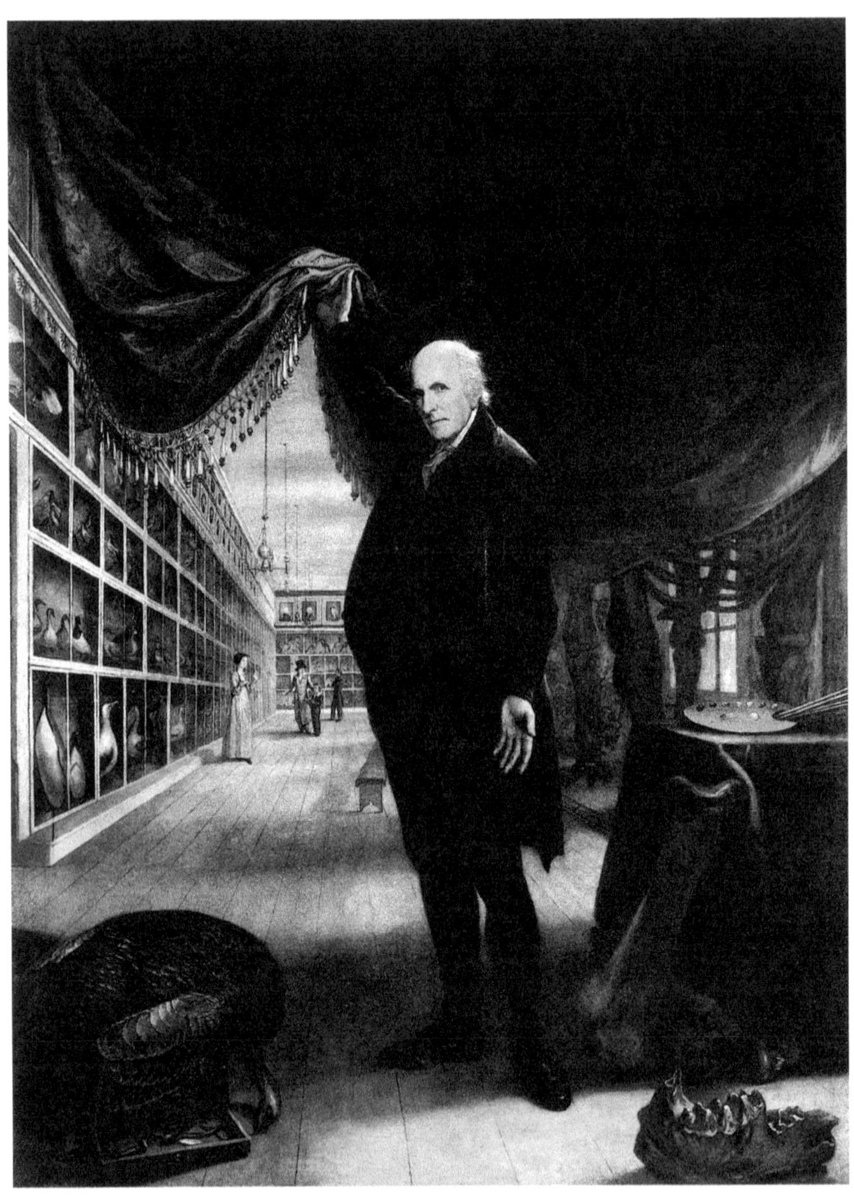

Plate 10 Charles Willson Peale (1741–1827), 'The artist in his museum'. Full-length self-portrait by Charles Willson Peale, an American painter, inventor and museum founder. Oil on canvas, 1822. Courtesy of the Granger Collection, New York.

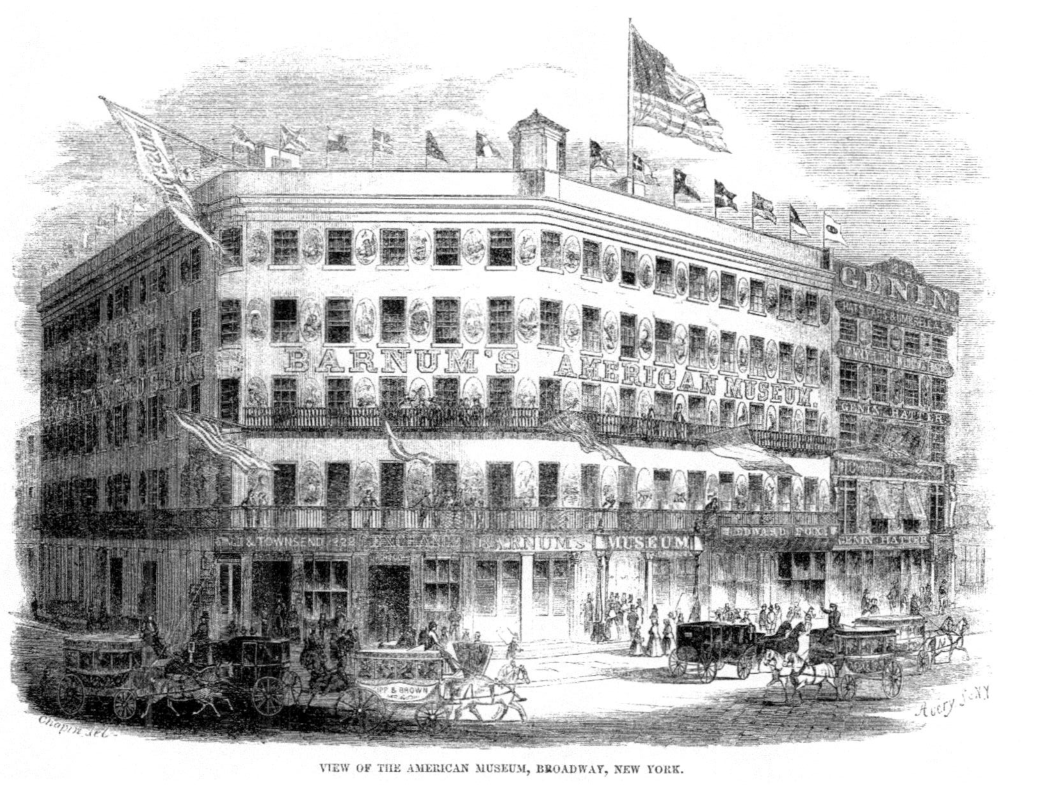

VIEW OF THE AMERICAN MUSEUM, BROADWAY, NEW YORK.

Plate 11 Barnum's Museum, 1853. View of P.T. Barnum's American Museum on Broadway, New York City. Wood engraving, American, 1853. Courtesy of the Granger Collection, New York.

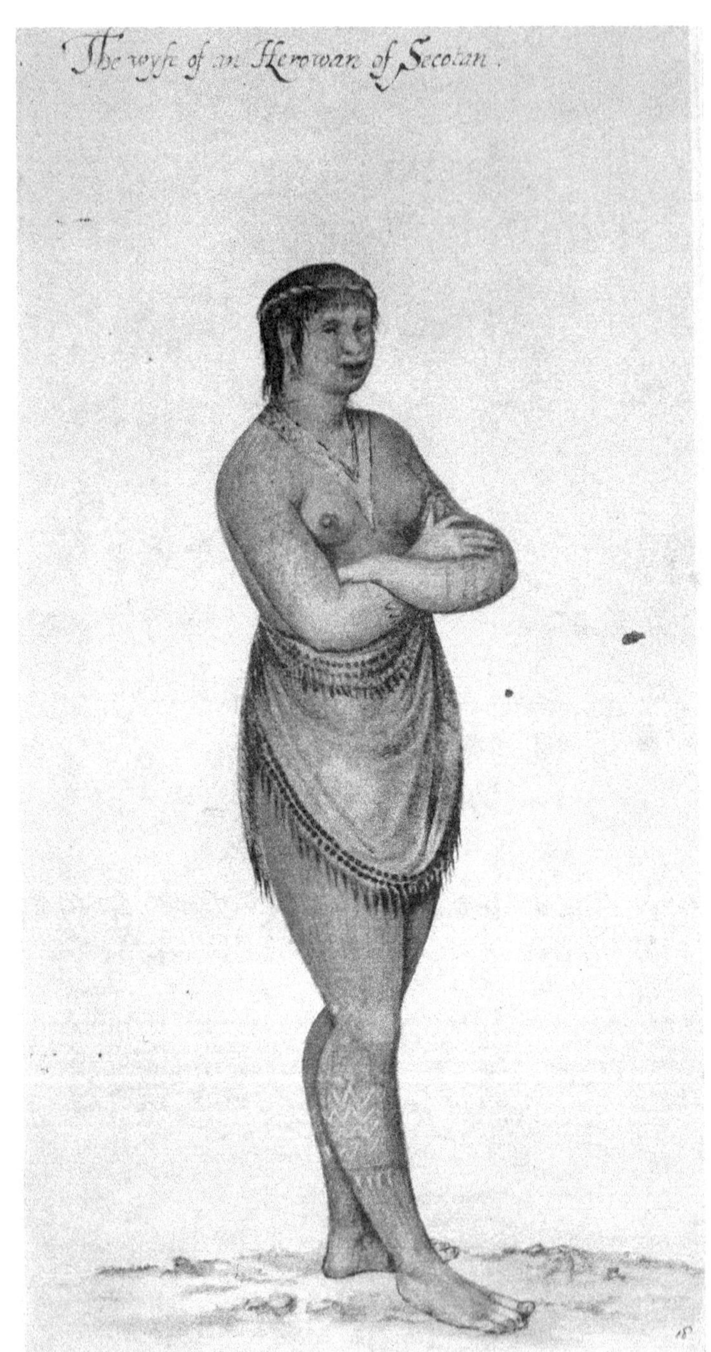

Plate 12 'Algonquian woman,' 1585. A Carolina Algonquian Indian woman of Secoton: watercolor, c.1585, by John White. Courtesy of the Granger Collection, New York.

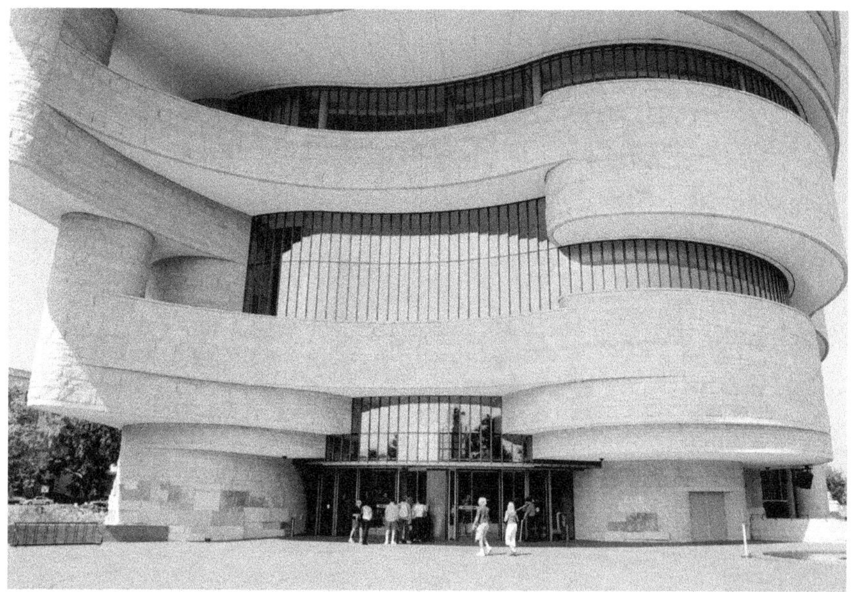

Plate 13 Smithsonian National Museum of the American Indian, Washington DC. Photograph by Pam Meecham.

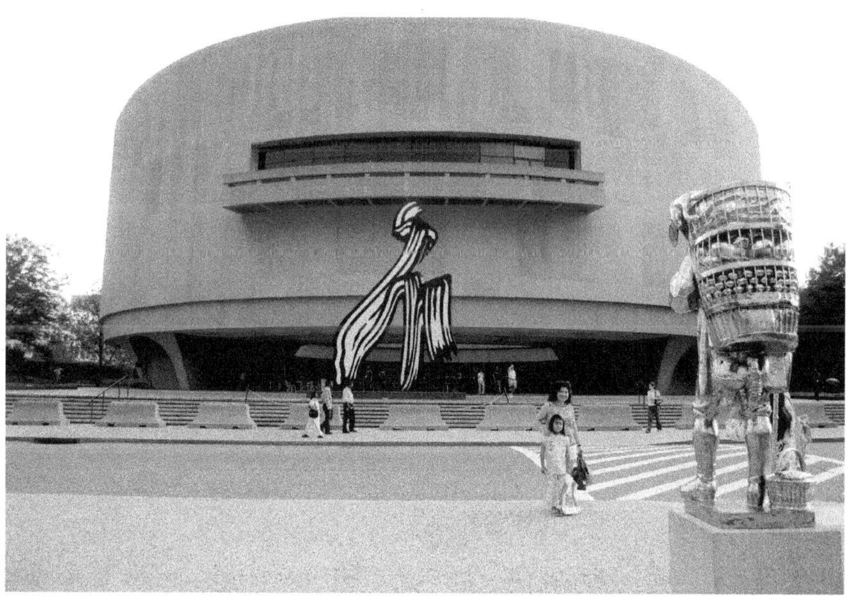

Plate 14 Jeff Koons's sculpture, 'Kiepenkerl' (pedlar), 1987, outside the Hirshhorn Museum, Washington. Photograph by Pam Meecham.

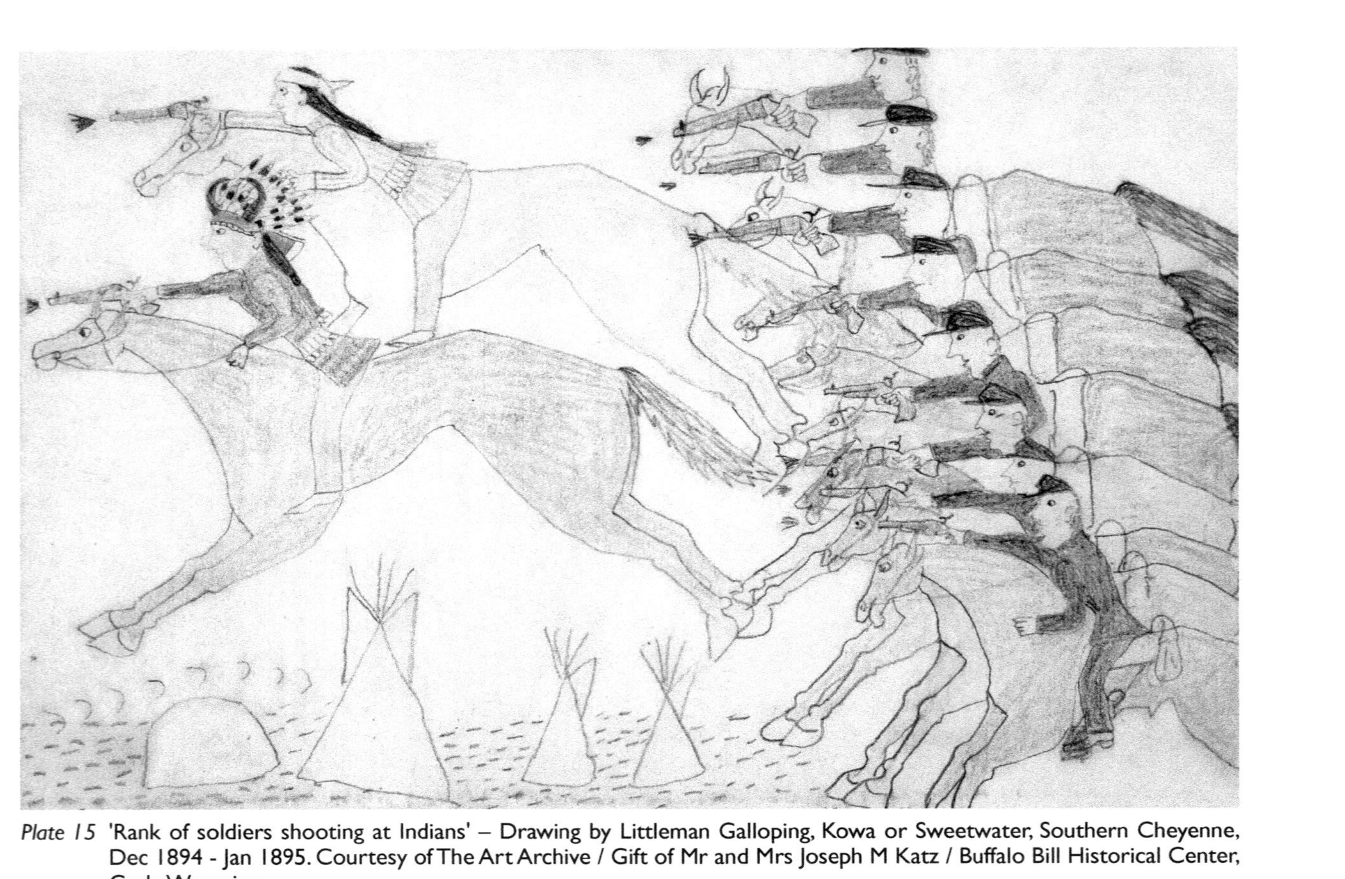

Plate 15 'Rank of soldiers shooting at Indians' – Drawing by Littleman Galloping, Kowa or Sweetwater, Southern Cheyenne, Dec 1894 - Jan 1895. Courtesy of The Art Archive / Gift of Mr and Mrs Joseph M Katz / Buffalo Bill Historical Center, Cody, Wyoming.

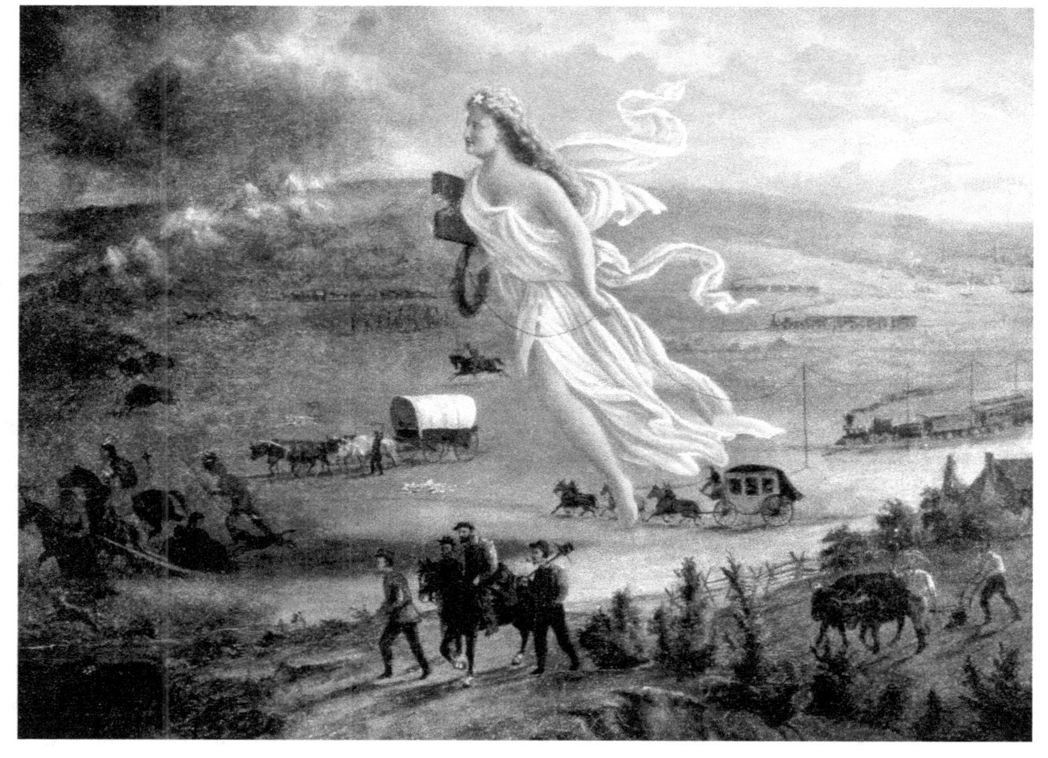

Plate 16 John Gast (1872) 'American progress', an allegorical respresentation of manifest destiny. Oil on canvas, 1872. Courtesy of the Granger Collection, New York.

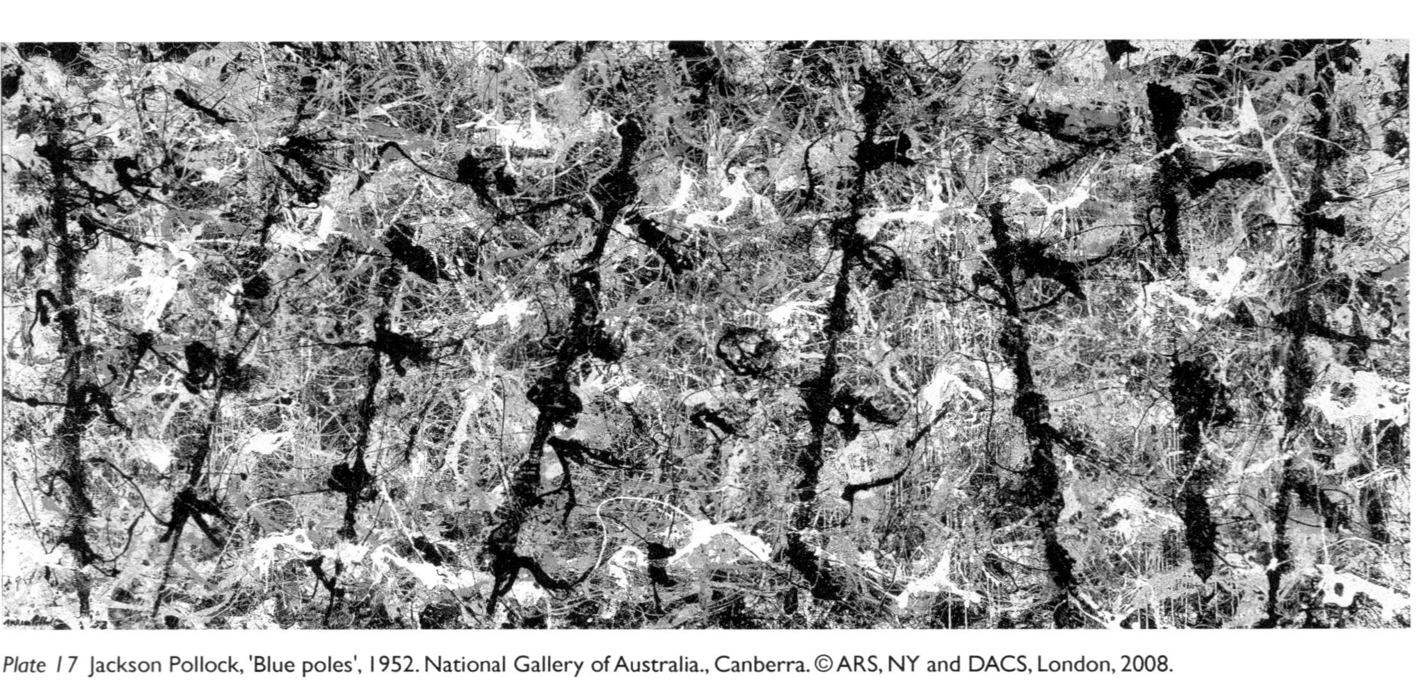

Plate 17 Jackson Pollock, 'Blue poles', 1952. National Gallery of Australia., Canberra. © ARS, NY and DACS, London, 2008.

was subsequently invited to be the guest artist to Ferdinand Hayden's 1871 government-sponsored geological survey of Yellowstone. The survey party included the official artist Henry Wood Elliott and the photographer, William Henry Jackson. Jackson's 300 images from the 1871 Yellowstone expedition are quite remarkable given the limitations of equipment, necessitating the moving of a cumbersome wooden camera and developing solutions, the creation of a portable darkroom, and the transport of fragile glass negatives. Moran completed numerous watercolour sketches at Yellowstone in preparation for later studio paintings. His attachment to Yellowstone was to be underlined by his decision to sign his work with a three-letter colophon (TYM) standing for his professional name, Thomas 'Yellowstone' Moran. One of the key outcomes of the professional attachment to the area was Moran's monumental painting (84 x 144 inches), the *Grand Canyon of the Yellowstone*, completed in 1872 – the year that Yellowstone was declared America's first national park – which was purchased for the nation for $10,000. That the first congressional acquisitions of landscape painting for the Capitol should be Moran's paintings of the American West (coupled with the price paid for Moran's first Yellowstone painting) demonstrated the importance of the West to American nationalism.[19]

The extent to which Moran's art featured in the decision of Congress to establish Yellowstone as America's first national park is debatable.[20] Hayden certainly appears to have presented Moran and Jackson's watercolours and photographs as part of his petition to Congress when he returned to Washington, DC in the autumn of 1871.[21] The fate of Yosemite meanwhile is often linked to Albert Bierstadt. John F. Sears cites the self-conscious decision to develop Yosemite and Yellowstone as tourist destinations in the 1860s and 1870s as evidence that tourism had become 'well-established both as a cultural activity and as an industry' by the middle of the century (1989: 123). However Yosemite had been conspicuously absent from the itineraries of the Great Surveys. Nor was Yosemite on the itinerary of the first tourists, only registering 653 visitors between 1856 and 1864 (Fifer 1988: 236). Indeed there are no surviving images of the area before the

19 Congress later purchased a second landscape by Moran, *Chasm of the Colorado*, painted following the artist's 1873 trip with John Wesley Powell to the Grand Canyon of the Colorado River. In 1875 Moran completed the third of his great western landscapes, *Mountain of the Holy Cross*, a view of a famous Colorado peak.

20 See especially Kinsey's *Thomas Moran and the Surveying of the American West* (1992: 60–1) for an analysis of the debate over Moran's role.

21 Hayden also used Moran's images in his article 'The wonders of the West II, more about the Yellowstone', which appeared in the February 1872 issue of *Scribner's Monthly*, and his official report of 1872, *Preliminary Report of the United States Geological Survey of Montana and Adjacent Territories*, also included Moran's engravings.

1850s, and Yosemite, for example, failed to inspire Thomas Moran (Boag 1998: 58).[22]

The painter most often connected with early representations of Yosemite was Thomas Hill (1829–1908). Hill painted in excess of 5,000 views of Yosemite, and several of his large panoramas were painted for wealthy Californian collectors. His commitment to Yosemite was such that he built a studio there in 1883, where he lived during the summer months. Although Hill is the prototype artist of Yosemite, it was Albert Bierstadt who became the archetypal painter of the area. He also established a studio in San Francisco, and made paintings, including several of the Yosemite Valley, which it is always supposed contributed to the setting-up of Yosemite National Park. But it was arguably the photographers Eadweard Muybridge and Ansel Adams who provided some of the key views of Yosemite. Muybridge's photographs and stereographs of Yosemite of the 1860s became among the most celebrated images taken of the valley. In one Muybridge photographed himself positioned on top of Contemplation Rock at Glacier Point. It shows the photographer seated at the edge of a precipice to one of Yosemite's deep chasms. He appears virtually in silhouette against the light-saturated cliffs of the valley.[23]

Adams (1902–1984) visited Yosemite every year from 1916 until his death. A member of the Sierra Club, the Wilderness Society and an activist in the nascent conservation movement, he routinely photographed landmarks. His highly evolved sense of the preservation of wilderness coupled with his resistance to 'resortism' led him to become an outspoken critic of the national parks movement. Adams was employed by the US Department of Interior to photograph the Western national parks in 1941 and 1942 for a scheme to decorate the department's new museum in Washington, D.C with enlarged photographic murals of scenes from the national parks.

Frontier

> The American nation is not like the others. Its nationalism is that of an ideological nation. Its history is separate. It accepts no comparison with others, and so it has been the most nationalistic of all the major nations. Not only politicians and public men but also the people themselves constantly assert its superiority over all the others, as if the virtue of its Constitution[24] were proof of permanent national success.
>
> (Pfaff 1993: 161)

22 The first trailblazers in Yosemite were not artists, and it was not until tourists such as Thomas A. Ayres passed through the area that any drawings were made.

23 This photograph of Muybridge was used as part of the evidence presented in support of his plea of insanity at his trial for the murder of his wife's lover.

24 The American Constitution was drawn up in 1787, followed by the nineteen amendments of the Bill of Rights in 1791.

American attitudes to, and justification for, expansion in the West were expressed in terms of the Puritan notion of covenant, combined with an understanding of America's 'unique destiny'. The first governor of New England, John Winthrope, summed up the vision of a new world. Perry Miller maintained that Winthrope, 'stands at the beginning of our consciousness.... His legacy, a form of Covenant with God, identified a programme of enterprise that committed a new nation to a conscious realisation of citizenship and specific good works' (1962: 38). The logic went that since the New World was not reproducing the old iniquitous social hierarchies of Europe, it would be given 'Divine Providence to the extent that it fulfils the Covenant'. In effect, Miller argues that Winthrope's doctrines led to the concept of 'God's Own People'. The Covenant became impractical, however, but the legacy of it remained, leaving a residual sense of personal sin and a punishment ethos.

This early sense of 'self' is crucial to any understanding of the rhetoric that surfaces in the identification of an authentic, visibly American culture. Received wisdom simply posits a nation anxious to overcome its colonial roots, and break the ties of a corrupt, overly sophisticated European heritage to form a uniquely American voice. However Sacvan Bercovitch, like Miller, sees the origins of America and the construction of the American self as conditioned by the individualism and moral imperatives of John Winthrope. Bercovitch (1975) draws on an early American work, Cotton Mather's hagiographic biography *The Life of John Winthrope*, as paradigmatic of the imperative to construct an American identity consistent with what he describes as 'a comprehensive social-divine selfhood'.

The post hoc reasoning that became known as the Turner thesis was originally a lecture delivered by the historian Frederick J. Turner in 1893 at the Chicago World's Fair, *The Significance of the Frontier in American History*. Although it has slipped in and out of fashion since, the thesis remains a tenacious presence in popular and academic US thinking. The theory interpreted the social and political development of the United States in relation to settlements that moved westwards, instead of accounting for democratic developments as being an extension of European influences. It was born out of a frustration at the continual referencing of European institutions in Eastern states as crucial to constitutional development, and an almost total marginalising of any 'homespun' influences.[25] The frontier was declared closed in 1890, when for the purposes of the Census it was no longer granted a place (Turner 1893: 199), and it is important to note that the thesis coincided

25 The theory met with virulently polarised pro and anti-sympathies. The extremes of reaction testify to the innovative quality of Turner's work: by 1903, he had honed the ideas to write *Contributions of the West to American Democracy*.

with the official closure of the frontier as a physical space and its subsequent entry into imagination.

Arguably the final American frontier was the state of Alaska. The Klondike gold rush entered the world's imagination through Jack London's novels *Call of the Wild* and *White Fang*, published in 1903 and 1906 respectively, which played out their canine dramas in the white frozen Yukon.[26] London observed men 'penetrating the land of desolation and mockery and silence, puny adventurers bent on colossal adventure, pitting themselves against the might of a world as remote and alien and pulseless [sic] as the abysses of space'(1906/1992: 114). In the white vastness, men 'perceived themselves finite and small, specks and motes, moving with weak cunning and little wisdom amidst the play and inter-play of the great blind elements and forces' (1906/1994: 114). London's books still resonate today in film and literature.[27] Parts of Alaska, protected through the Alaska National Interest Lands Conservation Acts since 1980, have doubled the size of the area controlled by the National Park Service.

Nash points to irreconcilable differences over the urge to civilise such extreme wilderness. Wilderness itself is a Eurocentric term not shared by the indigenous population of Alaska. While there have been major land-rights issues in Alaska, the late date at which the state joined the Union precluded the wholesale slaughter or removal of existing populations, which characterised the same process in other states. However just what to preserve of Alaska has been the subject of passionate debate, with suggestions ranging from 'total lock up', to development along Californian lines, to the right to live off wild land. The extreme, hostile wilderness was thought by some advocates of limited development to be protection enough from 'encroaching civilisation'. For others tourism, rather than a threat to preservation, could be seen as a reason to keep a pristine wilderness. Alaska thus came to represent, as Nash reminds us, a powerful place in the American consciousness even among those who would never visit it. According to Nash, the American imagination was fuelled by John Muir's nineteenth-century transcendentalism and Thoreauesque rhetoric to become the 'purest' of places in the priorities of environmentalists, recreation seekers, ecologists and hunters (Nash 1967/2001).

The Alaskan wilderness had been painted by artists in the nineteenth century: for example, by Henry Wood Elliot (1846–1930) and Sydney Mortimer Lawrence (1865–1940). Kesler Woodward's *Sydney Laurence, Painter of the North* (1990) claims that Lawrence defined Alaska as the last frontier through his images of Mount McKinley. Claire Fejes (1920–1998),

26 The Klondike and Yukon Territories are in British Columbia on the border of Alaska.

27 In 2007, a film adaptation was made of Jon Krakauer's best-selling book *Into the Wild*. Krakauer also wrote 'Death of an innocent: how Christopher McCandless lost his way in the wilds' in *Outside* magazine, January 1993.

born in New York, a member of the Student Arts League and part of the WPA during the New Deal in the 1930s, went to Fairbanks Alaska in 1946, and painted Alaskan native people, Inupiat and Athabascans. Fred Machetanz (1908–2002), whose landscape paintings of Alaska became iconic, was voted American Artist of the Year in 1981 by *American Artists* magazine not uncoincidentally in a period when Alaska was designated a wilderness. However, important landscape painting had been to the development of a specifically American art, Alaskan painters remain outside the general history of American art as the genre faded in importance in the twentieth century, except as a vehicle for avant-garde experimentation.

Bringing the West back East

The remoteness from nature of people in the cities of America also led to a craze for images of the West. As Rebecca Solnit has put it; 'What was vanishing as ecology was reappearing as imagery. Landscape showed up in the stereoscope cards in parlors, in the floral patterns on dresses and saddles and silverware, in the scenery engraved on pocket watches' (2003: 66). The affection for and interest in the West was stoked by popular literature. *Scribner's* and *Harper's Weekly* were two of many magazines that published engravings after paintings of wilderness. Sensational dime novels, the stories of Daniel Boone, Jedediah Smith, and Buffalo Bill's Wild West Congress of Rough Riders, all contributed to a myth of the West.

Post hoc renditions of the West compensated for the lack of visual documentation about the first trailblazers. For example, there are few images of the early pioneers like Daniel Boone (1734–1820) and Jedediah Smith (1799–1831). Instead the presence of the trailblazer in the west was retrospectively illustrated. Cole's *Daniel Boone sitting at the door of his cabin on the Great Osage Lake, Kentucky* (1826) is a posthumous painting,[28] as is George Caleb Bingham's *Daniel Boone escorting settlers through the Cumberland Gap* (1851–2). In combination with successful publications about Boone, such as Timothy Flint's *Biographical Memoir of Daniel Boone, the First Settler of Kentucky* (1833), the mythmaking around Boone's life far exceeded his own recorded statements on his life.

In 1775 Boone was part of a team of 30 other woodsmen employed to 'trailblaze' between the Carolinas and the West, a route that became known as the 'Wilderness Road'. This peripatetic life along the Wilderness Trail, around 300 miles in length, was celebrated by the publication of *Daniel*

28 Log cabins are an important attribute in Boone's personal iconography, and several surviving log cabins claim to have once been home to him. Harold R. Shurtleff has recognised the long 'emotional association of the log cabin with the American spirit' (1939: 214). At the Centennial Exhibition in Philadelphia log cabins were popular exhibits.

Boone's Adventures by John Filson in 1784, immortalizing Boone the frontiersman as an American legend. Another legendary trailblazer, Jedediah Smith too, achieved as many distinctions – he led the first overland party from the East to California, and laid the way for the Oregon Trail wagons. Smith was essentially a businessman running a company searching for new beaver streams in the West, but his adventures, including encounters with Blackfoot natives and a grizzly bear, are the stuff of legend, sealed when he was killed by Comanches as he led a wagon train taking goods to California down the Santa Fe Trail in 1831. In the absence of a visual record of Smith's activities, Frederic Remington invented one. His illustration of *Smith and men in the Mojave Desert in 1826, as imaginatively painted* (c. 1905), although not strictly illustrative of the adventures as such, hints at the topography of the desert, and the hazards of the expedition are implied in the faded areas at the edge of the composition.

We have seen how promoters exhorted Americans to settle in the West or visit its sights. However, even though many Americans were mobilised in the nineteenth century to see the West for themselves, many were also happy to connect to their Western heritage at a distance. One item that came back from the West to the East was a set of specimens for East Coast museums and botanical gardens. For example, the Botanic Garden of New York published its first catalogue in 1806, and listed nearly 4,000 species. The East Coast museums also exhibited large animal and mineral specimens. The Smithsonian's first activities were to conduct a meteorological survey and publish the first volume of *Contributions to Knowledge* in 1848. Its first pursuits were mostly scientific: a collection of ancient monuments of the Native Americans of the Mississippi Valley, a study of the orbit of Neptune and treatises on birds' eggs and air humidity.

In New York the Natural History Museum has an extensive collection of habitat group dioramas. Karen Wonders has attributed the popularity of dioramas in the United States to the American tendency to romanticise the wilderness, while Donna Haraway has compared them to morality plays. The dioramas were noted, and continue to be noted, as reliably mounted specimens seen against carefully rendered and geographically precise painted backdrops. Sixty years later many of the environments they represent and the animals natural to their habitat have been changed irrevocably. As the museum puts it, 'The viewer of a habitat group diorama is able to travel not only across continents, but also, in some cases, through time.' This compression of time and space in the halls of the Natural History Museum permits the visitor the conceit of transcontinental and indeed global 'travel', sensitive to the ecology and geography of each exhibit.

One of the exhibits, the *Alaska Brown Bear* in the Hall of North American Mammals, is a meticulous recreation of the bears' natural habitat. A pair of specimen bears, one standing on hind legs to illustrate the size of the creatures, is arranged on replicated foliage and grassland, in a generous space within the museum's display.[29] The large backdrop to the diorama was painted by Belmore Browne (1880–1954) in 1941 (Plate 9). Browne was a fine artist trained at the New York School of Art and the Academie Julian in Paris. He was equally a naturalist, and as part of his career as a wildlife illustrator, Browne participated in expeditions to Alaska on behalf of the American Museum of Natural History. Despite Browne's educational pedigree his work falls short of the dimensions of the twentieth-century avant-garde and rarely merits a line in conventional art histories, falling into the category of wildlife and landscape illustrator.

Revisions to the West

The Conestoga wagon we encountered confidently heading westward in Gast's *American progress* also appears in formation in Edward Ruscha's *A certain trail* from 1986. The painting shows the familiar iconic wagon train and stewarding cowboys heading west from right to left, but towards an ill-defined horizon that takes the party in a downwards path. The blurred black and white acrylic on canvas, airbrushed and soft-focus, seems to demythologise the expansion westward rendered so precisely in the nineteenth century images dealing with the 'course of Empire'. Ruscha's artwork is symptomatic of a more recent impulse to revise assumptions that carried over from the nineteenth-century formation of the West.

In an edition of essays entitled *Independent Spirits* (Trenton 1995), contributors reinstate the place of women artists in the narrative of American art in regions of the West such as New Mexico, southern and northern California, Arizona and Texas. For example, Joni L. Kinsey's essay, 'Cultivating the grasslands: women painters in the Great Plains', demonstrates how women artists were able to work as landscape artists at a time when landscape art was typified as masculine. Katherine Morrissey, among many, has remarked of the gendering of American identity as masculine in the ideology of the West; the cast of characters inhabited and shaping the West is conceived of as male and their activities of 'conquering a "virgin" land, subduing Indians, building railroads, ranching, farming, logging, establishing governments – are those perceived as "men's work"' (1992: 133). Although many standard histories have presented the West as a masculine and Caucasian space, the impact of women and of native Americans on the West has been reassessed in the last ten or so years. The West was a place of danger in lurid fiction and sensational art. Carl Wimar's *The abduction of Daniel Boone's daughter* (1853) and his *Attack on an emigrant train* (1856), show the West as a place where white settlers are in danger from marauding natives. John Vanderlyn's *The murder of Jane McCrea* (1803–4) shows two

29 Robert Rockwell sculpted the Alaska brown bear for the diorama.

lithe and powerfully built Iroquois with tomahawks about to despatch the hapless, porcelain-skinned women dressed as if for a European dining room.

Far from the stereotypical images of barbaric natives and helpless white women presented by Wimar and Vanderlyn, there are many surviving graphic representations of women in the West and Native Americans that refute the kind of melodramatic presentations given by sensationalist art and literature. There is for example evidence of women on cattle drives, women driving stagecoaches, women owning and running cattle ranches, women sharpshooters and women bandits. It is well known that a Native American woman, Sacajawea, accompanied the Lewis and Clark expedition. The reappraisal of the veracity and validity of this kind of information in the history of art has gone some way towards a revisionist history of the image-making process of the West.

Jimmie Durham, a sculptor, writer and poet of Cherokee heritage, lives and works in Europe. Durham deploys ironic strategies to attack mythologies that stereotype Native Americans in, for example, television Westerns of the 1950s such as *Wagon Train* (1957–65) and *The Rifleman* (1956–62), which formed the image of the West for the post-war generation in Great Britain, Australia and America.[30] For example, co-curating *The American West* at Compton Verney in England, he confounded viewer expectations about cowboys and Indians by presenting a history of resistance. However an earlier exhibition that attempted to contexualise the west beyond the formulaic battle of heroic settler verses the wilderness ran into difficulties. In 'The battle over "The West as America" Alan Wallach makes it clear just how much is at stake in curating an exhibition that shatters long held ideological assumptions (1998a: 105–17). This exhibition, held at the National Museum of American Art in Washington, DC in 1991, explored themes such as 'Inventing the Indian' and 'Repainting the past'. According to Wallach, 'in conquering the West, palette and paintbrush were as much instruments of domination as Colt revolvers or the pony express' (1998a: 106). Citing Frederic Remington's 1903 painting *Fight for the water hole* as an image which revisionist and traditional historians and art historians have contested, Wallach shows that the charge of political correctness that has haunted the 1990s is not really the issue. What Wallach thinks is problematic is the organisers' apparent failure 'to prepare for the inevitable clash of viewpoints over subject matter that for most Americans remains compelling and highly controversial' (1998a: 114–15).

30 William Body in 'Sixty million viewers can't be wrong': the rise and fall of the television Western', estimated that by 1958–9 television Westerns such as *Gunsmoke* represented 26 per cent of total network prime time. He summarised that 'the 570 hours of TV Westerns in the 1958–9 season were estimated to be the equivalent of 400 hours of Hollywood features a year' (1998: 119).

Andy Warhol's late work *Cowboys and Indians* (1986), a portfolio of serigraphs included portraits of a Native American mother and child, John Wayne, Annie Oakley, an elderly Geronimo, General Custer and Teddy Roosevelt, and artefacts from the Museum of the American Indian in New York. Assimilated into celebrity culture and playing with stereotypes, these images revel in the kitsch of the Western myth. However, more recent images of Native Americans by Native Americans have taken the principle of revision and parody further. Kent Monkman's *Artist and model* (2003) replays the artist model myth in the context of cowboy and Indian myths. Set in an indeterminate landscape, the male artist is dressed provocatively in pink high heels, armbands, scant clothing and a long headdress, painting at an easel, brush in one hand, bow and arrow in the other. Tied to a tree, the model, and subject of the schematic representation on the easel, is a St Sebastian-like figure, familiarly pierced by arrows but unfamiliarly depicted with an erect penis, cowboy hat and jeans at the ankles over a pair of cowboy boots.

The contemporary and frequent use of conceptual and performance art has resulted in a range of high-profile public assaults on normative Caucasian values. Performance art has been amply used by aboriginal peoples to comment upon the limited repertoire of 'types' offered by a majority culture. Lori Blondeau's 1997 performance *The lonely surfer squaw* featured a Native American woman in mukluks and fun-fur bikini posing with a huge pink phallus-like surfboard next to a river running through the snow-covered Saskatchewan landscape. The work critiques the stereotyping of aboriginal women as either squaw or Indian princess against the Californian ideal of the blonde beach babe. Another artist, Shelly Niro, a Mohawk from the Six Nations, films her performances and reworks them for the gallery space and catalogue afterlife. In *The shirt* from 2003, nine light boxes record a near life-size Hulleah Tsinhnanjinnie wearing a US flag as a headband and one of America's most successful fashion items, the T-shirt. The slogans across the shirts read, 'My ancestors were annihilated exterminated murdered and massacred', 'They were lied to cheated tricked and deceived', 'Attempts were made to assimilate colonize enslave and displace them' 'And all I get is this shirt'. Niro is concerned by the roles allocated to aboriginal people, and in the photographic exhibition *This land is mime land* she poses family and friends in a range of guises: Marilyn Monroe, (in *The Seven Year Itch*) a character from *Star Trek,* Santa Claus and an Elvis impersonator. In similar vein, but this time subverting language, the Native American conceptual artist James Luna's *The end of the frail* (1993) performance work disrupts the nostalgic and maudlin sentimentalism of James Fraser's 1915 *The end of the trail* at the National Cowboy Museum in Oklahoma City. Coco Fusco and Guillermo Gómez-Peña's performance *Two undiscovered Amerindians visit the West* (1992) was enacted during the anniversary of Columbus's discovery of the Americas. Fusco and Gómez-Peña were presented, caged, to an international public by a guide. The two new 'specimens' (*Guatinaui*) were explained to visitors as if they were new anthropological discoveries.

The special place of key landscape paintings in American art museums is telling: there is a reverential etiquette to display of the most iconic landscapes from the history of American painting in American museums.[31] At the Smithsonian American Art Museum, Bierstadt's painting *Among the Sierra Nevada, California*, is set in a recess to the main corridor of the gallery, framed by a swag of red velvet curtains. A sofa positioned in front of the painting allows two people to simultaneously admire and contemplate the painting. Of course, this is partially a knowing reference to the original terms of display, where Bierstadt would literally have unveiled his work to a paying audience. But the conceit also attests to its place in the cultural and emotional life of Americans.[32]

In her exploration of landscape and national identity entitled *The Empire of the Eye*, Angela Miller has seen a tension in the will towards an artistic nationalism that was 'as ideologically conflicted as political nationalism in its intention of recomposing the elements of individual or local experience into a unitary whole' (1993: 105). Although approaches to landscape art may vary, there is a consistency in the view that landscape is a carrier of powerful meanings about America. Paintings of the West have been important components in the activities of pressure groups to preserve the West and other wilderness areas. If we accept the apocryphal tales as emblematic rather than actual, then a painting could turn a cause with Congress, so that Moran's art helped to establish Yellowstone National Park and Bierstadt's did the same for Yosemite. In fact Moran was described in obituaries as the 'the father of the national parks'. His *The last of the buffalo* led to government legislation to protect the buffalo, and as we showed, Alaska too had its artistic advocates. The capacity that landscape has to marshal causes and shift positions shows how far landscape has the power to communicate a sense of national belonging.

31 Andrew Wyeth's iconic painting, *Christina's world* is not currently so reverentially displayed at MoMA. However, curators are sensitive to its popularity and are reluctant to remove it from permanent display.

32 It was not until 2002 and the showing of *American Sublime: Landscape Painting in the US 1820–1880* at Tate Britain that many Europeans saw classic American landscape paintings first hand and in any number. The show was a revelation to many critics, and it received positive reviews, punctuated with expressions of surprise.

Chapter 5

Accommodating American art

> Cultural categories reflect social distinctions and transform them symbolically from social accomplishments to natural facts.
>
> (DiMaggio 2004: 461)

The struggle to establish permanent national collections in a new country presents the opportunity to start over: to present cultural achievements within frameworks and structures that reflect local aspirations and ideologies. The ideological and material dimensions of an authentically American museum were not however easily determined. The founding father of the new Republic and author of the Declaration of Independence, Thomas Jefferson, was clear that a specifically American form of civic architecture should not draw upon English precedents, but be redolent of democratic virtue. Drawing a veil over its colonising conquests, Jefferson found his progenitors in Imperial Rome, borrowing its rotundas and columns to particular effect for his Virginia State Capital (1791) in Richmond. However, American Roman revival architecture, with its hybrid architectural forms, emerged as much in debt to English as to Roman architecture. This can be seen specifically in buildings that owed much to English Palladian architecture, even if their columns are often adorned with capitals decorated with corn-cobs and tobacco leaves.

If Jeffersonian architecture aspired to be uniquely American, the history of American art also aspired to a manifest destiny that marks an immigrant nation's ideological origins. The quest for an art distinct from European art, separate and yet neither inferior nor derivative, was to embody the 'American democratic experiment'. In 'Telling the Story of America', guiding visitors to the Smithsonian American Art Museum, Elizabeth Broun observed, 'Our national ideal – creating a fair and equal society, with as many freedoms as possible – is a kind of case study for the larger world' (Carbonell 2004: 300). Writing in 1996 in 'Some thoughts about national museums', Roger G. Kennedy (former director of the National Museum of American History, Smithsonian Institution) mused on the diversity that characterised the American experiment while recognising the contradiction inherent in the terms 'nation' and 'national' when used to convey homogeneity. He suggests:

> that citizens of the United States have a responsibility to bring to other peoples the benefits of their special experience in diversity. The best elements of their history demonstrates that, despite our foolishness and cruelties, we have learned from many peoples fiercely determined to retain their apartness while respectfully learning from each other. A national museum in the United States is, or may be, a vastly different place from a national museum in a country more uniform racially or historically. It is a place demonstrating that diversity of cultures can be as fecund of blessings as diversity of species.
>
> (Kennedy 2004: 306)

The burden of creating a national identity in national museums is apparent in the tensions that emerged, particularly in the post-revolution and again the post-bellum period, as the nation came to terms with its own diversity.

Despite the rhetoric presented by Kennedy and Broun there are anomalies, tensions and contradictions in the presentation of American culture in its museums. Writing in the same period as Kennedy, Karen Mary Davalos argued that the formation of the national galleries was predicated on a commitment to Western civilisation, and that visitors were presented with a:

> European-centred vision of what is referred to as an 'American' cultural heritage, a patriotic and sanitized interpretation of the nations' past, an authoritative account of taste. In the public history museums, commitments to founding fathers, heroes of war, and men of capital create an institution that resembles a shrine to patriarchy and capitalism, excluding the role of internal conflict, inequality, and women in the nation.
>
> (Davalos 2004: 521)

The artist in his museum: Charles Willson Peale

The first American *museum* (rather than collection) was conceptualised by the artist and scientist Charles Willson Peale, and housed in Pennsylvania State House, Philadelphia above the room where the Declaration of Independence was signed. The museum can be glimpsed in Peale's 1822 life-sized self-portrait *The artist in his museum*, painted when he was in his eighties (Plate 10). Peale uses the theatrical device of the drawn-back curtain to invite the viewer into the picture and museum beyond. Behind the curtain there are cased natural history specimens lining the museum walls and ordered in Linnaean classification terms.[1]

1 'Linnaeus had regularized the species empirically into clearer groupings, though the idea of a fixed number of species, unvaried since Creation, none added, none disappearing, goes back to Aristotle and was part of the heritage of eighteenth-century classifiers and theorists of species, in American as well as in Europe' (Stein 1998: 57).

In the foreground to the left of Peale is a dead wild turkey ready for taxidermy and transformation into a specimen. The turkey came from the Stephen Long expedition to the Rocky Mountains (1819–20), and was already a candidate for the national emblem (there is another national emblem in the form of the bald eagle positioned above it) in the landmark publication John James Audubon's 1827 folio *Birds of America*, the first plate was of the indigenous wild turkey. The turkey is important for reasons beyond the mere documenting of American wildlife. George-Louis Buffon (1707–1788) and other European naturalists such as Cornelius De Pauw[2] (1734–1799) had underestimated the richness of American natural history, going so far as to argue that populated with regressive peoples, plants and animals, species degenerated in the New World.

Peale was an internationalist rather than a nationalist, but was passionate about America's natural history, and so foregrounding the turkey can be read as a defiant gesture in relation to European hegemony and presumptions about American inferiority. On the dark side of the canvas behind Peale's back is a dimly lit specimen, an indistinct mastodon. This is an important reference for Peale, since he celebrated the discovery of the first specimen in 1806 in *The exhumation of the mastodon*. He had placed the dedication 'Mammoth – the first of American animals, in the first of American Museums' in a pamphlet written by Rembrandt Peale. The mastodon was eventually taken on tour to a sceptical Europe by one of Peale's sons.

So what lessons can be learned from the picture of Peale and his museum? Stein argues that it was not just an exemplification of a set of ideas about American natural history, but was actually about 'shaping consciousness, a way of seeing, a mode of cognition' (1998: 66). In Stein's formulation, Peale was not like dependent European artists, who were usually subject to their patrons' whims; he was instead 'a polymathic citizen seeking to engage the interests of the American public' (Stein 1998: 67). Natural history was a relatively socially inclusive, even classless, pursuit in the nineteenth century, and Peale's private museum of 'natural curiosities promoted his museum as being of use to a wide cross section of society including farmers, merchants and mechanics' (Conn 1998: 35–7). Peale designed his museum as part of a particular epistemology which has its origins in John Locke and the Enlightenment. Locke's empiricist doctrine emphasised experience in the pursuit of knowledge, an important trope in American thought. Locke was a key figure for a new nation trying to define itself, as philosophically he was committed to the 'modern' and rejected the traditional reverence bestowed on the classics. Locke's (1690) *Essay Concerning Human Understanding*

2 See Cornelius De Pauw, *A General History of the Americans* (1771) and A. Gerbi, *The Dispute of the New World* (1955).

supports, through *evidence* of an enormous range of customs and beliefs, the idea that there is no universally innate knowledge, ethical ideas or truths but rather all must be experienced and not imposed by religious (or any other) dogma.

Christopher Looby makes connections between Peale's design for the museum and notions of natural harmony and constructions of social and political order in the nascent nation state. Looby suggests that post-revolutionary America was too diverse to constitute a nation, stating:

> The American republic was as yet a factitious entity, a concocted political framework that gathered together people whose primordial loyalties were attached to local, ethnic, sectarian, and linguistic communities, rather than to the vaguely conceived society. Having established a new state, the revolutionary leaders discovered to their dismay that they had not succeeded in creating a new nation.
>
> (Looby 2004: 145)

Nature was called upon to help conceptualise a nation through its apparent structures and taxonomies, the study of which were in the eighteenth century the subject of considerable debate and false starts. Nonetheless the Linnaean system of classification, which was considered by men such as Jefferson to express a universal language, became annexed to the problem of social unity, or what might be characterised as the adoption of empirical science as a social model. Moreover the Linnaean system, based on exterior and visible characteristics and fixed principles, offered in a natural harmony, a buffer against the social chaos of post-revolutionary disintegration. Looby maintains that in Peale's museum we can see explicitly 'the relation between taxonomic natural sciences and political order' (2004: 154). The authorisation for this presentation came from 'portraits Peale had painted of the heroes of the Revolution, presiding over the rational order of things, of which they were the superior extension' (Looby 2004: 154).

Forming a national museum

It would not be unreasonable to expect a national museum to follow in the wake of Peale's early nineteenth-century museum in Philadelphia – particularly given Peale's appeal 'To the citizens of the United States of America', a letter written as a respectful address and published in Dunlap's *American Daily Advertiser*, Philadelphia on 13 January 1792. 'Bent on enlarging the collection...promising to be useful in advancing knowledge and the arts; ... all that is likely to be beneficial, curious or entertaining to the citizens of the new world', Peale wished through the generosity of other patrons to see 'this tender plant ... grow into full maturity, and become a *National Museum*' (original italics) (Peale 1792/2004: 130). However, Alan Wallach argues that the plans for the formation of a national museum in the antebellum period were a series of 'thwarted impulses towards the institutionalisation of high art' (1998c: 18). In short, the political kept getting in the way of any unified vision.

One way forward was for art to be divested of its political and social implications and presented purely – that is, without context. The complex role of education within the art museum often clashed with the aspirations to develop taste which rid museums of any pedagogic obligation:

> Thus, during the post-Civil War period, as a national upper class emerged, the public art museum – with its promise of canonical histories of art a relatively uniform set of aesthetic criteria – became not only an urgent necessity but also, given the class's new strength, a real possibility.
>
> (Wallach 1998c: 21)

Wallach's point is that in the six decades leading up the Civil War, 'Upper-class Americans may have dreamt of an American Louvre but elites were … far too weak and divided to cooperate in the creation of national cultural institutions' (1998c: 9). Drawing on the sociologist DiMaggio, he argues that three conditions needed to coexist in order for permanent national institutions to emerge: first, *elite entrepreneurship*, second, *classification*, and third, *framing* (1998c: 10–11). Crucially what needed to be established in the public's consciousness, rather than merely affirmed in a minority elite, was a clear distinction between high art and popular art.

P. T. Barnum's American Museum

Davalos (2004) has remarked on the low status of 'the side show, the circus, and the curio shop' compared with the high status of the museum. The struggle to create and maintain firm distinctions between high and popular culture can be read out of the colourful history of P. T. Barnum's American Museum (Plate 11). Barnum's enterprises, from museum to sideshow to circus, blurred the now familiar separation of entertainment (frivolous) and the art museum (worthy). At least until the early 1930s the museum and circus were fellow travellers. In the years leading up to the Civil War, Phineas Taylor Barnum (1810–1891), the self-declared 'prince of humbug', was best known as the showman behind 'The Greatest Show on Earth'. However Barnum was also a pioneer in what is currently termed 'edutainment', and an astute business man alert to marketing strategies.

P. T. Barnum's American Museum was housed from 1841 to 1865 in lower Manhattan. The building, festooned with flags and banners, advertised its wares accompanied by bands playing in the street. Quite unlike early modernism's enthusiasm for specialisation and secure classification, Barnum's museum was an eclectic mix, perhaps with roots in European medieval markets with their concoction of display, knowledge and amusement. Without the hierarchy that we have come to expect of modern museums, Barnum shared a belief in a moral and pedagogic purpose coupled to albeit often gratuitous, uplifting fervour. Twenty-five cents would buy the visitor an eccentric jumble of sensational 'freak show', instructional displays of natural history (some stuffed animals were purchased from Charles Willson Peale's collection), Shakespearian plays (but shorter), as well as morally improving history paintings. The museum assembled an aquarium, menagerie and waxworks as well as displays on temperance reform. The commerce between men of science and the showman is a measure of the lack of firm distinction in categories: professional and wondrous curio. Scientists were called upon to add validation, provenance or genealogy to dodgy specimens and unclassified curiosities, or add credibility to the account of many a fraudulent 'freak'. Even Peale had displayed human curiosities, although he eventually rejected the extraordinary body in favour of less sensational and more scientific displays. However it was not unusual to *display* Native Americans and African-Americans, who often attracted the attention of the burgeoning scientific and philosophical societies attending Barnum's extravaganzas.

By the mid-1800s museums and showmen had to compete for customers. Barnum's American Museum had a reputation for sensational exhibits including Tom Thumb, Siamese twins and fraudulent specimens such as the Fejee (sic) Mermaid (in reality a 'combine' made up of a monkey and a fish). However, it can also be argued that the American Museum represented a distinctly new urban experience which allowed differing social classes to mix freely. The museum was, for instance, one of the few places that middle-class women could go alone without censure. However, as the country moved towards civil war, racial tensions can also be read out of the museum's admission policy. In New York, the gradual emancipation of black people had been achieved but that did not stop segregation or the tendency to form social hierarchies based on race. Most public entertainment spaces were white only: Barnum's American Museum was no exception. However by 1849 Barnum advertised:

> Notice to Persons of Color – In order to afford respectable colored persons an opportunity to witness the extraordinary attractions at present exhibited at the Museums, the Manager has determined to admit this class of people on Thursday next, March 1, from 8 A.M. till 1 P.M.
>
> (Cook n.d.)

Contemporary theory suggests that the showing of 'freaks' keyed into the dominate group's need to confirm its own normalcy: that is, a reassurance that white Anglo-Saxon values were ascendant. And although Barnum (who was also a politician) renounced his former slave owning and proposed universal male suffrage in an amendment to the Connecticut Constitution in 1865, *difference* and *exoticism* between peoples were the hallmarks of his spectacles of living curiosities.

Barnum's first museum burned down spectacularly in 1865 and so too did a second in 1869. He then began his touring shows, which were discussed briefly in Chapter 3. DiMaggio noted in relation to the transformation of the Boston Museum of Fine Arts to firmer and more elevated classification systems, that in its early years:

> The bulk of its holdings consisted of reproductions. Charles Sumner had given a set of Curiosities, another donor had provided seven Egyptian mummies, and others had loaned such objects as a Philippine chain cutlass, a buffalo horn, and an old sled from Freisland and Zulu weapons .... While the casts [plaster casts of mostly European sculpture] remained central, the more Barnumesque items were soon discarded.
>
> (DiMaggio 2004: 463)

Drawing on contemporary newspaper reports of the deaccessioned parts of the collection, it was noted caustically that '"The common people will turn to [the items] gladly, if they are not appreciated by those of artistic and travel-improved taste"' (DiMaggio 2004: 463). DiMaggio also noted that as early as the 1880s museums had started to distance themselves from the amateur and the commercial: and of course Barnum excelled at both. Donna Haraway has also written about the distance that the taxidermist Akeley (whose legendary dioramas are still the highlight of a visit to the National History Museum in New York) put between himself and fakery. 'He stuffed Barnum's Jumbo' [killed by a train in 1885], she wrote, 'but he wanted no part of the great circus magnate's cultivation of the American popular art form, the hoax' (1984: 40).

One of the effects of the transformation of museums into more elevated classification systems was to relegate (or even not purchase) American art. It was damned twice: once through its association with commercial activity and second because it lacked the authority of European art. Such a move also reinforced the distinctions between high and low art, between the popular and fine art. While we cannot offer a comprehensive history of the American museum within the limits of this publication, it is worth noting that the dime museums that were popular until the turn of the century extended across the whole country, and were still up to the 1940s advertising freak shows and live acts, in stark contrast to the quiet reverence that was beginning to haunt the orthodox museum, as the side-show and 'freak' headed for the circus and theatre. Museums headed for firmer classification against their association with the circus, but they continued to be advertised as travelling museums in tandem with the circus.

Robert Bogdan notes the blurring of the taxonomic boundaries: issuing from the dime museum 'even into the [1940s] there were probably a dozen traveling freak shows with the word museum in their titles' (1988: 38). Moreover, he notes that museums began to travel with the circus as concessions. As early as 1837 the first circus 'to advertise as a menagerie, circus and museum was Waring, Raymond and Co' (Bogdan 1988: 41). The range of attractions at P. T. Barnum's Museum, Menagerie and Circus of the early 1870s, where the museum was prominent in the form of a sideshow, included 'twenty vans of waxworks, dioramas, mechanical figures' (Bogdan 1988: 41). The fate of the dioramas, waxworks and other forms of reproduction, placed in the museum alongside the authentic and acceptable to most in the eighteenth and early nineteenth century, came increasingly under pressure as museums became apologists for the national character and signifiers of power on an international stage. It was not until the mid-1870s and the arrival of the 'The Greatest Show on Earth' that 'museum' disappeared from Barnum's title. In 1871 the travelling museum was still paraded under the banner 'P. T. Barnum's Grand Traveling Museum, Menagerie, Caravan & Hippodrome'.

The Barnum Museum in Connecticut (originally a Barnum enterprise) is housed in an eclectic building drawing on Byzantine, Islamic, Gothic and the Romanesque motifs. It opened in 1893 under the perhaps surprising title of the Barnum Institute of Science and History. Although it has had a chequered history it still retains something of Barnum's showmanship, with a replica of his library and a 1,000 square foot miniature of Barnum's circus. It includes 3,000 miniature figures, an exhibition about Tom Thumb and a 2500 year old Egyptian mummy, testament to an age of curiosity unfettered by subject boundaries and the incursions of science that explained human differences 'by medicalizing human variation' (Bogdan 1988: 67) and added to the disenchantment of the world and an end to the display (at least in this form) of 'others'. The point is an important one: as well as the display of 'oddities' Barnum was the most successful entrepreneur to establish differences, which included the display of Native Americans, African-Americans and Asians ('the Korean Twins' and 'Chang, the Chinese giant'), and Australians – all contributing to knowledge of 'what we are not'. Linked to scientific and news stories of the day, 'freaks' were presented within popular quasi-journalistic and pedagogic modes. Half-absorbed scientific facts were wilfully connected with the fraudulent and the fanciful. What is perhaps important is that many *foreign* people were displayed alongside people with disabilities, and through narratives of differences in customs and eating habits, while others were eroticised and exoticised as 'other', as 'wild, weird and wonderful'. In a nation of immigrants it is interesting to speculate on how this was received and assimilated.

Tattooed bodies as changing signifiers

Tattooed bodies were often a feature of freak shows in Europe and America, one of the wonders of the eighteenth-century exploration of the world. In particular tattooed people from the Far East, the South Sea islands and South America were identified as primitive by the nineteenth century. We see in the earliest images of Native Americans, the Inuit, the North Carolina Algonquians and the Timucuans of Florida recorded by Jacques Le Moyne de Morgues around 1564, widespread use of body painting and tattoos. Pictured by John White in the 1580s and diminished by water damage, his paintings nonetheless show clearly that body adornment was related to class and power in much the same way that it was in Europe. In *The wyfe of an Herowan of Secotan*, Wingina was 'pownced': that is, tattooed in blue on her face, arms and legs (Plate 12).

It has been argued by Joyce E. Chaplin in 'Roanoke counterfeited according to the truth' (the latter phrase borrowed from White's description of his work) that White's images of non-threatening, smiling natives placed in a theatrical setting were a counterfeit staged to encourage colonisation: a 'propaganda campaign intended to promote the tiny English outpost' (2007: 51). In the first encounter with the Roanoke Algonquins by the English lead party in 1584, Amadas, Barlowe and Ferdinando brought a report of 'very handsome, and goodly people, and in their behaviour as mannerly, and civil, as any of Europe' (Morison 1971: 624). Moreover, far from the savage, tattooed and bloodthirsty Indian of nineteenth century legend, Barlowe wrote that:

> Wee found the people most gentle, loving and faithful, void of all guile and treason, and such as lived after the manner of the golden age. The earth bringeth foorth all things in aboundance, as in the first creation, without toile or labour.
>
> (quoted in Morison 1971: 624)

The references to the Garden of Eden and the golden age recur throughout the early years of European first encounter, and indeed predate the actual landings, as in imagination America (or what was perceived as the land to the East) was variously perceived as Eldorado, Edenic, Paradise and so on. What is important here is that the native body complete with painted or tattooed adornment could be overwritten before adornment became war-paint, and did not always signify as primitive and violent, at least during the optimistic days of colonisation when local knowledge was a precondition to survival.

The tattooed native also appears in Benjamin West's revolutionary depiction of a modern heroic 'history' painting, *The death of General Wolfe* (1770). In the foreground appears a powerfully built, tattooed Native

American, a model of restraint reflecting in *Thinker*-like pose on the unfolding of a seminal moment, the British army's defeat of the French at Quebec. If the Americanness of the painting lies in West's rejection of Roman dress, the traditional form of classicising historical subjects, for the actual details of the day, the native remains something of an enigma in the work.

Subsequently the Native American painted body in the days of frontier disputes was reconfigured to contribute to the image of the primitive. Although white bodies sporting tattoos by the 1800s could be a profitable sideshow, especially accompanied by an exotic and erotic narrative about how they were come by, it is the depiction of the tattooed body in paintings that concerns us here. Tattooed bodies were routinely advertised as 'The Living Picture-Gallery': Barnum used the phrase to promote tattooed exhibits in dime museums and side shows, and the American Museum exhibited a new exotic, a white tattooed person, as early as 1840 (before Barnum took over) (Bogdan 1988: 243). Fuelled by changing ideas about the ways physical and psychic attributes were connected, the tattoo has changing significations. Initially it was seen as evidence of status and power, but early anthropologists and Charles Darwin rewrote the tattoo as a sign of primitivism, evident in the ability to bear pain for the purposes of decoration and paganism. By the mid-1800s it had become a sign of sexual permissiveness and criminality, a conception particularly evident in the work of the crimionologist and anthropologist Cesare Lombroso (1890s). As the practice of tattooing offered alternative career prospects, women increasingly displayed their living human art galleries for viewing with the added frisson of an erotic charge. Interestingly stories of the enforced acquisition of tattoos were an important part of the narrative supporting the bodily display, and by the 1880s women regularly told of tattoos forced upon them when captured (and then miraculously saved) in encounters with hostile natives in the Wild West (Bogdan 1988).

Cast galleries: the pianola of the arts[3]

> The number of casts in US collections was enormous: by 1890 the Boston Museum of Fine Arts owned 777, the third largest in the world after the Royal Museum in Berlin (2,271) and the University at Strasbourg (819).
>
> (Wallach 1998b: 41)

As we have seen, throughout much of the nineteenth century casts after works of art were not considered to be secondary or diminished experiences

3 A phrase taken from Whitehill (1970: 202).

of an original work. On the contrary, cast courts were often the jewel in an American museum's crown. So although it would be tempting to consider the enthusiasm for a replica of Michelangelo's *David*, or a full-scale Parthenon frieze, as compensation for an 'impoverished' culture far removed from European civilisation, such a view would miss the distinctive ways that such works functioned historically. Wallach insists that 'Cast collections were not an oddity or a transient fashion but the central attraction of American art museums during the years between 1874–1905' (1998b: 46). He further argues that cast collections were 'neither anomalies nor stopgaps but integral to their [the museums'] purpose, some of which was popular education' (1998b: 49). They were also part of a developing American culture in competition with Europe and 'staking ... claim to the heritage of western civilisation, symbolized above all by the sculpture and architecture of Greco-Roman antiquity and the Italian Renaissance' (1998b: 46).

DiMaggio, writing about the cast collection at Boston's Museum of Fine Arts (MFA), commented upon the 'battle of the casts' (2004: 465). He distinguished between casts as an educational tool, and mechanically reproduced to boot, and the powerful belief that art had to be original to be a transcendent object of contemplation. Prosaic education and the need for a quiet aesthetic experience were seen, not for the last time, as irreconcilable. While this argument was also heard in Europe, particularly in the notion of *significant form* and the appeal to sensibility rather than learning in the work of Roger Fry and Clive Bell in Edwardian England, in America the stakes were higher. In a culture unencumbered by an aristocracy and still bound to democratic idealism and now the purchasing power to improve the 'quality' of the collections, the decision to banish the 'mechanical sculpture' of casts to the basement and to consider art in terms of aesthetic experience alone (Whitehill 1970: 202) was an important one.

The vanquished cast courts and the urge to buy usually foreign artworks had far-reaching consequences. The collection at MFA bereft of its cast collections was organised into a classification system based on period and nation, and the division between high art and popular was enshrined and legitimated. This pattern was repeated in most but by no means all museums, one result being a narrowing of canonical art and the development of a more class-based audience. The new aestheticism required leisure time and class confidence in the ineffable and the ambiguity of the unspoken, and so in the main became the preserve of upper and middle-class taste. What is important is the understanding that classification systems, including the divisions between genres and high and popular art, were ideological rather than *natural*, and need not have taken the forms of exhibiting that they did.

The first casts in America played the same civilising role of refining the brutish and bringing solace and beauty to the labouring poor as they had done in Europe. But cast collections, which often comprehensively displayed works that it was not possible to view as originals, were also about learning skills, understanding proportion and ideal beauty, and the values and beliefs attributed to earlier civilisations. By the early 1900s the great plaster cast collections had been dismantled and disowned as in need of constant correction 'by reference to the ... original ancient sculptures in the classical galleries' (Wallach 1998b: 50). Accounting for the about-turn and seemingly aesthetic embarrassment, Wallach conjectures that the rise of wealth of the 'robber barons'[4] resulted in the financial ability to collect originals, and so the distinction between original and 'fake' became an important one.

In drawing up a composite picture of 'the ideal museum visitor', Wallach proposes an individual 'no longer a man steeped in classical learning but the gentleman art lover, an amateur, a man of aristocratic taste, perhaps even a connoisseur who took pleasure in his unique ability to discern aesthetic quality'. The acquisition of taste therefore 'served as a cornerstone of elite or upper-class culture, distinguishing it from all that was commonplace and ordinary' (1998b: 108). Interestingly it was only the unique artwork that groomed the facility for taste. The demise of cast collections, as we saw in Chapter 2, coincided with several other national and international revisions about the role and function of the museum. The late nineteenth century European collections had been partially annexed to social reform, self-improvement, linked to enhanced performance in industry, particularly furniture and domestic decoration. The slightly later museums in America were quick to pick up on many aspects of the links between industry and art, as seen in the Arts and Industry Building in Washington and even in Boston's original Museum of Fine Art. By the early twentieth century the cast courts were dispersed or deaccessioned under the belief that only encounters with original artworks could transport the viewer out of the ordinary and everyday. The charge of crass materialism, all too easily laid at the door of American industrialists, could be leavened by a retreat to a secular space freed from the troubling commerce of daily life.

The enthusiasm for a cast of a significant classical sculpture has been revived in the shopping mall ethos of major galleries. The Metropolitan Museum of Art in New York had its own reproduction studio, and often museums swapped casts to make up a full set.[5] However, as originals came to replace copies and as casts acquired a greater pedagogical role, 'there was a concomitant and increasing subject specialisation, such as also occurred in ethnography: once the preserve of the curious, doctors and amateur travel-

4 'Robber baron' is the term given to the monopoly capitalists of the Gilded Age (a term coined by Mark Twain), who gained huge wealth from the development of industrialisation.

5 For instance 'In 1819 the trustees of the British Museum were approached by the French for a set of casts of the Elgin Marbles in return for one of the Parthenon metopes' (Wilson 2002: 127).

ler, transformed into a discipline with its own university chair and museum' (Marchand 2000: 195). The transformation of ethnography gave 'rise to prominence of stylistic analysis' as a means of understanding objects. This is not a deviation from the development of art collections, but central to the later development of aesthetics and museum design and display, as a comprehensive understanding of *style* came to dominate museum collections, and the impulse to organise and explain material culture overcame the dominance of classicism, which survives only in pale imitation.

The fall of the cast collections was important as a staging post in refocusing the art museum away from education and learning, and towards the acquisition of taste, therefore the effective preserve of middle-class elites. The Victoria and Albert museum in London kept its cast courts, but they were dismantled in the United States as they were in Europe, as a more authentic experience rather than learning was sought. Much was made of the democratic and nation-building potential of the museum through citizenship (see Preziosi 2003), and education was therefore foregrounded (indeed early educational initiatives including the development of docent tours in Boston Museum of Fine Art for the general public were instrumental in increasing museum audiences). In tandem with much of Europe, by the 1920s museums in the United States were becoming apologists for class-based elitism. Therefore by the mid-twentieth century education was dispatched to the basement and became the almost exclusive preserve of women and volunteers.

The American Wing

> AMERICAN ART REALLY EXISTS. Collection in New Wing of the Metropolitan Museum Refutes Critics of U.S. Culture.[6]

In 1924 the 'American Wing' was opened in the Metropolitan Museum, New York. An extension to the structure of the original museum, the American Wing (subsequently extensively remodelled) included a set of period rooms featuring domestic interior decoration of the nineteenth and twentieth centuries. The American Wing was instrumental in disseminating popular knowledge about America's artistic past and Americana. In Dianne H. Pilgrim's formulation, 'Americans first had to become convinced that they had a culture before that culture could be promoted' (1978: 4). Americans, mobilised by the growth of the automobile industry in the 1920s, were now able to visit historic houses and reconstructions of communities

6 Headline taken from an illustration in Marshall B. Davidson, 'Those American things' (1970).

such as Williamsburg and Sturbridge, and the American Wing reflected the growing national interest in American heritage.

The confirmation of the existence of American art, announced in the jubilant headline of one newspaper, through the opening of the period rooms at the Metropolitan Museum was oddly out of date. R. T. H. Halsey (1865–1943), curator for the American Wing, had an anti-modernising agenda. As Kaplan has observed, 'The American Wing was Halsey's hymn to individual achievement and his rejection of the values of the machine age.' (1982: 47). Kaplan suggests that the designation of the year 1825 as the 'cutoff date' for the period installations in the American Wing was meaningful, signalling Halsey's view that industrialisation had destroyed the craftsmanship of early Americana, rendering all that followed uncollectable. This was quite contrary to the prevailing modernism and machine aesthetic. In 1925 the International Exposition of Decorative Arts and Modern Industry in Paris had a lasting impact upon American manufacture of consumer goods.[7] MoMA the nation's first major museum devoted to modern art opening in 1929 took a contrary view to Halsey, setting up the world's first curatorial department devoted to modern architecture and design in 1932. The collection is a showcase of the modern design movement, which demonstrates its Arts and Crafts roots and highlights its seminal designs. Significantly MoMA's 1934 exhibition *Machine Art* demonstrated that tenable links between art and industry were being drawn in a fine-art context. *Machine Art* was a corrective to the period rooms, where industrial gadgets – engines, pistons and propellers – were exhibited as aesthetic objects and placed on pedestals and mounted on walls, in just the same way as curators exhibit paintings and sculptures.

Period rooms became popular at the beginning of the twentieth century, gaining a fillip through the national displays at the World's Fairs. Although they were initially set up to improve design and manufacturing of domestic goods, it is their use as a site of patriotism that is the focus here. According to McClellan, 'Recognition of the patriotic potential of period rooms quickly spread across Europe to the United States where their popular appeal qualified them for the indoctrination of new immigrants' (2003: 16). As evidence he cites from documentation published at the opening of the American Wing at the Metropolitan Museum in New York in 1924. It states:

> The American Wing cannot fail to revive [memories of past traditions] for here for the first time is a comprehensive, realistic setting for the

7 Jane N. Law has demonstrated the impact of the 1925 International Exposition of Decorative Arts and Modern Industry in Paris on American manufacture of consumer goods. See 'Designing the dream' (1986).

> traditions so dear to us and so invaluable for the Americanization of our many people, to whom much of our history is little known.
>
> (quoted in McClellan 2003: 16)

On the anniversary of the opening of the American Wing in 1954, the Keeper Lydia B. Powel reflected, 'The American Wing grew and prospered because both historically and psychologically we had, as a nation, arrived at a moment when we could pause to look back and revalue our past' (1954: 194). The occasions and opportunities for Americans to reflect on their past had increased exponentially, with period rooms opening in museums in Brooklyn, Philadelphia and the public opening of Henry Francis du Pont Winterthur Museum in Delaware in 1951.

Period rooms of Americana served another insidious function, contributing to the processes of assimilating people new to America by example. The Daughters of the American Revolution (DAR) and the Society of Colonial Dames ran patriotic educational schemes which advocated 'a loyalty that consisted essentially of willing submissiveness' (Higham 1955: 236–7). In the DAR headquarters in Washington, DC there are multiple period rooms, each sponsored by a different state organisation of the national society. Importantly the period rooms represented regional characteristics and identity, and they were also an induction into consumer culture and the rapid assimilation of immigrants into an Anglo-Saxon definition of an American.

To return to the opening addresses of 1924 we find a more modest ambition for period rooms. The various speakers applauded the opening of a specifically American wing in the vast spaces of the Metropolitan Museum, which was largely a showcase for a vast collection of European and Asian arts, for a range of distinct reasons. First it was an act of patriotism which recalled the founding of the American nation. Robert W. DeForest also wondered if 'American domestic art was not a chapter, or at least a paragraph, in the history of art' (in Carbonell 2004: 290). The speakers were aware of the difficulties such a novel move uncovered. First, was there anything distinctively American worth showing against the domestic achievements of, say, French furniture and the porcelains and jades of China? The solution of placing American domestic arts in period rooms was a response to the realisation that the 'homely productions of American household art quarreled with the great rooms of the Museum' (Honorable Elihu Root, in Carbonell 2004: 294) and domestic art of the American colonial period shown in individual cases 'lost [their] distinctive charm of simplicity and that it could be adequately shown only in the modest rooms for which it was made' (DeForest in Carbonell 2004: 290).

The rooms were shown in historic sequence from the earliest period to the first quarter of the twentieth century, while a modest colonial garden was fronted by the façade of the old Assay Office (bank). Regarded to be authentic *facts* of a previous age, the rooms were also considered to give to the nation's ancestors a human quality. While a history of American ancestors had emphasised self-reliance, love of liberty and so on, the exhibition was also considered to add warmth and beauty to an understanding of earlier lives:

> We get a new idea of the character of that wonderful formative power that has shaped the development of this great nation from the Atlantic to the Pacific, a power transcending the proportions of numerical relation and asserting itself over the vast multitudes of other races that have come in. We get a better understanding of that as we begin to understand the humanity of the people from whom it sprang.
>
> (Root, in Carbonell 2004: 294)

Extolling the virtues of simplicity (a constant theme in the formation of art and character) and crucially a belief in love of beauty without 'softness and luxury', (2004: 294) Root connects to a leavened Puritanism.

Seeking a perpetual or permanent museum

Although the permanent collection housed in a landmark building, increasingly associated with a celebrity architect, is desired as an international coming of age, as a marker of power it came much later to the United States than to France or England, Germany or Holland. What is now the Smithsonian American Art Museum (SAAM) was initiated in 1829, and became the first federal art collection. Growing out of a European collection belonging to Washington resident, John Varden, it was not until the rationalising of the museums of the Smithsonian in 1980 that it became the National Museum of American Art. In 2000 with congressional approval its current title, the Smithsonian American Art Museum, was taken, and it is now housed in the recently refurbished (2006) landmark Greek-Revival Patent Office Building dating from 1836.

Since the 1980s the collection has been committed wholly to the work of artists in the United States. It is situated with the National Portrait Gallery, a juxtaposition that acts as a reminder about the importance of portraiture in early American art, and that images of national character determine the formation of visual perceptions of Americans. It represents over 7,000 artists, and showcases works by established non-American-born artists such as David Hockney and Nam June Paik, reminding us that American identity is a liquid concept. Also represented are works and artists as diverse as the untrained James Hampton, who is represented by *The Throne of the Third Heaven of the Millennium General Assembly* (c. 1950–64) a colossal work of gold and silver aluminum foil; *La mano poderosa* [The all-powerful hand] attributed to Caban group c. 1875–1925); Justin McCarthy's *Washington crosses the Delaware variation of a theme no. 3* (c. 1963); and Edmonia

Lewis and Robert Rauschenberg. The strong representation of African-American art and Latino art, an assured presence, reflects recent American demographic changes, and also perhaps a reflection that previously invisible communities are less willing to remain mute when faced with publicly funded bodies that fail to represent the cultural plurality that is part of the radicalism of the United States. Also solidly represented are folk art, contemporary craft, and New Deal projects normally under-represented outside of specialist collections, as well as the familiar: American impressionism and abstraction.

The National Gallery of Art, located on the National Mall in Washington, DC, was formed from the collection of financier Andrew W. Mellon. Designed by architect John Russell Pope who also designed the Parthenon Gallery at the British Museum, the building opened in 1941 and was the largest marble structure in the world – and perhaps inevitably given Mellon's enthusiasm for the European museum model, neoclassical in style. Patronage played an important role in the formation of the collection. The received history and relatively narrow canon of American art is enshrined in the National Gallery. Such a history typically begins chronologically with the portraiture of colonial and federal American art, epitomised by Benjamin West, John Singleton Copley and Gilbert Stuart. It changed into a different register following the aspirations of the period after the Revolutionary War (1783), which sought a new sensibility that would celebrate and embody revolutionary liberty, allied to an enthusiasm for scientific naturalism. This tendency is found in the works of Charles Willson Peale and his ubiquitous family, with their Old Master names: Rembrandt, Raphaelle and so on.

Still following in chronological mode, the society's dominant ideals, based on European romanticism (particularly French romanticism, which chimed with the revolutionary imperatives of the American Revolution), were reinterpreted in America by West and his pupils Thomas Sully and John Trumbull. Landscape painting documented the growing awareness of native peoples and America's distinctive flora and fauna, particularly in the works of John James Audubon and George Catlin's extraordinary works documenting portraits of native Americans. Moving on, the nineteenth century invested in nationalistic expressions through landscape painting, particularly of the diminishing West, a style that found powerful advocates in the Hudson River school and Thomas Cole, George Caleb Bingham, Frederic Edwin Church and Albert Bierstadt. The necessity of a grand tour of Europe to search out the paintings of Turner and other artistic luminaries seems to mark American artists' dependency on European models of art practice.

At the time of the Civil War another form of realism took hold, through the works of Eakins and Homer. Notions of truth telling begin to seep into the literature. In tandem with the rise in urbanisation and huge numbers of immigrants, a new reality to be found in the excitement and discontent of city life was depicted by the Ashcan school and amongst others, Robert

Henri, Glackens and John Sloan. The history of twentieth-century American art is more contentious, as the urge to internationalism marked a move away from the perceived parochial to explore international avant-gardes. The tensions between those who still chose to depict homespun ideals (such as the much maligned regionalists of the 1930s and 1940s), other forms of realism represented by Edward Hopper and Bellows, and the abstractionists can be seen in the divisions in display in several major collections, where overtly American (in subject matter or style) material is displayed separately from works by artists whose Americanism was deemed capable of expressing international values. The influence of European modernists (particularly surrealists) escaping war-torn Europe is often credited with providing the theoretical and technical means through which American art comes of age. The art-historical argument asserts that by the 1950s, and crucially immediately after the Second World War, a unique form of American expression is ready to take centre international stage. By the 1970s American post war modernism has its own wing of the National Gallery, designed by I.M. Pei.

Community museums

In contrast to the tidy national display outlined above, Davalos accentuated the failure of new American museums to 'shake off the evolutionary model' which refers to non-European art as 'primitive, traditional, folk or exotic' (2004: 521). She offered ways forward in relation to community museums, while remaining cautionary. Handing control of representation to 'source people' may be one solution; self-representation in museums however can also reinforce stereotypes and merely replicate the repressive structures of traditional national museums. Established, legitimated taxonomies constructed as periods, schools and styles do not always fit neatly on to, for instance, Chicano and Mexicano museums with their emphasis on community and lack of firm distinctions between the categories of art and artefact.

Davalos was writing of the first Mexican museum in the Midwest: the Mexican Fine Arts Centre Museum (MFACM) which opened in 1987 in Chicago's largely Mexican Pilsen neighbourhood. She cites an early exhibition, *The Amart Tradition: Innovation and Dissent in Mexican Art* (1995), as an example of the 'mixing of aesthetic styles and display techniques ... [that] can rupture ... ethnographic or artistic approach(es) to objects' which use hybridity that could act as a message of 'affirmation, liberation and resistance' (2004: 529). *Amate* (bark paper) paintings, often forms of figurative realism with strong narratives, are made by Nahua artists from the Alto Balsas region in the state of Guerrero: *amates* are souvenirs, tourist art. However, in the exhibition, while *amates* were acknowledged as souvenirs they were also 'reposition[ed] ... as historically and politically situated objects of fine art' (Davalos 2004: 529). As well as landscapes, local and autobiographical scenes, *amates* often represent political and social dissent, a feature of the exhibition. In one instance such works highlighted images of protest over the contentious construction of a hydroelectric dam at San Juan Tetelcingo. Moreover the exhibition atypically emphasised the usually anonymous 'tourist souvenir artists' through the wide use of photographs. In the display the artists were given primacy and crucially context, a move away from traditional fine-art galleries' hagiographic individualism which accompanies the work of photographers. Davalos claims the exhibition 'interrogated the art/culture distinction and suggests an alternative hybrid location for the amate as souvenirs of resistance' (2004: 530). How and where to display the *amate* is a recent example of a historic problem. The rumbling discontent between advocates of community museums and populist art, and the apologists of the universal museum marked by distinction and the identification of excellence, make up some of the most interesting skirmishes in American art institutions' history. However questioning western cultural orders has become something of an orthodoxy in museums, as we shall see.

John Cotton Dana's New Museum

A pioneer of community museums, John Cotton Dana (1856–1929) was concerned that rather than developing a distinctly American set of values, the rapidly multiplying civic museums of the late nineteenth and early twentieth century replicated what he saw as inappropriate European models. On the funding of museums with taxpayers' money, he noted that:

> they [the people] would get no pleasure or profit out of the kinds of museums which kings, princes, and other masters of people and wealth had constructed; and so, being ruled by precedent or fashion, as were also their rich donors, their important citizen-trustees, and their architects, they voted for, or silently approved, spending public money for the old kinds of museums. They cared more to be in fashion than they did to get something useful and enjoyable.
>
> (Dana 1999: 190)

Dana, whose regard for culture was guided by Thorstein Veblen (1857–1929), believed that context was more important than aesthetics in the design of museum displays.[8] He founded the ground-breaking Newark Museum in 1909 and published his ideas in *The New Museum* in 1917.[9] Following European precedents, where the pedagogic foundation of the museums was being eroded by the cult of the curator and the shift away

8 In opposition to 'the object as contemplative piece', peddled by curators such as Boston's Benjamin Ives Gilman.

9 Republished in 1999 as *The New Museum: Selected Writings by John Cotton Dana* by the American Association of Museums.

from education to collecting, conservation and connoisseurship, Dana witnessed museums becoming storehouses for European art and playgrounds for the great and the good. Far removed from the ordinary, everyday American experience, Dana maintained that old European masters and precious objects from Asia, assiduously and jealously collected, were often irrelevant to the lives of working people.

Approaches to viewing art also fell under his scrutiny. Dana dismissed as cant the notion that merely gazing at great objects through aestheticism alone was enough to improve and elevate the viewer. According to Bruce Ford, 'He did not believe that any aesthetic norms were immutable' (2006: 2). Going against the grain of received taste and wisdom, which valorised the Ancients in relation to museum architecture, Dana 'went so far as to predict that in the future the architecture of ancient Greece might fall into disfavor' (Ford 2006: 2). For him, engagement, education and full public access were crucial to the democratising of culture, and therefore should be a museum's founding principles. An early advocate of what is once again being legislated as good museum practice, he also sought ways to increase cooperation between schools, libraries and museums as well as developing a pioneering museum studies course.

Deploring snobbery, Dana:

> boldly assert[ed] that beauty bears no relation to age, rarity, or price. To encourage recognition and enjoyment of beauty in commonplace things, he once exhibited well-designed pottery that he had procured from a five-and ten-cent store, proudly announcing that not a single piece had cost more than twenty-five cents.
>
> (Ford 2006: 2)

Dana's display bore comparison with a department store aesthetic, approaching visitors as 'customers' in a non-elitist environment which embraced the building, the collection and approaches to education. Indeed he stated that 'A great department store, easily reached, open at all hours, is more like a good museum of art than any of the museums we have yet established' (Hadley 1943: 68). His mantra of 'Learn what aid the community needs ... and fit the museum to those needs' (Weil 2002: 190) was in sharp contrast to the rapidly developing national museums. Moreover, Dana, who tellingly was also a pioneer in librarianship, campaigning for public access to open stacks without chaperoning by library staff, believed the public came before the collection.

Also fundamental to Dana's commitment to access was a firm belief in the power of art and artefact to enrich people's lives. That did not simply mean aping the manners and language of Europeans and increasingly an American elite. Aligning himself with personal freedom and cultural pluralism, Dana was dissatisfied with curator's prioritising of collection over audience: 'Dana

... chided both schools and museums for telling people what they ought to appreciate, maintaining that by doing so they encouraged hypocrisy – the greatest impediment to the genuine sensibility' (Ford 2006: 2). Of the many exhibitions that he was responsible for at Newark, one of the first was the 1912 show *Modern German Applied Arts*, of applied art produced by the Deutscher Werkbund. He also encouraged Holger Cahill to organise exhibitions of folk art, and in 1923 fronted a touring show on Chinese art.

Much of Dana's philosophy can be found in the expanded museum field developed during the New Deal era: Dana died in 1929 on the eve of the Great Depression that followed the Wall Street crash. But his 'apostle' Holger Cahill, who was national director of the Works Progress Administration/Federal Art Project (WPA/FAP) from 1935 to 1943, took much of Dana's philosophy into the community programmes that were the hallmark of his regime. Also like Dana, who was critical of the dismissive stance that many museums had adopted towards American art, that he purchased for the Newark Museum even when not to his taste, Cahill enthusiastically developed and promoted American art and artists.

Art for the millions[10]

During Franklin D. Roosevelt's administration, and more particularly from 1933 to 1943 in art programmes set up under the New Deal, we can see the two themes outlined above join together: the role of the community museum and the attempts to forestall the separation of high art from popular culture.

The New Deal of the 1930s provided a brief moment of state-sponsored art initiatives. While the country was faced with unemployment on a massive scale as banks failed at an astonishing rate, visual culture too was subjected to an overhaul. The arts, and specifically the task of the artist and the museum, were a small but significant part of an American call to order as the country plunged into economic turmoil. If the beginning of the century was marked by the radical formal innovations of artists such as John Marin, Milton Avery, Marsden Hartley and Georgia O'Keeffe, the artworks produced during the New Deal usually, but by no means always, took forms of a perceived 'democratic realism'. Also artworks were situated in publicly accessible spaces. During the Great Depression, art came out of the pampered hothouse of the art museum into schools, hospitals, prisons and federal housing projects. Even MoMA, a bastion of European modernism, was not immune to the New Deal projects: in 1938 showing an exhibition called *Subway Art* of Project murals done in glazed tiles. Crucially however,

10 Source: O'Connor (1973).

the concentration of art on the East Coast was ameliorated by nationwide initiatives.

In particular the New Deal saw a flourishing of wall mural art that related to local communities and the American scene, or bore witness to the triumphs of pioneer history and national heroes and heroines: images of Walt Whitman, muscular working men, resolute women, cotton pickers and miners abound.[11] Rejecting 'the prop symbol of the Greek goddess with cornucopia' (Siporin 1973: 67), artists such as Mitchell Siporin, working in the Midwest in Illinois, presented the 'rich life of our locale' and rejected the entire genealogy of American art up to the 1930s: 'the Greeks ... the Renaissance ... English portraitists ... and the swish of Bouguereau's nude descending from the bath [that] rustled through the art salons on the shores of Lake Michigan', granting a begrudging amnesty to the surrealists but dismissing all other modern European 'isms' (Siporin 1973: 64). Many artists working on 'native epic frescos' sought inspiration from pre-renaissance fresco painters Giotto and Masaccio, and the contemporary Mexican muralist Orozco (Siporin 1973: 64). The frescoes and wall paintings formed a bedrock of publicly funded projects that were often gently coercive in terms of pedagogy and nation building, although few survived beyond the 1950s (in part because mural painting in a culture given to rebuilding rather than renovation could not be a particularly long-term prospect). There were few voices raised against what Hilaire Hiler, working in the Aquatic Park Building in San Francisco, called the 'mural with a message'. Speaking from a minority position and producing a mural and floor decoration that functioned as 'primarily form and color', he argued in 'An approach to mural decoration' that :

> Historical subjects or social ones, whether they are called 'Cuirassiers at Waterloo', 'Don't Wake Grandma', 'Japanese Artillery in Action,' 'Sharecroppers,' 'The Mail Arrives at Porto Rico' fail to give me a thrill. Tons of news pulp, the movies, and the radio convinced me that mural painting as a means of special pleading could be absurdly feeble.
>
> (quoted in O'Connor 1973: 74)

Notwithstanding Hiler, and artists such as Arshile Gorky and Stuart Davis who preferred to work in semi-abstract modes, many of the WPA/FAP outputs bore a remarkable similarity in style, content and ideology to the socialist realism that was more familiar in the Soviet Union. The close affinity to left politics probably also accounts in part for their absence from standard art histories of the twentieth century. Philip Evergood, paying homage to the renaissance of mural painting in Mexico, noted:

11 Atypically Jackson Pollock painted *Cotton pickers* when working on the New York City Project in about 1937 (O'Connor 1973: 134).

> Whether our country's growing interest in the mural is predominantly the result of Mexican pollen ... wafted northwards on the breeze or due to an inner compulsion of our own artists to extend their appeal to a larger audience is a disputable point, but two things are certain: First, that our artists are unquestionably indebted to the Mexican artists who have brought to life the sound and permanent techniques of the ancients; second, that the economic depression and the consequent birth of the WPA/FAP has done more for the closer understanding between the American artist and his public through the medium of the mural than any individual efforts could have accomplished during a much longer period.
>
> (Evergood 1973: 49)

While according to Contreras, it would be reductive to search for a single unifying position during the New Deal, Holger Cahill saw it as an opportunity to return to a perceived antebellum national unity and:

> to a time when artist and society were not mutually excluded. To create a living present, his [Cahill's] search meant going back into the past to restore the values of an agrarian society – shattered by the impact of the Civil War. The mechanization of America in post-Civil War times challenged his goal; the ruthless newly rich looked to the stored-up treasures of Europe for their art, and the American artist became alienated in his or her own land.
>
> (Contreras 1983: 160)

Cahill owned one of Edward Hick's *The peaceable kingdom* series (c. 1840), pictures of a utopian vision of America where 'white and Indian lived in harmony; and the Shaker communities, founded by Mother Lee, where artisans created marvelous (sic) Shaker furniture for their communities' (Contreras 1983: 160). The realisation of Cahill's 'rediscovered' American unity would be accomplished through four programmes of the WPA/FPA: the establishment of community art centres, the compilation of an Index of American Design, the creation of WPA/FPA art for lending to tax-supported institutions, and nationwide travelling exhibitions of WPA/FPA art. In sum, Cahill designed a forceful intervention that held out the possibility of a democratic visual culture nationwide which would unite America. Core to that vision was *community*, realised in the establishment of over 100 WPA community art centres from Arizona to Wyoming. There were eighteen in Florida and ten in Wyoming, eleven in Oklahoma and three in New Mexico, while there were only four in New York, including Brooklyn, Harlem and Ridgewood, which was a testament to the policy of prioritising art venues beyond their concentration in urban centres (O'Connor 1973: 306–7). Cahill's support for home-grown art also resulted in national art exhibitions of WPA work, most notably *New Horizons in American Art*, which was shown at Museum of Modern Art, New York for one month in 1936, and *American Art Today*, shown in the 1939 New York World's Fair.

There are specific ideological positions to be drawn out of the rhetoric that informed the WPA community art centres. They were informed by a commitment to seeing art as enabling reconciliations between racial and social groups, and between American history and contemporary culture.[12] Society was perceived to be in a state of spiritual and even moral crisis, not just an economic one. The art centres, many set up in desert or other remote areas perceived as culturally deprived, were charged with bringing about artistic regeneration, restoring lost artisan skills and inculcating social cooperation. Artists were reconceptualised as social workers, their skills required to help forge social cohesion and stall young people's descent into crime. The democratic idealism of the WPA art projects, embodied in Cahill, was pitted against the transplanted European aristocratic elitism evident in traditional museums, and against the individualism of the European-derived modernist construction of the alienated artist. The projects, while embracing popular culture, distanced themselves from mass culture. Cahill in particular saw industrialisation and mass production as a threat to distinctly American values, as encapsulated in the Jeffersonian-Whitmanesque democratic idealism that underpinned the WPA. Part of the response to concerns about industrialisation was the creation of a massive documentary project: the Index of American Design, amassed between 1935–1943, which recorded over 20,000 pieces of American decorative arts including furniture, glass, pottery, textiles and metalwork (see Chapter 2).

The place for folk art

The validation of folk art through the institutionalising processes of the first half of the twentieth century represents a further commitment to American art. The connections between folk art and modernism have been widely remarked upon by commentators, who have argued that modernism gave permission for artists to look at folk art. Since modernism was decreasingly a display of academic virtuosity, the modernist need not be troubled by folk art's supposed lack of technical proficiency (Cahill 1932, Rosenberg 1975). Holger Cahill writer, curator and authority on folk art, was as we have seen influenced by Dewey and Veblen, both advocates of progressive and democratic thinking. Cahill worked at the Newark Museum in Newark, New Jersey, in the 1920s under its director Dana who, unusually for a museum

12 See in particular Jonathan Harris, 'Nationalizing art: the Community Art Centre Program' (1995: 44–63).

director in the period, was interested in both popular culture and the interface between art and industry.

Abby Aldrich Rockefeller's (1874–1948) passion for folk art was not exactly fired by the *American Primitives* exhibition at the Newark Museum (she had been collecting folk art in a modest way previously), but it did inspire her to systematically collect folk art under the guidance of Cahill and Edith Halpert. Cahill became a travelling agent, hunting out the best examples of folk art, until 1935 when she stopped collecting. Mrs Rockefeller's unrivaled collection was installed in the Abby Aldrich Rockefeller Folk Art Center just outside Colonial Williamsburg in 1957.

In 1932 and 1933, while Cahill was the acting director of the MoMA in New York, he devised an exhibition, *American Folk Art: The Art of the Common Man in America 1750–1900*, whose exhibits were drawn almost entirely from Mrs Rockefeller's collection. Cahill also staged *American Painting and Sculpture 1862–1932* and *American Sources of Modem Art*, which included Aztec, Incan and Mayan art, in order to demonstrate the impact of pre-Conquest art upon modernism. Cahill's writings in combination with his curatorial ideas articulated a theory about what was singular about American art.

The art of the everyday had an advocate in Henry Ford, who founded the Henry Ford Museum (now known as the Henry Ford Museum and Greenfield Village) in 1929. He was ostensibly making his vast collection of everyday objects visible to the public, but he was also making a statement of his regard for and belief in a particular history of the American people. Ford is often perceived as having a disregard for history (immortalised in his famous saying that 'history is bunk'), but Steven Conn argues that he was referring to conventional written history rather than the object-based epistemology he offered at his own museum (1998: 156).[13] In an interview in 1929 Ford explained that he wanted to 'give us a sense of unity ... through the generations, and to convey the inspiration of American genius to our youth'. The museum sits next to Greenfield Village, the largest outdoor museum in America, comprising around 100 relocated historical buildings from the seventeenth to the twentieth century, preserving a record of how Americans have lived and worked.

While he admits that Greenfield is a 'multi-levelled fiction' (Conn 1998: 158), Conn argues that Ford was attempting to contextualise his object-based collections by having, say, a blacksmith's workshop to explain blacksmith's tools. Ford was also a compulsive and completist collector, and Greenfield may be seen as encyclopedic collecting on an enormous scale. Numerous commentators have remarked on the apparent irreconcilability

13 What Ford actually said is 'History is more or less bunk', in an interview with Charles N. Wheeler, *Chicago Tribune*, 25 May 1916.

of Ford's nostalgic project at Dearborn, and his company's contribution to the eradication of the culture he was seeking to preserve.

A somewhat belated acknowledgement of Dana's commitment to community relevance and to the idealism of the New Deal, the Anacostia Neighborhood Museum, Smithsonian Institution, opened in 1967. Now called the Anacostia Community Museum and Centre for African American History and Culture, and initially located on Martin Luther King Jr. Avenue, it was the first federally funded community museum, and the idea of S. Dillon Ripley, then secretary of the Smithsonian Institution. Ripley conceptualised the Anacostia Neighborhood Museum as a 'drop-in' or 'storefront' museum rather than a temple of art. Using technology to bridge the gap between collections and audience, the museum has an On-line Academy which offers access to a database of artefacts, as well as lectures on the African-American historical and cultural experience. The museum's official website clarifies its position: it 'encourages the collection, protection, and preservation of materials that reflect the history and traditions of families, organizations, individuals and communities'. Edmund Barry Gaither, writing on the work of Rowena Stewart in '"Hey! That's mine": thoughts on pluralism and American museums', noted a significant departure from the normal museum collecting and interpretative strategies. Stewart, working at the Rhode Island Black Heritage Centre and the Afro-American Historical and Cultural Museum in Philadelphia, like Dana put people before objects and artefact holders, or 'keepers of the tradition', as the first interpreters and gatherers of associated materials (Gaither 1992: 61). The process of working with source communities involved dialogue with professionals that did not negate community ownership of tangible and intangible heritage.

The striving for museums that reflected homogeneous American values often excluded art and cultures that fell outside a constructed consensus. In a period currently uncertain about the possibility of representing overarching national values, and ever alert to the dangers of sliding from national pride into nationalism, what and who is represented have become more overtly problematic. The eighteenth and newest museum of the Smithsonian Institution, the National Museum of the American Indian, opened in 2004, is instructive here. Perhaps emblematically, the yellowing earth-coloured, curvilinear form of the museum's architecture, which evokes 'wind-sculpted rock formations of the American landscape' of the often-marginalised southwest (specifically the eroded sandstone of the Vermillion Wilderness in Arizona) stands resolutely on the National Mall in Washington opposite the (very late 1941) neoclassical temple of art, the National Gallery of Art (West Building), and close to the late modernism of the anti-humanist concrete façade of the imposing Hirshhorn Museum with its commitment to canonical modernism (Plate 13) & (Plate 14).

Based on the extraordinary collection of Native American art and artefact collected by wealthy New Yorker George Gustav Heye (1874–1957), the

NMAI represents a reconceptualisation of the relationship between the displayed and the museum: the right to self-represent an issue raised earlier. It is a landmark building, according to W. Richard West, Jr (Southern Cheyenne and member of the Cheyenne and Arapaho tribes of Oklahoma and the founding director of NMAI): 'at our heart we represent something intangible. We define a moment of reconciliation in American history, a time for Indian people to assume, finally, a prominent place of honor on the nation's front lawn' (quoted in Volkert *et al.* 2004: 7). The display is based on extensive discussions with Native American peoples, and the building is oriented to nature and set within specific celestial references. It has an east-facing main entrance and a dome open to the sky. There are built-in references to the pole star, Polaris and other celebrations of lunar events, solstices and equinoxes. It is also set within a landscape (given the location restrictions on the National Mall) with miniature areas representing, crops, meadows, wetlands and hardwood forests.

Seeking to avoid the pitfalls of ethnographic museums susceptible to situating indigenous cultures in an ahistoric homogenising 'primitive' past, and avoiding the art museum's tendency to transcend political and ideological foundations, the NMAI is not about a vanished or vanquished people but about the vast diversity within traditional communities and their ability to absorb continuities and change. Adaptations and achievements are visible in the art and artefacts chosen to represent living cultures. Rather than be a mausoleum to a mythical native authenticity, the exhibitions stress cultural crossovers. Unsurprisingly reproductions of John White drawings that we encountered earlier as the first surviving recordings of the Algonquians of North Carolina are on display: they are important documents that record early tribal customs, some of which survive today.

The display of drawing by native Americans, mostly Cheyenne military prisoners at Fort Marion in St Augustine, Florida between 1894 and 1895, also offers a different perspective on the received history. In the work by Littleman galloping (Kiowa or Sweetwater, Southern Cheyenne) depicting *Rank of Soldiers Shooting at Indians*, done on paper from ledger books rather than buffalo hide, the drawings tell of the campaign on the Great Plains to relocate or exterminate Native Americans that followed the Civil War (Plate 15).

The institutionally reflexive museum

Handing control of cultural representation to source peoples is not the only issue at stake in historically circumscribed collections. There are middle ways that are being negotiated. Although the art museum has displayed articles as aesthetic objects, when acquired they functioned in very different contexts. Gaskell has noted that 'art museums have proved to be very effective means of expunging the sacred qualities of objects' (2003: 150). He also noted that 'Museums might do well to reassess the Enlightenment assumptions under which they operate [and] that aesthetic and educational criteria alone justify the abstraction of sacred objects from their devotional or otherwise sacred contexts for deployment in an entirely secular domain' (2003: 150). The repatriation of scared artefacts is of course one issue, but museums charged also with conservation and public assess have found ways of partial restitution. For instance dance regalia belonging to the Hoopa Valley tribe, although displayed as art objects at the Peabody Museum of Archaeology and Ethnology at Harvard, while not used for the contemporary performances by Native Americans are brought out to 'attend' events, and so operate as both a living community resource and as a museum artefact (Gaskell 2003).

Conducting research with Native Americans on their interactions with museums, such as the Gene Autry Western Heritage Museum (now the Autry Museum of Western History), the Los Angeles County Museum of Natural History and the mission-style building of the Southwest Museum, that displayed their own culture and history, Wilson noted, as well as a lack of passivity in the face of their own presumed extinction, a marked difference in the use of artefacts to aid memory between Euro-Americans and Native Americans. Going someway to understanding that viewers through individual agency actively rewrites the museum's intentions, reinterpreting artefacts through their own experiences and memories often in potentially subversive ways, Wilson notes that Native Americans bring into the museum materials memory: 'linked to contiguous casualty is not necessarily a cognitive pathology but is part of a semiotic continuum of diverse possible ways for communicating and making sense' (Wilson 2000: 121).

Building on psycho-cultural practices of memory, the research also highlighted that memory itself is a constructed category, and that Euro-American literate memory practices and histories are constructed differently from Native American memories. They do not necessarily follow chronology or fact, and often involve 'embodied knowing and memory [that] is not necessarily true, and in fact ... can seem quite false to Euro-Americans' (Wilson 2000: 121). Truthfulness in opposition to a single scientifically knowable truth is useful here. However, resolving the hiatus between what Euro-Americans may regard as ahistorical fictions, such as that some artefacts are sentient, and the empirically fact-based curatorial endeavour to convert material culture into convincing evidence based narratives, is a compelling feature of the display of others which can be acknowledged in museums curated by source communities.

Although there has been a history of art quite separate from art's display, as if the hanging of art is incidental to its intrinsic worth and therefore not contingent upon anything, contemporary culture has increasingly sought to account for the experience of art within the context of the exhibition or site. Any encounter with art or artefact, it would seem, is mediated by its display.

Once thought to be a relatively neutral backdrop, the art museum and its curators, taxonomies, histories, architecture, acquisition policy and even trustees have been held up to scholarly scrutiny. If museums of anthropology have been an obvious focal point for an overhaul of displays of the primitive 'other', the seemingly benign art museum has not been immune to censure. Carol Duncan and Alan Wallach, in essays on the contemporary past including 'The museum of modern art as late capitalist ritual: an iconographic analysis' (Duncan and Wallach 1978), 'The universal survey museum' (Duncan and Wallach 1980) and *Civilising Rituals: Inside Public Art Museums* (Duncan 1995), have taken the art museum to task as the relationship between hanging and housing art has been theorised. In tandem with such critiques as Craig Owens's 'Discourses of others: feminists and postmodernism' (1990), they alerted a generation of cultural commentators to the politics of representation, and challenges to Western representation's authority and universalising claims.

On the museum's ruins by Douglas Crimp (1980) was part of the Foucauldian-derived critique of the museum as a place of confinement (continuing Foucault's historically based analysis of prisons and asylums) and even death (the mausoleum). It was also part of a then postmodern analysis of the inability of museums to present a coherent and defensible collection or display with a sustainable taxonomy. The focus for the approach was the new installation of nineteenth-century art in the André Meyer Galleries of the Metropolitan Museum in New York. The juxtaposing of 'self-evident' masterpieces with discredited salon works normally consigned to the basement caused disquiet for the art critic Hilton Kramer, as the prospect of a loss of standards and slide into valueless relativity loomed.[14] Part of an attack on received ideas begun in the nineteenth century by Flaubert, Crimp's essay undermined notions of originality, authenticity and presence to look at the endless possibilities of reproduction and quotation: the inauthentic. Looking at the inauthentic, the copy or the replica, had been part of a pattern of museum consumption long before the postmodern dismissal of the distinction between original and simulacra that haunted 1990s theory.

Women, modernism and the advancement of American art

While it was once possible to overlook women artists, it is impossible to overlook the influential women who helped created a climate of social acceptance for European modernism, and who determined that modern American art should have the status and purchasing power of European art, old and new. There was an almost collective determination to have new

14 See Hilton Kramer, 'Does Gérome belong with Goya and Manet? *New York Times*, 13 April 1980, s. 2, p.35

museums in which to put art that was regarded, following the Armory show of 1913, as dangerously un-American, even undemocratic. Already avid collectors of modern art, Abby Aldrich Rockefeller, Lillie P. Bliss and Mary Quinn Sullivan were the driving force behind the establishment of Museum of Modern Art, New York, which opened shortly after the stock market crash in November 1929. The museum set the gold standard for modern museums. Dubbed by Emily Genauer 'the fur-lined museum' and close to fashionable Fifth Avenue, haunted by the chic and wealthy, the museum has long been associated with money and avant-garde taste. Although the museum had considered pensioning or selling off works as they lost their cutting edge or were overturned by the new, it never happened, but it was not until 1958 that it opened a permanent exhibition of its own collection. Unequivocally modern, the flat, glass-fronted building is indistinguishable from a shop façade. MoMA's lack of a significant entrance with portico, steps and columns marked it out from its classical progenitors.

The Whitney Museum of American Art, also in New York, opened in 1931, was the project of Gertrude Vanderbilt Whitney. Juliana Force (1876–1948), a friend and collaborator of Whitney, was appointed as the museum's first director. Force and Whitney purchased American art widely, and some suggest indiscriminately, for their gallery on Eighth Street. Their operations were largely instinctive and intuitive, and their collecting policy, if indeed there was one, was informed by social networking and brokering. In spite of their lack of professional credentials, Ira Glackens noted that the opening of the Whitney Museum meant that 'American Art no longer needed to come in the back door' (McCarthy 1991: 240). Glackens may have been pleased to see that there was a door open for American art in New York, but in the 1930s MoMA was regarded as institutionally superior because of its international ambitions.

The Museum of Non-Objective Painting, which was effectively a nascent Guggenheim, opened in 1939, under the guidance of Baroness Hilla Rebay von Ehrenweisen who also wrote about modern art: Solomon R. Guggenheim provided the financial clout. There were other women to whom American artists owe a great debt. In a period of artistic turmoil during the 1950s Edith Gregor Halpert, director of the Downtown Gallery in New York, was also influential in keeping alive the artistic careers of artists who were still engaged in a social art practice. The Art of This Century on West 57th Street in New York, run by Peggy Guggenheim (then married to the surrealist Max Ernst), was foundational as the first gallery in the 1940s to allot solo shows to men who became legendary during the 1950s as the New York school or first generation of abstract expressionists: Jackson Pollock, William Baziotes, Mark Rothko and Clyfford Still.

As we have seen, the guiding light of the New Deal FPA project, Holger Cahill, influenced by John Dewey, had sought integration across all the arts rather than give fine art a privileged position. He argued that 'The importance of integration between the fine arts and the practical arts has been recognized from the first by the Federal Arts Project, as an objective desirable in itself and as a means of drawing together major aesthetic forces in this country' (quoted in O'Connor 1973: 18). And to a certain extent this can be seen at MoMA, which atypically collected design objects, photography and film as well as fine art. However the distinction between the hierarchies that Cahill sought to soften became more pronounced as MoMA gained a reputation so powerful that rather than just collecting existing works it was influential in their production.

Avoiding the passive display

The question of how to exhibit modern art taxed early advocates of modernism. Some designers and artists, such as El Lissitzky and Laszlo Moholy-Nagy, applied their work in theatre design to exhibition design: they 'attempted to integrate the dramatic organization of space in the theatre with graphic and typographic visual elements' (Henning 2006: 61). And of course there was the absurdist aesthetic of Duchamp, whose inventive approach to exhibition design involved disrupting the viewer and making access to works difficult: by having boys playing football during chic openings, or placing miles of string across the gallery impeding visitors' movement, or disrupting the opportunity to look with poor lighting.

Similarly, Frederick Keisler during the late 1930s applied his theory of design-correlation to Peggy Guggenheim's Art of this Century gallery, where he developed an inventive and noisy system for viewing surrealist works: part of a longer project to remove the separation between audience and performer. The gallery had three categories: abstract art, kinetic art and surrealism. Revealing Keisler's background in avant-garde theatre, the surrealist gallery had a tunnel or cave-like space. Keisler, who had also worked as a window designer, created an 'L and T system' which moved pictures off the walls into the middle of the display space, where the audience could swivel and adjust them. Paintings removed from their frames were shown projecting from the walls attached to an adjustable arm. They were lit alternately at three and half-second intervals, and periodically the lights went off, plunging the gallery into darkness. The disruption was compounded by the periodic sound of a train passing. This 'new reality', it can be claimed, collapsed the opposition of subject and object.

There have been attempts, such as MoMA's *Bauhaus 1919–1928*, designed by Bayer, to 'place[d] more emphasis on inviting the viewer to reflect on their own role in the interpretive process. Yet Bayer also conceived of his work in relation to consumption, as an act of persuasion similar to advertising' (Phillips 1988: 273, quoted by Hennings 2006: 67), the passive white cube aesthetic of MoMA came to dominate international display. It was not until Joseph Kosuth's *Brooklyn Museum Collection: Play of the*

Unmentionable that the assumed integrity of the establish modes of display was cogently questioned.

At the same time that the aesthetic approach to viewing grew, there was also a change in museum architecture, away from the neoclassical temples of art viewed as unsuitable for modern art, and from a patrician European culture, to a New World architecture. This was seen most famously in Godwin and Stone's department store façade to MoMA. With a change in façade came debate about how to organise and display modern art. Much has been made of the construction of the modernist canon conceptualised by Alfred Hamilton Barr Jr (1902–1981), which are visible in two schematic diagrams: *Torpedo Diagrams of the Ideal Permanent Collection, 1933–41* and the more familiar *The development of abstract art*, which was placed on the cover of exhibition catalogue *Cubism and Abstract Art* (for the exhibition at MoMA in 1936).

The *Torpedo Diagrams of the Ideal Permanent Collection* contain two torpedos drawn nine years apart. They were prepared by Barr to illustrate his 'Report on the Permanent Collection in 1933' and later for the Advisory Committee Report on Museum Collections in 1941. What is noticeable about the ideal permanent collection can be read out of revisions to Barr's schema. In the second diagram, nine years later than the first, the torpedo is still heading towards the 1950s but the balance in the diagram has changed. The torpedo's 'nose' contains with no hierarchy the United States and Mexico. The 'School of Paris' and the 'Rest of Europe' have now slipped behind, leaving Mexico and the United States firmly in the vanguard. Other casualties absent from the second, much streamlined, collection but contained in the propeller of the first are 'European prototypes and sources' and 'Non-European prototypes and sources'.

Schematically *The development of abstract art* delineates a genealogy for the development of abstraction. It follows a system of identifying *breakthrough* and *influence*, which leads compellingly to a complete narrative: the triumph of two forms of abstraction, non-geometrical abstraction and geometrical abstraction, by 1935. The historical framework is an important one in establishing a pattern of collecting for the permanent collection. The chart identifies in grid form the key masters of modern art and movements. Central to the lower part of the grid are 'Modern architecture' and the Bauhaus. The chart, although provisional, has been subject to controversy. Its teleology of modernism signposted the most significant movements in a trajectory that moved increasingly towards abstraction, as if art were in some way guided by external forces over which it had no control. The emphasis on a summative approach had the effect of relegating to the shadows art considered 'conservative' or implicated in forms of figurative realism.

The influence of MoMA is far-reaching: its collecting policy, curating and white-cube aesthetic set the standard for international museums world-wide for most of the second half of the twentieth century. Moreover by the 1950s and the arrival of William Rubin another form of permanence had been consolidated for western art. McCaughey states:

> What started as an intimate aesthetic experience wedded to a closely argued view of modern art became in time a tyrannous dogma until it tumbled into a parody of modernism where the arts of Paris and New York subsumed all the other stories. Excursions to Russia for constructivism, Italy for futurism, Germany for Expressionism and the Netherlands for de Stijl were brief, a diversion from the Grand Narrative.
>
> (McCaughey 1968: 126)

The provisional scheme developed by Barr has proved remarkably resilient. The Hirshhorn Museum in Washington, DC, while using celebrity artists and curators to reinterpret the collection, stays within an unapologetic commitment to the canonical modernism established by Barr. The permanent collection is a study in the acquisition of masterpieces of modernism, from French post-impressionism to American abstract impressionism and colour field painting, still (in 2007) displayed within a chronology with separate rooms to showcase such modernist luminaries as Max Ernst and Alexander Calder.

As key sites for the construction of American identity, twentieth century modern art museums in the United States are emblematic of an engagement with modernity. The recently reopened MoMA therefore provided a litmus test for more recent changes in society, such as lifestyle choices and celebrity curators, which notionally replace the Puritanism of the white cube. However, moving beyond a now middle-aged MoMA it is timely to look at the franchising of the art museum and its effects on local cultures. Using the Guggenheim museums as emblematic of global ambition, we review the ideological overhauls that are taking place in the reception of contemporary and modern art via the iconic postmodern building. The mantra of diversity and the constraints of corporate culture evident in the new museum order have dented some of the ambitions of conservation and scholarship, as the new museum is transformed from a palace to acquire 'cultural capital' to a place to invest in identity formation.

Changes in American museums

It is not long since the *American Century: Art and Culture 1900–2000* exhibition at the Whitney Museum of American Art reappraised American art and culture, and offered a more inclusive history: one that did not ride roughshod over artists and crucially artforms perceived as unworthy by an unforgiving art history written by apologists of avant-garde culture. The history presented in the Whitney exhibition was recuperative, and included what could be termed other vanguards, which embraced decorative arts, theatre and cinema.

Certainly the Whitney's century – in two parts, 1900–50 and 1950–2000 – seemed to offer a comprehensive picture. For instance, icons of US design like Louis Comfort Tiffany's turn of the century vessels and windows, and Paul Theodore Tranki's celebration of American modernity in his skyscraper bookcases from the 1920s, took their place alongside more female abstract expressionist painters (such as Grace Hartigan, Lee Krasner, Joan Mitchell and Elaine de Kooning) than audiences had been used to. Moreover the exhibition was interdisciplinary, crossing the boundaries of cartoon, photography, poetry, craft and design as well as movies, vaudeville and consumer culture.

The Whitney is not the only museum to rethink its exclusive attachment to avant-garde culture. In 2002, Frank Lloyd Wright's hymn to modernism, the Guggenheim Museum in New York, showed *Norman Rockwell: Pictures for the American People*, as the final venue for a exhibition that had travelled to seven museums starting in Atlanta: a show of over 400 works seen by more than a million people. Rockwell (1839–1978) was a sentimental and unashamed populist, and his paean to small-town America is familiar to several generations of Americans through the cover illustrations of the *Saturday Evening Post*. Although he also worked for *Look* magazine from the early 1960s, it is iconic images of family life extolling the virtues of the 'American way of life' that resulted in a lifetime of derision by serious art critics. The exhibition displayed all 322 of his *Saturday Evening Post* covers. Rockwell did paint images of lynching and of segregated schooling in paintings such as *The problem we all live with* from 1964, but his images of problematic social issues are rarely reproduced.

Inevitably critics were deeply divided by the Rockwell show, particularly as the timing came in a period of uncertainty, questioning of national identity and an outpouring of patriotism following the events of 11 September the previous year. Since Rockwell had been called upon during the Second World War to create an invented America, the show's scheduled stop in New York seemed timely. Writing in the *New York Times Art Review* under the heading 'Flags, Mom and apple pie through altered eyes', Michael Kimmelman referred to Rockwell's art in a time of national mourning as 'the perfect homely barometer of national self-identity'. Kimmelman also observed that with fashion designer Giorgio Armani's (2000–2001) show also at the Guggenheim, Rockwell was less at odds with the institution than he might have been several decades previously. It is noteworthy that the epithets 'illustrator' and 'storyteller' that dogged Rockwell have been subject to uneven revision.

Village Voice critic Jerry Saltz, in 'Middle Americana', was less convinced by the rhetoric surrounding Rockwell's rehabilitation as 'an artistic Benjamin

Franklin', and was concerned that 'the Guggenheim ... [is] trashing the reputation won for it by generations of artists, and [the exhibition] only underlines Rockwell's reputation as merely the maker of what he himself called "feel-good" "story-pictures"' (2001). The appearance of Rockwell's reproducible and illustrative art in a bastion of high art such as the Guggenheim also allowed a space for critics and theorists to reinforce their commitment to quality, and reaffirm the modernist critics' defence of the 'hard-won image' while railing against the newly discovered populism of erstwhile champions of 'elitist' culture. Alan Wallach argued that the preconditions for Rockwell's exhibition were threefold: first, the erosion of a traditional bourgeois culture which had itself been based upon aristocratic models; second, the waning of 'distinction' between classes in terms of taste; and finally the decline of modernism and along with it the devolution of the category of 'high art'. However, rather than see in such declines a greater form of democracy, Wallach saw in it the triumph of corporatisation, where 'corporate ideals of rationality, efficiency, functionality, impassivity ... and individualism' have replaced 'the days of genteel museum amateurism' (Wallach 2003: 106).

In tandem with the challenges to the purpose of the museum that demographic change and recent immigration and increasing competition from the leisure industries have brought, there has been a wholesale revision of what a museum should look like. In part a response to the changing function of the museum and a reversion to the nineteenth-century commitment to the public, the art museum is no longer a quest for the building with the neoclassical exterior. Whether audiences still enjoy the whole Grand Tour aesthetic, ascending a steep flight of steps to a temple of art and a quiet rummage around the ruins of European art, or prefer the all-singing all-dancing new museum, is a question of taste. However, collections historically circumscribed by period styles and schools of art, already subject to academic scrutiny, are further compromised by landmark or branded museums. Often artworks in their own right, such museums can outperform their collections.

Audiences might see the new buildings as being 'emancipated from the art exhibited inside' (Greub and Greub 2006), or as places where the art displayed rather than situated within the space looks awkward and misplaced: where the art is secondary to the buildings. It is noteworthy however that Yoshio Taniguchi's conservative, modernist addition to MoMA New York fits with the international style and aesthetic of Godwin and Stone's 1939 building and Cesar Pelli's 1984 galleries, Garden Hall and Museum Tower. Gehry, Liebskind and Lab One's enthusiasm for the 'great shape museum' simply did not fit.

If housing a national collection of canonical art from the Renaissance to the nineteenth century could err on the side of the conservative, with the architecture of choice the temple-like late neoclassical style familiar to

European nineteenth-century art lovers, housing modern art in America was to embrace significantly more radical solutions in both building and modes of display. Avant-garde art required avant-garde solutions. Pei's trademark pyramid designed to house modern American and international art in the East Wing of the National Gallery of Art in Washington stands in stark contrast to the neoclassicism of the earlier West Wing.

However, housing and displaying modern art was no more 'natural' or ideologically free than had been the display of 'the natural world' in dioramas or representations of the wilderness that we saw earlier. Moreover, displaying modern art quickly led to a narrow canon of acceptable art and orthodoxy in display, which has not been without controversy. The hard-won gains of modernism, now subject to revision, have helped put modernism's ritualistic gallery visit into historic perspective, the strengths and weaknesses of its protagonists and apologists easier to discern at a distance.

If in the 1970s uncovering the suppressed relationships between commerce and money had created artistic commentary, currently the economic and ideological basis of the art gallery is frankly exposed, witnessed most readily in the reinvention of Las Vegas, the self styled capital of kitsch, from naked commerce to naked commerce with an art gallery attached. In part a reconceptualisation to move into the luxury market, a Las Vegas hotel, the Bellagio, started to exhibit fine art in 1998, the first hotel to do so. If many museums had been funded by the third generation of robber barons who had gained kudos, respectability and taste, that is no longer the case. Las Vegas has built up its own unique blend of the inauthentic in art, with casts of Classical and Renaissance sculptures playing host to casino visitors, but the introduction of the real and authentic into the ersatz is a significant enterprise. Crow has argued that in this desert outpost, 'the cult that surrounds the displaced objects in all of America's museums reach a kind of pure extreme' (2006: 72).

Chapter 6

Writing about American art

In 1834 the painter, historian, playwright and theatre manager William Dunlap self-published his *History of the Rise and Progress of the Arts of Design in the United States* (Dunlap 1918), the first book to attempt to establish a credible genealogy for a distinctively American art. Like many other early nineteenth-century American projects, Dunlap's *History* created a model or framework for representing the history of art of a mythical unified nation. Drawing on what Van Wyck Brooks would later call 'a useable past' in relation to American literary culture, it can be argued that Dunlap's formulation of American art's history contributed to 'the origin and spread of nationalism' (Anderson 1991; Lyons 2005).

Dubbed 'the American Vasari',[1] the conjunction of Dunlap and Vasari is suggestive of America's appeal to established European art-historical procedure. Vasari's *Lives* is rooted in a humanist approach to recording art history which used the biography of the artist as a way of creating a genealogy for artworks. Both Dunlap and Vasari were artists, and their authorial voice was the arbitrating one of the connoisseur. But Dunlap's appellation, 'American Vasari', also signals the separation between the two ambitious projects. The 'Italian Vasari' was commissioned to write his *Lives* by Cardinal Farnese for Grand Duke Cosimo de' Medici to a tight organizational brief; the 'American Vasari' published his own *History*, and it is republican in conception and execution. Dunlap's outline of progress in painting has no debt to any authority other than the optimistic spirit of a new nation still seeking to distance itself from European modes of patronage and artistic production.

Maura Lyons suggests that Dunlap's *History* was informed by his allegiance to the National Academy of Design's 'emphasis on egalitarianism, professionalism, and national mission' (2005: 31). Vasari's theory of cyclical

1 Giorgio Vasari's *Lives of the Artists* was first published in 1550 and in an expanded version in 1568.

development[2] in art through the products of individual genius, supported by documentary evidence coupled with the uncanny ability of the connoisseur to select quality, is equally evident in Dunlap's organisation of content. Most notably his disregard for the social or historical context of art (beyond those affecting biographic details) in accounts of artistic development is an oversight that returns to haunt writing about American art.

Dunlap's eclectic writing style, close to oratory and autobiography in parts, might not appeal to later art-historical writing but his history of early American art has become an official, legitimate one, reprinted in 1965 and 1969 with a facsimile edition in 1970. Just as Vasari promoted his home region of Tuscany through his *Lives*, Dunlap's *History* limited its scope to artists largely drawn from his home region of New York state. As Lyons points out, Dunlap was not alone in conjuring 'up the national from the local' in an attempt to create a shared history. Although there were always alternative unofficial histories that intersected with the official histories in interesting ways, Dunlap's history nonetheless 'shifted the frame of reference for U.S. artists, removing them from the history of British art and placing them in a new narrative' (Lyons 2005: 2–3). Lyons's point is an important one. The impulse towards nationhood may have been a pressing one in the years following the American Revolution, but the separation of American art history from its European roots (and that is not to say just English or French roots) left Dunlap's *History* open to charges of distortion, which Whitehill (1965) suggests could lead to national chauvinism. It can be argued that early American art 'should be studied in terms of their European roots and of their relationship with the West Indies and the Maritime Provinces' (Lyons 2005: 10). The scant attention given to indigenous art in Dunlap's *Histories* also diminished the contribution of British, French and Spanish colonial art.

The ardent patriot Dunlap played down his years studying in London at the Royal Academy in the studio of the expatriate Benjamin West. As a resident New Yorker (although as we have seen he travelled widely as an itinerant portrait painter and artist-showman), Dunlap's allegiance was to New York. New York City was prospering, confident and growing – all preconditions for fine art to flourish. Dunlap's title *History of the Rise and Progress of the Arts of Design in the United States*[3] is not just a statement of his faith in New York's continued prosperity; it is also an affirmation of his allegiance to the National Academy of Design in New York, an organisation in dispute with the American Academy of Fine Art. His inclusion of 'Design' in the title of his book is perhaps a pointed gesture in this respect.

2 Vasari's cycle principally involved a childhood, youth and maturity model of artistic development: he rarely included any social or historical context in his account of artistic development.

3 The title is also an optimistic reworking of the Gibbon's pessimistic *Decline and Fall of the Roman Empire*.

Dunlap's partiality is also indicated by his presentation of a partial history, one where the influence of Boston and Philadelphia upon the rise and progress of the arts is diminished. What can be clearly read out of his *History* is the tendency to normalise the local as national. This is evident in his north-eastern bias towards the Hudson River school, an example of the local standing in for the national (Miller 1993). The final point to be gleaned from the writing of early American art histories such as Dunlap's is the way that North and South have been constructed:[4] the former is shown as lacking ideological imperatives and therefore synonymous with the national (the local as national), while the latter, even in the post-bellum period, retains its ideological and regional label. This is not to take Dunlap to task but rather to reflect and remark upon particular constructions of art history, which like all histories, including this one, are partial, local or contingent.

In much the same way that American art has often been discussed through the lens of European art history, the discipline of an American art history has been impeded by dominant European art histories. It is marked twice, from within and without. From within, the perceived parochial and derivative nature of American landscape painting, early portraits and early modernist abstract experimentation meant they were not deemed original or good enough to warrant their own history courses or scholarly publications. From without, writing about American art was often restricted to museum catalogues. Wanda Corn cites a range of examples of European dismissals of American art, ranging from Sydney Smith's question in 1820 'Who looks at an American picture and statue?' to Marcel Duchamp's waspish observation that America's only contribution to world culture was bridges and plumbing (Corn 1988: 190).

When, after 1945, American art does finally seem fit to enter the international stage, it is (as we saw in Chapter 3) at the expense of key early modernist artists such as John Marin and Arthur Dove. The dismissal of early twentieth-century American art was often achieved by Americans intent on promoting a triumphant coming of age for American art in the postwar period, when as Harold Rosenberg, speaking of the enormous interest in postwar abstraction, wrote, 'Is this the usual catching up of America with European art forms? Or is something new being created?' (1952/1990: 75–6). It has taken a considerable time to establish a critical mass of scholarship about pre-1945 American art. Corn recalls the paucity of specialist literature and academic interest when studying American art in the 1960s, but that by the late 1980s an academisation of American art history had taken place, with the first generation of university-trained art historians publishing widely. The discipline had, Corn contends, 'come of age', with

4 Lyons (2005: 37) cites Susan-Mary Grant, *North over South: Northern Nationalism and American Identity in the Antebellum Era*, in this respect.

internal scholars such as Michael Fried, Albert Boime and Robert Rosenblum writing on historical American art and 'replacing the self-tutored art historian who once dominated American art scholarship' (Corn 1988: 190).

Corn also maintains that the search for a national focus or American style is evident in the almost obsessive use of *American* in the title of collections, as in the National Museum of American Art. Although the imperative to construct an Americanness has enabled a discrete American art scholarship to emerge, it had a paradoxical effect: '"the Americanness of American art" approach also served to ghettoize the field within art history' (Corn 1988: 192). It was not until relatively late in the disciplinary field that American art history *on its own terms* was written about by non-Americans, most notably Jonathan Harris and Andrew Hemingway writing on the 1930s, and Australians Terry Smith and Robert Hughes.

Other nineteenth-century historians

Despite the observations above which suggest that writing about American art was a fugitive pursuit, there were scholarly, academic and literary forces in America that combined to shape the discipline of art history. Charles Eliot Norton (1827–1908) edited the *North American Review* with James Russell Lowell from 1864–8, and was a founder (1865) of *The Nation*.[5] He was from 1875 professor of the history of fine arts at Harvard, where he taught a number of courses, the most popular being 'The history of the fine arts as connected with literature'. The connection between the 'sister arts' is common in the nineteenth century, and art and literary criticism, frequently written by the same authors, appeared together in the same magazines and journal, such as the *Knickerbocker Magazine*, the *New-York Mirror*, the *North American Review* and the *Atlantic*. We saw a continuation of the commerce between writers and artists in twentieth-century surrealism in the introduction, even though high modernism demanded attention to subject specialisation and art's autonomy. Bourgeois readers of the opinion-forming press in the mid-nineteenth century, read art criticism in conjunction with editorials, leaders and articles debating and re-evaluating American cultural progress, and sometimes its superiority to Europe. Anne Farmer Meservey has summarised the debates around landscape art in nineteenth-century America as in the province of:

> 'cultural nationalists' and 'cultural universalists.' The isolationistic nationalists aimed to create an independent native culture without

5 *The Nation* was mainly a vehicle for political commentary, but some seminal art criticism was penned for it by Henry James, Bernard Berenson, Frank Jewett Mather, Jr and Clement Greenberg.

> relying upon European examples ... [promoting] realist art and ... specifically American landscapes, characters, and ways of life because they believed such art would stimulate patriotism and create popular pride in American customs and history. The cultural universalists ... [incorporated] the wisdom of European and classical civilizations and artistic traditions, supplementing it, perhaps, with native subjects. They believed the artist should strive to ennoble and refine the individual's taste and sensibility, favoring idealized, spiritually uplifting art themes and styles.
>
> (Meservey 1978: 73)

The contribution of art criticism to the creation of a national school of art in America was not just an exhortation to artists, it was equally directed at the art-loving public, and carried the suggestion that in America the taste for art could be cultivated. In the periodical literature landscape paintings were presented as poetic responses to the glories of indigenous nature, and genre scenes were presented as nationalistic beacons of the American way of life. Landscape art in particular continued to accrete nationalistic meanings as *the* subject of American art. There was a highly moralising content to art criticism in the mid-nineteenth century periodical press. Many critics had been irrevocably influenced by the English art critic John Ruskin. In the first instance, artists had been influenced by Pre-Raphaelitism, and the advocacy of its principles and practices were a regular feature of the magazine the *Crayon*. Begun in January 1855 as a weekly quarto of sixteen pages (expanding to thirty-two pages the following year), the *Crayon* was the leading art journal 'devoted to the graphic arts and the literature related to them'. The *Crayon*, in the spirit of the sister arts, began publishing many of the Hudson School's paintings to accompany literary works by writers such as Ralph Waldo Emerson and James Fennimore Cooper. It published letters from John Ruskin, and appointed William Michael Rossetti (the brother of the English painter, Dante Gabriel) as its English correspondent, so it regularly aired Pre-Raphaelite strictures about truth to nature. Roger Stein, in his study of the influence of Pre-Raphaelitism in America, distils 'The fundamental importance of Ruskin's writing' in antebellum America down to 'his identification of the interest in art with morality and religion as well as with the love of nature' (1967: 41). Ruskin's distinction between sensuous apprehension and moral judgment relegated the former and emphasised the latter, a distinction which Stein and others have argued appealed to Americans in the Puritan tradition.

While there may be some mileage in the connection between Puritanism and Ruskinism, the moralising tide of the mid-nineteenth-century American art press began to turn in the post-bellum period. The unchecked, sensuous apprehension of art so disparaged by Ruskin's American followers began to assert itself in the Aesthetic Movement. Aesthetes such as Bernard Berenson

(1865–1959), formerly a student of Norton's at Harvard, were less interested in art as an expression of morality than they were in the potential of art for art's sake. Berenson's collected *Essays in Appreciation* (1958) are revealing in this respect, a set of propositions for understanding and enjoying art devoid of moral responsibility. But Berenson was also a connoisseur, his professional expertise residing in his ability to identify the hand of the Old Master in a renaissance painting and to authenticate works of art for the collections of private individuals. The new spirit of scientific positivism, concurrent with aestheticism, also helped to ebb the tide of literary and moral art. The scholarly pursuit of art history, increasingly present in liberal arts curricula, demanded that the canon of art history be established and that works of art be assigned to schools or to artists. Moreover, Gilded Age collectors were buying up gilded paintings, early Italian art that had not yet been scooped up by European museums and galleries, and the question of attribution was important to the sale of paintings.

In early American art history there were few historians who were not Anglo-American. A notable exception was African-American critic and civil rights activist Freedman Henry Morris Murray (1859–1950), who wrote and lectured on American art.[6] By the same token, the lack of concentrated writing about non-European-derived art evident in Dunlap was alleviated by collectors such as the influential Aby Warburg:

> the festivals and artefacts of the Hopi, whom he sought out during an American sojourn in 1896, provide[s] the strongest early example of the bridge building required to render traditional Western fields of study commensurable with those devoted to the diverse cultures of the wider world.
>
> (Crow 2006)

Moreover, increasingly specialised divisions between disciplines meant that writers in the modern period have tended to refer to indigenous arts and crafts, rather than on their own terms, citing them as sources for the imagination of avant-garde American artists. In 1933 MoMA's *American Sources of Modern Art* exhibition and catalogue, for instance, sought to:

> show the high quality of ancient American art, and to indicate that its influence is present in modern art in the work of painters and sculptors some of whom have been unconscious of its influence, while others have accepted or sought it quite consciously.
>
> (Cahill 1933: 21)

6 See in particular his 'Emancipation and the freed in American sculpture' (1916) (Pohl 2002: 224).

Emigré scholars

While much has been written of the contribution to American art-making of European exiles such as the surrealists, rather less has been written of the ways in which American art history and art making itself was reconceptualised during the 1930s and 1940s following the exodus of academics from Europe. John Rewald was one of several émigré scholars escaping conflict who was welcomed into the United States. Rewald's 1946 *The History of Impressionism* may seem a strange choice for a discussion on writing about American art but it is relevant for several reasons. First published in 1946 with the support of MoMA New York and subsequently revised across five editions, it was a publishing phenomenon, although it was not published in Great Britain (or more widely) until 1973. There were sequels: in 1956 *Post-Impressionism-From Van Gogh to Gauguin*, again not published in Britain until 1978, and then *Gauguin to Matisse*, and numerous collections of letters by post-impressionists such as Cézanne and Gauguin. In a post-war period when publishing in many countries was still subject to rationing, Rewald's lavish book, 670 pages long, contained more than 600 illustration plates, over 80 in colour. The power and authority of the printed word should not be underestimated. If histories are written by victors, then art histories are validated through wide-scale publishing. John Tebbel, writing the history of the American publishing industry, identified a post-war boom between 1940 and 1980: what he termed a 'great change' to 'substantial growth' (1981: 536). He noted that the Metropolitan Museum, New York and MoMA in particular expanded their publishing developments through extensive collaborations with commercial publishers, and thereby greatly extended their readership (1981: 537).

Rewald's books confirmed the centrality of Paris to the development of modern art: Harold Rosenberg's 'cultural Klondike' and Walter Benjamin's 'capital of the nineteenth century'. The books also normalised, in the English language, a mythologising approach to the modern artist: artistic defiance against established norms is in *The History of Impressionism*'s opening sentence. It is followed by detailed accounts of the artist's *struggle* to gain critical and popular acceptance. Born in Germany, Rewald studied under the humanist art historian Erwin Panofsky in Hamburg and Fritz Saxl in Frankfurt and later in France. He was part of the Jewish diaspora arriving in America in 1941 under the sponsorship of Alfred H. Barr Jr, MoMA's director. Rewald, a professor of art history in Chicago and New York until the mid-1980s, also created the foundation that saved from oblivion Cézanne's studio at Aix-en-Provence, which became instead a place of homage.

Rewald's writing is notable for its intense concentration on the details of artists' lives. The books are illuminated with Rewald's photographs, showing where artists worked, their studios and favourite motifs (such as Cézanne's

Mont Sainte-Victoire). Empirical research around exhibitions together with the commentary of critics and public, numerous artists' quotes, diligently gleaned from letters, diaries, newspaper articles, and dealer's bids and interviews (with such luminaries as Matisse) are woven into a compelling story of official rejection and eventual artistic triumph. Citations are numerous, and part of Rewald's debt to the art-historical methodologies of the French historian Fustel de Coulanges, from whom he borrowed the notion that history is a pure science. Such a method:

> consists of stating facts, in analyzing them, in drawing them together and in bringing out connections. The historian's only skill should consist in deducting from the documents all that is in them and in adding nothing they do not contain. The best historian is he [sic] who remains closest to his texts, who interprets them most fairly.
>
> (Rewald 1973: 10)

Under this methodology Rewald and others hoped to uncover a pre-existing story interlocked in the lives of artists but separate from broader social and political considerations. In general, however, art historians of Rewald's generation rarely questioned the theoretical underpinning of their discipline. They operated within a hermetically sealed world of standards, defined by an elusive quality often designated to an artwork through a trained eye conditioned by familiarity with the object of study. Early twentieth-century art history, like much of the nineteenth-century, was also dominated by a methodology intent on tracing provenance and verifying authenticity via the lives of artists, and so the monograph and survey, such as Rewald's, were staple scholarly devices. He did not seek an art history without names, but in Gombrichian mode argued that: 'there is no art only artists'. What is notable about Rewald's approach to art history is the lack of detailed reading of the artworks themselves in deference to the immediate 'texts' that surrounded them. Nor did he engage in the psychoanalytical interpretations that feature strongly in more recent ways of writing about art. Rather he chose a more general psychobiography which often related the mental state of the artist closely to the artwork itself.

The discipline of American art history benefited in a variety of ways from the European émigrés who arrived in the 1930s. Finding teaching and research posts in American universities,[7] many 'émigré scholars, including Erwin Panofsky (who settled at Princeton in the Institute of Advanced

7 See in particular Thomas Crow's (2006) 'The practice of art history in America', which offers a reading of the influential art historians, from early twentieth century to the present, who have argued for significantly differing imperatives for art history and its objects of study.

Studies in the 1930s) rewrote what was a rather conservative discipline.[8] Importantly members of the influential Frankfurt Institute for Social Research (popularly referred to as the Frankfurt school) left Germany in the 1930s and after a brief period in Geneva settled first in New York from 1935, then in California from 1941, before returning to Germany in the 1950s. Herbert Marcuse (1898–1979), who with Theodor Adorno and Max Horkheimer founded the Frankfurt School, emigrated to the United States in 1934. Although Marcuse was not an art historian (he eventually became professor of philosophy at the University of California at San Diego), his writings influenced the New Left radicals of the 1960s, who overturned many of the normative and naturalised methodologies of the art histories on offer.

The New School for Social Research in New York, founded in 1919, was especially important in accepting refugee scholars. Created in 1933, the University in Exile, a graduate division, attracted scholars such as Hannah Arendt and Leo Strauss. Arendt (1906–1975) had studied with Martin Heidegger in Germany, eventually fleeing France under German occupation in 1941. Although not dealing directly with art history, Arendt's scholarship had far-reaching influence on social thought (not least because she translated the work of Walter Benjamin) and though her championing of structured liberal education (SLE) at Stanford University. Through works such as *The Human Condition* (1958), she theorised political action and a notion of freedom which she saw as public and associative, rather than concentrating on individualism, as was so prevalent in the United States. She reasoned that such freedom was possible in American townships if people engaged in civic culture, as Jefferson had idealised. Importantly for our purposes the New School supported the École Libre des Hautes Études, which employed French-speaking scholars such as Claude Lévi-Strauss. The school was responsible for the dissemination of continental philosophies (particularly of Horkheimer and Habermas), at odds with home-grown philosophers of aesthetics, such as Susanne Langer.[9] Many American artists and writers attended influential lectures, which played a key role in the development of the New Left, who then exerted huge influence on the making and writing of art during the latter half of the twentieth century.

Thomas Crow (2006) argued that a 'pedagogically reduced version of European art history largely set the limits for the entire discipline in its postwar American translation. An inherited social conservatism thereby joined itself to a structurally generated intellectual conservatism' (2006: 77). In discussing the relative invisibility of George Kubler's important contribution to American art history, 1962's *The Shape of Time: Remarks on the*

8 See in particular Erwin Panofsky's 'The history of art' (1953).

9 Langer's book *Feeling and Form: A Theory of Art* (1953) is making a belated re-entry into contemporary debates on emotions and the arts.

History of Things, Crow attributes this to the crisis in the Left and the political conservatism of the period. It was not until the 1970s, as we shall see, that American art history gained an intellectual energy born of radical social change.

Members of the Frankfurt school spent almost twenty years in America before returning to Germany in 1953. Often committed to neo-Marxism and critical of capitalism, they extended existing debates by American art historians such as Lithuanian-born Meyer Schapiro (1904–1996), who arrived in America at the age of 3. The relationships between high, popular and mass culture, and crucially the extent to which history could be brought to bear when reading artworks, were brought into a field that had excluded such transgressions. Schapiro, an art historian at Columbia University, New York, had met Walter Benjamin from the Frankfurt school while in Europe. He lectured at the New School for Social Research from 1936 to 1952, and offered the first course on modern art anywhere. Such historians engaged in Marxist theory problematised the notion that art history could be told in a straightforward, descriptive way divorced from wider political considerations such as issues of class, and the ideologies that sustained the construction of artists, institutions and critics. In short, they argued for 'a simultaneous consideration of observable facts and material conditions and their expression in class and gender ideology' (Eisenman *et al.* 1994: 11).

While we may today have become familiar with modern art and are no longer scandalised by its frank departure from fidelity to appearance and truth to nature, by the 1930s the need to explain modern art had become pressing as it was more widely exhibited and purchased. A lay public that could see no objective standard with which to be guided when judging the merits of modern art apparently needed an intercessor to *explain* the modern movement. The field had its most ardent theorists in formalist historians and powerful apologists such as Alfred H. Barr Jr. Barr's *Cubism and Abstract Art* (1936) and *What is Modern Painting?* (1943/1988), written for a lay public, were influential in promoting (erroneously) the view that representation in paintings (or simplistically, art that bore a resemblance to things in the world) was 'a passive mirroring of things and therefore essentially non-artistic, and that abstract art, on the other hand, is a purely aesthetic activity, unconstructed by objects and based on its own internal laws' (Schapiro 1978: 195).

The realism and abstraction debate from a forum that established reputations effectively marginalised what were termed more conservative forms of realism. However, in spite of some misrepresentation, modern art was never solely about abstract art, or even modern distortions. On the contrary it included a great deal of figurative work, which was technically in debt to Renaissance techniques. Publications such as *What is Modern Painting?* included early 'figurative' work by Stuart Davis, Orozco and Arthur Dove, and realists such as the self-taught John Kane and regionalist

Grant Wood. First published in 1943 and revised in 1947, 1952 and 1956, the book incorporated new trends and historic events such as the rise of fascism, and so acted as an index of MoMA's changing priorities over several decades.

Patricia Hills contended that Barr's revisions increasingly stressed formalism. Hills's principal argument was that through his revisions of *What is Modern Painting?* Barr systematically undermined realist art practice, as he inexorably moved the museum's taste towards abstract expressionism. Moreover, she claimed Barr's notion of artistic freedom found its antithesis in the realism of totalitarianism, which he associated first with Nazi Germany and then with communism. The revisions, Hills claimed, also moved further away from a figurative tradition defined as 'conservatism' rather than 'modern'. By 1956, according to her:

> [T]he message to artists was clear; to prove your independence from [if not your rejection of] communism you cannot work in realist styles but must be 'modern' which to Barr, meant working in abstract and expressive styles. It was a message not in contradiction to the museum's own acquisition policies.
>
> (Hills 2001)

Meyer Schapiro, writing in 1937, analysed the opposition of realist and abstract art. He contested as essentially 'unhistorical' Barr's claim that art has 'its own internal logic'. The accusation against Barr, whose approach in writing in defence of modern movements was to present a history of '-isms' with dates, was that the idea that (abstract) art was independent of historical conditions, realised the underlying order of nature and was an art of pure form without content, was illogical. The central paradox was that although Barr attempted to explain abstract art as developing chronologically, history was also irrelevant. Barr saw the removal of content from reading artworks as problematical, and he acknowledged that modern art was impoverished by the exclusion of the historical and political – but at least it was 'pure' (Barr 1987: 86). He stated that he 'preferred impoverishment to adulteration'.

Schapiro however insisted on a social basis for all art production, representational or not, maintaining that:

> as little as a work is guaranteed aesthetically by its resemblance to nature, so little is it guaranteed by its abstractness or 'purity'. Nature and abstract forms are both materials for art, and the choice of one or the other flows from historically changing interests.
>
> (Schapiro 1978: 196)

His key works were 'On the social basis of art' and 'The nature of abstract art', first published in *Marxist Quarterly* (January–March 1937). Schapiro, who was a medieval scholar before turning his attention to the modern, significantly critiqued the existing art historical procedures almost two decades before Rewald's work. Relating impressionist paintings to the activities of the leisured class:

> Schapiro argued, the aesthetic itself became identified with habits of enjoyment and release produced quite concretely within the emerging apparatus of commercial entertainment and tourism-even, and perhaps most of all, when art appeared entirely withdrawn into its own sphere, its own sensibility, its own medium.
>
> (Crow 2006: 82)

Schapiro was part of what were called the 'New York intellectuals', centred around the publication *Partisan Review*, edited by Phillip Rahv and Lionel Trilling.

The work of Schapiro was held in abeyance for several decades as the Left lost confidence in the intellectual commitments and forms of art practice of the 1930s following events in the USSR. In particular the Stalinist purges of the army and the Moscow show trials of opponents of the regime, held between 1935 and 1938, and in the following year the Hitler–Stalin Non-Aggression Pact, shook any residual faith in international socialism, leaving a deeply disillusioned Left. While formalism should not be seen as an outcome of such machinations (as a way of reading artworks it predates the 1930s), increasingly it became the dominant way of talking and writing about art. In the 1970s and 1980s Schapiro appealed to a new generation of historians dissatisfied with what they saw as the elitism of the trained eye, and institutional critique began to undermine any notion of objectivity in the selection of artworks.

While the criticism of Barr has some validity, he continues to be credited with creating a systematic structure for European modernism, through his chart in 1936 at a time when studying the modern period was not granted the same gravitas as studying the medieval or the Renaissance. For example, Rewald had difficulties publishing his work on the moderns. However as we saw in Chapter 5 developments at MoMA had far-reaching consequences, as did the publication of Barr's books, which explained modern art to a lay public. The difficulties that faced painters working in what were pejoratively termed social realist modes during the 1950s were exacerbated by hostility to the Soviet Union post-war and institutional moves away from supporting figuration. The charge most often laid at the door of MoMA and Barr as its first director was that of perpetuating a myth: that 'the more adventurous and original artists' had turned to abstraction 'because they had grown bored with painting facts' (Barr 1987: 84).

While there may be some evidence that Barr moved inexorably towards abstraction there is also evidence of his support for differing forms of realism, including the work of Shahn, Winslow Homer, William Gropper and John Kane (Barr 1958: 12–17). He also supported art that contained overt social and political imagery. In explaining modern art to the lay audience, he used Peter Blume's *The eternal city* (1937) as an example of an 'original and challenging painting ... attacked on all sides' (Barr 1958: 39). It is important to register Barr's defence of the work and the reasons for the condemnations, which he does not endorse: 'Some critics disliked its precise realistic technique and its elaborate use of symbolism and allegory; others attacked it because they felt art should have nothing to do with social and political questions; and [because it was] ... "inartistic"' (Barr 1958: 39).

Replying to set questions posed by the *Magazine of Art* in March 1949, Barr insisted that 'an actual "battle of styles" as for instance between realism and abstraction, is desirable only to those who thrive on partisanship. Both directions are valid and useful – and freedom to produce them and enjoy them should be protected as an essential liberty' (quoted in Sandler and Newman 1986: 212). Nonetheless MoMA became the focus of protest from realists and abstractionists alike. In 1952, fifty artists petitioned the museum over its overemphasis on non-objective art, resulting in the *Reality Manifesto*. They were supported philosophically by articles in *Masses and Mainstream* in 1952 which also attacked a perceived bias at MoMA. Concurrently, however MoMA was the focus of discontent from abstract artists, who charged it with artistic conservatism.

Taking American art seriously

The publishing machinery – from scholarly essay to artist-led magazines, manifesto and journalistic polemic – sustains and disseminates art practice. The archived published accounts of culture, many now down-loadable as exhibition aftermath, play an important part in what of events is remembered. Early in America's history a nascent publishing industry actively contributed to the dissemination of American art. Although they are not official art histories, the importance of art and literally journals such as the *Crayon*, the strong regional emphasis of Philadelphia's *Port Folio* (1801–27), *New-York Mirror* (1823–57), *Knickerbocker Magazine* (1833–62), the New York-based *American Monthly Magazine, American Review, New-York Review* and *Athenaeum Magazine* were all influential. The *New-York Mirror* included original compositions as well as prints with accompanying descriptions. The magazines operated on at least two levels. As well promoting particular constructions of artists and their work, they also taught the viewing public how to look at and understand American and European art.

There was considerable growth in journals throughout the twentieth century. The *Journal of Aesthetics and Art Criticism* is the quarterly publication for the American Society for Aesthetics, which began in 1941. Also influential and written in by Meyer Schapiro were the *New Masses*, *The Nation*, and *Dissent*, founded with Irving Howe and Michael Harrington. *Partisan Review* had been a vehicle for Marxism in the 1930s, publishing in 1939 Clement Greenberg's 'Avant garde and kitsch', which advocated art's removal from the world in the face of crass, mass culture: popular, commercial art, Rockwell's *Saturday Evening Post* covers and Tin Pan Alley. The little magazines of the twentieth-century should not be underestimated: the influential *Art News* for instance, by the 1950s was seen as the official organ of the New York school, providing critical support for the nascent movement. There were battles pitted across magazines as artists rallied to realism or abstract expressionism. The Reality group for instance published their defence of realism and their hostility to selections at MoMA, which seemed to favour non-objective work, in a short-lived magazine called *Reality* (1953). There were many other magazines, such as *Tiger's Eye*, which published articles such as Barnett Newman's 'The first man was an artist' (1947) arguing against the 'domination of science over the mind of modern man'. In a period of extraordinary interest in American art the magazines, some of which were artist-led, contributed to rich, highly partisan debates about the forms contemporary art should take.

Susan Noyes Platt has identified several examples of the dismissive attitude to the 1930s in *Art and Politics in the 1930's, Modernism-Marxism-Americanism: A History of Cultural Activism during the Depression Years* (1999). She maintains that John Baur's 1949 survey, *Revolution and Tradition in American Art*, is exemplary of a model of 1930s American art which saw it as 'a brief and disappointing interlude between American Modernism and Abstract Expressionism' (1999: xvi). The diminishment of the 1930s was reinforced by Sam Hunter's 1959 *Modern American Painting and Sculpture*, in which 'he does the New Deal and Mexican Muralists on one page' (Noyes Platt 1999: xvi). Noyes Platt then cited John Wilmerding's *American Art* (1976), which 'has only one sentence devoted to the New Deal and moves quickly from Regionalism on to Abstraction' (1999: xvi). To Platt's list can be added Norbert Lynton's later survey, which placed the New Deal in a short parenthesis (Lynton 1980: 227). Sam Hunter's later publication (1973) devoted only five pages of 470 to the art of the 1930s.

The theories that attempted to radicalise institutionally dominant art history by calling institutional practices and art history into question were often referred to as the 'new art history', and grew out of 1960s social unrest. The New Left in America, and scholars such as Carol Duncan, Alan Wallach and Max Kozloff, transformed the discipline with articles such as Kozloff's 'The Rivera frescoes of Modern Industry at the Detroit Institute of Arts: proletarian art under capitalist patronage' published in 1973, and Duncan and Wallach's 'The museum as late capitalist ritual: an iconographic analysis', published in *Marxist Perspectives* (1978).

The scholarly history of American art gained a fillip from the collection and publication of primary source materials in the mid-twentieth century. In 1968 Herschel Chipp (with contributions from Peter Selz and Joshua C. Taylor) published *Theories of Modern Art: A Source Book by Artists and Critics* in a response to a need by American art historians for the original sources that first recorded and discussed art. Although we might take issue with Chipp's statement that 'American art before the Armory Show is basically anti-theoretical and should be studied from a broader viewpoint that would include the social, political, and cultural environment' (1968: vi), art students have undoubtedly gained from working with primary sources, manifestos, letters, artist's statements, political speeches given in the United States of Representatives and so on. *Theories of Modern Art* is also notable for presenting a large section of American source material in addition to European texts, organising into one volume otherwise hard-to-find documentary material. However, Chipp also disseminated a particular view of the genesis of American art, which is evident in section ix, 'Contemporary art: the autonomy of the work of art', rather than situating artworks within a particular social context.

The 1996 *Theories and Documents of Contemporary Art: A Sourcebook of Artists' Writing* edited by Stiles and Selz marked a determined enterprise to reflect sweeping social changes and a widening of the parameters of art practice. It demanded, in effect, that publications about art be more representative of diverse voices: inclusive of women, ethnic minorities and non-mainstream artists working in new technologies and conceptual art. It also responded to the importation into art history and art practice of theory from other disciplines such as cultural studies and literature, which changed our understanding of the pathology of the artist. While it was still narrowly focused on European and American examples, female artists such as Yoko Ono, Adrian Piper, Faith Ringgold, Louise Bourgeois, Nancy Spero and Cindy Sherman were represented through primary source texts to a wide international audience. In the albeit smaller American section of Chipp's groundbreaking anthology, Elaine de Kooning is the solitary female voice. This was not necessarily to do with an increase in the numbers of women working in theory and/or as artists between 1968 and 1994, as many of the women transverse the period; it was more to do with an art culture wilfully oblivious to their presence. J. C. Taylor's *Nineteenth-Century Theories of Art,* published in 1987, and David and Cecile Shapiro's *Abstract Expressionism: A Critical Record* (1990) are also light on women, with just three again receiving mention: Elaine de Kooning, Dore Ashton and Anita Brookner.

Feminism and Linda Nochlin

Interpreters of Schapiro's methodology came during the 1960s, with historians such as Linda Nochlin, who cites Schapiro's 'Courbet and popular imagery: an essay on realism and naiveté' (1941) as crucially important for historians trained in the 1950s and 1960s, offering an alternative methodology to the standard formalism on offer at Vassar and New York University's Institute of Fine Arts (Nochlin 1991: xiii–xiv). Her 'bricolage' of a methodology which flexibly uses what seems appropriate contributed to 'thinking art history Otherly', and she maintained that 'what really displaces, repositions, and transforms the disciplinary object itself most drastically – are the questions raised by feminism' (Nochlin 1991: xvi). Her 1971 'Why have there been no great women artists? began with a prolonged focus on the representation of women, and more recently she was 'Dislocating tradition : women artists and the body, from Cassatt to Whiteread'.[10] Also influential was her work on *Realism* (1971), *Women, Art and Power* (1989) and *Representing Women* (1999), which included a look at women such as Florine Stettheimer (1871–1944), whose work, executed in an eccentric blend of art deco and art nouveau, celebrated patriotic themes and locations such as parades on Broadway and Wall Street: specifically *The cathedrals of Broadway* (1929).

In 1991's *The Politics of Vision* Nochlin states her position which, while methodologically it owes much to Rewald and his colleagues, is self-consciously aware of the political dimensions on three levels: first the political position of the art historian herself, second the position of the artwork within society, and third the politics and history of the politics of art history. If Rewald's methodology consisted objectively 'of stating facts, in analyzing them, in drawing them together and in bringing out connections' (Rewald 1973: 10), for Nochlin 'the very act of producing art history implicates the art historian politically' (Nochlin 1991: xv).

As well as refuting claims to objectivity, it was against the over-reliance on the art historical methodology of formalism that Nochlin and other feminists pitted themselves. Drawing on a wide range of models and methodologies – psychoanalytic theory, structuralism, Marxist theory, literary criticism and aspects of traditional art history and its revised modes – feminist art history 'reproblematizes and reconstitutes the central issue of how meaning is produced in form within the work of art' (Nochlin 1991: xvii).

The discipline is in debt to a number of women art historians, such as Anne Wagner, who have opened up the terrain of art history not just to establish the reputations of women artists but to uncover the operations and structures of art history and the academy. In particular such writers have looked not at women alone but at the ways that the experience of being a woman artist intersects with race, class and sexuality. Lucy R. Lippard's 1995 *The Pink Glass Swan: Selected Feminist Essays On Art*, also drew together a range of writing from the 1970s to the 1990s both scholarly and

10 In the Luce annual lecture on creativity, Royal Academy, London, January 2008.

popular, crossing the boundary between political activism and women's art, and sometimes looking at taboo subjects and women artists' responses to them. Whitney Chadwick's populist history *Women, Art and Society* (1990) also did much to introduce women artists to an audience beyond the studio or academe.

Queer studies, too has belatedly impacted on art history, often through its cross-over with cultural and media studies: film theory applied to art history. In particular queer theory calls into question the fixity of heterosexual and homosexual identities. Judith Butler (of the University of California), a post-structuralist philosopher, has had a major impact on writing about art, in particular through her delineation of performativity, a theory that is widely used to create new meanings around the relationship between desire, sexuality and meaning-making with visual images. She also problematises notions of the pre-existing self: her philosophic position has been amply deployed in re-reading images.

Post-structuralism has informed new readings from the perspective of gender and queer politics. For instance Jennifer Doyle reinterprets the life and work of Thomas Eakins in 'Sex, sodomy, and scandal: art and undress in the work of Thomas Eakins' (2006: 15-44). *Pop Out: Queer Warhol*, an edited book by Doyle, Flatley and Munoz from 1996, explores new ways of writing about previously taboo subjects. Munoz's *Disidentifications: Queers of Colour and the Performance of Politics* (1999) gives voice and photographic visualisation to a range of ephemeral queer theatre performances.

A less didactic present?

Janet Wolff's *AngloModern: Paintings and Modernity in Britain and the United States*, written in 2003, pays attention to the exchanges between Europe and the United States, and remarks on the hasty rewriting of art history in recent years to be inclusive of the realist and figurative traditions which had been 'rendered invisible by museum practice and art-historical discourse' (2003: 1). The post-war 'triumph' of American painting was achieved at the expense of seemingly more democratic and 'realistic' modes of painting, such as works endorsed by the public work projects of the 1930s. From the political realism of Philip Evergood, Jacob Lawrence and Ben Shahn to the 'anecdotal realism' of Norman Rockwell or Andrew Wyeth and the mystical realism of West Coast painter Morris Graves, many artists felt the scorn of critics committed to formalist values (Phillips 1999: 31). David Craven maintains that future studies of abstract expressionism will have to address:

> not only how painters of the New York School related to ... other groups of Abstract Expressionists from Canada, Europe and Latin America, but also how the social concerns of the Abstract Expressionist

> were sometimes interrelated with those of figurative artists on the left, such as Shahn or Evergood.
>
> (Craven 1999: 86)

Beyond studying abstract expressionism, American art history has moved towards a critical approach, rejecting the simple binary division of modernism versus realism, to look again at commonalities.

Contemporary art historians and critics are unlikely to be as confident or as prescriptive as partisan advocates of formalism and the social history of art in the twentieth century. In 2004, the authors of *Art Since 1900: Modernism, Antimodernism, Postmodernism* (Foster *et al.* 2004), contributors to the influential journal *October*, offered four art historical methodologies with no particular hierarchy: psychoanalysis in modernism and as method, the social history of art, formalism and structuralism, and post-structuralism and deconstruction (2004:5). Acknowledging a lack of confidence in their own tools and that models were 'hardly thriving' (2004: 679), the authors saw the current lack of a single force as positive.

The importance of psychoanalysis is foregrounded in *Art Since 1900* the timeline beginning with Sigmund Freud's *The Interpretation of Dreams* (1900). However Foster and colleagues (2004) note that European psychoanalysis was reworked at a local level, arguing that while in Europe surrealism's concern with the unconscious was about broad political concerns, in America it was reduced to 'ego psychology'. It was 'stunted' and even in its Jungian manifestations wilfully self-referred. Such intensity led to a rejection by minimalists such as John Cage and Robert Rauschenberg of the private ego approach of the abstract expressionism generation. Psychoanalytic theory has been used in postcolonial theory, queer theory, and by feminists in particular to explore the workings of subjectivity and sexuality. Rediscovered in the 1970s, especially by post-minimalists such as Eva Hesse, it has been readily applied to works such as *Contingent* (1969), the ethereal beauty of which has lent itself to readings that have stressed variously vulnerability and carnality.

There are however, some clear contemporary allegiances, with Frances K. Pohl for instance titling her 2002 survey *Framing America: A Social History of American Art*. Her diverse and inclusive text, thematically and chronologically driven, 'highlights the different ways in which art historians have approached the study of American art – e.g. through the use of biography, stylistic analysis, the study of patronage and/or the locations of artistic production within struggles for political or personal power' (Pohl 2002: 9). It has an acknowledged debt to Arnold Hauser's four-volume *The Social History of Art* (1951). Like other social histories of art, Pohl's history of American art is less perhaps about the personal struggles Rewald conceptualised, than about 'the place of art within the struggles for power in both the public and private realms, and with rethinking the category "art" itself ...

combining research on art institutions ... with attention to the critical discourses surrounding them' (Pohl 2002 :11).

'Is art history?'[11]

A generation of writers on American art received a fillip from the arrival in the 1980s of the English art historian T. J. Clark, whose early seminal works on French modernism effected a paradigm shift. The methodology that it ushered in may be termed the social history of art. At its most obviously reductive, artworks were read as ideological documents, often shackled to moral indignation. This is a vexed area: as we have seen many artworks, even the most seemingly benign such as botanical drawings and epic landscapes, are invested by author and viewer with national and personal ideology. According to Martin Berger's *Sight Unseen: Whiteness and American Visual Culture* (2005), even representations without figures in them have the possibility of perpetuating dominant ideologies and racism, so the Left have been quick to seize upon readings that uncovered the stereotypes embedded in representations of, say, the African-Americans in antebellum America. The casualty of such an approach has been the artwork as an artwork: that is to say, as a relatively autonomous aesthetic object.

Clark's more recent *The Sight of Death: An Experiment in Art Writing* (2006) has returned to the aesthetic, to look again at artworks as things in themselves. He was perhaps uncomfortable with the ways in which his earlier methodology was bowdlerised and used exclusively to cite instances of historical injustice and prejudice. A minor discontent, or a reversal of Clark's earlier priorities, his book does give primacy to the work of art over its contexts or the work's conditions of production. The utopianism of the social history of art spawned in the 1970s, which saw art as part of an emancipatory social project, seems to have run aground. Clark and others' responses to how we currently write about art are more complex than just issues of artworks being annexes to 'every tawdry ideology' or causes. In raising the stakes on the aesthetic again, Clark asks what our relationship is to it, and why has it been so neglected in academic circles. In part it is because the aesthetic was perceived as elitist, and so its neglect (or diminishment) was an article of faith for the Left. Powerful theoreticians had also eroded any confidence in an ideology-free aesthetic. In America, where so much rhetoric around egalitarianism has resulted in powerful civil rights movements, a methodology that searched works for evidence of the arts confirming the status quo found fertile ground.

Clark also returns to the ways in which a diary entry, sometimes in the form of a poem, can illuminate a work of art: 'uncover the magic of seeing'

11 A question first asked by Svetlana Alpers (1977).

(2006: 237). His concern that we are engaged in 'writing pictures to death' (2006: 8) is in part an acknowledgement that there is a gap between forms, that writing can only be an analogy of a painting and anyway 'language is always too specific and discriminating ... when it tries to mimic this first idiotic appropriation of the visual' (2006: 9). But perhaps most importantly, Clark returns to first-person accounts of his close observations, inflected by the light and ambience of the Getty in Los Angeles: 'The first thing that caught my eye this afternoon in "Landscape with a Calm"[12] was the placing of ...' (2006: 15).

12 A painting by Poussin (1650–1).

Chapter 7

End notes

Henry Luce's editorial 'The American century', published in *Life* magazine in 1941 prior to America's involvement in the Second World War, was a call to arms. For the publishing magnate, international isolationism was no longer an option. The editorial was marked by a variation on the belief in manifest destiny that has distinguished much of America's history, identifying America's 'nobility of health and vigor' as essential qualities for progress in the wider world (Luce 1941: 64). Luce's 'magnificent purpose'[1] in promoting democracy (and American financial systems) abroad, and his vision for American expansionism or even empire-building, were not shared by the majority, but the epithet 'the American century' stuck, and was widely reused in the twentieth and twenty-first centuries. The Whitney Museum of American Art's survey of twentieth-century American art in 2000 reused the term to headline the show. The rhetoric of Luce's journalism now looks less triumphalist than in the 1940s: the twenty-first century is less secure. Art has rarely been a significant force in world affairs but it has not been immune to greater world events, as we have seen.[2] This chapter looks at the recent past and the contemporary American scene to see how artists have responded to the challenges of a less certain world.

Any summary of contemporary American art is confounded, as the much-trumpeted diversity, even randomness, of current art practice is open to interpretation: utopian or a new conformity. Besides this, art history has a way of reducing the diversity of the past to a streamlined, manageable story. In particular, that officially sanctioned in the twentieth century, presented an avant-garde that rarely reflected (even within mainstream modernism) the huge range of artistic practices that actually took place. We have seen that early American modernists, 1930s and 1940s Mexican art, and forms of 1950s figuration were often casualties of what Raymond Williams termed

1 Luce's philosophy was conditioned by his Christian commitments: he was a Presbyterian and the son of missionaries.

2 David Craven, writing in defiance of conventional wisdom, demonstrates the ways in which art has been used in Latin America to create social and political change.

'the machinery of selective tradition' (1989: 69). Nonetheless, as we shall see there are currently identifiable traits in contemporary art criticism: a renewed interest in aesthetics, a nostalgia for recalibrating past art forms, boundary spanning, and pioneering strategies to demobilise notions of the nation-state and unitary citizenship. Historical subject matter and arcane artforms reappear in a new range of guises to play an important part in the current repertoire. Ostensibly such plurality could lead the way to greater freedom of practice and critical diversity. However, some critics and historians are concerned that 'our paradigm has also abetted a flat indifference, a stagnant incommensurability, a consumerist-touristic culture of sampling' (Foster *et al.* 2004: 679). Looking back to more certain times, the quandary is, 'is this posthistorical default in contemporary art any great improvement on the old historicist determinism of modernist art à la Greenberg and company?' (Foster *et al.* 2004: 679).

The artist too has been subject to revision, not least because the current vigorous collaborations across disciplinary boundaries undercut notions of authenticity and originality, and have propelled the artist back into the curatorial arena that preoccupied the early surrealists. Moreover compelled to engage in dialogue at international biennial, triennial and quinquennials, often talking about complex installation work or transnational justice and cultural translation from 'platforms'[3] or 'stations', artists have become ethically, socially and politically accountable. Often akin to the travelling artists of the eighteenth and nineteenth century and the artist as social worker of the 1930s New Deal, many artists work without studios, being instead location and project-based. These are referred to as itinerant artists by Miwon Kwon; she notes that 'the increasing institutional interest in current site-oriented practices that mobilize the site as a discursive narrative is demanding an intensive physical mobilization of the artist to create works in various cities throughout the cosmopolitan art world' (2006: 45).

The anxious object?

When Harold Rosenberg wrote after the Second World War of the *Anxious Object* (1966), he was extending an existential anxiety and personal alienation close to French sensibilities, to the work of art. A sense of anxiety does pervade much of contemporary American art, although it takes a different form. Contemporary anxieties may perhaps be most easily read out of West Coast painter Ed Ruscha's *Course of empire*, which represented the United States at the 51st Venice Biennale in 2005. Ruscha, at the forefront of pop

3 Okwui Enwezor's 2002 *Documenta II*, held in Kassel in Germany, constellated international platforms for discussions that foregrounded political debate: new technologies enabling forms of interaction and rendering the international art show globally peripatetic.

art and associated with defining the 1960s 'LA look', reconceptualised American landscape painting (and eschewed East Coast aesthetics) with billboard-like images of filling stations (*Standard Station, Amarillo, Texas*, 1963) and ubiquitous flat-roofed industrial buildings. Ruscha trained at commercial art school, taking much of the context, forms and techniques into fine art, as is sometimes seen in his slick airbrushed paintings with their homage to photography and typography.[4]

Ruscha's Venice work can be read as an elegiac, if bleak, commentary not just on Thomas Cole's 1836 landscape series of the same name (without the definite article) but on the rapidly changing recent American urban landscape. Ruscha put together five horizontal black and white canvases, with five new colour ones being shown separately in the two wings of the pavilion. The former, done in 1992, were from his *Blue Collar* series: drawings of drab grey industrial units with words such as TECHCHEM on them. The reworked colour versions, such as *The Old Tech-Chem Building* (2003), show the same buildings renovated. Others in this landscape series visualise buildings such as *The Old Tool and Die Building* (2004), stencilled (reminiscent of sign-painting), with commercial words such as 'Trade School' and 'Telephone'.

The response to the first series, mirrored in the colour canvases, was of a more dystopian globalised world, the brash confidence of the earlier series gone. The paintings now revisit the obsolete or redundant, which are covered with graffiti and even a swastika, the new words on the block, looking like pan-Asian characters, are the artist's invention. One building with 'Fat Boy' writ large across it is overshadowed by a glowering Colesque red sky. Economic success signified by the mass-produced industrial units of Los Angeles' commercial buildings now looks in doubt as the productive strength of the United States migrates to Asia. And yet Cole's five canvases of magisterial mountains from the nineteenth century (as we saw in Chapter 4) showed an imagined future rather than a reality. While there is a sense of ruined, uncertain empire in the veteran Ruscha's work, some (like Kunitz 2005) have seen the move from black and white to colour as positive, and the range of changes taking place in the renovated buildings as not entirely negative.

A younger generation of artists, while not always sanguine, is dealing with a perceived new world order in different ways. The pathology of the artist has been reconceptualised, with artists more likely to collaborate and cross boundaries with subject domains such as science and anthropology. Moreover, they are likely to return to the past through more interdisciplinary means than Ruscha's painted *Course of empire*.

4 Ruscha was educated at the influential Chouinard Art Institute.

Appropriating appropriation

> Almost every work of serious contemporary art recapitulates, on some explicit or implicit level, the historical sequence of objects to which it belongs. Consciousness of precedent has become very nearly the condition of major artistic ambition. For that reason artists have become avid, if unpredictable, consumers of art history.
>
> (Crow 1996: 212)

Crow's claim that knowledge of art history is a precondition of contemporary art practice stands in stark contrast to the ambition of high modernists (in the early to mid-twentieth century) who authenticated their practice upon a mythic and unadulterated originality. In summary, if modernism was predicated on a search for individual self-expression, then what followed was recognition of the futility of such a search, and an acceptance that the self (and art) are constructed categories. That is not to say that modernists were unaware of their precedents: they were simply irrelevant except as a counterpoint to their own search for a unique signature style or as something to be overturned in pursuit of the new.

From the late 1970s what was termed appropriation art became an insider strategy, with artists flagrantly plagiarising the work of others, often motivated by revised notions of the real and simulacra. It is entirely consistent therefore that the most prominent exponents of such strategies should work with the photographic image. More recently a second generation of appropriation artists has gained a fillip as the dissemination of images in a digital age has meant a reconceptualisation of modes of reproduction, and opened up the democratic potential of art for all. In 1979 Sherrie Levine rephotographed Walker Evans's seminal images of Depression America from an exhibition catalogue *First and Last* to create part of the *After* series, which knowingly appropriates the work of often male artists. In 2001 Michael Mandiberg revisited the same photographs and created AfterWalkerEvans.com and AfterSherrieLevine.com, sites from which to download and print out an image complete with certificates of authenticity. Democratic idealism with artworks for all, or yet more irony or overt commentary on new modes of art distribution, the revisiting of once-radical gestures is not without pitfalls. The effectiveness of the second generation of appropriation artists has been questioned, as has the continuity of the conceptually related practice of institutional critique (in that they both question normative values).

The institutionalization of the benign institutional critique?

The phenomenon of the 'institutional critique' has led to considerable questioning of the ways in which the past has been stored, disseminated and displayed. Artists' critiques of the institutions that house, classify and sell their work are not new: they are readily traced to Dada in Europe and the influence of Marcel Duchamp and the American surrealists. The politics of institutional critique were central to social unrest in the late 1960s. By the 1970s, many artists had turned their sceptical gaze to the fabric of the art museum, exposing the operations of these seemingly civilized and benign cultural venues. From performances such Mierle Laderman Ukeles's *Maintenance art* in 1973, which involved washing the steps of the Wadsworth Athenium (in Hartford, Connecticut), to Hans Haacke's inventions uncovering the relationship between museum trustees and slum landlords, artists were engaged in making transparent the structures that supported what some perceived to be corrupt institutions at worst, apologists for elitist bourgeois values at best.

Collections too came under scrutiny, most famously in Andy Warhol's *Raiding the icebox* of 1970. In an act of curatorial vandalism, Warhol displayed the entire shoe collection from the basement of the Rhode Island School of Design's museum. His typically ambiguous gesture has been interpreted variously as a commentary on consumerism, revisiting the rejected (Wollen 1993), or in his incoherent display, an assault on the unwarranted confidence in the museum's classification systems.

By the 1990s institutional critique gained momentum as it was cogently formulated in Fred Wilson's seminal 1992 *Mining the museum* in Baltimore. By placing slave manacles, unexplained, amongst the metalwork display of exquisitely decorated drinking vessels and jugs from the eighteenth and nineteenth century, Wilson sought to expose the ideological nature of the museum display. The African-American Renée Green (b. 1959) has also turned her attention to the way in which cultural ambience can mask hidden histories. In *Mise en scène II* (ICA London, 1992[5]), Green recreated an eighteenth-century salon, rather like a period room in a museum. With Handel's *Fireworks* emanating from a sound box labelled 'Ambience', the viewer is confronted with another history woven into the fabric on the furniture. In sharp contrast to the civilised mood of the room (a metaphor for the sanitised history on offer in many museums), the fabric, (toile) covering the chairs depicts troubling scenes of revolt. A French imperial soldier is lynched by a Haitian revolutionary in a reversal of the commonplace scenes of lynching. In contention over the *Code Noir*, French legislation to prevent miscegenation, the revolt is rarely recorded. In Green's work the rebellion is repositioned to ask questions about the telling of history.

Institutional critique and artists as interventionists in the museum and gallery space were theorised and given widespread authority at the New York School of Visual Arts by theorists such as Craig Owens (1990) and

5 *True stories: part two* by Mark Dion and Renée Green was shown at the ICA London, 4 November–6 December 1992.

Douglas Crimp, whose *On the museum's ruins* (1993), with photographs by Louise Lawler, received widespread academic exposure. Crimp and Owens taught artists such as Mark Dion (b. 1961). However, in 'From the critique of institutions to an institution of critique' (2005), Andrea Fraser concludes that we are complicit:

> It's not a question of being against the institution: We are the institution. It's a question of what kind of institution we are, what kind of values we institutionalise, what forms of practice we reward, and what kinds of rewards we aspire to.
>
> (Fraser 2005, reprinted in Horowitz and Sholis 2006: 38)

The effectiveness of the current generation of artists working on institutional critique has been lessened by the ability of liberal art galleries and museums to adjust to criticism. Such adjustments have resulted in benign, sanctioned interventions into gallery spaces rather than wholesale overhaul of institutional practice. Corporate culture seems to be a permanent fixture in the art museum, with Fraser observing that MoMA opened its new temporary exhibition galleries (2004) with a corporate collection, causing concern about the independence of exhibition selections and further concerns about corporate censorship of controversial artists and artworks. However Fraser also suggests 'we' stop speaking of the institution as other than us:

> the very institutionalization that marked [the failure of the historical avant-garde to abolish autonomous art and integrate into the praxis of life[6]] became the condition of institutional critique. Recognizing that failure and its consequences, institutional critique turned from the increasing bad-faith efforts of neo-avant-gardes at dismantling or escaping the institution of art and aimed instead to defend the very institution that the institutionalization of the avant-garde's 'self-criticism' had created the potential for: an institution of critique.
>
> (Fraser 2005: 39 in Horowitz and Sholis)

Accepting institutionality within the constraints of funding applications may require a greater self-reflexivity from the artist. However, do-it-yourself approaches (also characterised as garage or basement approaches) that are oppositional to mainstream institutional values still exist. Unsanctioned interventions into the museum do still take place. While identity politics and well-publicised guerrilla tactics such as those of the Guerrilla Girls in the 1980s, which pointedly asked if women had to be nude to get into the Metropolitan Museum of Art, have ensured a more equitable distribution of

6 Fraser was referring to Peter Bürger's 1984 *Theory of the Avant-Garde*.

artists, unsanctioned popular culture in the museum space can still cause a stir. Break-dancing across Carl Andre's flat minimalist, steel grid sculpture, laid out on the floor of the San Diego Museum of Contemporary Art in 2000, Juan Capistran took what was then a counter-cultural form, unannounced and uncaptioned, into the museum; the event, *The breaks*, was recorded in a series of photographs.

Unpacking the museum

Despite the current rethinking about the status of interventions into the museum, museums continue to be sites of some of the most visually compelling works, in part because they often reuse existing artworks/artefacts. In debt theoretically to earlier notions of institutional critique, artists have usefully unravelled authoritative fictions such as museum classification, often finding rich inspiration in displays at natural history museums. The working practices of artists such as Dion, whose work from the late 1980s resembles fieldwork, involves collecting specimens, the use of the scientific notebooks and the apparatus of the naturalist or archeologist as much as the traditional artist's paraphernalia. Dion works across the world, from rainforests in Belize to the River Thames in London, in collaboration with others, eschewing the unique signature style of individualised creativity. Using the theories and procedures of ethnography, anthropology and archaeology, the interdisciplinary works often operate as a palimpsest: the uncovering of layers of the past, rather than giving attention to the 'surface' which had so dominated high modernism.

Dion's artworks, such as the early 1989 *Extinction* series, included *Black rhino, with head.* A real rhino head in a wooden crate was displayed as a specimen ready to be dispatched to a collector, in one of several containers marked 'fragile' in stencilled lettering, adorned with photographs of poached rhinos and a map of Africa. Together with a photograph of Theodore Roosevelt hunting the now rare animal, the series could be read as a commentary on the relationship between colonialisation, animal importation, extinction and the subsequent loss of biodiversity, and also on what Donna Haraway calls 'Teddy bear patriarchy' (1984).

Critical of the presumed radicalism of the ecological movement, Dion, an amateur naturalist, also collects and has a natural history collection that includes the habitat diorama. He admits however to being 'more interested in Poe than Thoreau' (Corrin, Kwon and Bryson 1997: 33), and combines an interest in the natural world with pre-Enlightenment classification systems, the *Wunderkammer* and the cabinet of curiosity, as well as the display of the dead in the contemporary Enlightenment natural history museum. Many 'projects' such as Dion's are engaged in political and social issues, calling into question art-making as an autonomous activity, and preferring to conceptualise artworks through process and relations with sites rather than making decontexualised objects. Avoiding the perils of art for arts sake and formalism, but also sidestepping the charge of art as social work, has taxed artists in recent years.

While appropriation artists have revisited iconic artworks of the past, others have returned to outmoded, even arcane, subjects and media, often exploring the taxonomies of the past. For instance, the performance group La Pocha Nostra has turned its sceptical eye on the historical diorama in performances where audiences become living tableaux. Dion too as we saw returns to the outmoded, a strategy that flies in the face of a cultural history and practice of visual art in America which has been obsessed with the new. America has been preoccupied with the technologically and conceptually new, in contradistinction to the Old World's obsession with the past. The new in America had been a signifier of radicalism, an article of faith for a country distancing itself from the old Europe. Perhaps more than in many other cultures, new forms of consumerism and their methods of distribution have been extensively explored by American artists. So such widespread reworking of old forms marks a significant departure.

While a sense of unease may be found in many of the artworks since at least the beginning of the twenty-first century, it would be easy to date attention to the events of what is universally called 9/11: pre 9/11 and post 9/11 are used to mark out economically, socially and artistically distinct timeframes. However, many artworks were exhibiting a *fin de siècle* anxiety in the 1990s. As well as general unease about the future of the United States, there have been tangible anxieties in the art world, which has been disproportionately affected by HIV/Aids. Robert Gober's *Untitled* (1991) features a pair of legs from an apparently face-down body, severed by a painted landscape at the buttocks. Candles have been fitted into the legs, a disquieting tactic that explores the abject, sexuality and death. Like several other artists in this summary, Gober's work evokes the diorama, and he commented that his part-tableau installations are 'natural history dioramas about contemporary human beings' (quoted in Foster *et al.* 2004: 646).

The absent female body

Since the nineteenth century artists have found alternative sites for making and displaying artworks. In particular women sought alternative sites in part because institutional bias privileged patriarchal values. Women in the 1960s turned the body itself into a site of contention and expression. Barbara Kruger's *Your body is a battlefield* demonstrates that the political body is still a force in recent art, used as a vehicle to explore and expose the ways in which cultures construct categories such as gender, race and sexuality. While there are continuities with the identity politics of the twentieth century, a third generation of feminists have revisited the work of first and second-generation feminists, but the rules of engagement have been re-conceptualised.

Although powerful feminist works such as Carolee Schneemann's *Interior scroll* and Judy Chicago's *Dinner party* had been criticised for biological essentialism, such complaints have been revisited. In 'The serial spaces of Ana Mendieta' (2007), Susan Best argues that Ana Mendieta's best known earth/body work, the *Silueta* (silhouette) series produced by Mendieta between 1973 and 1980, overcomes the charge of essentialising and ahistoricism that has haunted her reputation and this series in particular. Over 100 siluetas were made by Mendieta, using her own body, often in an ancient goddess-like pose, and recorded in film and photography: documentation of her stated aims to 'become one with the earth'. Although she does 'appear' literally in some works, more typically she is absent: only the impression of her indistinct body temporarily remains.

The Cuban-American's close identification of the female body with the earth, and a reinforcement of the concept of Mother Earth, can be seen as a form of biological reductionism, implying that women are nature to men's culture. Such a position has a long history, going back at least to the eighteenth century. The issue of the gendering of nature as female has been problematic for women seeking to account for why men and women are allocated or occupy different spheres of social activity. Certainly Mendietia's work can be played out against the more overtly masculine earthworks of artists such as Robert Smithson,[7] whose *Spiral jetty* (1970), a colossal 1,500 feet coil of black basalt earth in the Great Salt Lake, Utah, was formed by earth-moving equipment. However both artists were interested in pre-Columbian traces, and Smithson's new art form which he termed Earthworks had its roots in literature, particular a Brian Aldiss novel of ecological disaster, also called *Earthworks*.

Mendieta in particular drew on Mexican, Latin American, Catholic and Neolithic sources. Her silhouettes had little environmental impact, and for the most part were created to disappear back into the landscape through natural organic breakdown:

> In recent feminist art history essentialism has generally been regarded as a term of abuse or an approach to avoid at all costs. In feminist philosophy, however, the inescapability of using essentialist, or universal notions has been widely canvassed. If essentialism is inescapable, as many argue, then one of the challenges for feminist theory is to distinguish between varieties of essentialism and their efficacy for feminist ends.
>
> (Best 2007: 57)

7 The exhibition *Earthworks* organised by Robert Smithson at the Dwan Gallery in New York in 1968 is credited with starting the Land Art movement.

Mendieta's deployment of essentialism, Best suggests, serves such ends. Best and others have tried to bring Mendieta's work back into prominence by exploring theoretical positions such as Butler's performativity[8] and eco-theories, and a call to reinvent the essentialist terms in which women have been characterised.

From apolitical camp to gender insurgency

If many artists have presented an overt image of femininity or masculinity and an uncomplicated relationship to American values, others have used camp to represent their ambivalence about normativity, American values and the overt masculinity often pictured in portraits of the artist as American. For instance observed in legendary film footage dressed as a working man in T-shirt and jeans, Jackson Pollock became a public figure following photographs published in *Life* magazine. In 1949 under the provocative headline 'Is he the greatest living painter in the United States?' Pollock in paint-smeared jeans and denim jacket, cigarette in mouth, is pictured against his wide, horizontal canvas *Summertime no. 9A* (1948) with an inset showing a detail of tangled skeins of paint from *Number twelve*. What was striking about the photograph was the way Pollock was imagined as American: the painter Willem de Kooning said of the image that 'he looks like some guy who works at a service station pumping gas' (Naifeh and Whitesmith 1989: 595). In the popular imagination Pollock became the quintessential American painter – taciturn and troubled, he was superficially related to James Dean and Ernest Hemingway, sharing their dress, nature or alcoholism.

Parodic camp has a long history in American culture, and offered an alternative vision of the American artist. Camp is often defined as a performance or even a form of cultural appreciation that is capricious in expression. In the context of the 1950s and 1960s, predating the New York Stonewall[9] rebellion of 1969 and the subsequent Gay Rights movement, camp could be seen as an assault on normative gender constructions which were particularly polarised after the war. Theatricality and playfulness were the hallmarks of camp, where according to Susan Sontag's 'Notes on "camp"' of 1964, the 'whole point ... was to dethrone seriousness' (1964: 527). Famously she asserted camp's triumph of style over content, maintaining that 'the Camp sensibility is disengaged, depoliticized – or at least apolitical' (1964: 517).

8 See in particular *Ana Mendieta: Earth Body, Sculpture and Performance, 1972–1985* (curated by Olga Viso), Whitney Museum, New York, 2004.

9 The New York Stonewall rebellion is named after the site of conflict between police and protestors at the Stonewall Inn in Greenwich Village on 28 June 1969. Up to that time police regularly arrested people for cross-dressing or drinking in groups of more than three.

Camp, particularly parodic camp, was used by many outsider groups as we saw in Chapter 4, and was never the preserve of gay culture, although many successful exponents of camp were gay men. However the presumed apoliticality of camp, drag and cross-dressing which often lampooned women brought the charge of misogyny and lost much of its cachet during the politicised 1990s. Moreover, sections of gay culture gained visibility on television and in mainstream film, and while many do not wish for or find total acceptance or tolerance, homosexuality has been legislatively sanctioned. Less secure has been the increased visibility of transgender identities or gender queerness, although during the 1960s Warhol's entourage included transvestites and drag queens such as Candy Darling, and accentuated difference.

Present expressions of gender difference are intent on dissolving categories of male and female rather than seeking to pass one gender off as another. Wolf suggests that:

> queer culture was transformed by the increasing visibility of transgender identity, shifting gender pronouns, gender-neutral names, and – perhaps most radically – with surgery. In the past few years, this gender frontier has expanded, thanks to FTM (female to male) trannies, who dissolve or translate lesbian or butch codes and sensibilities into a non-normative transman, trannyfag, or androgynous identities.
>
> (Wolf 2006: 114)

Tara Mateik, an educator and artist with a background in electronic arts, founded the Society of Biological Insurgents (SBI) in 2002. Through installations and video such as *Video Kourous* (2002), which looks at the sea horse, the only animal where the male reproduces, and in performances such as the *Battle of the sexes* in which Mateik plays both Billie Jean King and Bobby Riggs,[10] Mateik and collaborators 'wage strategic operations to overthrow institutions of compulsory gender'. Mateik sometimes works with the Yes Men, an 'identity correction' collective which disrupts biologically determined gender identities.

Described as 'a proto-totalitarian artist – a small-time Richard Wagner who mythifies the catastrophic conditions of existence under late capitalism' (Foster *et al.* 2004: 673), performance artist Mathew Barney also turns his attention to normative identities. Blurring the boundaries of gender and animals has not been the preserve of gay activists. Barney has also turned his attention to species boundaries, most famously with the camp and bizarre

10 A tennis match dubbed the battle of the sexes was played in Houston, Texas in 1973 between Billie Jean King, then the leading female tennis player in the world, and a former Wimbledon champion, Bobby Riggs, who maintained that he could beat any woman. He lost in three straight sets.

occasionally zombiesque film-cycle *Cremaster*[11] from 1994 to 2002. In the films Barney is transformed into a satyr and even the Loughton ram. The five films were shown in the cinema, and presented narratives that can be read as a satire on gender roles but particularly that assigned to men and played out in its most masculine formation. Much is made of the moment of sexual differentiation, as part of a narrative on creation and death (including the execution of Gary Gilmore), traversing geographic locations as far apart at Barney's native Idaho, New York, the Isle of Man and Budapest in Hungary. Although the films evade any easy reading, they have been seen as commentary on a crisis precipitated by the changing nature of gender roles and women's empowerment (Hopkins 2000: 245).

Post-nostalgia for the American dream

In part the present artistic uncertainty is the logical conclusion of forces set in motion by conceptual art rather than a response to events external to the art world. Conceptual art (that is, an art of ideas rather than a finished marketable object) was, as Crow suggests, 'Against visual culture' (1998b: 212). Although America cannot lay claim to the genesis of conceptual art, some of its best-known exponents have worked in the United States. Appropriation art, full of knowing irony, had become a self-referential form of parody that was difficult to read without a knowledge of previous art styles and artists. Moreover, artworks were often motored by theoretical considerations, inexplicable to many. That is not to say that earlier artworks were not in thrall to one theory or another, but in the late twentieth century theoretical concerns placed the very basis of art production into doubt. There was also a fragmentation: put simply, artworks were made up of many segments, sometimes losing the overall visual coherence that we had come to expect of monumental or epic art. Works such as Rachel Harrison's *This is not an artwork* (2006) sum up the doubts about what constitutes an artwork: an uncertainty that has haunted both modernism and contemporary art.

To reiterate: If the very artwork itself is insecure, then that insecurity has been made manifest by artists who appropriate the work of other artists. During the 1980s and early 1990s, Cady Noland often worked with 'ready-mades', referencing a mythic American past, its cowboys and guns and its icons, Diet Pepsi and Budweiser, in works such as *The American trip* (1988) and *Cowboy blank with showboat costume* (1990). Noland's work typically critiques the dark side of American culture, exploring masculinity and a dysfunctional culture. Noland also revisited classic American subjects such as Patty Hearst and a seemingly national obsession with serial killers. Her work

11 The title referes to the cremaster muscle, which functions to raise and lower the scrotum. The muscle also plays a part in regulating the temperature of the testis, and so is important in determining the gender of any progeny.

was the focus of a 'recreation' when in *Cady Noland Approximately: Sculptures and Editions 1984–1999* at Triple Candle, New York (2006), two artists recreated works from photocopies in flagrant disregard of the original.

Changing visions of the American self

In *Only Skin Deep: Changing Visions of the American Self* (2003), Coco Fusco and Brian Wallis have raised issues of race that have punctuated the history of American art. They offer a distinctly different perspective on American identity from that presented by writers such as Samuel P. Huntington, who wrote *Who Are We? The Challenges to America's National Identity* in (2004) Unhappy with the increased numbers of Hispanic immigrants to the United States, Huntington commented in an interview with Walter Ellis that:

> America was created, by and large, by British Protestant settlers .... Would America be the same country it is today if in the seventeenth and eighteenth centuries it had been settled by French, Portuguese or Spanish migrants? The answer is no. It would be Quebec, or Brazil, or Mexico.
> (quoted in Ellis 2004: 17)

Ellis adds, 'Huntingdon's thesis contends that contemporary Latino immigrants do not en masse wish to buy into the existing US, but intend setting up their own parallel language and culture, is necessarily doom-laden' (2004). There were many voices raised against what was perceived as a racist stance. The book raised the stakes on issues of origins and the formation of the United States under East Coast Puritan values, which had been explored by artists since at least Edward Hicks's *Peaceable kingdom* series of the 1830s.[12]

Laying to rest the shade of Cotton Mather[13]

If Barbara Rose, reviewing art in Los Angeles in 1966, thought Cotton Mather[14] could be laid to rest, she was wrong, for his spirit has remained

12 Edward Hicks (1780–1849), a Quaker preacher, made over one hundred versions of *Peaceable kingdom*, which was based on a biblical source.

13 A quote slightly adapted from Barbara Rose's 'Los Angeles: the second city' (1966: 114).

14 Cotton Mather (1663–1728), a Puritan minister, was influential through the prolific publication of books and pamphlets. He wrote *Magnalia Christi Americana* (The Great Works of Christ in America) in 1702, a collection that included 'The life of John Winthrop'. He is best know for his association with the Salem witchcraft trials of 1692. A slave owner, he also wrote *The Negro Christianized* in 1706. His influence reached far beyond the late seventeenth and early eighteenth century in establishing the centrality of New England Puritan theological values for the coming Republic following the American Revolution.

remarkably robust. Still ousting residual Puritanism forty years later, Sam Durant recycled the waxwork figures from the obsolete Plymouth National Wax Museum. Durant's 2006 *Scenes from the pilgrim story: natural history* resituated the waxworks, once the pedagogic staple of a museum visit, in an art context. The relocation to an art space does not remove, but rather redoubles, the pedagogic impulse, as 'natural history' is revisited, calling into question national myths of origin, in part through the use of largely discredited art forms. Durant, who works in Los Angeles, placed on white plinths the life-size, dismembered models of Puritans.

This was not Durant's only skirmish with the past, explored through forms of representation. His philosophically related project, *Proposals for new monuments*, appeared in 2007/8 in the exhibition *Un-monumental* at New Museum, New York. Durant's *Proposal for White and Indian Dead Monument transpositions, Washington D.C., 2005* is made up of thirty replicas of obelisks (modelled to about one-third of their original size) painted a uniform battleship grey. The obelisks vary in size and detail but conform to the essential form of the ancient symbol. Durant's criteria for selection was that the monument should be based on some similarity to the landmark obelisk, Washington's Monument in Washington, DC. Research was an important element of this work, as Durant searched for numerous massacre monuments that commemorated death caused by conflicts between indigenous people and settlers. The time-span covered the earliest conflicts through to the twentieth century. Notable was the disparity in scale (if that can be used as a value judgement) between the white and Indian memorials, with greater size allocated to numerically smaller deaths in the white monuments. Durant's conviction that art has a powerful place within a critical discourse is evident in his claim that the proposed monument could take its place amongst the numerous monuments on the Mall in Washington:

> it [the Monument proposal] served to make the point that America is based on violence and conquest – not on democracy as we are taught to believe (and is repeated ... in the corporate media). So it makes a certain historical point which could be used to understand current situations. For instance one might view the war in Iraq as a continuation of the historical pattern of colonial war and aggression, rather than swallowing the Administration's now obviously bogus justifications. I've found the more I know about history the less I believe what the government says. This ... would be the opposite of what a 'conventional' monument is supposed to do ... my Monument Proposal would be understood as an anti-monument.
>
> (quoted in LeKay 2007)

The publicly situated 'don't touch' monument has been the subject of technological intervention. Sandra de la Loza's video animated a frieze of terracotta figures at the Fort Moore Pioneer Memorial in Los Angeles, an intervention giving a significantly different account of history.

The status and exploits of non-Americans aspiring to live in America have also been explored by several contemporary artists. Julio César Morales's 2005 *Undocumented interventions* graphically documents unsuccessful attempts to emigrate from Mexico to the United States in figurative, hand-coloured drawings. They include 'x-ray' images of a man concealed inside a car seat or hidden in the bodywork. More generally his work looks at issues of labour and surveillance. We discussed earlier foreign artists who considered the impact of America within their own 'borders'. Mexican artist Daniel Guzmán draws on 'low' culture and countercultures, including comic book aesthetics and urban consumer culture, to radically critique the post-colonial present specifically found in vast metropolitan conurbations such as Mexico City. His misleadingly titled video *New York groove* (2004) shows a man dancing in busy streets to a Kiss soundtrack. He is seemingly aping New York culture through badly executed dance steps. It is filmed in Mexico City, and a commentary on the supposed buffoonery and lack of sophistication of the Mexican stereotype sometimes perpetrated by North American culture. But it is also a commentary on the erosion of local culture through the persistent presence of American culture. Guzmán sees his inability to master the steps as an act of defiance, stating:

> I belong to a city of the third world in which poverty and misery take over one's imagination, intuition, and ideas as tools to deal with the day to day .... I see myself as a kind of garbage man playing with notions about the exotic and faraway.
>
> (quoted in Blazwick 2004: 316)

The New Barbarians

> Dear visitor: Welcome to the New Barbarian collection, a new concept of presenting live art created by a consortium of global corporations catering to your innermost cultural fears, sexual desires and revolutionary aspirations .... This is a temporarily de-colonized zone. Observe your own projections VERY carefully. North, South, East ... delete All political, racial, historical, medical and ethical implications have been carefully extracted from the bodies on display for your own comfort.
>
> (British MC at the 2007 performance of *The New Barbarians Collection Fall 2007: Designer primitives on the runaway runway*, Arnolfini, Bristol)

Guillermo Gómez-Peña, a founder member of the transnational San Francisco-based La Pocha Nostra, 'a conceptual institute of hybrid art and cross-over jam culture' (www.pochanostra.com), creates works that may be described as utopian at the same time as exploring cultural anxieties in the West in the new millennium. Censorship and nationalism are recurring themes in the loose international group, which was set up to support Chicano artists marginalised by the Anglo avant-garde. According to their manifesto, 'Through our performance praxis and pedagogy ... we try to build more open, fluid and tolerant communities defying dysfunctional or dated notions of identity, nationality, language and art making' (La Pocha Nostra 2008). Performers such as Violeta Luna and Roberto Sifuentes, appearing with Gómez-Peña in a piece entitled *The New Barbarians Collection Fall 2007: Designer primitives on the runaway runway*, sought to erase boundaries such as those between art and spectator, and art and politics, as well as undermining fixed notions of identities: gender, artist and race.

The internationally toured series[15] of performances called *The New Barbarians* reused the fashion catwalk as 'X-treme fashion' in a more politicised context: the naked bodies of performers are sold as the show unravels. Pop culture finds itself under scrutiny during these performances, as the protagonists reveal the sometimes self-serving appropriation of 'otherness' the pop industry deploys. The lack of boundaries and categories is particularly evident in the sources and methods used by La Pocha Nostra. Drawing on an aesthetic they describe as 'robo-baroque' and 'ethno techno-cannibal aesthetics', they 'sample and devour' eclectically, fusing disparate cultural forms from 'border and Chicano pop culture; TV; film; rock and roll; hip hop; comics; journalism; anthropology; pornography; religious imagery ...and the history of visual and performing arts' (La Pocha Nostra 2008). The results of such archiving and mixing are then reinterpreted for live audiences in performances that sometimes recall the sideshow and dioramas of an earlier age. Moreover, while the new America has given some cause for pessimism, committed to presenting a different face of America, La Pocha Nostra's manifesto conceptualises the future quite differently with 'No homeland; no fear; no borders; no patriotism; no nation-state; no ideology; no censorship' (La Pocha Nostra 2008). If early identity artists were concerned with establishing who and where they are, then a younger generation of Chicano and Hispanic artists are working in mainstream conceptual art, and are less likely to define themselves by race and more likely to look at issues of art practice.

The legacy of modernism

The Hirshhorn Museum, in Washington DC as we saw in Chapter 5, like many other galleries, was set up for and continues to display the modernist

15 Other performance artists collaborate with La Pocha Nostra, which is a loose federation or rebel artists' collective.

canon, which with few deviations moves inexorably to American high modernism and colour-field painting. But outside the Hirshhorn's uncompromising late modernist building stands *Kiepenkerl* (pedlar), Jeff Koons's steely shiny statue from 1987 (Plate 14). Invited to produce a work in Germany, Koons recast an existing sculpture of a traditional figure sited on the Potsdamer Platz in Munster Town centre. *Kiepenkerl*, like much of Koons's work, is a paradox. The pipe-smoking pedlar, dressed in a linen smock, carrying a walking stick, touted his wares on his back, from town to village, a familiar figure historically, but an anomaly in modernity. And yet outside the Hirshhorn he reappears in a celebration of banality, kitsch and nostalgia, conceptualised by a former commodity broker and master of self-publicity.

Koons's self-publicizing hype, playfulness, cynicism and celebration of kitsch are a far-cry from the serious endeavours of high modernism – perhaps it could be seen as a closer but more polished and financially successful neo-Dada. Although often seen as a product of the 1980s, the commodification and even banality of art exemplified by Koons continues. In the polish and glamour of Koons's makeover of modernism there is a touch of the side-show or fairground baroque, which is a hallmark of his celebration of celebrity. The commodification of culture was foretold as early as 1900, when in *Philosophy of Money*, Georg Simmel wrote of culture under capitalism and its inability to evade commodity status. Under modern capitalism all forms of human creativity would be reduced to the vagaries of the marketplace, a view encapsulated in Barbara Kruger's 1980s slogan, 'When I hear the word culture, I take out my checkbook.'

The hiatus we (or those who lived through modernism's greatest triumphs and failures) inhabit is in part because the legacy of modernism is still undecided. Some find the passing of the certainties of modernism's determinism painful. Moreover the collapse of the binary between avant-garde culture and the kitsch of mass culture has left an uneasy vacuum. The distinction (even if determined by a subjective 'eye') discerned where quality, and crucially where opposition to dominant paradigms, lay: so lack of boundaries and interdisciplinarity can be interpreted as a loss. This is especially so if many younger artists' embrace of commodification and institutional acceptance are seen negatively. Being repelled by institutional authority was a precondition of entry into the nineteenth and twentieth-century avant-garde. Moreover, making art for money, while necessary, was not a precondition of making art.

In a roundtable discussion the four authors of 2004's *Art Since 1900* (Foster, Krauss, Bois and Buchloh) articulated their misgivings about the inability of culture to defend art's autonomy. Distressed by increasing standardisation and the inability of artists to sit outside of a homogenising apparatus, they fear 'commodity production, investment portfolio, and entertainment', the realisation of Guy Debord's integrated spectacle and the 'susceptibility of art to integration and therefore ideological control' Foster *et al.* 2004: 673).

Much of their position is based on European philosophy of the twentieth century, and in particular Debord's *The Society of the Spectacle* (1967/1994). A member of an anarchic but politically unaffiliated confederation of artists and intellectuals called the Situationists, which developed around the Paris student-led unrest of the 1960s, Debord foregrounded in revolutionary terms the relationship between capital and image. According to Debord, within advanced capitalism everything becomes spectacle mediated by the superficial image, where reality is cast into doubt and everything enters a world of appearances and commodification. However, although it can be argued that people become passive and manipulated under spectacle, that does require a passive consumer. But spectacle can also offer emancipation, since it has subversive potential (Debord famously supported the counter-culture strategy of graffiti). A return to the use of spectacle's potential to radicalise or control through commodification lies at the heart of much recent debate. Retort[16] returned to the central premise of Debord and the Situationists International to 'make them [the society of the spectacle and the colonization of everyday life], instruments of political analysis again, directed to an understanding of the powers and vulnerabilities of the capitalist state' following the attacks on the United States on 11 September 2001 (Boal *et al.* 2006: 162). Writing as a collective the authors rage against over-commodification, the inability to learn from an albeit constructed past, and the realisation of Debord's predictions in the spectacle of 11 September (Debord 1994: 24).

Technology, media and phantom sightings[17]

The effects of the information age and concerns about media monopolies have preoccupied many theorists, historians and artists since the early days of television. More pressing now that the spectacle and the proliferation of images dominate American lives to an unprecedented extent, artists have continued critiquing our responses to screen culture. The utopian and dystopian impact of technology on the everyday are equally celebrated or mourned: held up for scrutiny by artists who use technology as a platform to communicate or use technology as a new creative tool. Under the influence of numerous theorists technology is also called to account for the ways in which identities are formed and mediated through screen culture.

Technologised commodification, consumerism and over-consumption via

16 A collective consisting of Iain Boal, T. J. Clark, Joseph Matthews and Michael Watts.

17 The title is a reference to LACMA's *Phantom Sightings: Art and the Chicano Movement 2007*, touring southwest America in 2008.

television extends to the commodification of the body, particularly the racial body. Paul Pfeiffer (born in Honolulu) in *The long count* (2000/1) revisits three boxing matches: their reworked titles, *I shook up the world, Rumble in the jungle* and *Thrilla in Manila*, reminding even the least sports-conscious viewer of Muhammad Ali's legendary matches against Sonny Liston, George Forman and Joe Frazier from the mid-1960s to the 1970s. The three monitors that relive the fight do not however allow us full access to the past. The images are digitally erased in a 'translucent negative' (Blazwick 2004: 302). We can hear the sound of the fights but are not allowed to 'consume' them. Instead we are made aware of our own spectatorship. The spectacle of the African-American stereotype of the sportsman/women is foregrounded here; but we are made aware of the role of media technology in the representation of others.

Early pioneer of video art Nam June Paik's *Electronic superhighway: Continental U.S., Alaska, Hawaii,* originally created in 1995, was reconstructed in Washington at the Smithsonian American Art Museum (SAAM) in 2007. Its configurations vary but in essence it is a 40 ft wide map with each American state structured and defined by neon-tubes. Within each neon-lit state, flickering monitors bring the viewer a chaotic collage of sound and image, mostly drawn from clichés of American media and mass culture, mixed with significant speeches on issues such as human rights (Martin Luther King Jr vies with movie soundtracks). At its most literal Kansas is imaged through fragments of *The Wizard of Oz*. The image is on the cover of this book, and it is also, along with *Electronic moon times 2* and *Lostsputnik,* viewable on YouTube (2008). Paik's colossal work can be read in many ways: that technology homogenises national and global cultures is just one possibility. His work since 2000 he termed 'post-video': it involves the use of laser technology projected onto a range of surfaces: material and cascading water. Site-specific collaborative works (with Norman Ballard) transformed the rotunda of Frank Lloyd Wright's Guggenheim Museum in New York, with laser projections that passed through a waterfall cascading seven storeys.

Iñigo Manglano-Ovalle also works in an interdisciplinary way which combines art with architecture, politics and science. *The storm* (2007), installed at the Citizenship and Immigration Services building in Chicago, uses technology to create a commentary on the current US immigration process, which has scaled up its activities since the 'war on terror' post 9/11. The large-scale sculpture of two thunderstorm clouds builds on earlier work such as *Random sky* (2006), which used computer-generated data to visualise representations of the weather.

32 cars for the 20th century play Mozart's Requiem quietly by Nam June Paik consists of classic cars, sprayed silver, with their engines replaced by sound equipment that plays Mozart's *Requiem.* With the cars devoid of their original function and transformed into aesthetic objects, the work can be read as a commentary on built-in obsolescence and innovations for the consumer, but it can also say something about the ways in which the American automobile industry dominated twentieth-century living in the Western world. Our dependence on the car and our profligate use of power have returned many artists to issues raised by Robert Smithson's earthworks of the 1970s. Smithson's philosophical position finds echoes in the ecologically charged works of Agnes Denes, another artists engaged in interdisciplinary work whose environmental project, a living sculpture (1982) *Wheatfield – a confrontation* consisted of a two-acre field of wheat grown on a vacant lot in lower Manhattan. The harvested grain was redistributed around the world as part of the International Art show for the End of World Hunger. Formally the impact of such a work in a built-up city with its attendant urban spectacles of neon signs and billboards was immense, underpinning global concerns, an example of artists' attempts to reconcile the demands of art with outward responsibilities.

We saw in the introduction an uncertain States of America being promoted in academic literature and exhibitions outside America. The artworks found in such exhibitions of young artists working in America are often critical of lifestyles, and certainly the artist's body and the body of others are still at the forefront of practice. However, there is a discernible move away from the racialised body towards a greater acknowledgement of hybridised identity and the importance of genetics.

Laurie Anderson, the pioneering multimedia performance artist, was the first artist in residence at NASA. *The end of the moon*, second in a trio of solo works, was the result of the encounter and toured internationally in 2006. In a departure from her earlier work, which often involved complex technological combinations such as split-screen video projections, she moved to a low-tech response to contemporary American culture. Using songs, stories and music, Anderson created a poetic travelogue-cum-commentary on many of the issues raised above: consumerism, war, freedom and the idea of beauty. The work is grand, even epic in scope, combining personal narrative with theory, research and ideas around spirituality. The low-tech collage of Anderson's work bears some comparison to Cornell's *Americana fantastic*, which we encountered in the introduction. But there are other continuities with the history of American art. The search for the self and the specifically American self, the competing demands of technological progress and the transcendent, reverberate in her works. The challenges facing contemporary art in America include a consideration of relational concepts and the reconciliation of art with social and historical constructions. The move to more interactive user-friendly works judged within relational concepts is also a marker of the current diversity and energy of American art.

Bibliography

Abbott, E. R. (1917) 'Report on reproductions', *Bulletin of the College Art Association of America* 3: 16–21.

Allentown Art Museum (nd) *Contemporary American Painting: A Selection from the James A. Michener Foundation Collection*, Allentown, Pa.: Allentown Art Museum.

Alpers, Svetlana (1977) 'Is art history?' *Daedalus* 106, part 3.

Anderson, Benedict (1991) *Imagined Communities: Reflections on the Origins and Spread of Nationalism*, 2nd edn, London: Verso.

Anderson, Nancy K. (1992) 'Curious historical artistic data: art history and Western American art', pp. 1–36 in Jules David Prown et al. (eds), *Discovered Lands, Invented Pasts: Transforming Visions of the American West*, New Haven, Conn. and London: Yale University Press.

Anderson, Nancy K. (1998) 'The kiss of enterprise: the Western landscape as symbol and resource' in Marianne Doezema and Elizabeth Milroy (eds), *Reading American Art*, New Haven, Conn. and London: Yale University Press.

Anderson, Patricia (2001) *Elwyn Lynn's Art World*, Sydney: Pandora Press.

Arendt, Hannah (1958) *The Human Condition*, Chicago, Ill.: University of Chicago Press.

Arnheim, R. (1983) 'On duplication', pp. 274–84 in D. Dutton (ed.), *The Forger's Art*, Berkeley, Calif.: University of California Press.

Arrington, Joseph Earl (1968) 'Godfrey N. Frankenstein's moving panorama of Niagara Falls', *New York History* 49 (April): 169–99.

Asma, Stephen T. (2001) *Stuffed Animals and Pickled Heads: The Culture and Evolution of Natural History Museums*, Oxford: Oxford University Press.

Austfield, M. L. and V. M. Mecklenberg (1984) *Advancing American Art: Politics and Aesthetics in the State Department Exhibition 1946–48*, Montgomery, Ala.: Museum of Fine Arts.

Avery, Kevin J. and Peter M. Fodera (1988) *John Vanderlyn's Panoramic View of the Palace and Gardens of Versailles*, New York: Metropolitan Museum of Art.

Baignell, M. (1980) *Dictionary of American Art*, London: John Murray.

Banes, S. (1998) *Subversive Expectations: Performance Art and Paratheater in New York, 1976–85*, Ann Arbor, Mich.: Michigan University Press.

Barnard, H. (1906) *Pestalozzi and his Educational System*, Syracuse, N.Y.: C. W. Bardeen.

Barnhill, Georgia Brady, Diana Korzenik and Caroline F. Sloat (1997) *The*

Cultivation of Artists in Nineteenth-Century America, Worcester, Mass.: American Antiquarian Society.

Barr, Alfred H. Jr (1936) *Cubism and Abstract Art*, New York: Museum of Modern Art (MoMA).

Barr, Alfred H. Jr (1958), *What is Modern Painting?* 3rd edn, New York: MoMA/ Simon & Schuster.

Barr, Alfred H. Jr (1987), *What is Modern Painting?* rev. edn, New York: MoMA.

Barr, Alfred H. Jr (1988) *What is Modern Painting?* 9th edn, New York: MoMA.

Barr Papers. Unpublished documents, New York: Museum of Modern Art. No 3, Political Controversy (index 3–1270, no. 4, Soviet Matters (index 128–1376); File 28, US Exhibition in Moscow, Record Group no. 8.

Barthes, Roland (1957) 'The great family of man', pp. 100–2 in *Mythologies*, London: Vintage.

Baudrillard, Jean (1988) *America*, New York and London: Verso.

Baudrillard, Jean (1993) *Simulations*, New York: Semiotext(E).

Beam, Philip C. and James M. Carpenter (1943) 'The limitations of color slides', *College Art Journal* 2(1): 35–40.

Bedell, Rebecca (2002) *The Anatomy of Nature: Geology and American Landscape Painting, 1825–1875*, Berkeley, Calif.: University of California Press.

Benjamin, Walter (1999) 'The work of art in the age of mechanical reproduction', pp. 211–44 in H. Arendt (ed.), *Illuminations: Essays and Reflections*, London: Pimlico.

Bennett, Michael J. (1996) *When Dreams Came True: The G.I. Bill and the Making of Modern America*, New York: Brassey's.

Bercovitch, S. (1975) *The Puritan Origins of the American Self*, New Haven, Conn.: Yale University Press.

Berenson, B. (1893) 'Isochromatic photography and Venetian Pictures', *The Nation* 57(1480) (Nov.): S.346–7 (reprinted in Roberts 1997).

Berenson, Bernard (1958) *Essays in Appreciation,* London: Chapman & Hall.

Berger, Martin (2005) *Sight Unseen: Whiteness and American Visual Culture*, Berkeley, Calif.: University of California Press.

Berman, Avis (1990) *Rebels on Eighteenth: Juliana Force and the Whitney Museum of American Art*, New York: Athenaeum.

Berry, Nancy and Mayer, Susan (eds) (1989) *Museum Education: History, Theory, and Practice*, Reston, Va.: NAEA.

Best, Susan (2007) 'The serial spaces of Ana Mendieta', *Art History* 30(1): 57–82.

Birch, Thomas H. (1998) 'The incarceration of wildness: wilderness areas as prisons', p. 449 in J. Baird Callicott (ed.), *The Great New Wilderness Debate*, Athens, Ga.: University of Georgia Press.

Birnbaum, Daniel, Gunnar B. Kvaran and Hans Ulrich Obrist (2006) *The Uncertain States of America Reader*, ed. N. Horowitz and C. Scholes, New York: Sternberg.

Bjelajac, David (2000) *American Art: A Cultural History*, New York: Laurence King.

Blackman, Charles Arthur Boyd, David Boyd, John Brack, Robert Dickerson, John Perceval, Clifton Pugh and Bernard Smith (1959) *The Antipodean Manifesto*, Melbourne: Victorian Artists' Society.

Blair, Karen J. (1994) *The Torchbearers: Women and Their Amateur Arts*

Associations in America, 1890–1930, Bloomington, Ind.: Indiana University Press.

Blazwick, Iwona (2004) *Faces in the Crowd, Volti nella Folla* Castello di Rivoli, Whitechapel Gallery and Milan: Skira SpA.

Boag, Peter (1998) 'Thomas Moran and Western landscapes: an inquiry into an artist's environmental values', *Pacific Historical Review* 67(1): 40–66.

Boal, Iain, T. J. Clark, Joseph Matthews and Michael Watts (2006) 'The state, spectacle, and September 11', pp. 162–72 in N. Horowitz and B. Sholis (eds), *The Uncertain States of America Reader*, New York: Sternberg.

Bode, Carl (1959) *The Anatomy of American Popular Culture, 1840–1861*, Berkeley, Calif.: University of California Press.

Body, William (1998) 'Sixty million viewers can't be wrong: the rise and fall of the television western', pp. 119–40 in Edward Buscome and Roberta E. Pearson (eds), *Back in the Saddle Again: New Essays on the Western*, London: British Film Institute.

Bogart, Michele (1981) 'The development of a popular market for sculpture in America, 1850–1880', *Journal of American Culture* 4(1):3–27.

Bogdan, Robert (1988) *Freak Show: Presenting Human Oddities for Amusement and Profit*, Chicago, Ill.: University of Chicago Press.

Boime, Albert (1971) *The Academy and French Painting in the Nineteenth Century*, London: Phaidon.

Boime, Albert (1990) *The Art of Exclusion: Representing Blacks in the Nineteenth Century*, Washington, DC and London: Smithsonian Institute Press.

Boime, Albert (1991) *The Magisterial Gaze: Manifest Destiny and American Landscape Painting, c. 1830–1865*, Washington: Smithsonian Institution Press.

Bolin, Paul E. (1990) 'The Massachusetts Drawing Act of 1870: industrial mandate or democratic maneuver?' in Donald Soucy and Mary Ann Stankiewicz (eds), *Framing the Past: Essays on Art Education*, Reston, Va.: National Art Education Association.

Bolin, Paul E. (1995) 'Overlooked and obscured through history: the legislative bill proposed to amend the Massachusetts Drawing Act of 1870', *Studies in Art Education* 37(1) (Autumn): 55–64.

Boorstin, Daniel (1961) *The Image: A Guide to Pseudo-Events in America*, New York: Vintage.

Bourgeois, Louise (1998) *The Destruction of the Father, The Reconstruction of the Father: Writings and Interviews, 1923–1997*, Cambridge, Mass.: MIT Press.

Brooks, Van Wyck (1918) 'On creating a usable past', *Dial* 64 (11 April): 337–41.

Broun, Elizabeth (2004) 'Telling the story of America', pp. 296–301 in Bettina Messias Carbonell (ed.), *Museum Studies: An Anthology of Contexts*, Oxford: Blackwell.

Brown, C. B. (1805) 'Plan for the improvement and diffusion of the arts', *Literary Magazine* (March): 113–15.

Brownell, W. C. (1879) 'The art schools of Philadelphia', *Scribner's* 17: 737–50.

Brundage, W. Fitzhugh (2003) 'Meta Warrick's 1907 "Negro tableaux" and (re) presenting African American historical memory', *Journal of American History* 89(4): 1368–1400 [online] http://www.historycooperative.org/journals/jah/89.4/brundage.html (accessed 23 May 2008).

Buff, Barbara Ball (1987) *American Paradise: The World of the Hudson River School*, New York: Metropolitan Museum of Art and Harry N. Abrams.

Bunce, Michael (1994) *Countryside Ideal: Anglo-American Images of Landscape*, London: Routledge.

Burleigh, Nina (2003) *Stranger and the Statesman: James Smithson, John Quincy Adams, and the Making of America's Greatest Museum, The Smithsonian*, New York: Harper Collins.

Burn, Ian (1975a) 'The art market: affluence and degradation', *Artforum* (April): 34–7.

Burn, Ian (1975b) 'Buying cultural dependency: a note on the crazed thinking behind several Australian collections', *The Fox* (New York) 1(1) (April): 141–4.

Burn, Ian, Nigel Lendon, Charles Mereweather and Ann Stephen (1988) *The Necessity of Australian Art: An Essay about Interpretation*, Sydney: Power Institute, University of Sydney.

Burns, Sarah (1996) *Inventing the Modern Artist: Art and Culture in Gilded Age America*, New Haven, Conn. and London: Yale University Press.

Burns, Sarah (2004) *Painting the Dark Side: Art and the Gothic Imagination in Nineteenth-Century America*, Berkeley, Calif.: University of California Press.

Burroughs, Alan (1936) *Limners and Likeness*, Cambridge, Mass.: Harvard University Press.

Butler, Judith (1990) *Gender Trouble: Feminism and the Subversion of Identity*, London: Routledge.

Butler, Judith (1993) *Bodies that Matter: On the Discursive Limits of 'Sex'*, London: Routledge.

Butler, Judith (1997) *Excitable Speech: A Politics of the Performative,* London: Routledge.

Byrd, Gibson (1963) 'The artist-teacher in America: his changing role in our institutions', *Art Journal* 23(2) (Winter): 130–5.

Cahill, Holger (1932) 'Folk art: its place in the American tradition,' *Parnassus* 4 (March): 1–4.

Cahill, Holger (1933/1969) *American Sources of Modern Art,* New York Museum of Modern Art: Arno Press.

Camnitzer, L. (1996) *Beyond The Fantastic: Contemporary Art Criticism From Latin America*, Cambridge, Mass.: INIVA, MIT Press.

Campbell, Catherine H. (1981/2004) 'Albert Bierstadt and the White Mountains', *Archives of American Art Journal* 21(3): 14–23.

Carbonell, Bettina Messias (ed.) (2004) *Museum Studies: An Anthology of Contexts*, Oxford: Blackwell.

Catlin, George (1848) *A Descriptive Catalogue of Catlin's Indian Collection, Containing Portraits, Landscape, Costumes, &c., and Representations of the Manners and Customs of the North American Indians. Collected and Painted by Mr. Catlin, During Eight Years' Travel Amongst Forty-Eight Tribes, Mostly Speaking Different Languages*, London: Published by the Author.

Chadwick, Whitney (1990) *Women, Art and Society,* London: Thames & Hudson.

Chalmers, F. Graeme (1996) 'The early history of the Philadelphia School of Design for Women', *Journal of Design History* 9(4): 237–52.

Chaplik, Dorothy (1989) *Latin American Art: An Introduction to the Works of the 20th Century*, New York: McFarland.

Chaplin, Joyce E. (2007) 'Roanoke counterfeited according to the truth', pp. 51–63 in Kim Sloan (ed.), *A New World: England's First View of America*, London: British Museum Press.

Chapman, John Gadsby (1847) *The American Drawing Book: A Manual for the Amateur, and Basis of Study for the Professional Artist*, New York: J. S. Redfield, Clinton Hall.

Charlot, Jean (1950) 'Diego Rivera at the Academy of San Carlos', *College Art Journal* 10(1) (Autumn): 10–17.

Chomsky, N. (1992) *Deterring Democracy*, London: Vintage.

Chipp, Herschel B. with Peter Selz and Joshua C. Taylor (1968) *Theories of Modern Art: A Source Book by Artists and Critics*, Berkeley, Calif.: University of California Press.

Clapper, Michael (2002) 'I was once a barefoot boy!: cultural tensions in a popular chromo', *American Art* 16(2) (Summer): 16–39.

Clark, Deborah (1999) 'Tachistes, action painters, geometric abstractionists, abstract expressionists and their innumerable band of camp followers', in Ewen McDonald (ed.), *The Antipodeans: Challenge and Response in Australian Art 1955–1956*, Canberra: National Gallery of Australia.

Clark, Manning (1986/1963) *A Short History of Australia*, 2nd edn, Ringwood, Vic: Penguin.

Clark, T. J. (1999) *Farewell to an Idea: Episodes from a History of Modernism*. New Haven, Conn. and London: Yale University Press.

Clark, T. J. (2006) *The Sight of Death: An Experiment in Art Writing*, New Haven, Conn. and London: Yale University Press.

Clarke, I. (1885) *Art and Industry*, Vol. I, Washington, DC: Government Printing Office.

Clayton, Virginia Tuttle (ed.) (2002) *Drawing on America's Past: Folk Art, Modernism and the Index of American Design*, Chapel Hill, NC: University of North Carolina Press.

Cockcroft, Eva (1985) 'Abstract expressionism: weapon of the cold war', pp. 125–133 in Francis Frascina (ed.), *Pollock and After: The Critical Debate*, London: Paul Chapman.

Cole, Thomas (1836) 'Essay on American scenery,' *American Monthly* I: 1–12.

Comfort, George Fisk (1867) 'Esthetics in collegiate education', *Methodist Quarterly Review* (October): 572–93.

Comfort, George Fisk (1870) *Art Museums in America*, Boston: Houghton.

Committee of the College Art Association (John Alford, Henry R. Hope, Amy Woller, McClelland and Wolfgang Stechow) (1946) 'The practice of art in a liberal education', *College Art Journal* 6(2) (Winter): 91–7.

Conn, Stephen (1998) *Museums and American Intellectual Life 1876–1926*, Chicago, Ill.: University of Chicago Press.

Contreras, Belisario R. (1983) *Tradition and Innovation in New Deal Art*, Lewisburg: Bucknell University Press.

Conwill, Kinshasha Holman (1991) 'In search of an 'authentic' vision: decoding the appeal of the self-taught African-American Artist', *American Art* 5(4) (Autumn): 2–9.

Cook, James W. (nd) 'Race and race relations in P. T. Barnum's New York City',

New York: The Lost Museum [online] http://chnm.gmu.edu/lostmuseum/ lm/117/ (accessed 1 February 2008).
Corn, Wanda M. (1988) 'Historical scholarship in American art', *Art Bulletin* 70(2) (June): 188–207.
Corn, Wanda M. (1999) *The Great American Thing: Modern Art and National identity 1915–1935*, Berkeley, Calif.: University of California Press.
Corrin, Lisa Graziose, Miwon Kwon and Norman Bryson (1997) *Mark Dion*, London and New York: Phaidon.
Counihan, Noel (1967) Sydney Tribune, 5 July.
Cowdrey, M. B. (1953) *American Academy of Fine Arts and American Art-Union*, New York: New York Historical Society.
Cox, John D. (2005) *Traveling South: Travel Narratives and the Construction of American Identity*, Athens, Ga.: University of Georgia Press.
Crane, Diana (1987) *The Transformation of the Avant-Garde: The New York Art World, 1940–1985*, Chicago: University of Chicago Press.
Crane, Susan A. (ed.) (2000) *Museums and Memory*, Stanford, Calif.: Stanford University Press.
Craven, David (1999) *Abstract Expressionism as Cultural Critique: Dissent During the McCarthy Period*, Cambridge, Mass.: MIT Press.
Craven, Thomas (ed.) (1939) *A Treasury of American Prints*, New York: Simon & Schuster.
Craven, Wayne (1971) 'Asher B. Durand's career as an engraver', *American Art Journal* 3(1) (Spring): 39–57.
Crimp, Douglas (1980) 'On the museum's ruins', reprinted as pp 43–56 in Hal Foster (ed.) (1990) *Postmodern Culture*, London: Pluto.
Crimp, Douglas with photographs by Louise Lawler (1993) *On the Museum's Ruins*, Cambridge, Mass.: MIT Press.
Crofutt, George A. (1883) *Crofutt's New Overland Tourist and Pacific Coast Guide over the Union, Central and Southern Pacific Railroads, their Branches and Connections, by Rail, Water and Stage,* Omaha, Nebr. and Denver, Colo.: Overland.
Cronon, William (1995) 'The trouble with wilderness; or, getting back to the wrong nature', pp. 69–90 in William Cronon (ed.), *Uncommon Ground: Rethinking the Human Place in Nature*, New York: W. W. Norton.
Crow, Thomas (1996) *Modern Art in the Common Culture*, New Haven, Conn. and London: Yale University Press.
Crow, Thomas (2006) 'The practice of art history in America', *Daedalus* (Spring): 70–90.
Cummings, T. S. (1865) *Historic Annals of the National Academy of Design*, Philadelphia, Penn.: George W. Childs.
Dalton, Pen (2001) *The Gendering of Art Education, Modernism, Identity and Critical Feminism*, Buckingham and Philadelphia, Penn.: Open University Press.
Dana, John Cotton (1999) *The New Museum: Selected Writings by John Cotton Dana*. Washington, DC: American Association of Museums.
Daniels, Stephen (1993) *Fields of Vision: Landscape Imagery and National Identity in England and the United States*, Cambridge: Polity Press.
Danto, Arthur (1999) 'Degas in Vegas', *The Nation*, 1 March.
Davalos, Karen Mary (1998/2004) 'Exhibiting mestizaje: the politics and experience

of the Mexican Fine Arts Centre', reprinted as pp. 521–40 in Bettina Messias Carbonell (ed.), *Museum Studies: An Anthology of Contexts*, Oxford: Blackwell.

Davidson, Abraham A. (1994) *Early American Modernist Painting 1910–1935*, New York: Da Capo.

Davidson, Marshall B. (1970) 'Those American things', *Metropolitan Museum Journal* 3: 219–33.

De Pauw, Cornelius (1771/1806) *A General History of the Americans, of their Customs, Manners, and Colours. An History of the Patagonians, of the Blasards, and White Negroes. History of Peru. An History of the Manners, Customs, etc. of the Chinese and Egyptians*. Selected from M. Pauw by D. Webb, Rochdale, NY: T. Wood.

Dearinger, David (ed.) (2000) *Rave Reviews: American Art and Its Critics (1826–1925)*, New York: National Academy of Design.

Debord, Guy (1967/1994) *The Society of the Spectacle*, trans. Donald Nicholson-Smith, New York: Zone.

Denevan, William M. (1992) 'The Americas before and after 1492: current geographical research', *Annals of the Association of American Geographers* 82(3): 369–85.

DeVorkin, David and Robert W. Smith (2004) *The Hubble Space Telescope: Imaging the Universe*, Washington, DC: National Geographic Society.

Dewey, John (1934/2005) *Art as Experience*, New York: Berkeley.

Dickson, Harold E. (1973) 'Artists as showmen', *American Art Journal* 5(1): 4–17.

DiMaggio, Paul (1982/2004) 'Cultural entrepreneurship in nineteenth-century Boston, Part ll: The classification and framing of American art', reprinted as pp. 461–82 in Bettina Messias Carbonell (ed.), *Museum Studies: An Anthology of Contexts*, Oxford: Blackwell.

Dippie, Brian W., George Gurney and Therese Thau Heyman (2002) *George Catlin and His Indian Gallery*, Washington, DC: Smithsonian American Art Museum and W. W. Norton.

Doezema, Marianne and Elizabeth Murray (eds) (1998) *Reading American Art*, New Haven, Conn. and London: Yale University Press.

Dolmetsch, J. D. (1981) 'Colonial America's elegantly framed prints', *Antiques* 129: 1106–1112.

Doss, Erica (1991) *Benton, Pollock and the Politics of Modernism: From Regionalism to Abstract Expressionism*, Chicago, Ill.: University of Chicago Press.

Doss, Erika (2002) *Twentieth-Century American Art*, London: Thames & Hudson.

Dow, Arthur Wesley (1889/1997) *Composition: A Series of Exercises in Art Structure for the use of Students and Teachers*, with an new intro. by Joseph Masheck, Berkeley, Calif.: University of California Press.

Dow, Arthur Wesley (1912) *Theory and Practice of Teaching Art*, 2nd edn, New York: Teachers College Press.

Dow, Arthur Wesley (1918)'A course in fine arts for candidates for the higher degrees', *Bulletin of the College Art Association of America* 1(4): 114–118.

Doyle, Jennifer (1999) 'Sex, scandal, and Thomas Eakins's *The Gross clinic*', *Representations* 68 (Autumn): 1–33.

Doyle, Jennifer (2006) *Sex Objects: Art and the Dialectics of Desire*, Minneapolis, Minn.: University of Minnesota Press.

Doyle, Jennifer, Jonathan Flatley and José Esteban Muñoz, (eds) (1996) *Pop Out: Queer Warhol*, Durham, N.C.: Duke University Press.

Duncan, Carol (1995) *Civilizing Rituals: Inside Public Museums*, London and New York: Routledge.

Duncan, Carol and Alan Wallach (1978) 'The museum of modern art as late capitalist ritual: an iconographic analysis', *Marxist Perspectives* 1(4) (Winter): 28–51.

Duncan, Carol and Alan Wallach (1980) 'The universal survey museum', *Art History* 3(4) (December): 448–69.

Dunlap, W. (1918). *A History of the Rise and Progress of the Arts of Design in the United States*, vols 1–2, Boston, Mass.: C. E. Goodspeed.

Durham, Jimmie, Richard William Hill and John Leslie (eds) (2005) *The American West*, Compton Verney: Compton Verney Gallery.

Duro, Paul (1986) 'The 'demoiselles à copier' in the Second Empire', *Woman's Art Journal* (7)1 (Spring–Summer): 1–7.

Duro, Paul (1988) 'Copyists in the Louvre in the middle decades of the nineteenth century', *Gazette des Beaux-Arts* 91 (April): 249–53.

Dutton, D. (ed.) (1983) *The Forger's Art. Forgery and the Philosophy of Art*, Berkeley, Calif.: University of California Press.

Eagle, Mary and John Jones (1994) *A Story of Australian Painting*, Melbourne: Macmillan.

Earle, Edward W. (1979) *Points of View: The Stereograph in America – A Cultural History*, Rochester, NY: Visual Studies Workshop Press in Collaboration with the Gallery Association of New York State.

Eco, Umberto (1995) *Faith in Fakes: Travels in Hyperreality*, London: Minerva.

Edelson, Bob (1999) *New American Street Art*, New York: Soho.

Efland, A. D. (1976) 'The school art style: a functional analysis', *Studies in Art Education* 17(3): 37–44.

Efland, A. D. (1983) 'School art and its social origins', *Studies in Art Education* 24(3): 149–57.

Efland, A. D. (1985) 'Art and education for women in 19th century Boston', *Studies in Art Education* 26(3): 133–40.

Efland, A. D. (1990) *A History of Art Education: Intellectual and Social Currents in Teaching the Visual Arts*, New York: Teachers College Press.

Eisenman, Stephen F., Thomas Crow, Brian Lukacher, Linda Nochlin and Frances K. Phohl (1994) *Nineteenth Century Art: A Critical History*, London: Thames & Hudson.

Elderfield, John (ed.) (1994) '*The Museum of Modern Art at Mid-Century: At Home and Abroad*', *Studies in Modern Art 4* New York: MoMA.

Elderfield, John (ed.) (1995) 'The Museum of Modern Art at mid-century continuity and change', *Studies in Modern Art 5*, New York: MoMA.

Ellis, Walter (2004) 'Welcome to the United States of Latin America', *Times Higher Education Supplement*, 18 June: 17.

Emerson, R. W. (1971) *Collected Works of Ralph Waldo Emerson*, ed. Alfred R. Ferguson and Robert E. Spiller, 2 vols, Cambridge: Belknap Press and Harvard University Press.

Evergood, Philip (1973) 'Concerning mural painting', p. 180 in Frances V. O'Connor (ed.), *Art for the Millions: Essays from the 1930s by Artists and Administrators of the WPA Federal Art Project*, Boston: New York Graphic Society.

Fawcett, Trevor (1983) 'Visual facts and the nineteenth-century art lecture', *Art History* 6(4): 443–60.

Fawcett, Trevor (1986) 'Graphic versus photographic in the nineteenth-century reproduction', *Art History* 9(2): 185–212.

Fenton, James (1990) 'Evolution of lantern slides', *New England Journal of Photographic History* 128 (Summer): 16–19.

Fernadez-Armesto, Felipe (2003) *The Americas: The History of a Hemisphere*, London: Weidenfeld & Nicolson.

Fifer, J. Valerie (1988) *American Progress: The Growth of the Transport, Tourist and Information Industries in the Nineteenth Century West : Seen Through the Life and Times of George A Crofutt*, Chester, Conn.: Globe Pequot.

Fine, Gary Alan (2004) *Everyday Genius: Self-Taught Art and the Culture of Authenticity*, Chicago, Ill.: University of Chicago Press.

Finemore, Brian (1968) *Australian Impressionists*, Melbourne: Longmans.

Fink, Lois and Joshua C. Taylor (1975) *Academy: The Academic Tradition in American Art*, Washington, DC: Smithsonian Institute Press.

Flexner, J. T. (1947) *History of American Painting*, New York: Dover.

Flexner, James (1969) *First Flowers of Our Wilderness: American Painting, the Colonial Period*, New York: Dover.

Foote, Henry Wilder (1935) 'Mr. Smibert shows his pictures March, 1730', *New England Quarterly* 8(1) (March): 14–28.

Ford, Bruce E. (2006) *A Champion of Individual Liberty: John Cotton Dana 1856–1929*, Newark, N.J.: Newark Public Library [online] http://www.npl.org/Pages/ProgramsExhibits/Dana/Champion_Dana.pdf (accessed 23 May 2008).

Ford, Charles Henri (ed.) (1943) *View*, 'Americana Fantastica' ser. ll(4) [online] http://www.bibliopolis.net/cote/viewno4.htm (accessed 20 November 2007).

Foreman, Carolyn T. (1943) *Indians Abroad: 1493–1938*, Norman, Okla.: University of Oklahoma Press.

Forest, Robert W. de, Grosvenor Atterbury and Elihu Root (1924/2004) Addresses on the occasion of the opening of the American Wing, the Metropolitan Museum of Art, New York, reprinted as pp 290–5 in Bettina Messias Carbonell (ed.), *Museum Studies: An Anthology of Contexts*, Oxford: Blackwell.

Forman, Dave (1998) 'Wilderness areas for real', pp. 404–5 in J. Baird Callicott (ed.), *The Great New Wilderness Debate*, Athens, Ga.: University of Georgia Press.

Foster, Hal (ed.) (1983/1990) *Postmodern Culture*, London: Pluto.

Foster, Hal (1995) 'The artist as ethnographer, pp. 170–203 in *The Return of the Real*, Cambridge, Mass.: MIT Press.

Foster, Hal, Rosalind Krauss, Yve-Alain Bois and Benjamin H.D. Buchloh (2004) *Art Since 1900: Modernism, Antimodernism, Postmodernism*, London: Thames & Hudson.

Fox, Charles Philip and Tom Parkinson (1969) *The Circus in America*, Waukesah, Wisc.: Country Beautiful.

Fraser, Andrea (2005) 'From the critique of institutions to an institution of critique', *Art Forum* 44(1) (September), repr. as pp. 32–9 in N. Horowitz and B. Sholis (eds), *The Uncertain States of America Reader,* New York: Sternberg Press,.

Freitag, Wolfgang M. (1979) 'Early uses of photography in the history of art', *Art Journal* (Winter): 117–23.

Freitag, Wolfgang M. (1987) 'Art reproductions in the library: notes on their history and use', pp. 349–63 in Gabriel Wiesberg and Laurinda Dixon (eds), *The Documented Image: Visions in Art History*, Syracuse, N.Y.: Syracuse University Press.

Friedman, J. and R. Berenholtz (1992) *Inside New York: Discovering New York's Classic Interiors*, Oxford: Phaidon.

Froehlich, H. and B. Snow (1904) *Text Books of Art Education*, Books I and II, New York: Prang Educational.

Fryberger, Betsy G. (ed.) (2003) *The Changing Garden: Four Centuries of European and American Art*, Berkeley, Calif.: University of California Press.

Fusco, C. and B. Wallis (2003) *Only Skin Deep: Changing Visions of the American Self*, New York: Harry N. Abrams.

Gaither, Barry (1992) "Hey! that's mine': thoughts on pluralism and American museums', pp. 56–64 in Ivan Karp, Christine Mullen Kreamer and Steven D. Lavine (eds), *Museums and Communities: The Politics of Public Culture*, Washington , DC and London: Smithsonian Institution Press.

Gale, Peggy (ed.) (2004) *Artists Talk: 1969–1977*, Halifax: Press of the Nova Scotia College of Art and Design.

Gandelsonas, Mario (1999) *X-Urbanism: Architecture and the American City*, New York: Princeton Architectural Press.

Gaskell, Ivan (2003) 'Sacred to profane and back again', in Andrew McClellan (ed.), *Art and its Publics: Museum Studies at the Millennium*, Oxford: Blackwell.

Gerbi, Antonello (1955) *The Dispute of the New World: The History of a Polemic 1750–1900*, trans. Jeremy Moyle, Pittsburgh, Penn.: University of Pittsburgh Press.

Gerdts, William H. (1969) 'The influence of Ruskin and Pre-Raphaelitism on American still-life painting', *American Art Journal* 1(2): 80–97.

Gerdts, William H. (1971) 'Marble and nudity,' *Art in America* 59 (May June): 63–67.

Gerdts, William H. (1974) *The Great American Nude*, New York and Washington, DC: Praeger.

Gerdts, William H. (1983) 'The American 'discourses': a survey of lectures and writings on American art, 1770–1858', *American Art Journal* 15(3): 61–79.

Glick, Paula F. (1995) 'The first appearance of Chevreul's color theory in America', *American Art Journal* 27(1/2): 101–5.

Godkin, E. L. (1870) 'Autotypes and oleographs', *The Nation*, 10 November: 317–18.

Godkin, E. L. (1895) *Reflections and Comments, 1865–1895*, New York: Scribner's.

Goetzmann, William H. (1999) 'Mountain man as Jacksonian man', pp. 83–96 in Walter Nugent and Marin Ridge (eds), *The American West: The Reader*, Bloomington and Indianapolis, Ind.: Indiana University Press.

Gombrich, Ernst (1950/1972) *The Story of Art*, Oxford: Phaidon.

Goodman, N. (1983) 'Art and authenticity', in D. Dutton (ed.), *The Forger's Art. Forgery and the Philosophy of Art*, Berkeley, Calif.: University of California Press.

Goodrich, L. (1959) *Paintings and Sculpture from the American National Exhibition in Moscow*, New York: Whitney Museum of American Art.

Goodrich, Lloyd (1967) *The Artist in America*, compiled by the editors of *Art in America*, New York: W. W. Norton.

Grafton, J. (1977) *New York in the Nineteenth Century: 321 Engravings from Harpers Weekly and Other Contemporary Sources*, London: Dover.

Gramsci, Antoni (1971) *Selections from the Prison Notebooks of Antoni Gramsci*, London: Lawrence & Wishart.

Grant, Susan-Mary (2000) *North over South: Northern Nationalism and American Identity in the Antebellum Era*, Lawrence, Kan.: University of Kansas.

Green, Harry (1966) 'Walter Smith: the forgotten man', *Art Education* 19(1) (January): 3–9.

Green, Vivien M. (1982) 'Hiram Powers' "Greek slave:" emblem of freedom', *American Art Journal* 14(4) (Autumn): 31–9.

Greenberg, Clement (1939/1992) 'Avant-garde and kitsch', pp. 21–32 in Frances Frascina and Jonathan Harris (eds), *Art in Modern Culture: An Anthology of Critical Texts*, London: Phaidon.

Greenberg, Reesa, Bruce W. Ferguson and Sandy Nairne (eds) (1996) *Thinking About Exhibitions*, London: Routledge.

Greub, Suzanne and Greub, Thierry (2006) *Museums of the Twenty-first Century: Concepts Projects Buildings*, Munich: Prestel.

Gritton, Joy L. (1991) 'The Institute of American Indian Arts: a convergence of ideologies', pp. 22–29 in *Shared Visions: Native American Painters and Sculptors in the Twentieth Century*, Phoenix: Heard Museum.

Gritton, Joy L. (1992) 'Cross-cultural education vs. modernist imperialism: the Institute of American Indian Arts', *Art Journal* 51(3): 28–35.

Groseclose, Barbara (2000) *Nineteenth-Century American Art*, Oxford: Oxford University Press.

Gross, S. and Susan Daley (1993) *Old Greenwich Village: An Architectural Portrait*, New York: Preservation Press.

Gruber, J. Richard (1998) *Thomas Hart Benton and the American South*, Georgia: Morris Museum of Art.

Guilbaut, Serge (1980) 'The new adventures of the avant-garde in America: Greenberg, Pollack, or from the Trotskyism to the new liberalism of the "vital centre"', pp. 153–66 in Frances Frascina and Jonathan Harris (eds), *Art in Modern Culture: An Anthology of Critical Texts*, London: Phaidon.

Guilbault, Serge (1983/1987) *How New York Stole the Idea of Modern Art: Abstract Expressionism, Freedom and the Cold War*, Chicago, Ill.: University of Chicago Press.

Hadley, C. (1943). *John Cotton Dana: A Sketch*, Chicago: American Library Association.

Hagen, O. (1940) *The Birth of the American Tradition in Art*, New York: Scribner's.

Halsey, R. T. H. (1935) 'Prints Washington lived with at Mount Vernon', *Bulletin of the Metropolitan Museum of Art* 30: 63–5.

Hamber, Anthony J. (1996) *'A Higher Branch of the Art': Photographing the Fine Arts in England 1839–1880*, Amsterdam: Gordon & Breach.

Hamber, Anthony (1989–90) 'The photography of the visual arts, 1839–1880', Parts 1–4, *Visual Resources*, 1989, 5(4): 289–310; 1989, 6(1): 19–42; 1989, 6(2):165–80; 1990, 6(3): 219–42.

Hanners, John (1981) '"The great three-mile painting": John Banvard's *Mississippi Panorama*', *Journal of American Culture* 4(1): 28–42.

Haraway, Donna (1984) 'Teddy bear patriarchy: taxidermy in the Garden of Eden, New York City, 1908–1936', *Social Text* 11 (Winter): 20–64.

Haraway, Donna (1989) *Primate Visions: Gender, Race and Nature in the World of Modern Science*, London: Routledge.

Harpur, Royston (1968) 'An important academy', *The Field*: 92–3.

Harris, Ann Sutherland (1973) 'Women in college art departments and museums', *Art Journal* 32(4) (Summer): 417–19.

Harris, Emma, Christopher Benfey, Eva Diaz, Edmund de Waal and Jed Perl (2005) *Starting at Zero: Black Mountain College 1933–57*, Bristol: Arnolfini Bristol and Cambridge: Kettle's Yard.

Harris, Jonathan (1995) *Federal Art and National Culture: The Politics of Identity in New Deal America*, Cambridge: Cambridge University Press.

Harris, Mary Emma (1987) *The Arts at Black Mountain College*, Cambridge, Mass.: MIT Press.

Harris, Neil (1966) *The Artist in American Society: The Formative Years, 1790–1860*, New York: George Braziller.

Harrison, Charles and Paul Wood (eds) (2003) *Art in Theory 1900–2000: An Anthology of Changing Ideas*, Oxford: Blackwell.

Hart, Deborah (1991) *John Olsen*, Sydney: Craftsman House.

Haskell, Barbara (1999) *The American Century: Art and Culture 1900–1950*, New York: Whitney Museum of American Art.

Haskell, Francis and Nicholas Penny (1981) *Taste and the Antique: The Lure of Classical Sculpture, 1500–1900*, New Haven, Conn.: Yale University Press.

Hauser, Arnold (1951/1962) *The Social History of Art*, 4 vols, New York: Routledge.

Havice, Christine (1981) 'In a class by herself: 19th-century images of the woman artist as student', *Women Artists Journal* (Spring–Summer): 35–40.

Haynes, Sam W. and Christopher Morris (eds) (1997) *Manifest Destiny and Empire: American Antebellum Expansionism*, College Station, Tex.: A & M University Press.

Hemingway, Andrew (1994) 'Meyer Schapiro and Marxism in the 1930s', *Oxford Art Journal* 17(1): 13–29.

Hemingway, Andrew (2002) *Artists on the left: artists and the American communist movement, 1926–1956*, New Haven, Conn.: Yale University Press.

Henderson, H. W. (1911) *The Pennsylvania Academy of the Fine Arts*, Boston: L. C. Page.

Hendricks, Gordon (1971) 'Durand, Maverick and the 'Declaration'', *American Art Journal* 3(1) (Spring): 58–71.

Hendricks, Gordon (1974) *Albert Bierstadt, Painter of the American West*, New York: Harry N. Abrams.

Henning, Michelle (2006) *Museums, Media and Cultural Theory*, Maidenhead: Open University Press/McGraw-Hill Education.

Henshaw, John (1967) 'A Second Look at the art of the New World', *The Australian*, 29 July 1967.

Hietala, Thomas R. (1997) ''This splendid juggernaut': westward a nation and its people', in Sam Haynes and Christopher Morris (eds), *Manifest Destiny and*

Empire: American Antibellum Expansionism, College Station, Tex.: A&M University Press.

Higham, J. (1955) *Strangers in the Land: Patterns of American Nativism, 1860–1925*, New Brunswick, N.J.: Rutgers University Press.

Hilaire, Hiler (1973) 'An approach to mural decoration', pp. 74–5 in Frances V. O'Connor (ed.), *Art for the Millions: Essays from the 1930s by Artists and Administrators of the WPA Federal Art Project*, Boston: New York Graphic Society.

Hill, Richard William (2005) 'Cowboy justice: an American trip', pp. 148–65 in Jimmie Durham, Richard William Hill and John Leslie (eds), *The American West*, Compton Verney: Compton Verney Gallery.

Hills, Patricia (2001) *Modern Art in the USA: Issues and Controversies of the 20th Century*, Englewood Cliffs, N..J: Prentice Hall.

Horne, Donald (1964/1967) *The Lucky Country: Australia in the Sixties*, rev. edn, Ringwood, Victoria: Penguin.

Hoopes, Donelson F. and Wend von Kalnein (1972) *The Düsseldorf Academy and the Americans*, Atlanta, Ga.: High Museum of Art.

Hopkins, David (2000) *After Modern Art 1945–2000*, Oxford: Oxford University Press.

Hoppin, Martha J. (1981) 'Women artists in Boston, 1870–1900: the pupils of William Morris Hunt', *American Art Journal* 13(1) (Winter): 17–46.

Hough, Katherine Plake and Michael Zakian (1992) *Out of Place: Restoring Identity to the Regional Landscape*, New Haven, Conn.: Yale University Press.

Howard, Seymour (1977) 'Thomas Jefferson's art gallery for Monticello', *Art Bulletin* 59(4) (December): 583–600.

Howat, John K. (1968) 'Washington crossing the Delaware', *Metropolitan Museum of Art Bulletin*, New Series, 26(7) (March): 289–99.

Huber, Christine Jones (1973) *The Pennsylvania Academy and its Women, 1850 to 1920*, Philadelphia: Pennsylvania Academy of Fine Arts.

Hughes, Anthony and Erich Ranfft (eds) (1997) *Sculpture and its Reproductions*, London: Reaktion.

Hughes, Robert (1997) *American Visions: The Epic History of Art in America*, London: Harvill.

Hults, Linda C. (1989) 'Thomas Moran's "Shoshone falls": a Western Niagara', *Smithsonian Studies in American Art* 3(1) (Winter): 88–102.

Hunter, S. (1958) pp. 283–332 in Marcel Brion, Sam Hunter, Giulio Carlo Argan, Nello Ponente, Umbro Apollonio, Otto Bihalij-Merin, Will Grohmann, Herbert Read, H. L. C. Jaffe and J. P. Hodin, *Art Since 1945*, New York: Harry N. Abrams.

Hunter, S. (1959) *Modern American Painting and Sculpture*, New York: Dell.

Hunter, S. (1963) *New Directions in American Painting*, Waltham, Mass.: Poses Institute of Fine Arts, Brandeis University.

Hunter, S. (1973) *American Art of the 20th Century*, New York: Harry N. Abrams.

Huntington, Samuel P. (2004) *Who Are We? The Challenges to America's National Identity*, New York: Simon & Schuster.

Huth, Hans (1950) 'The American and nature', *Journal of the Warburg and Courtauld Institutes* 13(1/2): 101–49.

Hyde, Anne Farrar (1990) *An American Vision: Far Western Landscape and National Culture, 1820–1920*, New York: New York University Press.

Hyman, Linda (1976) 'The Greek slave by Hiram Powers: high art as popular culture', *Art Journal* 35(3) (Spring): 216–23.

Irvine, Betty Jo (1974) *Slide Libraries: A Guide for Academic Institutions and Museums*, Littleton, Colo.: Libraries Unlimited.

Ivins, Williams (1969) *Prints and Visual Communication*, Cambridge, Mass.: MIT Press.

Iyer, Pico (2007) Article in *Sydney Morning Herald*, 5 January: 9.

Jachec, Nancy (2003) 'Transatlantic cultural politics in the late 1950s: the Leaders and Specialists Grant Program', *Art History* 26(4) (September): 533–55.

Jackson, K. T. (1995) *Encyclopedia of New York City*, New Haven, Conn. and London: Yale University Press.

Jacobs, Michael (1985) *The Good and Simple Life: Artist Colonies in Europe and America,* London: Phaidon.

Jakle, John A. (1985) *The Tourist: Travel in Twentieth-Century North America,* Lincoln, Nebr. and London: University of Nebraska Press.

Jarves, James Jackson (1861) *Art Studies: The 'Old Masters' of Italy; Painting*, New York: Derby & Jackson.

Jarves, James Jackson (1871) 'Progress of American sculpture in Europe', *Art Journal* 10: 7.

Jensen, Joan (1995) *One Foot on the Rockies: Women and Creativity in the Modern American West*, Albuquerque, N.M.: University of New Mexico Press.

Johns, Elizabeth (1983) 'Thomas Eakins and "pure art" education', *Archives of American Art Journal* 23(3): 2–5.

Johnson, Ellen H. (ed.) (1982) *American Artists on Art from 1940–1980*, New York: Icon.

Josephson, Matthew (1934) *The Robber Barons,* San Diego, Calif.: Harvest.

Kaplan, Louis (2005) *American Exposures: Photography and Community in the Twentieth Century,* Minnesota, Wisc.: University of Minnesota Press.

Kaplan, Wendy (1982) 'R. T. H. Halsey: an ideology of collecting American decorative arts', *Winterthur Portfolio* 17(1) (Spring): 43–53.

Kaprow, Allan (1966) *Assemblage, Environments and Happenings*, New York: Abrams.

Karp, Ivan, Corinne A. Kratz and Tomás Ybarra-Frausto (eds) (2006) *Public Cultures/Global Transformations*, Durham, N.C. and London: Duke University Press.

Karp, Ivan, Christine Mullen Kreamer and Steven D. Lavine (eds) (1992) *Museums and Communities: The Politics of Public Culture,* Washington, DC and London: Smithsonian Institution Press.

Kasson, Joy S. (2000) 'Conclusion: performing national identity', pp. 265–73, 297–99 in *Buffalo Bill's Wild West: Celebrity, Memory, and Popular History*, New York: Hill and Wang.

Kemenov, V. (1959) ' US contemporary art on exhibition in Sokolniki Park: realistic trend suppressed and weakened', *Sovietskaya Kultura* [*Soviet Culture*], Moscow (transcript 11 pages, MoMA archives).

Kennedy, Brian (1998) 'Introduction', to *Catalogue, National Gallery of Australia*, Canberra: National Gallery of Australia.

Kennedy, Roger G. (1996/2004 'Some thoughts about national museums', repr. as pp. 302–6 in Bettina Messias Carbonell (ed.), *Museum Studies: An Anthology of Contexts*, Oxford: Blackwell.

Kerr, D. B. and Max Harris (eds) (1941) *Angry Penguins* No. 1, April.

Kimball, F. (1944) 'Jefferson and the arts', *Proceedings of the American Philosophical Society* 83: 238–45.

Kimmelman, Michael (1994) 'Revisiting the revisionists: the modern, its critics, and the cold war', pp. 38–56 in John Elderfield (ed.), *The Museum of Modern Art at Mid-Century: At Home and Abroad*, studies in American Art New York: MoMA.

Kimmelman, Michael (2001) 'Flags, mom and apple pie through altered eyes' , *New York Times* Art Review, 2 November.

Kinsey, Joni Louise (2006) *Thomas Moran's West: Chromolithography, High Art, and Popular Taste*, Kansas: University Press of Kansas.

Kinsey, Joni Louise (1992) 'The Hayden Geological and Geographical Survey of the Territories', pp. 43–67, 182–90 in *Thomas Moran and the Surveying of the American West*, Washington, DC and London: Smithsonian Institution Press.

Kornhauser, Elizabeth Mankin (1996) *American Paintings Before 1945 in the Wadsworth Athenaeum*, 2 vols, New Haven, Conn. and London: Yale University Press.

Kozloff, Max (1967) 'The "Poetics of softness"', pp. 26–30 in Maurice Tuchman (ed.), *American Sculpture of the 60's*, New York: New York Graphic Society.

Kozloff, Max (1973) 'The Rivera frescoes of Modern Industry at the Detroit Institute of Arts: proletarian art under capitalist patronage', *Artforum* 12(3) (November): 58–63.

Kozloff, Max (1985) 'American painting during the cold war', pp. 107–23 in Francis Frascina (ed.), *Pollock and After: The Critical Debat*e, London: Paul Chapman.

Kramer, Hilton (1955) 'On the horizon: exhibiting Family of Man', *Commentary* 20(4): 365–7.

Krauss, Rosalind (1977) *Passages in Modern Sculpture,* London: Thames & Hudson.

Kubler, George (1962) *The Shape of Time: Remarks on the History of Things*, New Haven, Conn.: Yale University Press.

Kuenzli, R. E. (1986) *New York Dada*, New York: Willis Locker & Owens.

Kunitz, Daniel (2005) 'Ed Ruscha's American optimism', *New York Sun*, 17 November.

Kupperman, Ordahl Karen (2000) *Indians and English: Facing Off in Early America*, Ithaca, N.Y.: Cornell University Press.

Kwon, Miwon (2006) 'Itinerant artists', pp. 45–51 in N. Horowitz and B. Sholis (eds), *The Uncertain States of America Reader*, New York: Sternberg.

Lambert, Susan (1987) *The Image Multiplied: Five Centuries of Printed Reproductions of Paintings and Drawings,* London: Trefoil.

Langa, Helen (2004) *Radical Art: Printmaking and the Left in 1930s New York*, Berkeley, Calif.: University of California Press.

Langer, Susan (1953) *Feeling and Form: A Theory of Art*, New York: Charles Scribner's sons.

Lankevich, G. J. (1998) *American Metropolis: A History of New York City*, New York: New York University Press.

Lansell, G.R. (1967) 'Where the action is', *Art* 18.

Larkin, Susan G. (2001) *The Cos Cob Art Colony: Impressionists on the Connecticut Shore,* New York: National Academy of Design Museum, and New Haven, Conn.: Yale University Press.

Law, Jane N. (1986) 'Designing the dream', pp. 18–36 in Fannia Weingartner (ed.), *Streamlining America: A Henry Ford Museum Exhibit*, Dearborn, Mich.. Henry Ford Museum and Greenfield Village.

Leighton, Howard B. (1984) 'The lantern slide and art history', *History of Photography* 2 (April–June): 107–18.

Leja, Michael (1993) *Reframing Abstract Expressionism: Subjectivity and Painting*, New Haven, Conn.: Yale University Press.

LeKay, John (2007) Interview with Sam Durant [online] http://www.heyokamagazine.com/HEYOKA.3.SCULPT.SAM%20DURANT.htm (accessed 1 March 2008).

Levine, Lawrence W. (1988) *Highbrow/Lowbrow: The Emergence of Cultural Hierarchy in America*, Cambridge, Mass.: Harvard University Press.

Limbach, Russell T. (1973) 'Lithography: stepchild of the arts', pp. 145–7 in Frances V. O'Connor (ed.), *Art for the Millions: Essays from the 1930s by Artists and Administrators of the WPA Federal Art Project*, Boston: New York Graphic Society.

Lindey, Christine (1990) *Art in the Cold War: From Vladivostock to Kalamazoo, 1945–62*, London: Herbert Press.

Lipman, Jean (ed.) (1963) *What is American in American Art*? New York: McGraw-Hill.

Lipman, Jean (1976) *Bright Stars: American Painting and Sculpture Since 1776*, New York: E.P. Dutton.

Lippard, Lucy (1966) 'American painting 1946–1966: cult of the direct and the difficult', pp. 5–6 in *Two Decades of American Painting*, New York: MoMA.

Lippard, Lucy R. (1993) 'Jimmie Durham: postmodernist savage', *Art in America* 81(2): 62–9.

Lippard, Lucy R. (1995) *The Pink Glass Swan: Selected Feminist Essays on Art*, New York: New Press.

Lipton, Leah (1983) 'The Boston Artists' Association, 1841–1851', *American Art Journal* 15(4) (Autumn): 45–57.

Littleton, Taylor D. and Maltby Sykes (1989) *Advancing American Art, Painting, Politics and Cultural Confrontation at Mid-Century,* Alabama: University of Alabama Press.

Lloyd, Michael and Michael Desmond (1992) *European and American Paintings and Sculptures 1870–1970 in the Australian National Gallery*, Canberra: Australian National Gallery.

Locke, John (1960/1997) *An Essay Concerning Human Understanding*, New York: Penguin Classics.

Logan, F. M. (1955) *Growth of Art in American Schools*, New York: Harper & Brothers.

London, Jack (1906/1994) *White Fang*, London: Puffin.

Looby, Christopher (1987/2004) 'The constitution of nature: taxonomy as politics in Jefferson, Peale, and Bartram', pp. 143–58 in Bettina Messias Carbonell (ed.), *Museum Studies: An Anthology of Contexts*, Oxford: Blackwell.

Loring, Philip A. (2007) 'The most resilient show on earth: the circus as a model for viewing identity, change, and chaos', *Ecology and Society* 12(1): Art. 9 [online] URL: http://www.ecologyandsociety.org/vol12/iss1/art9/ (accessed 11 November 2007).

Lubin, David (1994) *Picturing a Nation: Art and Social Change in Nineteenth-Century America*, New Haven, Conn.: Yale University Press.

Luce, Henry (1941) 'The American century', *Life*, 17 February.

Lueck, Beth L. (1997) *American Writers and the Picturesque Tour: The Search for National Identity, 1790–1860,* Garland Studies in 19th Century American Literature, New York: Garland.

Lynes, Russell (1973) *Good Old Modern: An Intimate Portrait of the MOMA,* New York: Athenaeum.

Lynn, Elwyn (1964) 'The travelling exhibition of selected paintings from the James A. Michener Foundation Collection', *Art and Australia* 2(3) (December): 204–9.

Lynn, Elwyn (1967) 'Puritans in Affluent America', *The Bulletin*, July 22, 1967.

Lynn, Elwyn (1968) Untitled essay in *The Field*: 84–5.

Lynton, N. (1980) *The Story of Modern Art,* Oxford: Phaidon.

Lyons, Maura (2005) *William Dunlap and the Construction of an American Art History*, Amherst and Boston, Mass.: University of Massachusetts Press.

MacDonald, S. (1970) *History and Philosophy of Art Education*, New York: American Elsevier.

Malraux, André (1953/1974) *The Voices of Silence*, pp. 13–127, trans. Stuart Gilbert, St Albans: Paladin.

Marantz, Irving J. (1973) 'The artist as a social worker', pp. 197–8 in Frances V. O'Connor (ed.), *Art for the Millions: Essays from the 1930s by Artists and Administrators of the WPA Federal Art Project*, Boston: New York Graphic Society.

Marchand, Suzanne (2000) 'The quarrel of the Ancients and Moderns in the German museums', pp. 179–99 in Susan A. Crane (ed.), *Museums and Memory*, Stanford, Calif.: Stanford University Press.

Marshall, R. and Robert Mapplethorpe (1986) *50 New York Artists: A Critical Selection of Painters and Sculptors Working in New York*, New York: Chronicle.

Martin, K. A. (1994) 'The university and arts education', *Metropolitan Universities* (Spring): 35–40.

Marzio, P. C. (1976) *The Art Crusade: An Analysis of American Drawing Manuals, 1820–1860*, Washington, DC: Smithsonian Press.

Marzio, Peter (1979) *The Democratic Art: Pictures for a 19th-Century America*, Boston: David Godine.

Masley, Alexander (1949) 'Fine art and art education', *College Art Journal* 8(4) (Summer): 279–87.

McCarthy, Kathleen D. (1991) *Women's Culture: American Philanthropy and Art, 1830–1930,* Chicago, Ill.: University of Chicago Press.

McCaughey, Patrick (1968) 'Experience and the new abstraction', *The Field*: 88–9.

McClellan, Andrew (ed.) (2003) *Art and its Publics: Museum Studies at the Millennium*, Oxford: Blackwell.

McDermott, John Francis (1958) *The Lost Panoramas of the Mississippi*, Chicago: University of Chicago Press.

McDonald, Ewen (ed.) (1999) *The Antipodeans: Challenge and Response in Australian Art 1955–1956*, Canberra: National Gallery of Australia.

McKinsey, Elizabeth (1985) *Niagara Falls: Icon of the American Sublime*, New York and Cambridge: Cambridge University Press.

McLanathan, Richard B. K. (1960), 'Art in Moscow', *The Atlantic* (May): 73–8.

McLanathan, R. (1968) *The American Tradition in the Arts,* New York: Harcourt, Brace & World.

McLuhan, Marshall (1964) *Understanding Media: The Extensions of Man*, New York: McGraw-Hill.

McNulty, J. Bard (ed.) (1983) *The Correspondence of Thomas Cole and Daniel Wadsworth*, Hartford: Connecticut Historical Society.

McNutt, James K. (1990) 'Plaster casts after Antique sculpture: their role in the elevation of public taste and in American art instruction', *Studies in Art Education* 3: 158–67.

Meecham, Pam and Julie Sheldon (2005) *Modern Art: A Critical Introduction*, London: Routledge.

Meiland, J.W. (1983) 'Originals, copies, and aesthetic value', pp. 115–30 in D. Dutton (ed.), *The Forger's Art: Forgery and the Philosophy of Art*, Berkeley, Calif.: University of California Press.

Mendelowitz, Daniel M. (1960) *A History of American Art*, New York: Holt, Rinehart & Winston.

Meservey, Anne Farmer (1978) 'The role of art in American life: critics' views on native art and literature, 1830–1865', *American Art Journal* 10(1) (May): 72–89.

Meyer, Peter G. (ed.) (2001) *Brushes with History: Writing on Art from The Nation, 1865–2001*, New York: Thunder's Mouth Press.

Millen, Ronald (1965) 'Shotgun wedding in Venice', *Art and Australia* 2(4) (March): 282–7.

Miller, Angela (1989) 'Thomas Cole and Jacksonian America: the course of empire as political allegory', *Prospects* 14: 65–92.

Miller, Angela (1993) *The Empire of the Eye: Landscape Representation and American Cultural Politics 1825–75*, Ithaca, N.Y.: Cornell University Press.

Miller, P. (1962), 'The shaping of the American character: Ezra Pound and Walt Whitman', in H. R. Pearce (ed.), *Whitman: A Collection of Critical Essays*, Englewood Cliffs, N.J.: Prentice-Hall.

Miller, Stephen G. (2005) *Plaster Casts at Berkeley. Collections of the Hearst Museum of Anthropology & Department of Classics at UC Berkeley. An Exhibition of Rare Plaster Casts of Ancient Greek and Roman Sculpture*, 2nd edn [online] http://repositories.cdlib.org/ucbclassics/CastsCatalogue/ (accessed 1 February 2008).

Milner, Clyde A. II, Anne M. Butler and David Rich Lewis (eds) (1997) 'Meriwether Lewis views the Great Falls of the Missouri, 1805', pp. 117–122 in *Major Problems in the History of the American West*, 2nd edn, Boston and New York: Houghton Mifflin.

Morison, Samuel Eliot (1971) *The European Discovery of America: The Northern Voyages A.D. 500–1600*, New York: Oxford University Press.

Morrison, J. (1973) *The Rise of the Arts on the American Campus*, New York: McGraw-Hill.

Morrissey, Katherine G. (1992) 'Engendering the West', in *Under an Open Sky: Rethinking America's Western Past*, New York: W. W. Norton.

Moses, L. C. (1996) *Wild West Shows and the Images of American Indians 1883–1933*, Albuquerque, N.M.: University of New Mexico Press.

Mosquera, Gerardo (1994) 'Meyer Schapiro, Marxist aesthetics, and abstract art' , trans. David Craven and Colleen Kattau, *Oxford Art Journal* 17(1): 76–80.

Mumford, L. (1952) *Art and Technics*, New York: Columbia University Press.

Muñoz, José Esteban (1999) *Disidentifications: Queers of Color and the Performance of Politics,* Minneapolis, Minn.: University of Minnesota Press.

Myers, Kenneth (1988) *The Catskills: Painters, Writers, and Tourists in the Mountains, 1820–1895*, Yonkers, N.Y.: Hudson River Museum of Westchester/ University Press of New England.

Naifeh, Steve and G. W. Whitesmith (1989) *Jackson Pollock: An American Saga*, New York: Clarkson N. Porter.

Nash, Roderick (1967/2001) *Wilderness and the American Mind*, New Haven, Conn.: Yale University Press.

Neihardt, John (1932) *Black Elk Speaks: Being the Life of a Holy Man of the Ogalala Sioux*, New York: William Morrow. Repr. University of Nebraska Press (1979), intro. Vine Deloria, Jr.; repub. as *The Sixth Grandfather: Black Elk's Teachings Given to John G. Neihardt,* ed. and intro. Raymond J. DeMallie, Lincoln: University of Nebraska Press (1984).

Nelson, Robert S. (2000) 'The slide lecture, or the work of art 'history' in the age of mechanical reproduction', *Critical Inquiry* 26(3) (Spring): 414–34.

Nenn, Beth and Adam D. Weinberg (1999) *Frames of Reference: Looking at American Art, 1900–1950*, New York: Whitney Museum of American Art/ Berkeley, Los Angeles and London: University of California Press.

Newman, Amy (2000) *Challenging Art: Artforum 1962–1974*, New York: Soho Press.

Newman, Barnett (1947) 'The first man was an artist', *Tiger's Eye* 1(1) (October): 57–60.

Nochlin, Linda (1971) *Realism*, Harmondsworth: Penguin.

Nochlin, Linda (1971/1973) 'Why have there been no great women artists?' pp. 1–43 in Thomas B. Hess and Elizabeth C. Barker (eds), *Art and Sexual Politics*, New York: Collier.

Nochlin, Linda (1973) 'The realist criminal and the abstract law', *Art in America* 61 (Sept.–Oct.): 54–61.

Nochlin, Linda (1989) *Women, Art and Power and Other Essays,* London: Thames & Hudson.

Nochlin, Linda (1991) *The Politics of Vision: Essays on Nineteenth-Century Art and Society,* London: Thames & Hudson.

Nochlin, Linda (1994) 'Issues of gender in Cassatt and Eakins' , pp. 255–73 in Steven F. Eisenman (ed.), *Nineteenth Century Art*, London: Thames & Hudson.

Nochlin, Linda (1999) *Representing Women*, London: Thames & Hudson.

Noguchi, Isamu (1987) *The Isamu Noguchi Garden Museum*, New York: Harry N. Abrams.

Novak, Barbara (1968/1969/1979) *American Painting of the Nineteenth Century:*

Realism, Idealism, and the American Experience (vars edns), New York: Praeger.

Novak, Barbara (2007) *Nature and Culture: American Landscape and Painting 1825–1875*, Oxford: Oxford University Press.

Noyes Platt, S. (1999) *Art and Politics in the 1930's, Modernism-Marxism-Americanism. A History of Cultural Activism during the Depression Years,* New York: Midmarch Arts Press.

Nugent, Walter and Marin Ridge (eds) (1999) *The American West: The Reader*, Bloomington and Indianapolis: Indiana University Press.

Nye, David E. (1996) *American Technological Sublime*, Cambridge, Mass.: MIT Press.

Nye, David E. (1997) *Narratives and Spaces : Technology and the Construction of American Culture*, Exeter: University of Exeter Press.

Nye, David E. (2004) *America as Second Creation: Technology and Narratives of New Beginnings*, Cambridge, Mass.: MIT Press.

O'Brian, John (ed.) (1986) *Clement Greenberg: The Collected Essays and Criticism*, 4 vols, Chicago: University of Chicago Press.

O'Connor, Francis V. (ed.) (1973/1975) *Art for the Millions: Essays from the 1930s by Artists and Administrators of the WPA Federal Art Project*, Boston: New York Graphic Society.

O'Hara, Frank (1965) 'Introduction', in *Abstract Watercolours by 14 Americans* (exhibition 15 October–10 November), Sydney: Art Gallery of New South Wales.

O'Sullivan, John L. (1845) 'Annexation', *Democratic Review* 17(1) (July–August): 5–10.

Oedel, William T. (1992) 'After Paris: Rembrandt Peale's Apollodorian Gallery', *Winterthur Portfolio* 27(1) (Spring): 1–27.

Oettermann, Stefan (1997) *The Panorama: History of a Mass Medium,* rpt. and trans., New York: Zone.

Olds, Elizabeth (1973) 'Prints for mass production', pp. 142–4 in Francis V. O'Connor (ed.), *Art for the Millions: Essays from the 7930s by Artists and Administrators of the WPA Federal Art Project*, Boston: New York Graphic Society.

Orvell, Miles (2003) *American Photography*, Oxford History of Art series, Oxford: Oxford University Press.

Owens, Craig (1990) 'Discourses of others: feminists and postmodernism', pp. 57–77 in Hal Foster (ed.), *Postmodern Culture*, London: Pluto.

Panofsky, Erwin (1953) 'The history of art', pp. 85–8 in W. R. Crawford (ed.), *The Cultural Migration: The European Scholar in America*, Philadelphia: University of Pennsylvania Press (repr. New York: Arno Press, 1977).

Papadakis, A. C. (1989) *New York, New Art*, Art and Design Series, London: Academy.

Parker Tyler, Robert (1943) Editorial, *View* 2(4) (January).

Parry, Ellwood C. III (1988) 'Thomas Eakins's 'Naked series' reconsidered: another look at the standing nude photographs made for the use of Eakins's students', *American Art Journal* 20(2): 53–77.

Parry, Ellwood C. III (1988) *The Art of Thomas Cole*, Newark, Del.: University of Delaware Press.

Paternosto, C. (1988) 'North and South connected: an abstraction of the Americas', in C. de Torres (ed.), *North and South Connected: An Abstraction of the Americas*, Dalton, Mass.: Studley Press.

Patin, Thomas (1999) 'Exhibitions and empire: national parks and the performance of manifest destiny', *Journal of American Culture* 22(1): 41–60.

Patton, Sharon F. (1998) *African-American Art*, Oxford: Oxford University Press.

Paz, Octavio (1987) *Essays on Mexican Art*, trans. Helen Lane, New York: Harcourt Brace.

Peale, Charles Willson (1792/2004) 'To the Citizens of the United States of America', in *Dunlap's American Daily Advertiser*, Philadelphia, 13 January 1792; repr. as pp. 129–30 in Bettina Messias Carbonell (ed.), *Museum Studies: An Anthology of Contexts*, Oxford: Blackwell.

Peck, Daniel H. (2005) 'Unlikely kindred spirits: a new vision of landscape in the works of Henry David Thoreau and Asher B. Durand', *American Literary History* 17(4) (Winter): 687–713.

Peet, Phyllis (1990) 'The art education of Emily Sartain', *Woman's Art Journal* 11(1) (Spring–Summer): 9–15.

Pestalozzi, J. H. (1903) *ABC der Anschaung*, Zurich and Bern: J. G. Cotta.

Pestalozzi, J. H. (1801/1898) *How Gertrude Teaches her Children*, trans. L. E. Holland and F. C. Turner, Syracuse, N.Y.: C. W. Bordeen.

Pevsner, N. (1973) *Academies of Art Past and Present*, New York: Da Capo Press.

Pfaff, W. (1993) *The Wrath of Nations: Civilisation and the Furies of Nationalism*, New York: Touchstone/Simon & Schuster.

Phillips, C. (1988) 'The judgement seat of photography', in A. Michelson R. Krauss, D. Crimp and J. Copiec (eds), *October: The First Decade 1976–1986*, Cambridge, Mass.: MIT Press

Phillips, Lisa (1999) *The American Century: Art and Culture 1950–2000*, New York: Whitney Museum of American Art.

Phillips, Lisa (2007) *Unmonumental: The Object in the 21st Century*, London and New York: Phaidon.

Pilgrim, Dianne H. (1978) 'Inherited from the past: the American period room', *American Art Journal* 10(1) (May): 4–23.

Pinson, Peter (2002) *Elwyn Lynn: Metaphor and Texture*, Sydney: Craftsman House.

Plumwood, Val (1998) 'Wilderness skepticism and wilderness dualism', in J. Baird Callicott (ed.), *The Great New Wilderness Debate*, Athens, Ga.: University of Georgia Press.

Pohl, F. K. (1981), 'An American in Venice: Ben Shahn and the U.S. Foreign Policy at the 1954 Venice Biennale', *Art History* 4(1) (March): 80–113.

Pohl, F. K. (1989), *Ben Shahn: New Deal Artist in a Cold War Climate (1947–1954)*,Austin: University of Texas Press.

Pohl, Frances K. (1994) 'Black and white in America', in Steven F. Eisenman, *Nineteenth Century Art*, London: Thames and Hudson.

Pohl, Frances K. (2002) *Framing America: A Social History of American Art*, New York: Thames & Hudson.

Pointon, Marcia (ed.) (1994) *Art Apart: Art Institutions and Ideology across England and North America*, Manchester: Manchester University Press.

Polcari, Stephen (1991) *Abstract Expressionism and Modern Experience*, Cambridge: Cambridge University Press.
Pollock, Jackson (1944) Interview, *Art and Architecture* 49 (February): 7–8.
Powel, Lydia B. (1954) 'The American Wing', *Metropolitan Museum of Art Bulletin*, New Series 12(7) (Mar.ch): 194–216.
Pratt, Mary Louise (1992) *Imperial Eyes: Travel Writing and Transculturation*, London: Routledge.
Prescott, K. W. (1973) *The Complete Graphic Works of Ben Shahn*, New York: Quadrangle/New York Times Book Co.
Prescott, K. W. (1982) *Prints and Posters of Ben Shahn*, New York: Dover.
Preziosi, Donald (2003) *Brain of the Earth's Body: Art, Museums, and the phastasms of modernity*, Minneapolis: University of Minnesota Press.
Prieto, Laura (2001) *At Home in the Studio: The Professionalization of Women Artists in America*, Cambridge, Mass.: Harvard University Press.
Prince, J. N. (1990) *The Arts at State Colleges and Universities*, Washington, DC: American Association of State Colleges and Universities.
Quinn, Stephen (2006) *Windows on Nature: The Great Habitat Dioramas of the American Museum of Natural History*, New York: Harry N. Abrams.
Quirarte, Jacinto (1973) *Mexican American Artists*, Austin: University of Texas Press.
Rainey, Sue (1994) *Creating 'Picturesque America': Monument to the Natural and Cultural Landscape*, Nashville, Tenn.: Vanderbilt University Press.
Rather, Susan (1997) 'Carpenter, tailor, shoemaker, artist: Copley and portrait painting around 1770', *Art Bulletin* 79(2) (June): 269–90.
Ravaisson, F. (1857) 'Instruction in drawing in schools of art and design', *Bernard's American Journal of Education* 2: 419–34.
Read, Herbert (1954) 'The museum and the artist', *College Art Journal* 13(4) (Summer): 289–94.
Reality (1953) 1(1) (Spring).
Reality (1954) 1(2) (Spring).
Reality (1955) 1(3) (Summer).
Reeves, Richard (1982) *American Journey: Traveling with Tocqueville in Search of Democracy in America*, New York: Simon & Schuster.
Reinhardt, Ad (1953) 'The artist in search of an academy' *College Art Journal* 12(3), Spring: 249–51.
Rewald, John (1973) *The History of Impressionism*, London: Secker & Warburg.
Reynolds, Sir Joshua (1997) *Discourses on Art*, ed. Robert R. Wark, New Haven, Conn. and London: Yale University Press.
Richardson, E. P. (1956a/1963) *A Short History of American Painting*, New York: Crowell.
Richardson, E. P. (1956b) *Painting in America: The Story of 450 Years*, New York: Crowell.
Roberts, Helene E. (ed.) (1997) *Art History Through the Camera's Lens*, Amsterdam: Gordon & Breach.
Roberts, John (1998) *The Art of Interruption: Realism, Photography and the Everyday*, Manchester: Manchester University Press.
Robertson, Bryan (1960) *Jackson Pollock*, New York: Harry N. Abrams.

Rodman, S. (1951) *Portrait of the Artist as an American: Ben Shahn, A Biography with Pictures*, New York: Harpers & Brothers.

Rojek, Chris and John Urry (eds) (1997) *Touring Cultures: Transformations of Travel and Theory,* London: Routledge.

Rose, Barbara (1966) 'Los Angeles: the second city', *Art in America* 54 (January–February): 114.

Rose, Barbara (ed.) (1967) *Readings in American Art since 1900: a documetary survey,* London: Thames & Hudson.

Rose, Barbara (1969) *American Painting: The Twentieth Century*, London: Macmillan.

Rose, Barbara (1975) *American Art since 1900: A Critical History,* New York: Frederick A. Praeger.

Rosenberg Harold (1966) *Anxious Object: Art Today and its Audience*, New York: Horizon.

Rosenberg, Harold (1952/1990) 'The American action painters', pp. 75–6 in David and Cecile Shapiro (eds), *Abstract Expressionism: A Critical Record*, Cambridge: Cambridge University Press.

Rosenberg, Harold (1973) 'Educating artists', pp. 91–102 in G. Battock (ed.), *New Ideas in Art Education*, New York: E.P. Dutton.

Rosenberg, Harold (1975) *Art on the Edge: Creators and Situations*, Chicago, Ill.: University of Chicago Press.

Rotskoff, Lori E. (1997) 'Decorating the dining-room: still-life chromolithographs and domestic ideology in nineteenth-century America', *Journal of American Studies* 31(1): 19–42.

Rourke, C. (1942) *The Roots of American Culture,* New York: Harcourt, Brace.

Rubenfeld, Florence (1998) *Clement Greenberg: A Life,* New York: Scribner.

Rubinstein, Charlotte Streifer (1982) *American Women Artists: From the Early Indian Times to Present,* Boston, Mass.: G. K. Hall.

Rubinstein, Charlotte Streifer (1990) *American Women Sculptors: A History of Women Working in Three Dimensions*, Boston, Mass.: G. K. Hall.

Rugoff, Milton A. (1971) *Prudery and Passion: Sexuality in Victorian America,* New York: Putman.

Russell, Charles (ed.) (2001) *Self-Taught Art: The Culture and Aesthetics of American Vernacular Art*, Jackson, Miss.: University Press of Mississippi.

Rydell, Robert W. and Rob Kroes (2005) *Buffalo Bill in Bologna: The Americanization of the World, 1869–1922*, Chicago, Ill.: University of Chicago Press.

Saltz, Jerry 2001 'Middle Americana' *Village Voice.*

Sandler, Irving (1966) 'The will to renewal', pp. 3–5 in *Two Decades of American Painting*, New York: MoMA.

Sandler, Irving (1970) *The Triumph of American Painting: A History of Abstract Expressionism*, New York: Praeger.

Sandler, Irving (1978) *New York School: The Painters and Sculptors of the Fifties*, New York: Harper.

Sandler, Irving and Amy Newman (eds) (1986) *Defining Modern Art: Selected Writings of Alfred H. Barr, Jr.*, New York: Harry A. Abrams.

Sanford, Charles L. (1957) 'The concept of the sublime in the works of Thomas Cole and William Cullen Bryant', *American Literature* 28(4) (Jan.): 434–48.

Sanford, Charles L. (1961) *The Quest for Paradise: Europe and the American Moral Imagination,* Urbana, Ill.: University of Illinois Press.
Saunders, Richard H. (1995) *John Smibert, Colonial America's First Portrait Painter,* New Haven, Conn.: Barra Foundation/Yale University Press.
Schapiro, Meyer (1936) 'Race nationality and art', *Art Front* 11 (March).
Schapiro, Meyer (1937/1978) 'The nature of abstract art', Marxist Quarterly 1 (Jan.–Mar.); repr. in Meyer Schapiro (1978) *Modern Art: 19th and 20th Centuries: Selected Papers*, New York: George Braziller.
Schapiro Meyer (1941) 'Courbet and popular imagery: an essay on realism and naiveté', *Journal of the Warburg and Courtauld Institutes* 4: 164–91.
Schapiro, Meyer (1978) *Modern Art: 19th and 20th Centuries: Selected Papers,* New York: George Braziller.
Schapiro, Meyer (2003) 'On the social basis of art', in Charles Harrison and Paul Wood (eds), *Art in Theory, 1900–2000*, Oxford: Blackwell.
Schoelwer, Susan Prendergast (1992) 'The absent other: women in the land and art of mountain men', pp.134–65, 203–7in Jules David Prown *et al.* (eds), *Discovered Lands, Invented Pasts: Transforming Visions of the American West,* New Haven, Conn. and London: Yale University Press.
Scribner's (1876) 'The art collection of Vassar College', *Scribner's Monthly* 11(4) (February): 593–4.
Schwartz, H. (1996) *The Culture of the Copy*, New York: Zone.
Searing, H. (1982) *New American Art Museums,* New York: Whitney Museum of American Art/University of California Press.
Sears, John F. (1989) *Sacred Places: American Tourist Attractions in the Nineteenth Century,* New York: Oxford University Press.
Sekula, Allan (1984) 'The traffic in photographs', pp. 96–101 in *Photography Against the Grain: Essays and Photoworks*, Halifax: Press of the Nova Scotia Scotia College of Art and Design.
Sellars, Charles Coleman (1947) *Charles Willson Peale*, 2 vols, Philadelphia, Penn.: American Philosophical Society.
Sellin, David (1975) 'The first pose: Howard Roberts, Thomas Eakins, and a century of Philadelphia nudes', *Philadelphia Museum of Art Bulletin* 70(311/312) (Spring): 1–2, 5–56.
Senie, Harriet F. and Sally Webster (eds) (1992) *Critical Issues in Public Art: Content, Context and Controversy,* New York: Harper Collins.
Sennett, Robert S. (1986) 'Early photographic catalogues: an untapped resource', *Visual Resources* 3(2) (Summer): 75–96.
Shahn, Ben (1953) 'The Artist and the politicians', *Rights* 1(1): 4–8, and *Art News* (September): 7.
Shahn, Ben (1968) Interview with Forrest Selvig, unpublished manuscript in the Ben Shahn papers, New York Archives of American Art.
Shapiro, David and Shapiro, Cecile (1990) *Abstract Expressionism: A Critical Record,* Cambridge: Cambridge University Press.
Shipp, Steve (1996) *American Art Colonies, 1850–1930: A Historical Guide to America's Original Art Colonies and their Artists*, Westport, Conn.: Greenwood.
Shurtleff, Harold R. (1939) *The Log Cabin Myth: A Study of the Early Dwellings of*

the English Colonists in North America, Cambridge, Mass.: Harvard University Press.

Sides, Hampton (2007) *Blood and Thunder*, New York: Little, Brown.

Sill, Geoffrey M. and Roberta K. Tarbell (eds) (1992) *Walt Whitman and the Visual Arts*, New Brunswick: Rutgers University Press.

Simon, K. (1978) *Fifth Avenue: A Very Social History*, New York: Harcourt Brace.

Singerman, Howard (1999) *Art Subjects: Making Artists in the American University*, Berkeley: University of California Press.

Siporin, Michell (1973) 'Mural art and the midwestern myth', pp. 64–7 in Frances V. O'Connor (ed.), *Art for the Millions: Essays from the 1930s by Artists and Administrators of the WPA Federal Art Project*, Boston: New York Graphic Society.

Siqueiros, D. A. (1934/1992) 'Towards a transformation of the plastic arts', pp.412–14 in Charles Harrison and Paul Wood (eds), *Art in Theory 1900–2000: An Anthology of Changing Ideas*, Oxford: Blackwell.

Siqueiros, D. A. (1975) *Art and Revolution*, trans. Sylvia Calles, London: Lawrence & Wishart.

Slotkin, Richard (1981) 'The "Wild West"', pp. 27–44 in David H. Katzine et al. (eds), *Buffalo Bill and the Wild West*, New York: Brooklyn Museum, Museum of Art, Carnegie Institute, and Buffalo Bill Historical Center.

Slotkin, Richard (1973) *Regeneration Through Violence: The Mythology of the American Frontier, 1600–1860*, Norman, Okla.: University of Oklahoma Press.

Slotkin, Richard (1988) 'Introduction', to James Fennimore Cooper, *Last of the Mohicans*, New York: Penguin.

Slotkin, Richard (1998) *The Fatal Environment: The Myth of the Frontier in the Age of Industrialization, 1800–1890*, Norman, Okla.: University of Oklahoma Press.

Smith, Bernard (1962) *Australian Painting Today: The John Murtagh Macrossan Memorial Lecture, 1961*, St Lucia, Qld: Queensland University Press.

Smith, Bernard (1984) *The Boy Adeodatos: The Portrait of a Lucky Young Bastard*, Ringwood, Vic: Penguin.

Smith, Bernard (2002) *A Pavane for Another Time*, South Yarra: Macmillan.

Smith, Gayle L. (1985) 'Emerson and the luminist painters: a study of their styles', *American Quarterly* 37(2) (Summer): 193–215.

Smith, Gordon M. (1973) 'The Shaker arts and crafts', pp. 173–5 in Frances V. O'Connor (ed.), *Art for the Millions: Essays from the 1930s by Artists and Administrators of the WPA Federal Art Project*, Boston: New York Graphic Society.

Smith, John Rubens (1822/1843) *The Juvenile Drawing Book, Being the Rudiments of the Art in a Series of Progressive Lessons*, Philadelphia, Penn.: J. W. Moore.

Smith, P. (1996) *The History of American Art Education: Learning about Art in American Schools*, Westport, Conn.: Greenwood.

Smith, Peter (1986) 'The ecology of picture study', *Art Education* (Sept): 48–54.

Smith Terry (1974) 'The provincialism problem', *Artforum* 13(1) (September): 55–9.

Smith, Walter (1872) *Art Education, Scholastic and Industrial*, Boston: J. R. Osgood.

Smithson, Robert (1966) 'Entropy and the new monuments', *Artforum* (June): 27.

Smyth, Craig Hugh and Peter M. Lukehart (1993) *The Early Years of Art History in the United States*, Princeton, N.J.: Department of Art and Archaeology, Princeton University.

Soby, J. T. (nd, c. 1962–71) *My Life in the Art World*, unpublished manuscript, New York: Archives of the Museum of Modern Art.

Solnit, Rebecca (2003) *Yosemite in Time, Ice Ages, Tree Clocks, Ghost Rivers: Photographs by Mark Klett and Byron Wolfe*, San Antonio, Tex.: Trinity University Press.

Solnit, Rebecca (2004a) *Motion Studies: Time, Space and Edward Muybridge*, London: Bloomsbury.

Solnit, Rebecca (2004b) *River of Shadows: Eadweard Muybridge and the Technological Wild West*, Harmondsworth: Penguin.

Sontag, S. (1964) 'Notes on "camp"', *Partisan Review* 31: 515–30.

Sontag, Susan (1977) *On Photography*, New York: Penguin.

Spindler, Robert P. (1988) 'Windows to the American past: lantern slides as historic evidence', *Visual Resources* 5(1) (Spring): 1–15.

Standing Bear, Luther (1928/1975) *My People the Sioux*, ed. Richard N. Ellis and E.A. Brininstool, Lincoln, Nebr.: University of Nebraska Press.

Staniszewski, M. A. (1998) *The Power of Display: A History of Exhibition Installations at the Museum of Modern Art*, Cambridge, Mass.: MIT Press.

Stankiewicz, Mary Ann (1993) 'Virtue and good manners: toward a history of art history instruction', in Craig Hugh Smyth and Peter M. Lukehart (eds), *The Early Years of Art History in the United States*, Princeton, N.J.: Princeton University Press.

Stankiewicz, Mary Ann (1985) 'Mary Dana Hicks Prang: a pioneer in American art education', in Mary Ann Stankiewicz and Enid Zimmerman (eds), *Women Art Educators II*, Bloomington, Ind.: Mary Rouse Memorial Fund.

Stankiewicz, Mary Ann (1982) 'The creative sister: an historical look at women, the arts, and higher education', *Studies in Art Education* 24(1): 48–56.

Stankiewicz, Mary Ann (1984) '"The eye is a nobler organ": Ruskin and American art education', *Journal of Aesthetic Education* 18(2) (Summer): 51–64.

Stankiewicz, Mary Ann (1985) 'A picture age: reproductions in picture study', *Studies in Art Education* 26(2) (Winter): 86–92.

Stankiewicz, Mary Ann (1999) 'Chromo-civilization and the genteel tradition (an essay on the social value of art education)', *Studies in Art Education* 40(2) (Winter): 101–13.

Starita, Joe (1995/1996) *The Dull Knives of Pine Ridge: A Lakota Odyssey*, New York: G. P. Putnam/New York: Berkley.

Steichen, Edward and Carl Sandberg (1955) *The Family of Man*, New York: Museum of Modern Art/Harry N. Abrams.

Stein, Roger B. (1967) *John Ruskin and Aesthetic Thought in America, 1840–1900*, Cambridge, Mass.: MIT Press.

Stein, Roger B. (1998) 'Charles Willson Peale's expressive design: the artist in his museum', in Marianne Doezema and Elizabeth Milroy (eds), *Reading American Art*, New Haven, Conn. and London: Yale University Press.

Stephen, Ann, Andrew McNamara, and Philip Goad (eds) (2007) *Modernism and Australia: Documents on Art, Design and Architecture 1917–1967*, Melbourne: Meiegunyah Press.

Stern, Robert, Thomas Mellins and David Fishman (1997) *New York 1960: Architecture and Urbanism Between the Second World War and the Bicentennial*, New York: Taschen.

Stiles, K. and Selz, P. (1996) *Theories and Documents of Contemporary Art: A Sourcebook of Artists' Writings*, Berkeley: University of California Press.

Stone, Clayton (1987) 'Antique casts in America', *Sculpture Review* 36(1–2): 26–31.

Stott, William (1973) *Documentary Expression and Thirties America*, Oxford: Oxford University Press.

Sussman, Elizabeth (ed.) (1996) *City of Ambition: Artists and New York, 1900–1960*, New York: Whitney Museum of Art.

Swenson, G. R. (1966) 'A view of an exhibition', in *Two Decades of American Painting*, New York: MoMA.

Szarkowski (1994) 13 'The Museum of Modern Art at mid-century: continuity and change', in John Elderfield (ed.), *Studies in Modern Art 5: The Museum of Modern Art at Mid-Century: Continuity and Change*, New York: MoMA.

Taft, Lorado (1903/1924) *The History of American Sculpture*, new edn, New York: Macmillan.

Tagg, J. (1976) 'American power and American painting', *Praxis* 1(2) (Winter): 59–79.

Tagg, J. (1992) *Grounds of Dispute: Art History, Cultural Politics and the Discursive Field*, London: Macmillan.

Talbot, Carl (1998) 'The wilderness narrative and the cultural logic of capitalism', in J. Baird Callicott (ed.), *The Great New Wilderness Debate*, Athens, Ga.: University of Georgia Press.

Tarr, Patricia (1989) 'Pestalozzian and Froebelian influences on contemporary elementary school art', *Studies in Art Education* 30(2) (Winter): 115–21.

Tashjian, Dickran (1995) *A Boatload of Madmen: Surrealism and the American Avant-Garde 1920–1950*, New York: Thames & Hudson.

Tatham, David (1981) 'Samuel F. B. Morse's "Gallery of the Louvre": the figures in the foreground', *American Art Journal* 13(4) (Autumn): 38–48.

Taylor, G. R. (1956) *The Turner Thesis: Concerning the Role of the Frontier in American History*, New York: D. C. Heath.

Taylor, J. C. (1976) *America as Art*, London: Harper & Row.

Taylor, J. C. (ed.) (1987) *Nineteenth-Century Theories of Art*, Berkeley, Calif.: University of California Press.

Tebbel, J. (1981) *A History of Book Publishing in the United States, Vol. IV, The Great Change, 1940–1980*, New York: R.R. Bowker.

Thayer, Donald B. (1976) 'Early anatomy instruction at the National Academy of Design: the tradition behind it', *American Art Journal* 8(1) (May): 38–5 1.

Thistlewood, David (ed.) (1993) *American Abstract Expressionism*, Critical Forum Series 1, Liverpool: Liverpool University Press and Tate Gallery Liverpool.

Thomas, Laurie (1976) *The Most Noble Art of Them All*, Brisbane: University of Queensland Press.

Thoreau, David Henry (1864) *The Maine Woods*, Boston, Mass.: Ticknor and Fields.

Tilden, Freeman (1965) *The National Parks: What They Mean to You and Me*, New York: Alfred A. Knopf.

Tilden, Freeman (1977) *Interpreting Our Heritage,* North Carolina: Chapel Hill Books.

Tocqueville, Alexis de (1959) 'Quinze jours au désert', in George Wilson Pierson, *Tocqueville in America*, New York: Doubleday, Anchor.

Tocqueville, Alexis de (1835/40 / 1980) *Democracy in America,* 2 vols., trans. Henry Reeves, rev. Francis Bowen, New York: Alfred A. Knopf.

Tocqueville, Alexis de (1971) *Journey to America*, ed. J. P. Mayer, trans. George Lawrence, New York: Doubleday, Anchor Books.

Tocqueville, Alexis de (1985) *Selected Letters on Politics and Society*, ed. Roger Boesche, trans. James Toupin and Roger Boesche, Berkeley, Calif.: University of California Press.

Trenton, Patricia (ed.) (1995) *Independent Spirits: Women Painters of the American West, 1890–1945*, Los Angeles: Autry Museum of Western Heritage and Berkeley, Calif.: University of California Press.

Trollope, F. (1839) *Domestic Manners of the Americans*, London: Richard Bentley.

Troyen, Carol (1991) 'Retreat to Arcadia: American landscape and the American Art-Union', *American Art Journal* 23(1): 20–37.

Turner, F. J. (1893) *The Significance of the Frontier in American History*, Irvington Reprint Series, History Reprint h–214, North Stratford: Irvington.

Turner, James (1999) *The Liberal Education of Charles Eliot Norton*, Baltimore and London: Johns Hopkins University Press.

'Tyro' (1831) 'Letter on the chanting cherubs', *New England Magazine* 1(1) (July): 20–6.

Vanderbilt, Kermit (1959) *Charles Eliot Norton: Apostle of Culture in a Democracy*, Cambridge, Mass.: Belknap Press.

Vanneman, R. and L. W. Cannon (1987) *The American Perception of Class*, Philadelphia, Penn.: Temple University Press.

Venn, Beth and Adam D. Weinberg (1998) *Unknown Terrain: The Landscapes of Andrew Wyeth,* New York: Whitney Museum of American Art, Harry N. Abrams.

Venn, Beth and Adam D. Weinberg (1999) *Frames of Reference: Looking at American Art 1900–50*, Berkeley, Calif.: University of California Press.

Volkert, James Martin, R. Kinda and Amy Pickworth (2004) *National Museum of the American Indian, Smithsonian Institution Washington, D.C. Map and Guide*, London: Scala.

Walker, A. J. (1998), *Cultural Offensive: America's Impact on British Art Since 1945,* London and Sterling, Va.: Pluto.

Walker. John A. (2007) 'Art Czar: the rise and fall of Clement Greenberg, Alice Goldfarb, Marquis', *The Art Book* 14(2) (May): 50–2.

Walker, Peter and Melanie Simo (1994) *Invisible Gardens: The Search for Modernism in the American Landscape,* Cambridge, Mass.: MIT Press.

Wallace, David H. (1972) 'The art of John Rogers: "so real and so true"', *American Art Journal* 4(2) (Nov.): 59–70.

Wallach, Alan (1996) 'Wadsworth's tower: an episode in the history of American landscape vision', *American Art* 10(3) (Fall): 8–27.

Wallach, Alan (1998a) 'The Battle over "The West as America"', pp. 105–17 in *Exhibiting Contradiction: Essays on the Art Museum in the United States*, Amherst, Mass.: University of Massachusetts Press.

Wallach, Alan (1998b) 'The American cast museum: an episode in the history of the institutional definition of art', pp. 38–50 in *Exhibiting Contradiction: Essays on the Art Museum in the United States*, Amherst, Mass.: University of Massachusetts Press.

Wallach, Alan (1998c) *Exhibiting Contradictions: Essays on the Art Museum in the United States*, Amherst, Mass.: University of Massachusetts Press.

Wallach, Alan (2001) 'Oliver Larkin's "Art and Life in America": between the Popular Front and the cold war', *American Art* 15(3) (Autumn): 80–9.

Wallach, Alan (2002) 'Thomas Cole's River in the Catskills as antipastoral', *Art Bulletin* (June): 334–50.

Wallach, Alan (2003) '"Norman Rockwell" at the Guggenheim', pp. 96–115 in Andrew McClellan (ed.), *Art and its Publics: Museum Studies at the Millennium*, Oxford: Blackwell.

Walls, Nina de Angeli (2001) *Art, Industry, and Women's Education in Philadelphia*, Westport, Conn.: Greenwood.

Wardlaw, A. *et al.* (1989) *Black Art: Ancestral Legacy, the African Impulse in African-American Art*, Dallas, Tex.: Dallas Museum of Art.

Warsager, Hyman (1973) 'Graphic techniques in progress', pp. 139–47 in Frances V. O'Connor (ed.), *Art for the Millions: Essays from the 1930s by Artists and Administrators of the WPA Federal Art Project*, Boston, Mass.: New York Graphic Society.

Watson, Rymer Bayly (dir.) (2000) *Poles Apart: The Blue Poles Controversy*, movie, 52 mins.

Weil, Stephen E. (2002) *Making Museums Matter*, Washington, DC: Smithsonian Institution Press.

Wein, Jo Ann (1981) 'The Parisian training of American women artists', *Woman's Art Journal* 2(1), (Spring–Summer): 41–4.

Weinberg, H. Barbara (1991) *The Lure of Paris: Nineteenth-Century American Painters and Their French Teachers*, New York: Abbeville.

Welter, B. (1966) 'The cult of true womanhood: 1820–1860', *American Quarterly* 18: 151–74.

Wertkin, Gerard C., Elsa Longhauser, Harald Szeemann and Lee Kogan (1998) *Self-Taught Artists of the Twentieth Century: An Anthology*, New York, Museum of American Folk Art and San Francisco: Chronicle Books.

White, Gabriel (1959) 'Preface' in *The New American Painting as shown in eight European Countries 1958-1959*, New York: MoMA.

White, Robert R. (ed.) (1983) *The Taos Society of Artists*, Albuquerque, N.M.: University of New Mexico Press/Historical Society of New Mexico.

Whitehill, Walter Muir (1965) *The Arts in Early American History*, Chapel Hill, N.C.: University of North Carolina Press for Institute of Early American History and Culture.

Whitehill, W. M. (1970) *Museum of Fine Arts, Boston: A Centennial History*, Cambridge, Mass.: Harvard University Press.

Whiting, Cécile (1989) *Antifascism in American Art*, New Haven, Conn. and London: Yale University Press.

Williams, Raymond (1989) *The Politics of Modernism*, London: Verso.

Wilmerding, John (ed.) (1973) *The Genius of American Painting*, London: Weidenfeld and Nicolson.

Wilmerding, John (1976) *American Art*, New York: Puffin.

Wilson, Alexander (1818) *The Foresters: A Poem, Descriptive of a Pedestrian Journey to the Falls of Niagara, in the Autumn of 1804*, Newtown, Pa.: S. Siegfried & J. Wilson.

Wilson, David M. (2002) *The British Museum: A History*, London: British Museum Press.

Wilson, Diana Drake (2000) 'Realizing memory, transforming history: Euro/ American/Indians', pp. 115–36 in Susan A. Crane (ed.), *Museums and Memory*, Stanford, Calif.: Stanford University Press:.

Wilson, Raymond L. (1982) 'The first art school in the West: the San Francisco Art Association's California School of Design', *American Art Journal* 14(1) (Winter): 42–55.

Wilton, Andrew and Tim Barringer (2002) *American Sublime: Landscape Painting in the United States 1820–1880*, London: Tate Gallery Publications.

Wolf, Matt (2006)'New live queer art', pp. 107–19 in N. Horowitz and B. Sholis (eds), *The Uncertain States of America Reader*, New York: Sternberg.

Wolff, Janet (2003) *AngloModern: Paintings and Modernity in Britain and the United States*, Ithaca, N.Y.: Cornell University Press.

Wollen, Peter (1993) *Raiding the Icebox: Reflections on Twentieth Century Culture*, London: Verso.

Wonders, Karen (1993) *Habitat Dioramas: Illusions of Wilderness in Museums of Natural History*, Uppsala: Almqvist & Wiksell.

Woodward, Kesler E. (1990) *Sydney Laurence, Painter of the North*, Seattle: University of Washington Press/Anchorage Museum of History and Art.

Wright, Peter and John Armor (1989) *The Mural Project, with photography by Ansel Adams*, Santa Barbara, Calif.: Reverie Press.

Wygant, F. (1983) *Art in American Schools in the Nineteenth Century*, Cincinnati: Interwood Press.

Yount, Sylvia (2001) 'Braving (and bridging) the great divide: the academy and the museum', *American Art* 15(3) (Autumn): 2–7.

Zinn, H. (1980) *A People's History of the United States*, New York: Harper Perennial.

Index

NOTE: Page numbers followed by *n* refer to information in a footnote.

For Product Safety Concerns and Information please contact our EU representative GPSR@taylorandfrancis.com
Taylor & Francis Verlag GmbH, Kaufingerstraße 24, 80331 München, Germany

www.ingramcontent.com/pod-product-compliance
Lightning Source LLC
LaVergne TN
LVHW050510100826
845148LV00002B/286
* 9 7 8 0 4 1 5 4 2 0 7 0 9 *